THE NEW AGENDA FOR PEACE RESEARCH

The New Agenda for Peace Research

Edited by
HO-WON JEONG
Institute for Conflict Analysis and Resolution
George Mason University, USA

LONDON AND NEW YORK

First published 1999 by Ashgate Publishing

Reissued 2018 by Routledge
2 Park Square, Milton Park, Abingdon, Oxon, OX14 4RN
711 Third Avenue, New York, NY 10017, USA

Routledge is an imprint of the Taylor & Francis Group, an informa business

Copyright © Ho-Won Jeong 1999

All rights reserved. No part of this book may be reprinted or reproduced or utilised in any form or by any electronic, mechanical, or other means, now known or hereafter invented, including photocopying and recording, or in any information storage or retrieval system, without permission in writing from the publishers.

Notice:
Product or corporate names may be trademarks or registered trademarks, and are used only for identification and explanation without intent to infringe.

Publisher's Note
The publisher has gone to great lengths to ensure the quality of this reprint but points out that some imperfections in the original copies may be apparent.

Disclaimer
The publisher has made every effort to trace copyright holders and welcomes correspondence from those they have been unable to contact.

A Library of Congress record exists under LC control number: 98049093

ISBN 13: 978-1-138-33842-5 (hbk)
ISBN 13: 978-1-138-33846-3 (pbk)
ISBN 13: 978-0-429-44174-5 (ebk)

Contents

Contributors vii
Foreword by *Hayward R. Alker* xii
Preface xiv

Part I Introduction

1   Peace Research and International Relations   3
       Ho-Won Jeong

2   The Expanding Tool Chest for Peacebuilders
       Chadwick F. Alger   13

Part II Understanding War

3   Identity and the Outbreak of War
       Iver B. Neumann   45

4   War and Globality: The Role and
       Character of War in the Global Transition
       Martin Shaw   61

Part III Approaches to Peace

5   From Arms to Disarmament Races:
       Disarmament Dynamics after the Cold War
       Bjørn Møller   83

6   Conflict Resolution Roles in International
       Peacekeeping Missions
       Daniel Druckman, James A. Wall and Paul F. Diehl   105

7   From Conflict Resolution to Conflict Transformation:
       A Critical Review
       Raimo Väyrynen   135

8	Preventing Conflict Escalation: Uncertainty and Knowledge *Dan Smith*	161
9	Self-Determination and Minority Rights *Jennifer Jackson Preece*	179
10	Linking Conflict to Environmental Security *Ho-Won Jeong and Jyrki Käkönen*	211
11	Postdevelopment: Beyond the Critique of Development *Arturo Escobar and Ho-Won Jeong*	223
12	What is Peace Culture? *Michael N. Nagler*	233

Part IV Transformation of Global Order

13	Human Needs and the State *Dov Ronen*	261
14	The Emergence of Regional Civil Society: Contributions to a New Human Security Agenda *Timothy M. Shaw and Sandra J. MacLean*	289
15	Globalisation, Class and Cultural Identity at the End of Hegemony *Jonathan Friedman*	309

Bibliography	327
Index	355

Contributors

Chadwick F. Alger is Mershon Professor of Political Science and Public Policy Emeritus, the Ohio State University. He served as Secretary General, International Peace Research Association (1983-1987), President, International Studies Association (1978-79), and Chairperson, Consortium on Peace Research, Education and Development (1974-75). Professor Alger has published widely on the UN system based on first-hand research at the United Nations in New York and Geneva. His most recent book is *The Future of the United Nations System: Potential for the Twenty First Century* (1998).

Paul F. Diehl is Professor of Political Science at the University of Illinois, Urbana-Champaign. He has published widely on such topics as the causes of war, United Nations peacekeeping, international law, and arms control. His recent books include *Territorial Changes and International Conflict* (1992), *International Peacekeeping* (1993), and *The Politics of Global Governance* (1997). He served recently on the National Academy of Science Committee on Techniques for the Enhancement of Human Performance.

Daniel Druckman is Professor of Conflict Resolution at George Mason University's Institute for Conflict Analysis and Resolution, Fairfax. He directed National Academy of Science committees from 1985 to 1997. He has published widely on such topics as conflict resolution and negotiation, nationalism, group processes, non-verbal communication, and modelling methodologies. He sits on the boards of six journals, including the *Journal of Conflict Resolution* and the *American Behavioral Scientist* as well as *International Negotiation*.

Arturo Escobar is Professor of Anthropology at the University of Massachusetts, Amherst. His current research interests are political ecology and the anthropology of development, social movements, and science and technology. For the past five years, he has been working in the Pacific rainforest region of Colombia on the issues of cultural politics and biodiversity conservation. He is the author of *Encountering Development: The Making and Unmaking of the Third World* (1995).

Jonathan Friedman is Professor of Social Anthropology at the University of Lund, Sweden. He has done research on Southeast Asia and the Pacific. His theoretical work concentrates on the study of long-term historical processes and the relations between a global process and cultural identity. He has been President of the European Society of Oceanists and has editorial functions on several journals such as *Identities, Critique of Anthropology, Review of International Political Economy*. Among his books are *Modernity and Identity* (co-edited with Scott Lash, 1992), *Cultural Identity and Global Process* (1994), *Consumption and Identity* (1994), *Hawaii: Return to Nationhood* (co-edited with James Carrier, 1995).

Ho-Won Jeong is on the Faculty of the Institute for Conflict Analysis and Resolution, George Mason University. Dr. Jeong is Editor of *International Journal of Peace Studies* as well as *Peace and Conflict Studies* sponsored by the Network of Peace and Conflict Studies. He has written extensively on international political economy and organisations, environmental conflict, conflict resolution and peace research.

Jyrki Käkönen is Director of Tampere Peace Research Institute, Finland. His current research interests are environmental security, regionalisation and civil society. His edited volumes include *Perspectives on Environmental Conflict and International Relations* (1992) and *Green Security or Militarized Environment* (1994).

Sandra J. MacLean is Assistant Professor of International Development Studies and Research Fellow at the Centre for Foreign Policy Studies, Dalhousie University, Halifax, Canada.. Her research interests include new security issues, democratisation and civil society. She has published recently in *Canadian Journal of Development Studies, New Political Economy,* and *Journal of Contemporary African Studies.*

Bjørn Møller is Senior Research Fellow, Project Director and on the Board of the Copenhagen Peace Research Institute and Associate Professor of International Relations, Institute of Political Science, University of Copenhagen. He currently serves as Secretary General of the International Peace Research Association, member of the UNIDIR Expert Group on Confidence-Building in the Middle East, Project Director of the Global Non-Offensive Defence Network funded by the Ford Foundation and Editor of *NOD and Conversion.* He is the author of *Resolving the Security Dilemma in Europe* (1991), *Common Security and Nonoffensive Defense* (1992) and *Dictionary of Alternative Defense* (1995).

Michael N. Nagler is Professor Emeritus at University of California, Berkeley where he founded the Peace and Conflict Studies Program and still regularly teaches the upper-division non-violence course. Professor Nagler has spoken and written widely for campus, religious, public and special interest groups on the subject of peace and non-violence for twenty-five years in addition to his career in classics. He has consulted for the US Institute of Peace and many other organisations and is President of Centers for Nonviolence Education. He is the author of *America Without Violence, The Upanishads* (with Sri Eknath Easwaran).

Iver B. Neumann is on leave from his job as head of the Russian Centre at the Norwegian Institute of International Affairs and is presently working on the Planning Staff of the Norwegian Foreign Ministry. His most recent books are *The Future of International Relations* (co-edited with Ole Wæver, 1997) and *Uses of the Other: The 'East' in European Identity Formation* (1998).

Jennifer Jackson Preece is Lecturer in European Nationalism at the European Institute, London School of Economics and Political Science. She has published widely on nationalism, minority rights and ethnic conflict. Dr. Preece is the author of *National Minorities and the European Nation States System* (1998).

Dov Ronen has been affiliated with various programmes at Harvard University, including Center for International Affairs and Department of Psychiatry. He served as Chairman of the Ethnicity and Politics Research Committee of the International Political Science Association and Advisor of UNESCO's Project, Management of Social Transformations. Dr. Ronen has published numerous academic journal articles as well as five books, including *The Quest for Self-Determination* (1979), *Pluralism and Democracy in Africa* (editor, 1986), and *The Challenge of Ethnic Conflict: Democracy and Self-Determination in Central Europe* (1997).

Martin Shaw is Professor of International Relations and Politics at the University of Sussex, England. He previously held Chair in Sociology at the University of Hull. His books include *Post-Military Society: Militarism, Demilitarization and War at the End of the Twentieth Century* (1991), *Global Society and International Relations* (1994), *Civil Society and Media in Global Crises: Representing Distant Violence* (1996) and *Dialectics of War: An Essay on the Social Theory of War and Peace* (1998).

Timothy M. Shaw is Director of the Centre for Foreign Policy Studies and Professor of Political Science and International Development Studies at Dalhousie University. He has taught at universities in Japan, Nigeria, South Africa, Uganda, Zambia, and Zimbabwe. His recent articles have been published in such journals as *Canadian Journal of Development Studies, International Peacekeeping, Journal of Contemporary African Studies,* and *New Political Economy*. He has served for a decade as

General Editor of the Macmillan/St Martin's Press Series on International Political Economy.

Dan Smith has been Director of the International Peace Research Institute (PRIO), Oslo since 1993, Chairperson of the Board of the Institute for Journalism in Transition, London and Prague, and Chair of the International Advisory Board of the Foundation for Research of Societal Problems, Ankara, Turkey. He was Director (1991-3) and Associate Director (1988-91) of the Transnational Institute, Amsterdam. Dr. Smith has edited and co-edited several volumes on problems of peace and conflict and is the author of over 100 articles and chapters in anthologies. He has published *Pressure: How America Runs NATO* (1989) and *The State of War and Peace Atlas* (1997).

Raimo Väyrynen is John M. Regan Jr. Director of Joan B. Kroc Institute for International Peace Studies and Professor of Government and International Relations at the University of Notre Dame. He served as Secretary-General of International Peace Research Association (1975-79) and Dean of Faculty of Social Sciences at the University of Helsinki (1990-93). Dr. Väyrynen has published numerous scholarly books and articles on international security, international political economy, and conflict studies. His most recent book is *Global Transformation: Economics, Politics, and Culture* (1997).

James A. Wall is Professor of Management in the College of Business and Public Administration at the University of Missouri, Columbia. He has published widely on negotiation and mediation, including a number of studies on mediation in several Asian countries. He is the author of *Negotiation Theory and Practice* (1986) and *Bosses* (1987). He has served as President and Executive Director of the International Association of Conflict Management.

Foreword

Reading through the chapters of Ho-Won Jeong's 'New Agenda' brings to mind earlier efforts to define and update an internationally oriented, normatively focussed, yet academically acceptable inter-discipline of peace research. In the 1940s, Quincy Wright's *A Study of War* and Louis F. Richardson's writings helped do this for many in the English speaking world. Starting in 1957, the first few issues of the *Journal of Conflict Resolution* heralded for many Americans and their academic followers such an interdisciplinary approach, which was given a more epistemologically tolerant, European focus by the *Journal of Peace Research*, edited in Scandinavia since 1963. Starting in the 1960s, Johan Galtung's pioneering writings extended and dialectically reformulated the behavioural approaches of Wright, Richardson and others to take into account both the dialectical epistemologies of Marxist and non-Marxist thought, and the alternative cosmologies of both Eastern and Western cultures of inquiry. Since their inaugural meeting in Groningen in 1965, the multi-disciplinary, multi-sphere conferences and proceedings of a scientifically self-defined International Peace Research Association have born a similarly inclusive set of concerns. More recently, the many publications of the World Order Models Project coordinated by Richard Falk and Saul Mendlovitz (and including Galtung's impressive *The True Worlds*) conveyed a kindred, humanely oriented, globally conceived concert of different voices speaking to common goals of peace, justice, the respect for diversity and the need for sustained environmental viability. And there have been more journals dedicated to peace research, education and practice.

Having participated in Peter Wallenstein's edited overview of *Peace Research* of ten years ago, I am struck by the innovation in post-Cold War themes that this 'New Agenda' presents. Not surprisingly, the many volumes of the United Nations University's project on Multilateralism and the UN System, directed by Robert W. Cox, share

'New Agenda's concern with and for a possibly emergent, socioeconomically global, culturally pluralistic and politically post-hegemonic, multilateral world order. And the critical onslaught against the adequacy of state-centric security notions is constructively reflected here in linked discussions of human needs, minority rights, cultural/regional identities, environmental security and alternative development. Within more conventional security concerns, be they understanding and preventing war decisions, disarmament, peacekeeping and peacebuilding, a culturally sensitive, transformative approach characteristic of contemporary, mature peace research is readily in evidence. So is the discourse-based focus on identity-constitutive relations, known in earlier Hegelian-Marxist literatures as 'internal' relations.

Would it be too much to hope that in another decade or two, these value-focussed lines of serious inquiry would become even more central in the preoccupations of concerned scholars than they are today? Then we could look back on the present volume as containing many rich contributions from pioneering citizen-scholars to a new world order where peace, fairness, sustainable development and human cultural diversity were highly valued.

Hayward R. Alker
Los Angeles
September 1998

Preface

Peace research has broadened our understanding of global problems over the last several decades. Whereas the prevention of a nuclear war between the US and Russia is no longer an overarching security concern, new sets of problems such as internal conflict, environmental degradation and the impact of neoliberal economic order on human well-being have drawn more close attention. As peace research embraces diverse issues, the boundaries of the field have become loose. This book intends to add new dimensions to our thinking about peace by incorporating theoretical development which is taking place in international relations and other areas of social science and humanities. Conceptual and theoretical issues are discussed in the context of promoting global peace and human security.

By examining evolving peace strategies in a changing global system, this volume also seeks to make a contribution to a policy-making community. Peace research deals with both intellectual and practical problems. Long term policy perspectives would not be achieved without systematic analysis of behavioural patterns as well as structural conditions. The contributors integrate policy concerns in their conceptual understanding.

Editing this book proved to be an intellectually fruitful experience. I have been extraordinarily fortunate to collect chapters from some of the most distinguished scholars in the field. I appreciate their contributing excellent pieces of academic work despite busy schedules. Hayward Alker generously wrote a very informative foreword that suggests the future directions of peace research.

I owe great personal debts to J. Martin Rochester, Dennis Sandole, Courtney Smith and my other colleagues who read part of the manuscripts and offered valuable comments. The timely completion of this book has been made possible by a research grant from the Institute for Conflict Analysis and Resolution, George Mason University. I feel deep gratitude to Kevin Clements and Christopher Mitchell who offered collegial support and enthusiasm. Special thanks to Emily Fitzsimmons and Lynn Kunkle who contributed their time and talent to the editorial process of this book. I also very much appreciate Landon Hancock, Chad Ford and Alex Scheinman who have been involved in the various stages of this project.

I am also grateful to John Irwin of Ashgate Publishing, for recognising the importance of this project and helping to get it off the ground. Appreciation also needs to be expressed to Pauline Beavers and Ann Newell who offered helpful advice and comments on the final production of the manuscripts.

I wish to dedicate this book to friends and colleagues who have contributed to developing the field of peace and conflict studies. They include the late Paul Smoker, Linda Groff, Michael True, Mary Clark, Glenn Paige, Miles Wolpin, Luc Reychler and many others whom I met at various places. I have known most of them for many years, and their personal support was critical for my journey to peace research. Finally, this book could not have been accomplished without the support and patience of Mary and Nimmy who allowed me to concentrate my time on editing and writing.

August 1998

Ho-Won Jeong

Part I
Introduction

1 Peace Research and International Relations

HO-WON JEONG

In order to draw a map of the field of peace research, we need to ask various sets of conceptual and normative questions since divergence and convergence of ideas cut across epistemological, ontological and normative boundaries. The goals and objectives of researchers influence the specific nature of research programmes, methodological foundations, and their policy relevance. The evolution of major theories and concepts in peace research has, to a great extent, benefited from debates in international relations while sociology, anthropology, psychology, and other disciplinary areas have also made important contributions.

Based on a reflective assessment of the status of the field, this book suggests the future agenda for peace research. Conceptual problems are linked to specific policy issues such as disarmament, peacekeeping, conflict resolution, preventive diplomacy, nonviolent social change, development and environmental security. These issues are highlighted by globalisation, identity formation, requirements for the satisfaction of basic needs, regional developmentalism and civil society which characterise the structural transition of global politics toward the 21st century.

Epistemological Community

The development of peace research reflects a complicated process, compounded by several concurrent scientific as well as social developments in scattered locations throughout the world. It is, in part, attributed to changes in the field of international relations which, after having its formative phase between the two world wars, obtained a relatively independent scientific status. In the fifties when the science of international relations was in a stage of dynamic development, a strong impulse was felt to establish a new area of study with a focus on the problems of violent conflict. These efforts soon resulted in creating the field of peace research in the modern social science tradition.

Peace research has also been influenced by social and political consciousness. There was a growing willingness among researchers to respond favourably to social needs for a scientific, but at the same time socially relevant study. As some researchers were interested in nonviolent social change, there were close connections between peace researchers and peace movements in the early stages of the field. However, the separation between peace research and peace movements was inevitable with the evolution of peace research as an academic discipline.

For the last several decades, peace and conflict studies have been taught in various disciplinary areas, including but not limited to psychology, sociology, anthropology, political science, and geography. Causes and prevention of violence at individual, group, and international levels have been examined by various methods such as simulation and content analysis. Efforts were also made to integrate social and psychological theories of conflict. The multi-disciplinary approach brought diverse methodological traditions to peace research.

The growing quest for a new science devoted to peace had been affected by scientific studies of foreign policy and conflict behaviour in the 1960s. Some who were influenced by the revolution of behavioural sciences have been more eager to adopt a scientific approach to peace research. The behavioural school stresses raw data, highly deductive propositions, and empirical verification. The shared belief behind early scientific research efforts was that verifiable theories and empirical methods can contribute to the establishment of a peaceful world (Richardson, 1960). The main research agenda of behaviouralists was to explain conflictual behaviour with formal models. Attempts were also made to explain order in international relations in terms of system theories (Kaplan, 1957; Modelski, 1978). In understanding factors leading to war, some researchers focused on the psychological and behavioural characteristics of individuals. Studies of Korean War decision making and the Cuban Missile Crisis were based on the presumption that regularities in human behaviour can be explained and even generalised (Allison, 1971; Paige, 1968). The emphasis on systematic analysis of social phenomena and methodological rigor encouraged research on world system models, simulation, games, and causal models between economic factors and war (Guetzkow and Alger, 1963; Singer and Small, 1972). The proponents of scientific approaches believe that theories on crisis decision making can be used to predict the occurrence of war. Quantitative studies of the arms race and formal decision making models are designed to help understand the behaviour of decision makers.

It did not take long for behaviouralist traditions to be criticised. One of the original mistakes of scientific peace research was to place too much emphasis on empiricist methods (Galtung, 1975). Scientific approaches ignore substantive problems which are not amenable to quantitative analysis. Peace research lacks a framework for synthesis in linking different issues to each other. Peace science has not failed in the areas of accumulation of more data on manifest violence, arms race and military coups. However, adequate conceptual frameworks to explain causes of violence have not emerged from the data-gathering process.

It is also argued that the scientific approach to research on peace and conflict has failed to provide alternative perspectives. Very little attention has been devoted to understanding the underlying conditions required for building peaceful societies. Behavioural methodology cannot remove the uncertainty of politics nor comprehend it. Pursuing the systematic analysis 'to the point of eliminating individual creativity and responsibility may well mire us in cyclic determinism' (Forcey, 1989, p.13).

Researchers should be able to point out obstacles to structural changes if peace research is considered as an emancipatory project. It needs to contribute to the transformation of a world filled with violence. Examining the structural conditions of repression and exploitation is crucial for dealing with the root causes of violent conflict (Burton and Dukes, 1990). Evaluation of the prospects for change requires analysis of the connections between modes of production and hierarchical political structures (Cox, 1996). Since individual behaviour and responsibility cannot be examined without reference to political and social collectivity in historical contexts, value explicit inquiry is considered more desirable.

As reviewed above, there are diverse views on how to study peace and war. The way we define peace research has different implications for the nature, content, and scope of theory as well as the methods of analysis. Given the fact that the field is characterised by variations of methods to investigate human experiences at different levels and in different empirical domains, it would be a difficult task to develop a single all embracing conceptual scheme that ties specialised research areas into a tightly woven package. Overall, the field of peace research, broadly defined, would remain a methodologically pluralistic community with emanicipatory interest in transformative possibilities for the improvement of human well-being as well as the prevention of violence. On the other hand, the different methodological traditions may possibly be integrated by a research orientation called 'emancipatory empiricism', which stresses the data of experience, its practical interpretation and reconstructive analysis (Alker, 1996, p. 338). In the study of Korean War decision making, for instance, the overall explanatory analysis could be concentrated on the substantive content of crisis decisions which led to the acceptance of a violent response, rather than on the processual characteristic of a high consensus decision (Paige, 1977).

Theoretical Traditions

Different interpretations of a world order generate diverse views on research agendas. In strategic studies, security is seen as the protection of nation states, and war might be needed to defend national interests and maintain peace. Strong military forces, therefore, ought to be ready to prevent attacks from another state. Even arms control should serve the same goal as the development and deployment of weapons systems in improving military strength. Strategic studies have traditionally stressed the protection of state institutions and advocated the monopoly of elites over security decision making. Political leaders should be prepared for the use of military force to promote national interests.

Peace research takes a critical view of traditional international relations theories which interpret the world in terms of competition between nations. The power politics framework of realist and neorealist paradigms is not easily integrated into peace theories which include social justice. A multicultural basis of understanding is essential for resolving conflict and building peace. The criticisms of values and norms of dominant state institutions result in the rejection of the nuclear balance of terror as well as the support of dictatorships in maintaining a global strategic alliance.

To a great extent, peace research was influenced by the idealist tradition of functional cooperation. Hope for peace can be generated by a greater participation of individuals and subnational groups in global problem solving. Contrary to realist assumptions of a world order, idealist perspectives emphasised that peace can be achieved only through cooperation among nations designed to promote human wellbeing. The ultimate resolution of conflict does not come from fear and competition for power.

Peace and conflict studies must now respond to new priorities in a changing world order. Multinational corporations, nongovernmental organisations, and supranational institutions such as the European Union play a critical role in shaping a future world order in such areas as human rights and the environment. The assumptions of international anarchy and a struggle for power are replaced by the notion of voluntary cooperation in the pursuit of the common good for humanity (Mitrany, 1966). In idealist traditions, peace is more than the concern of state elites. Interstate relations are simply a historical deviation produced by the birth of a modern state system. The problems of society existed before the rise of sovereign states. How to organise human associations is a major concern for peaceful coexistence between different societies.

The relationship between peace studies and Marxism is inherently dialectical. Both are wholeheartedly committed to a vision of progressive social change. The Marxist explanation of human alienation in a social process engendered the concept of structural violence. Peace studies also generally disagree with a conventional development model which generates large income gaps between the rich and the poor. By exploring critical issues raised by Marxism such as exploitation, alienation and marginalisation, peace and conflict studies can best articulate the inherent contradictions within a dominant social structure. With respect to the strategies of social change, however, peace studies has been more affected by the nonviolent traditions of Tolstoy and Gandhi than by Marxist revolutionary theories.

The analysis of the causes and consequences of war leads to an emphasis that conflict should and can be resolved peacefully. The prevention of violence requires an understanding of theories and techniques of managing, reducing, and resolving conflict. The adoption of nonviolent means for change is essential for constructing peace. While negative peace focuses on the absence of war and other types of physical violence, it does not specifically investigate the structural causes of violence. Positive peace has an emphasis on change for social progress. Peace research has broadened the agenda by including the elimination of poverty and injustice in its definition of peace.

Despite divergences in the main focus, a common ground might be created between the different conceptual approaches to peace. The division between negative and positive peace has been narrowed since the fall of the Berlin Wall. Human security is enhanced by the disarmament process. Such alternative security systems as non-offensive defence and civilian-based defence depart from deterrence strategies. Positive peace goals can be realised by the reduction of military budgets and conversion of military production for civilian use.

The symbiotic relationships between positive and negative peace would not be understood without having a broad notion of human security. The concept of security binds together individuals, states, and the international system so closely that the conditions of peace can be treated in an integrative manner. It includes non-military sources of threats such as environmental degradation, migration and poverty. The concept of security for the global community is needed to articulate concerns with global ecology. The visualisation of collective existence on the planet can be made possible by understanding a new set of spatial, metaphysical and doctrinal constructs. Since the underlying premise of ecology is holism and mutual dependence of parts, ecological security defies the traditional boundaries of modern territoriality.

In theoretical traditions of peace research, hierarchical institutions and violent culture are more important explanatory variables for war and domination than evil human nature. This interpretation leads to a more critical analysis of the present social system. While negative peace issues such as the prevention of the proliferation of nuclear weapons are still a pressing concern, sustainable development and social justice should be fully integrated into a theoretical understanding of a peaceful world order. One of integrating themes for future peace studies would be a critical examination of state centric paradigms in the areas of alternative military security, the environment, and human rights.

Reconfigurations and Reformulations

If disciplinary self-understanding needs to reflect social ontologies, reformulations of theories can be made in a way to critically examine reality and explore transformative possibilities in the realms of human action. Theoretical reasoning is important in the understanding of human intentionality and experience as well as the structural analysis of problems. In dealing with policy-oriented questions of how to prevent and control violence, the emancipatory goal of peace research would remain intact as a normative core.

Beyond general policy discourse, however, knowledge cumulation needs to be based on the reconfiguration of research programmes which would result from the elaboration of conceptual strategies, specification of empirical content, revisions of methodological assumptions and proliferation of theoretical ideas. In examining particular facets of social world, both opportunities and provocations can be provided by a new intellectual and political environment. Dialogue between competing theories could be encouraged by an agreement on and shared concerns with normative realities.

To move beyond problem-solving to the goal of human emancipation, existing approaches have to be reassessed for their reformulations. The contributors to this volume explore the pragmatic possibilities for change by critically looking at past practice and theories. Following this chapter, Chadwick Alger provides a comprehensive map of a set of peace tools, ranging from control of military power, economic equity to ecological balance. These peace tools were invented to deal with a specific threat to peace interpreted in the historical and social context.

In understanding war, theoretical reformulations can be pursued along the inherent knowledge interest of globality and identity. In Chapter 3, Iver Neumann connects the transformation of identity with the process of violisation. The outbreak of war is then interpreted as a way of representing identity. In Chapter 4, Martin Shaw explains that state relations and war play a large part in constituting globality. At the same time, war is seen as part of the global transition.

In recent years, there has been recognition of the multifaceted sources of violent conflict, including human rights abuses, poverty, environmental degradation and refugee flows. Serious attention has been paid to the control of regional arms races, humanitarian intervention, peacekeeping and enforcement, non-military solutions to internal wars through conflict resolution, culture of peace and environmental security. Part III focuses on these emerging sets of problems and provides strategies to deal with them. Bjørn Møller (Chapter 5) explains the persistence of arms race problems on a regional scale in terms of action-reaction dynamics. A defensive restructuring of armed forces is needed to mitigate the security dilemma.

In Chapter 6, Daniel Druckman, Jim Wall and Paul Diehl propose that peacekeeping strategies need to be designed to create conditions for conflict resolution. They observe that peacekeeping would be ineffective in resolving protracted conflict without peacemaking and peacebuilding activities. Raimo Väyrynen (Chapter 7) finds that traditional conflict resolution methods mislead us in understanding the nature and cause of conflict in failed states by ignoring such factors as culture and power. Dan Smith (Chapter 8) demonstrates that successful preventive policies require adequate knowledge bases for intervention. According to Jennifer Jackson Preece (Chapter 9), management of ethnonational tension and conflict should be based on minority rights regimes voluntarily assumed and sustained by internal state actors.

Theories on development, conflict and security can be reformulated in terms of identity and culture. In Chapter 10, Ho-Won Jeong and Jyrki Käkönen suggest that environmental conflict needs to be understood in terms of various types of threats to the referent objects and the process of perceiving these threats. Chapter 11, by Arturo Escobar and Ho-Won Jeong, conceptualises postdevelopment in terms of noncapitalism and politics for the survival of place-based cultures. Michael Nagler (Chapter 12) highlights principled non-violence built in reconciliation as a means to change a culture saturated with violence.

In Part IV, the authors illustrate structural configurations in a global political space and their implications for human security. According to Dov Ronen (Chapter 13), states will be made an obsolete form of political entity in the future global order which will be shaped by the drive for the satisfaction of basic needs. Timothy Shaw and Sandra MacLean (Chapter 14) observe that regional civil society emerges in response to inequalities and social disruptions that are features of dominant neoliberal order. The 'bottom-up' forms of regionalism will promote human security. Jonathan Friedman (Chapter 15) points out the paradoxes of globalisation by looking at vertical polarisation in the global system.

Overall, this book aims to explain, first, the nature of violence and war, then moves on to approaches to managing and preventing violence and finally assesses structural changes. We analyse the conditions related not only to physical violence, but also to domination sustained by cultural norms, development practice and environmental policies. All the chapters offer critical analysis rather than mere observation or identification of changes that we have been experiencing in the new global environment. The recent developments in the social sciences and humanities such as critical security studies, political economy of globalisation, cultural politics and poststructural analysis of discourse and identity are reflected in many chapters.

As new images and ideas are emerging, it remains an important task to promote theoretical understandings of structural trends and explore new directions for action. Peace research can be established as an integrative project by developing a conceptually coherent map which helps to reveal the locations and sources of violence, examine strategies to deal with them and illuminate structural transitions to a non-hierarchical world order. The themes in various chapters of this book can be submerged under the disciplinary goal of peace research which links the control and elimination of violent conflicts to nonviolent structural transformations.

2 The Expanding Tool Chest for Peacebuilders

CHADWICK F. ALGER

A Peace 'Tool Chest'

The basic premise of this chapter is that we have learned much more about building peace in the 20th century, through research and practice, than we normally tend to apply. Therefore, we will attempt an inventory of the available instruments for pursuing peace. Twenty-four peace 'tools' will be presented -- two that were inherited from the 19th century, and twenty-two that have been developed in this century. Applying the concept 'tools' as a label for these twenty-four approaches can help to create a practical orientation toward their application. The enumeration of the tools in six rectangles in Figure 1 can be viewed as six toolboxes.

Figure 1: The Peacebuilders' Tool Chest

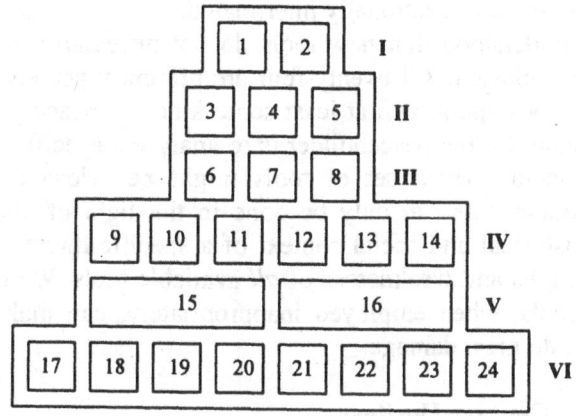

If they were stacked on top of each other, they would be familiar to the auto mechanic as six drawers in a mechanic's tool chest. If you told auto mechanics that six drawers of tools were indispensable to the peace 'mechanic', both as a result of learning through practice and because the world is becoming increasingly complicated as a result of new technology, they would quickly understand. The tool chest of the auto mechanic has ever more drawers because new technology is making automobiles increasingly complicated.

We will present the tools in chronological order mainly to demonstrate that new tools arose out of experience that revealed the shortcomings of older tools. Practitioners of any trade or profession that employs tools can understand this -- not only mechanics but also plumbers, carpenters, electricians, surgeons, etc. Of course, it will be obvious that our chronological presentation is very simplified. Innovation in history is very complex. We are never completely certain when a new idea first arises. In some respects all ideas embedded in peace tools are very old. While we would assert that the learning process revealed in Figure 2 (see page 16) certainly is reflected in the experience of some people, it is not based on intensive research on the deep historical origin of peace-related ideas. The basic purpose of Figure 2 is to offer an orderly context in which to learn about the twenty-four tools and the fact that they are functionally interrelated.

It must be understood that new tools do not necessarily make old tools useless or irrelevant. All twenty-four are presently perceived to be useful by *some*, for coping with at least some kinds of peace problems. Thus, the challenge for the peacebuilder is to analyse a specific threat to peace and to decide which set of tools might be relevant for that situation. Of course, this can only be done in the light of knowledge about (1) the historical and social context of a specific threat to peace, and (2) the strengths and weaknesses of *all* available tools. We certainly know that all tools, when employed inappropriately, can make things worse, and even do great damage.

Our Nineteenth Century Heritage

As we entered the 20th century, the state system had *Diplomacy* (1), a significant human achievement that deserves considerable credit for the fact that states have peaceful relations with others much of the time. The system of embassies that each country has in the capitals of other countries has developed over many centuries. Formerly consisting primarily of career diplomats representing their Foreign Ministry, now many embassies include representatives of other government departments responsible for health, labour, education, trade, environment, etc. Of course, this expansion of diplomatic representation reflects the impact of new technologies on relations between states.

There are significant limitations in the capacity of the inter-state diplomatic system to permit sustained contact among all states. Large states have embassies in virtually all other states -- some 185. And all of the smaller states tend to have embassies in the large states. But many smaller states cannot afford to have permanent embassies in all other states, and sometimes they may not really need permanent representation in distant small states. Instead, one embassy may be accredited to a number of states in a region. Thus, it is important to understand that there are limitations in the capacity of the diplomatic system to sustain linkage among all states.

Although we have emphasised that the inter-state diplomatic system preserves peace most of the time, nevertheless disputes do arise and create situations in which states fear aggression by others. In such cases, *Balance of Power* (2) may be used to deter aggression. In the sense in which we are using the term, the employment of balance of power means that a state attempts to acquire sufficient military and related capacity to deter aggression, or attempts to deter aggression by making alliances with other states. In some cases, when balance of power is employed as a deterrent, it does indeed deter aggression. On the other hand, reciprocal application of balance of power does sometimes lead to arms races. Many believed that balance of power and accompanying arms races contributed significantly to the outbreak of World War I.

In the aftermath of World War I, states created the first world organisation (members from Africa, Asia, Europe and North and South America) devoted to preserving peace. As many as 63 states became members of this League of Nations, but there were never more than 58 members at any one time. Although the League only made modest contributions to restraining inter-state violence, as the first world 'laboratory' devoted to inter-state peace, it made significant contributions toward the development of the United Nations in 1945.

16   The New Agenda for Peace Research

	19th Century	1919	1945	1950-1989	1990 -	
		League Covenant	UN Charter	UN Practice	UN Practice	NGO/Peoples Movements
		Collective Security (3)	Collective Security	Collective Security	Collective Security	
				Peacekeeping (9)	Peacekeeping	
		Peaceful Settlement (4)	Peaceful Settlement	Peaceful Settlement	Peaceful Settlement	Track II Diplomacy (17)
	Diplomacy (1) Balance of Power (2)	Disarmament/ Arms Control (5)	Disarmament/ Arms Control	Disarmament/ Arms Control	Disarmament/ Arms Control	Conversion (18)
					Humanitarian Intervention (15)	Defensive Defence (19)
	I	II			Preventative Diplomacy (16)	
			Functionalism (6)	Functionalism	Functionalism	Nonviolence (20)
			Self-Determination (7)	Self-Determination	Self-Determination	Citizen Defence (21)
			Human Rights (8)	Human Rights	Human Rights	Self Reliance (22)
				Economic Development (10)	Economic Development	Feminist Perspectives (23)
				Economic Equity (NIEO) (11)	Economic Equity (NIEO)	Peace Education (24)
				Communication Equity (12)	Communication Equity	
				Ecological Balance (13)	Ecological Balance	
				Governance for Commons (14)	Governance of Commons	
			III	IV	V	VI
	NEGATIVE PEACE			POSITIVE PEACE		

Figure 2: The Emergence of Peace Tools

The League of Nations Covenant

The League of Nations Covenant, which came into force in 1920, provided members with three main peace tools. First, *Collective Security* (3) was devised to overcome the weaknesses of balance of power as a deterrent to aggression. Collective Security obligated all who were members of the League to 'undertake to respect and preserve as against external aggression the territorial integrity and existing political independence of all Members of the League'. Those who advocated collective security believed that the pledge of *all* to resist aggression by *any* member would be such an overwhelming deterrent that none would have reasonable ground for fearing aggression. But the obvious common sense of collective security in the abstract ignores that *all* may not be able or willing to resist aggression by *any* other member. This may be explained by longstanding friendships and alliances and perhaps by fear of retribution by powerful neighbours. Also, when the aggressor is very powerful, the practice of collective security in the pursuit of peace may produce an even larger war than the initial aggression. For reasons such as these, collective security did not prevent aggression by Germany, Japan, and Italy that led to World War II.

The second main peace tool in the League Covenant was *Peaceful Settlement* (4), intended to prevent the outbreak of violence in those instances when routine diplomacy fails to do so. In cases where a dispute may 'lead to a rupture', the Covenant requires states to 'submit the matter either to arbitration or judicial settlement or to inquiry by the [League] Council'. In other words, members involved in a dispute agree to involve certain 'third parties' when they alone cannot control escalating hostility. In employing third parties, states are drawing on human experience in a variety of other contexts: labour-management disputes, disputes between buyers and sellers, marital disputes, etc. In giving third party approaches a place in the Covenant, the League obviously drew on earlier provisions for employment of third parties developed in the Hague Conferences of 1899 and 1907.

The third main peace tool in the Covenant was *Disarmament/Arms Control* (5). Some who believed that arms races had contributed to the outbreak of World War I thought that elimination, or at least reduction, of arms would enhance chances for peace. This was an effort to codify disarmament and arms control proposals that had been advanced in earlier times. Although Covenant provisions for disarmament/arms control never fulfilled the aspirations of advocates, they did provoke the negotiation of numerous arms control measures in the 1930s. These provided valuable experience, and also a great deal of scepticism, for those who would again face similar circumstances after World War II.

The United Nations Charter

Following World War II the victorious states once again endeavoured to create a world organisation that would maintain peace. When the United Nations Charter was drafted in San Francisco in 1945, it once again incorporated collective security, peaceful settlement and disarmament/arms control. Experience under the Covenant led to strengthening of collective security by explicitly providing for procedures through which members would make armed forces available for collective security response, and a Military Staff Committee that would plan for the use of these forces and advise and assist the Security Council in their employment. In some respects, means for pacific settlement are more fully defined. Although disarmament/arms control is again made available, the Charter emphasises it less than the Covenant.

But the most significant differences between the Covenant and the Charter consist of the addition of three peace tools. The first was *Functionalism* (6) in which states cooperate in efforts to solve common economic and social problems that might disrupt normal relationships and even lead to violence. Drafters of the Charter had in mind examples such as worldwide depression in the 1930s and the inability of states to collaborate in coping with this disaster. The depression led to strikes, extreme social unrest and violence in many countries and significantly contributed to the development of totalitarian governments and aggression in some cases. Emphasis on economic and social cooperation in the Charter is signified by the creation of the Economic and Social Council (ECOSOC) alongside the Security Council (responsible for collective security) which had been the only council in the League. ECOSOC was created 'with a view to the creation of conditions of stability and well-being which are necessary for peaceful and friendly relations among nations...' Its mission includes the achievement of higher standards of living, full employment, solutions of international economic, social, health and related problems and international cultural and educational cooperation. At the same time, ECOSOC has the responsibility of coordinating the activities of some 30 agencies in the UN system with responsibility for health, labour, education, development, environment, population, trade, atomic energy and a number of other global problems.

It is very important that we appreciate the degree to which the League 'laboratory' provided the knowledge and experience that led to the significant place that economic and social cooperation is given in the UN Charter. Although the League Covenant gave relatively slight attention to economic and social activities, in practice, the League became significantly involved in a great number of economic and social issues. Indeed, as the days of the League drew to an end before World War II, proposals had already been made to create a League economic and social council.

The second peace tool added by the UN Charter was *Self-Determination* (7). Here again the UN built on League experience. In granting independence to many nations formerly in the defeated Austro-Hungarian and Ottoman Empires, the World War I peace settlements recognised self-determination as a tool for building future peace. In addition, parts of the former Ottoman Empire outside of Europe and other colonies of defeated states were placed under a Permanent Mandates Commission of the League of Nations, including Iraq, Syria, and Lebanon in the Middle East; Cameroons, Rwanda, Urundi, Tanganyika, Togoland, Somaliland and Southwest Africa in Africa; and areas in the Pacific. These territories were administered by states that were members of the victorious coalition, with some attaining independence before World War II. It is very important that the Mandate system established reporting procedures through which administrating powers were responsible to the members of the League. This laid the foundation for later growth in the belief that those governing colonies have some responsibilities to the rest of the world. In the UN Charter, the Mandates were called Trusteeships, and placed under a third Council, the Trusteeship Council. But most important for self-determination in the Charter was inclusion of a 'Declaration Regarding Non-Self-Governing Territories', which covered the many overseas colonies not under trusteeship. This Declaration asserts that those administrating colonies are obligated 'to develop self-government...and to assist them in the progressive development of their free political institutions...'

Eventually this Declaration provided the foundation for prodding the overseas colonial powers to begin relinquishing control of their colonies.

This led to the 'Declaration on the Granting of Independence to Colonial Countries and Peoples' by the General Assembly in 1960. Both the Trusteeship Council and the General Assembly played a very significant role in the largely peaceful dismantling of overseas empires. In this respect, self-determination has proven to be a very useful peace tool. This remarkable transformation of the inter-state system more than doubled the number of independent states and the number of UN members.

Now the world confronts a new generation of self-determination demands by peoples in multi-nation states (as in Yugoslavia) and in multi-state nations (e.g., the Kurds). The UN system desperately needs to establish procedures whereby the legitimacy of these claims can be assessed, *before* severe disruption and violence occur. At the same time, those making self-determination claims deemed to be legitimate must guarantee the rights of minorities that are inevitably present in all political units. The numerous cases in which unscrupulous leaders employ self-determination strategies for personal gain is but one example of the fact that peace tools, as well as all other tools, can be used for both noble and depraved purposes.

The third peace tool added by the UN Charter was *Human Rights* (8). Although these words were never used in the League Covenant, human rights are mentioned seven times in the Charter, including the second sentence of the Preamble which announces determination 'to reaffirm faith in fundamental human rights, in the dignity and worth of the human person, in the equal rights of men and women and of nations large and small'. As in the case of economic and social cooperation, the Charter states that human rights shall be promoted in order to 'create conditions and well-being which are necessary for peaceful and friendly relations among nations...' Building on the brief references to human rights in the Charter, the UN General Assembly soon produced the Universal Declaration on Human Rights in 1947 which is now widely accepted as part of international common law and has even been applied by domestic courts in a number of states.

In order to strengthen the legal status of the Declaration, its principles were, in 1966, put in treaty form by the General Assembly, as the International Covenant on Civil and Political Rights and the International Covenant on Economic, Social and Cultural Rights. In addition, an array of more specialised treaties have been developed on genocide, racial discrimination, women's rights, children's rights, forced labour, cruel and inhumane punishment, rights of refugees and other human rights problems. All of these help to prevent the creation of unacceptable conditions of human depravity that may lead to severe unrest and even fighting.

Readers have noted that in Figure 2 peace tools 1 - 5 are placed in the category Negative Peace and tools 6 - 8 are in the category Positive Peace. Put in the simplest terms, Negative Peace is achieved by stopping violence. Positive Peace is achieved by building societies and inter-state relationships that do not generate conditions likely to precipitate violence or other causes of human suffering and deprivation. The first tends to depend largely on the expertise and activities of professional diplomatic and military people. The second draws on expertise in a diversity of professions coping with economic and social problems. The distinctive character of negative peace and positive peace cannot be pushed too far because they are intertwined. But it is important to understand that in this century practitioners learned that in applying tools that focused mainly on stopping the violence, or directly preventing it from breaking out, they often found themselves confronting overwhelming escalations of violence that could not be stopped. In other words, they learned that they were too late and realised that something should have been done earlier to cope with underlying causes of violence, before things got out of hand. This led to supplementing those peace tools employing a more negative peace emphasis with those more focused on positive peace.

Because the concept of power used to define power politics, super power and world power are frequently employed in works on international relations, it is useful to point out that our 20th century journey in the quest for peace has greatly expanded the instruments through which power can be exercised. This concept has been frequently associated with one kind of power, military power. Kenneth Boulding insightfully drew our attention to 'the three faces of power': (1) threat power -- the power to destroy, (2) economic power -- the power to produce and exchange, and (3) integrative power -- the power to create such relations as love, respect, friendship and legitimacy (Boulding, 1989). The peace tools invented in the 20th century apply a diversity of forms of economic and integrative power. Thus, self-determination employs the power of legitimacy in the quest for peace, and functionalism employs a variety of kinds of integrative power. In other words, our quest for peace has revealed that power employed in problem solving is often more effective than threat power.

United Nations Practice, 1950-1989

The post-World War II context in which the United Nations emerged provided two severe challenges to those attempting to apply the six peace tools incorporated into the Charter. First, the East-West conflict escalated into confrontation between two military blocs: the North Atlantic Treaty Organisation (NATO), led by the United States, and the Warsaw Pact, led by the Soviet Union. The Charter assumed that these states would collaborate in the Security Council in employing peaceful settlement and collective security in order to preserve peace. But instead, the 'policemen' threatened world war with each other and became indirectly involved in conflicts in Africa, Asia and the Middle East. There was particular danger that conflicts in the Middle East and the Congo (Zaire) would escalate into a world war. As a response, *Peacekeeping* (9) was invented. Although some variations have been employed, peacekeeping essentially involves a cease-fire, followed by the creation of a demilitarised corridor on each side of a truce line. This neutral corridor is patrolled by a UN peacekeeping force.

Peacekeeping is fundamentally different from collective security in several respects. Peacekeeping forces require the permission of states on whose territory they are based. Although big powers have provided logistical support, until quite recently the troops normally come from smaller states deemed to be politically acceptable by the parties to the conflict. The troops normally only carry small arms that are used in self-defence. Their primary protection is the fact that their blue helmets and the UN emblems on their jeeps are given legitimacy by the members of the UN under whose authority they are acting. UN peacekeeping forces have successfully kept peace in the Congo (Zaire), the Middle East, Cyprus and other places for many years. But there has not been equal success in resolving the conflicts that have made them necessary.

The second post-war challenge to the UN was the struggle for, and acquisition of self-determination by overseas colonies of European-based empires. This not only transformed the inter-state system but also brought fundamental changes in the United Nations. There was rapid doubling of UN membership, largely by addition of new members from Africa, Asia, the Caribbean and Pacific Islands. Widespread poverty has been very significant in most of the new states, thus creating a deeper gulf between rich and poor UN members. Other terms applied to the two groups have been Developed Countries (DC) and Less Developed

Countries (LDC). Also the term Third World has often been used for the poor countries of Africa, Asia and Latin America, as distinguished from the First World (free market, industrialised countries) and Second World (Soviet bloc).

Prodded by the growing divide between the rich and the poor in the United Nations, the three peace tools developed out of UN practice were largely a product of growing insight on the relevance of economic conditions and relationships for peace. *Economic Development* (10) became a growing policy concern both within the UN and outside. The basic idea was that the rich-poor gap could be diminished if the rich countries provided development aid to the poor countries so that they could 'take off' and become developed. It tended to be assumed that development in Third World countries should be patterned after the industrialised countries of Europe and North America. Emphasis was placed on heavy industry and economic infrastructure such as roads, railroads, airports and dams. In earlier efforts, food and agriculture tended to be given low priority. Aid was primarily provided by special development loan funds and technical assistance programmes that emphasised the transfer of know-how, often through providing technical experts and the tools they require. Economic development programmes were established not only by UN agencies and regional international governmental organisations but also by governments in industrialised countries. It was frequently argued that the multilateral programmes of the UN and other international organisations were more fruitful because they were more likely to be based on economic development criteria, but that bilateral programmes tended to be less economically productive because they tended to be more shaped by bilateral political factors.

Many people would argue that both bilateral and multilateral economic development programmes have often contributed to peace by diminishing poverty. But overall they did not diminish the rich-poor gap in the world. Indeed, as economic development programmes grew in the 1950s and 1960s, the rich-poor gap continued to grow. Critics of these development programmes began to argue that the gap was growing because of the nature of the economic relations between the developed countries and the Third World. In other words, they attributed the growth in the rich-poor gap to the international economic structure in which countries in the Third World were perceived to be dependent upon industrialised countries. From this perspective, it was seen that the growth in the gap would continue until this dependency relationship was overcome.

This led to Third World demands for *International Economic Equity* (11). The Third World movement for a more equitable international economic system was centred in (1) the Non-Aligned Movement, an organisation of some 100 countries from all parts of the world that were neither aligned with NATO states nor Warsaw Pact states and in (2) the United Nations conference on Trade and Development (UNCTAD). The latter began as a UN conference in 1964 and later became a permanent UN organisation, with headquarters in Geneva. The Third World caucus in UNCTAD came to be known as the 'Group of 77', although it eventually included some 120 states. In these two organisations the Third World devised a programme for a New International Economic Order (NIEO). Among their demands were (1) stabilisation of the prices of Third World commodities (coffee, tea, cocoa, etc.) in order to build a predictable economic base for development programmes, (2) pegging the price of these commodities to the price of manufactured products which the Third World buys from industrialised countries, (3) access of Third World products to First World markets, (4) Third World access to technology useful in their development programmes, and (5) international regulation of the activities of transnational corporations in Third World countries.

As revealed in the name of the new UN agency, UNCTAD, the basic thrust of these demands were that development aid would be less necessary in an international economy structured so that the Third World could 'earn a living'. Instead, it was asserted that the international economy is structured so that the benefits pile up in corporate headquarters and banks in industrialised countries, thus making it necessary for Third World countries to seek aid. Unfortunately, from a Third World perspective, although an extensive campaign was waged in the UN General Assembly for NIEO principles, for the most part, industrialised countries were very unresponsive. This has generated considerable animosity in the Third World as the gap between the rich and the poor continues to grow. At the same time, there was puzzlement over the apparent inability of the Third World to reach the people of industrialised countries with the reasonableness of their appeal. For example, there was a tendency for the press in the United States to picture Third World demands in the General Assembly as reckless demands for special privileges by an 'African-Asian-Latin American horde' which was not grateful for all of the aid that they had received.

Frustration over failure to convince people in industrialised countries about the justness of their NIEO appeal contributed to the demands of the Third World for *International Communications Equity* (12). Observing that the headquarters of the world news agencies (United Press, Associated Press, Reuters, etc.) were in industrialised countries, and citing examples of biased Third World reporting, Third World countries began to ask for a New International Information and Communications Order (NIICO). The demands for the NIICO was also stimulated by technological change in communication. In particular, using communication satellites in geostationary orbit makes it possible to reach into every country and virtually any village in the world. Of course, this technology has been developed, and is largely controlled, by giant communications corporations headquartered in industrialised countries.

The struggle for the NIICO has been largely waged in the United Nations Educational, Scientific and Cultural Organisation (UNESCO), with its headquarters in Paris. This dispute illuminates how technological change may transform the context in which a peace tool is applied and thereby generate conflict in its definition and use. The UNESCO Constitution, adopted in London in November 1945, asserted 'that ignorance of each other's ways and lives has been a common cause...of that suspicion and mistrust between peoples of the world through which their differences have all too often broken into war'. The Constitution asserted that these conditions could be overcome through education, pursuit of objective truth and 'the free exchange of ideas and knowledge'. The last would be employed 'for the purposes of mutual understanding and a truer and more perfect knowledge of each other's lives'. In practice, what was believed to be the essential spirit of these worlds was incorporated into the words 'free flow of communication'.

But as newly independent peoples in the Third World became increasingly sensitive to the quality of their recently won political independence, they developed a growing awareness of the one-way international flow of news, radio and TV broadcasts, films, books and magazines. Out of this dissatisfaction came a replacement for the earlier 'free flow' slogan: 'free and balanced flow of communication'. But how is 'balance' to be achieved while still remaining 'free'? This is a vitally important peace issue that must be resolved through international dialogue and debate. Ways must be found to structure communications in such a way that they foster peace rather than produce deeply felt animosity.

Although environmental issues have been a significant human problem at least since the Industrial Revolution in the late 18th century, *Ecological Balance* (13) became a widely recognised problem in world relations as a result of the UN Environment Conference held in Stockholm in 1972. But at this time there was tendency for industrialised countries to take the lead and for Third World countries to see it as a strategy to prevent them from industrialising too -- thus as a way to keep them poor. But by the time of the UN Conference on Environment and Development (UNCED) in Rio de Janeiro in 1992, all parts of the world agreed that ecological balance is a problem confronted by all peoples. Furthermore, whereas in 1972 very few tended to see ecological balance as a dimension of peace, this perspective is now widely shared.

The relationship between ecological balance and peace can be viewed from at least two perspectives. One perspective achieved widespread visibility during the UNCED Conference when disputes erupted about (1) who is responsible for global pollution, (2) which ecological problems should receive priority and (3) who should pay 'to clean up the mess'. In the context of growing pollution, and increasing sensitivity to the negative effects of pollution, these questions are likely to create increasing conflict in the future. Particularly acrimonious at the UNCED Conference was the debate between representatives of industrialised and Third World countries. The Third World drew attention to the fact that industrialised countries are the primary polluters. From this, they conclude that industrialised countries should accept special responsibility for paying for programmes to restore ecological balance. At the same time, Third World countries point out that these same countries have enjoyed the benefits of industrialisation while polluting air, water and land. Therefore, if Third World countries are to be deprived of the opportunity to develop in the same way as industrialised countries, but are to employ more costly approaches, industrialised countries have an obligation to provide financial support for 'sustainable development'.

A second perspective on the peace-ecological balance is that by disrupting normal relationships between specific human beings and their environment, pollution directly produces peacelessness for these people. In some cases, as with the destruction of the habitat of people in rain forests with bulldozers and explosives, it is as quick and devastating as war. The rapidly growing intrusion of new technologies on the commons makes provisions for *Governance for the Commons* (14) an increasingly significant peace issue. By the commons we refer to areas outside the territorial boundaries of states that tend to be assumed to be spaces available to all, a term early associated with the village green in the centre of small towns and also city parks. In the international context, the oceans and space are generally thought of as commons, and many would add Antarctica. We shall use the example of the oceans in our brief discussion, an exceedingly significant commons because it covers 70% of the surface of the globe. Before the days of more intrusive technology, the two main issues in the ocean commons tended to be establishing agreed upon borders of states, early set at a three mile limit, and insuring 'freedom on the seas' in all of the rest of the oceans. But new technologies for ocean transit, fishing, drilling for gas and oil, mining minerals on the seabed and ocean research -- as well as increased use of the oceans as dumping grounds for waste produced on land -- have raised a host of new problems with respect to the ocean commons.

A historic step in building positive peace was taken in 1982 with the completion of a comprehensive treaty for governance of the oceans, the United Nations Law of the Sea Treaty. Completed after 10 years of negotiation, a US negotiator, Elliott Richardson, called it the single most important development in international law since the drafting of the UN Charter. The treaty provides a new organisation in the UN system, the International Seabed Authority, with its own Assembly, Council and Secretariat, as well as an International Tribunal for the Law of the Sea and a branch to oversee the mining of manganese nodules on the sea bed. The International Seabed Authority became fully operational as an autonomous international organisation in June 1996, with headquarters in Kingston, Jamaica. The treaty also offers new approaches for peaceful settlement of disputes. Not only are there provisions for getting quick decisions from the International Tribunal, but states involved in a dispute are offered four different options for working toward a settlement: the International Tribunal, the International Court of Justice, an arbitral tribunal provided for in the treaty and special arbitral tribunals consisting of experts in the issue under dispute. If parties to a dispute cannot jointly agree on one of these four methods, they are then obliged to accept arbitration.

United Nations Practice, 1990 – Present

As the United Nations and its member states have responded to a number of international crises in the changed political context of the post-Cold War period, two additional peace tools have emerged out of the 'laboratories' of experience. *Humanitarian Intervention* (15) has evolved largely unannounced because it has often been called peacekeeping -- as exemplified by interventions in Somalia and Rwanda -- although it is a fundamentally different kind of peace tool. Humanitarian intervention differs from peacekeeping in that it may take place without the permission of the state involved, and thus it is occasionally referred to as Chapter VI 3/4, placing it between peacekeeping and Chapter VII enforcement. Recent humanitarian interventions include the UN Observer Mission in Haiti (UNMIH), UN Mission for Rwanda (UNAMIR) and UN Operation in Somalia (UNOSOM). In these operations the Security Council authorised a group of states to deploy military forces outside the UN context. But in other cases, including Somalia and Yugoslavia, enforcement was entrusted by the Security Council to the Secretary General or another international organisation such as NATO. Arend and Beck (1993, pp. 113-14) define humanitarian intervention as 'the use of armed force by a state (or states) to protect rights violations there'. It occurs within the borders of the target state without their explicit consent. Väyrynen, after citing the Arend and Beck definition of humanitarian intervention, reports that there is growing opinion that international law permits access to crisis areas in which egregious violation of human rights override domestic jurisdiction. Here, of course, he refers to the provision in Article 2(7) of the Charter prohibiting intervention 'in matters which are essentially within the domestic jurisdiction of any state' (Väyrynen, 1998, pp. 61-62).

But humanitarian intervention can also be used to prevent escalation of a domestic dispute that would jeopardise the security of other states. In this case, support of the Charter is easier, since these cases would seem to come under Article 39 of Chapter VII which applies to 'threats' to peace. In the case of application of enforcement measures under Chapter VII, Article 2(7) does not apply. But some might say that humanitarian crises seem to 'endanger' peace rather than be a 'threat' to it, calling for use of Chapter VI. By using Article 39, 'threat' to peace, N.D. White thinks that the Security Council has stretched the concept to meet humanitarian needs, and has developed a new political and legal justification for quick enforcement against 'rogue' states (White, 1993, pp. 38-49, cited by Väyrynen, 1998, p. 63). Although the development of humanitarian intervention as an acceptable peace tool is still in process, it seems to be widely acceptable that the limits of Article 2(7) have been considerably narrowed in practice, and in legal definitions.

There is a widespread commentary declaring that one of the prime failures in world politics has been the tendency of states, and inter-state organisations, to respond to crises rather than to anticipate and work to prevent them. Kittani (1995) reports that Boutros-Ghali presided over major innovations for institutionalising *Preventative Diplomacy* (16) in the UN Secretariat. They include the creation of regional desks within the Department of Political Affairs (DPA) charged with responsibility of monitoring developments around the world, creation of Task Forces on peace operations, and interdepartmental working groups. In his *Agenda for Peace*, Boutros-Ghali defines preventive diplomacy as 'action to prevent disputes from arising between parties, to prevent existing disputes from escalating into conflicts and to limit the spread of the latter when they occur'. For Boutros-Ghali, preventive diplomacy requires three elements: measures to create confidence, early warning based on information gathering, and informal or formal fact-finding. 'It may also involve preventive deployment and, in some situations, demilitarised zones' (Boutros-Ghali, 1995, pp. 46-51).

Not surprisingly, fact finding and early warning are emphasised by many practitioners and scholars. Some note the importance of information collected by the Secretary General in his contacts with governments, and with others, and his power to dispatch special envoys (Boutros-Ghali, 1995, pp. 47-48). The Commission on Global Governance welcomes the greater freedom the Secretary General now has to dispatch missions, but is concerned that he does not have the resources for doing the job (Commission on Global Governance, 1995, p. 99). There is increasing recognition that the kind of fact finding that is needed for competent early warning would have to draw systematically on the information resources of the *entire* UN system. Boutros-Ghali has drawn attention to the valuable UN networks of information on the environment, nuclear accidents, natural disasters, mass movements of populations, and threats of famine and disease. He underlines the need to synthesise these sources with political indicators, to assess threats to peace that they suggest, and to analyse action that might be taken (Boutros-Ghali, 1995, pp. 48-49).

Non-Governmental Organisations and People's Movements

The final drawer in the tool chest outlined in Figure 1 consists of non-governmental organisations and people's movements. The term non-governmental organisation (NGO) is a concept evolving out of international organisation research and practice to distinguish inter-state organisations such as the UN that have governments of states as members from international organisations whose members consist of national associations or individuals that are not government officials. Prominent examples are organisations such as the international professional associations (doctors and lawyers), international scholarly associations (political scientists and sociologists), international religious organisations (virtually all faiths and denominations), and international organisations focusing on specific issues such as Greenpeace, Amnesty International and World Federation of Mental Health. NGOs made up of members from a number of countries are often referred to as International NGOs (INGOs). More than 4,000 INGOs mirror virtually all those to be found within single countries. Many INGO movements arise to address specific peace issues such as disarmament, poverty, human rights and ecological balance. At times, these movements are coalitions of already existing NGOs and INGOs but they may also include, and may be led by, others who become mobilised in response to a specific issue. Thus, because of considerable overlap, we combine NGOs, INGOs and peoples movements in our discussion.

The growing involvement of people outside of government in world affairs, in general, and peace issues, in particular, can be broadly described as People's organisations (PO). POs have mobilised people for peace action by bringing pressure on governments to employ all of the peace tools that we have enumerated. For example, during the Cold War, it was often peace movements that kept disarmament and arms control on the public agenda at times when governments of both of the superpowers seemed disinterested. Many organisations have had sustained involvement in movements advocating economic aid and adjustment in international economic practices. Many would assert that the towering achievements in drafting and embryonic efforts at monitoring international human rights standards have been attained largely because of sustained PO initiatives and pressure on individual states and UN organisations. At the same time, many would give POs considerable credit for placing environmental issues high on the global agenda. Reflections of this were the widely reported activities of the assembled POs from all over the world at the UNCED Conference in Rio de Janeiro in 1992.

POs have also been the inventors and advocates of at least eight new peace tools. It must be made clear that these do not replace tools already employed, but they do illuminate weaknesses of old tools, or the fact that there is no tool for coping with specific causes of peacelessness. *Second Track Diplomacy* (17) addresses the limitations of diplomacy and peaceful settlement by recognising that negotiations stalled or broken off by governmental representatives may be revived by initiatives outside of government. Consisting at least, in part, of people outside of government, this approach offers a 'second track' that may reach into alternative representatives of governments, often at a lower level. This approach has been advocated and employed largely by scholars, often including those who have had wide governmental experience.

One form of second track diplomacy originated by an Australian diplomat turned scholar, John Burton (1990a), is given the name 'problem solving workshop'. Burton is concerned that representatives of states often do not *resolve* conflicts, but tend instead to arrange *settlements* that 'paper over' underlying grievances which will be the source of escalating conflict in the future. This is because representatives of states sometimes do not adequately represent the needs of all that will be affected by the settlement. To overcome this shortcoming, problem solving workshops assemble both governmental and non-governmental people who can widely represent the needs of all parties, including those not adequately represented by representatives of states. The workshops consist of meetings between these people and social scientists who help them to probe deeply into the basic roots of the conflict, stimulate dialogue between the parties in search of mutually acceptable solutions and introduce social science insights where they are deemed to be useful. Burton is particularly reluctant to have these social scientists pose solutions because he believes that viable solutions must come from the participants themselves. Not all practitioners of this approach share Burton's reluctance. This approach has been widely practised in international disputes, including Cyprus, the Middle East, Northern Ireland and the Argentine-British war over the Malvinas/Falkland Islands.

The exceedingly slow progress in disarmament/arms control negotiations has provoked the development of four approaches that could, in some instance, be viewed as supplements to negotiations and, in others as substitutes. These approaches sometimes diminish the need for specific kinds of weapons and, at other times, attempt to offer nonviolent substitutes for weapons.

Conversion (18) is targeted at the conversion of military production to that which satisfies civilian needs, such as housing, appliances, etc. This approach tends to illuminate the domestic sources of arms races in that arms production is often advocated as a way to create jobs for factory workers, engineers and researchers. It follows that the communities, in which those employed in arms development and production live, come to depend on arms production to keep the local economy prosperous. But arms production as a means for providing employment may, of course, contribute to arms races by provoking other countries into responding by building more weapons. Conversion plans, drafted largely by POs in local communities, advocate ways in which more jobs can be created through investment in civilian production than through less labour-intensive military production.

In the 20th century, the explosive power and geographical reach of weapons have increased to the point where virtually any place on earth might be reached with a nuclear missile. On the other hand, it is those who have this long-range destructive capacity that are most fearful that they may be destroyed. Why? Because Country A that has long-range nuclear weapons fears that Country B might destroy its weapons with their nuclear weapons. Why? Because Country B fears that Country A might make a 'first strike' against its weapons. To overcome the fact that those with the most powerful offensive weapons are least secure, some advocate *Defensive Defence* (19), that is, defence employing weapons that are defensive in nature. This approach has largely been advocated by POs and scholars in Europe.

There is no doubt that it is sometimes difficult to distinguish between defensive arms and offensive arms. On the other hand, there is also no doubt that some arms, such as intercontinental missiles, aircraft carriers and long-range bombers, have obvious offensive capacity. Other weapons, such as land mines and fixed shore batteries, can be employed in a strictly defensive capacity. In certain respects, weapons between these extremes could be used for either offence or defence. But it cannot be denied that certain arms are essentially defensive, such as short-range mechanised forces, interception aircraft and mobile anti-aircraft missiles (Fischer, 1984, pp. 47-62). Combined with other peace tools, efforts of State A to present a defensive posture to State B diminishes the fear of State B that A will be aggressive. This approach motivates states to acquire understanding, more than they often do, of how their weapons are perceived, and the consequences of this perception. At the same time, the defensive defence approach may stimulate arms designers to employ new technology in the design of weapons that are convincingly limited to defensive purposes. Instead, it would seem that up to this point new technology has largely been directed toward bigger and bigger weapons with ever more distant reach.

Nonviolence (20), used by POs in the pursuit of social change, can be viewed as a substitute for the use of arms. Employment of nonviolence diminishes the need for police, and military forces employed for internal security within a state, to use their weapons. This can diminish the need for and employment of armed forces in countries where the military are expected to make a significant contribution to maintaining internal order. Indeed, much of the arms trade in the world is less motivated by the fear of neighbouring states than by the fear of internal uprisings.

Presently there is a growing interest in nonviolence throughout the world as an increasing number of people acquire first-hand knowledge of the failure of the employment of arms to bring peace. Significant is the way in which nonviolence training gives those involved penetrating understanding of reasons for the often thoughtless impulse to respond with violence when provoked by others, and the long-term negative consequences of responding with violence. At the same time, they learn reasons why nonviolent responses are more likely to receive nonviolent responses in return. This restrains the launching of violence spirals which escalate into ever larger violent reactions.

Unfortunately, many people still tend to wrongly perceive nonviolent action as passive. Instead nonviolence actively engages in conflict, but without inflicting violence on others and without violating its fundamental values. This strategy is based on the insight that social change created by violence may establish institutions of violence that outlast the revolution and may put in power people who habitually use violence. Those who advocate nonviolence first try to reach opponents through petition, argument and discussion. If that fails, direct action such as non-cooperation with authorities, civil disobedience and fasting may be employed. But fundamental is the consistent recognition of opponents as fellow human beings. As stated by Gandhi in his campaign against British imperialism: 'Whilst we may attack measures and systems, we may not, must not attack men. Imperfect ourselves, we must be tender towards others and slow to impute motives' (Ambler, 1990, p. 201).

Citizen Defence (21) is closely related to nonviolence employed for social change, but this tool employs nonviolent techniques for national defence. Citizen defence goes one step further than defensive defence by also eliminating defensive weapons. Fundamental to civilian defence is deterrence through convincing a potential invader that there would be no payoff from invasion. Instead there would be a struggle in which the invader would be continually challenged. Citizen defence requires large scale, well-publicised organisation and planning for massive refusal to cooperate with the invader's military government. Police would refuse to arrest local patriots; teachers would refuse to introduce the invader's propaganda; workers would use strikes and delays to obstruct the invaders from acquiring their needs. Politicians, civil servants and judges would ignore the invaders' orders. Local plans would be made to maintain local media, schools and other local services.

This kind of resistance would have to be backed up by underground broadcasting stations and presses, storage for food, medicine, water and fuel, and plans for dispersion of people to places where these facilities would be located. Gene Sharp, a strong civilian defence advocate and strategist asserts that 'nonviolent action resembles military war more than it does negotiation; it is a technique of struggle. As such, nonviolent action involves the use of power' (Sharp, 1970, p. 21). At the same time, it requires patriots with courage, ingenuity, tenacity and unusual creativity.

People who have lived their entire life in societies in which there is an unquestioned reflex in which violence is responded to with violence frequently have difficulty in accepting the fact that nonviolent defence makes sense. But the argument for nonviolent defence is persuasive enough that it must be included in any peacemakers' tool box. After all, there is always the possibility that military defence will be perceived as potentially aggressive. What often begins as truly defensive precautions may inadvertently involve a state in an arms race. At the same time, arms production and employment always takes resources that could be devoted to human needs. Furthermore, armed defence in modern war almost always results in the destruction of cities, their populations and the economic and social infrastructure. These costs and likely consequences of military defence impel us to approach, with an open mind, an alternative that does not in any way threaten neighbours and that is focused primarily on defence of life and social institutions.

Sharp reports that there have been many instances of effective nonviolent defence, such as early resistance by American colonists, 1773-1775; Hungarian passive resistance against Austrian rule, 1850-1867; Finland's disobedience and non-cooperation with the Russians, 1898-1905; and resistance in several Nazi-occupied countries, especially Norway, the Netherlands and Denmark (Sharp, 1970, p. 20).

Self-Reliance (22) emerged as a peace tool in the context of a dialogue focused primarily on the economic dimensions of peace which evolved from functionalism, to economic development, to international economic equity -- each successive approach attempting to cope with limitations of preceding approaches. Some critics of the New International Economic Order's approach to obtaining international economic equity are critical of its emphasis on creating a more equitable trading system. They observe that this would tend to increase the utilisation of land in rural areas of the Third World for producing agricultural exports, thereby requiring those tilling small farms to become employees of large plantations. Thus, the rural masses would become dependent on trade in an international economic system in which profits would tend to gravitate to owners of agricultural industries, thereby increasing the gap between the rich and the poor. At the same time, rural people would become increasingly dependent on external sources for food and other necessities that had been produced at home. In making this argument, critics of the NIEO cite, as examples, African areas -- formerly self-sufficient in food production -- which now import food from abroad. Of course, the drastic change in local economies foreseen would also lead to equally dramatic changes in local culture which is intertwined with the local economy.

A very significant contribution of the self-reliance critique is that it shifts attention to the consequences of international economic relationships for the mass of individuals. It asks: what will the impact of economic development and international economic equity strategies be which are designed and implemented by decisions in national capitals, on the mass of individuals who have not participated in making these decisions? By raising these questions, insight is gained with respect to the fact that, although our discussions of peace tend to focus on relations between leaders of states and nations, the presence or absence of peace is most accurately measured by the degree to which the masses are experiencing peace in their daily lives.

Emphasised is the fact that self-reliance does not mean self-sufficiency, or the absence of trade, but it does mean 'reliance on oneself to the point that your own capabilities are so well developed that if a crisis should occur, then one could be self-sufficient'. Galtung is particularly concerned when a local community, country or region does not make sufficient use of its own potential but submits to long-term economic exchange in which primary products are exchanged for manufactured goods. In this case, he sees that there is enduring acceptance of a long-term inferior position in which it will be difficult to satisfy the basic needs of local people (Galtung, pp. 12-13).

Self-reliance is a useful example of the degree to which there are connections and overlaps between peace tools. We have already noted that self-reliance challenges development practices that might frustrate the full development of individual human potential and that might contribute to conflict produced by growing disparities in wealth. At the same time, self-reliance shares much with self-determination, although in this case, it is not applied to nationality and ethnic groups but to individual human beings and diverse economic units. Also, self-reliance, in its pursuit of human fulfilment, pursues some of the same goals as human rights, particularly those considered to be economic and social.

The *Feminist Perspective* (23) is particularly useful in shedding light on the degree to which values associated with militarism and military organisations permeate societies and how this came to be. At the same time, the feminist perspective provides a vision of alternative kinds of societies. It is necessary to consider the feminist perspective as a separate tool because women's perspectives and experiences have been largely omitted in most works on international relations and peace. One need not be a female in order to approach human behaviour with a feminist perspective, but there is no doubt that the actual experiences of women has sharpened their perceptions and understanding of the roots of violence. This understanding is provoked by the violence experienced by women from the hands of men within societies, through rape and family violence. At the same time, it is women, and their children, who suffer most extensively from militarisation and war. This includes not only the growing destruction of civilian societies by war but also the diversion of resources away from the needs of families into military weapons and organisations. Not insignificant is the fact that these military organisations are male-dominated and that they were created by political and military decisions made almost exclusively by men.

The feminist perspective takes note of male dependence on violence within societies, as a means for satisfaction of needs, for solving problems and for signalling individual significance and identity. Why are these attributes so prevalent in men and rare in women? Why are they much more prevalent in some cultures than in others? Why are they so prevalent in some men but not in others? In responding to these questions, feminists conclude that the tendency to employ violence as a tool for coping with problems in human relationships is learned through early socialisation of males in certain cultures. They are taught that to be a man, you must be aggressive and respond to provocative frustrations with violence. Not to reply with violence is not to be in control and to deny one's 'manhood'. This form of socialisation is then easily transferred in response to disappointments and frustrations in relations between gangs, between labour and management, and readily applied to questions of national and international peace and security.

Thus the fundamental contributions of the feminist perspective as a peace tool are (1) to question the inevitability of violence as a tool in the pursuit of peace and security, (2) to illuminate its negative consequences and (3) to provoke thought about where the roots of the 'violence habit' are to be found. From this, it follows that 'a feminist world security system would attempt to include all people and all nations based on a notion of extended kinship including the entire human family' (Reardon, 1990, pp. 138-139). It is very significant that the last question directs our attention, beyond arenas of inter-state conflict, to the daily life of individual societies, including our own.

In other words, the feminist vision of a peaceful world tends to begin with family and kinship relations and then extends the quality of these mutually nurturing relationships to the world. It is less inclined to make unquestioned assumptions about the need for a state/military apparatus to oversee these world relationships. Of course, once again, we are encountering an overlap with peace tools already presented. In essence, the feminist perspective offers insight on the need for positive peace tools. In this sense, the feminist perspective confirms and supports the need for peace tools such as nonviolence, self-reliance, economic equity and human rights. On the one hand, some have achieved their understanding of the need for these tools through experiences in the struggle for peace that revealed the shortcomings of negative peace tools, and of some positive peace tools as well. On the other hand, others (feminists) have attained similar insights by understanding the experiences of women in everyday life as well as in times of war. Of overwhelming importance is the fact that the feminist perspective not only illuminates the need for certain positive peace tools; feminine practice throughout the world also demonstrates that they work!

Peace Education (24) can be viewed as the obvious candidate to be the last tool to be presented because it obviously comprises all that has gone before. But it is certainly not last in importance. Indeed, the successful employment of all that we have learned about peacebuilding in the 20th century is dependent on peace education. Now broadened interdependence has directly involved *everybody* in diverse human enterprises that either contribute to or detract from peaceful human relations on a global scale. This is why it is now necessary that *all* begin to comprehend the peace potential generated in a variety of 'peace laboratories' in this century.

Over and over again in real-life 'experiments' with an array of peace tools, practitioners have found the need to probe deeper and deeper into the causes of peacelessness. At the end of the quest, a diversity of non-governmental/citizens movements were discerned to be a necessary 'drawer' in the 'peace tool chest' because the roots of peacelessness extend into domestic societies, local communities and even families. Thus, the seeds of peace must be planted, watered, nurtured and cultivated there. This means, of course, that *all* require peace education. Obviously it is not a subject essential only for present or future government leaders. Indeed, implementation of their peace plans requires the active support that only a citizenry with comprehensive peace education can provide. Furthermore, *comprehensive* peace education deepens insight on peace potential, particularly with respect to certain positive peace tools, and most specifically, those requiring broad participation. It is obvious that the full extent of this potential has not yet been realised. Most people have not been challenged to join the quest for peace. This should be the purpose of peace education.

There are those who tend to limit peace education to what they call conflict management or conflict resolution. Sometimes these approaches focus on managing or resolving conflicts in the schools, between neighbours, between business enterprises and their customers, and between labour and management. There are many community programmes that attempt to offer conflict resolution alternatives to the courts, thereby relieving overcrowded court agendas. These programmes are very helpful, both in resolving conflicts and in educating those involved about ways for diminishing the social disruption, and violence potential, of human conflict. But obviously these approaches are only one aspect of peace education. We believe that peace studies must offer comprehensive coverage of the diverse causes of peacelessness and their relationship. This encourages a long term perspective that illuminates strategies for removing the roots of disruptive peacelessness before they get out of control. History is replete with examples where conflict resolution approaches have offered too little, and too late. Even those practising the employment of only one peace tool, such as conflict resolution, need to understand where this tool fits in the full array of those available. After all, we would not prefer to have a personal surgeon who is not aware that some gallstones can now be eliminated by drugs and sound waves.

Finally, peace education with a comprehensive view is essential because it will probably be the only occasion in which young people are challenged to put into words their vision of a peaceful world. Because of the emphasis on extreme conflict and violence by the media, and because the academic study of international relations tends to emphasise the same phenomena, young people tend to assume that a world with widespread violence is inevitable. As a result, when students are asked to describe their personal vision of a peaceful world, they find it difficult to describe anything other than what they perceive the present world to be like. But peace education with a broad perspective cultivates the capacity of students to perceive widespread peace in the world, and significant achievements in efforts to diminish the scope of peacelessness. This enhancement of capacity to perceive peace potential makes it easier for students to employ their own values in envisioning their preferred peaceful world for the future.

Overview of Approaches to Peace

We have presented twenty-four peace tools in our survey of the quest for peace which has spread across the 19th and 20th centuries. The tools were somewhat arbitrarily gathered into six categories: 19th century, League Covenant (1919), UN Charter (1945), UN Practice 1950-89, UN Practice 1990 - present, and NGO/Peoples Movements. Figure 2 presented a complementary perspective in which the nine categories are based on the instrument, or means employed in the quest for peace.

The product of our historical inventory will be a list of the twenty-four peace tools filed in nine categories, based on the essential characteristics of each: (1) words, (2) limited military power, (3) deterrent military power, (4) reducing weapons, (5) alternatives to weapons, (6) protecting rights of individuals and groups, (7) collaboration in solving common economic and social problems, (8) equitable sharing of economic, communications and ecological systems, and (9) involvement of the population at large through peace education and organised participation. This product is presented in the conclusion of this chapter as Table 1 (see page 41).

Group I basically employs spoken and written *words*. The enduring significance of this approach was underlined by Jules Cambon (1931, p. 12) sixty years ago: 'The best instrument of a Government wishing to persuade another Government will always remain the spoken words of a decent man'. Fundamental is *diplomacy* through a worldwide system of embassies that has developed over many centuries. Very significant has been the development of procedures for widening the diplomatic dialogue to include a variety of *peaceful settlement* mediators, or 'third parties'. Another more recent innovation has been efforts to establish *second track diplomacy* by bringing in additional government officials, former officials, representatives of private groups and social scientists. Most recently, *preventive diplomacy* expands the tools available to diplomats for coping with emerging challenges through threat assessment, monitoring, fact finding and early warning.

Group II offers tools between the spoken word and a more traditional military response. *Peacekeeping* is a means for obtaining and maintaining a cease-fire so that negotiations can then be undertaken for coping with the conflict which precipitated the violence. *Humanitarian intervention* normally does not have the benefit of a cease-fire and endeavours to apply limited enforcement without slipping over the precipice into warfare.

Group III basically employs military power as a deterrent to aggression, in the form of *balance of power* exercised through alliances,

Table 1: Summary of Approaches to Peace

Name		Instrument
Diplomacy	I	Inter-State Communication
Peaceful Settlement		Good Offices, Conciliation, Arbitration, Courts
2nd Track Diplomacy		Non-State Actors
Preventative Diplomacy		Conflict Monitoring, Early Warning
Peacekeeping	II	Cease-Fire Patrol/Observation
Humanitarian Intervention		Armed Intervention to Protect Human Rights Within States
Balance of Power	III	Military Balance
Collective Security		Military Superiority under System-Wide Authority
Disarmament	IV	No Weapons
Arms Control		Reduce Weapons
Defensive Defence		Reduce External Threat of Defensive Weapons
Conversion		Convert to Civilian Production
Nonviolent Politics	V	Diminish Need for Weapons as Instruments for Social Change
Citizen Defence		Diminish Need for Weapons for National Defence
Self-Determination	VI	Autonomy/Independence for Identity Groups
Human Rights		Legitimise Transnational Standards for Economic, Social, Political, and Cultural Rights
Functionalism	VII	Collaboration to Solve Problems
Development		Overcome Poverty and Develop
Self-Reliance		Humans According to Their Needs
Int'l Communications Equity	VIII	Overcome One-Way Int'l Comm.
Ecological Balance		Overcome Destruction of Habitat
Governance for Commons		Sharing Equity in Use for the Commons
Feminist Perspectives	IX	Illuminate Roots of Violence in Society
Peace Education		Learn about the Causes of Peace
People's Movements		Broaden Opportunities for Participation in Efforts to Implement Peace

and the exercise of military superiority through a system-wide *collective security* system.

Group IV employs strategies for eliminating or reducing the number and destructive power of weapons through *disarmament, arms control, defensive defence* and *conversion*.

Group V attempts to diminish the need for weapons by providing alternative means for achieving social change (*nonviolent politics*) and for national defence (*citizen defence*).

Group VI basically employs protection of the rights of identity and *self-determination* for groups as well as protection of the *human rights* of individuals -- economic, social, political and cultural.

Group VII employs collaboration in solving common economic and social problems (*functionalism*). But in situations in which there are wide gaps between the rich and the poor, strategies are required to cope with poverty and widespread failure to satisfy basic human needs (*development*). Furthermore, strategies for overcoming these gaps require a concern for the *self-reliance* of those who are the targets of development strategies.

Group VIII basically employs approaches that seek to attain *equitable international economic, communications* and *ecological systems*. Inevitably this also requires collaborative problem solving in *governance for the global commons* (oceans, space, Antarctica) and equitable sharing in the use of the commons.

Group IX requires the linkage of the population at large to the quest for peace, through education and organised participation. *Feminist perspectives* illuminate the roots of militarism and violence within societies. *People's movements* offer opportunities for people to participate in the building of more peaceful societies. *Peace education* prepares people for enlightened participation and, at the same time, stimulates them to acquire their own vision of a peaceful world toward which their personal participation is directed.

Part II
Understanding War

3 Identity and the Outbreak of War

IVER B. NEUMANN

The international relations literature on identity is frequently assailed for being too abstract and the literature on the causes of war for being too rationalistic. This generates the need to overview how the two are implicated. This chapter investigates the intersection between the concepts of identity and war. Identification is considered as an aspect of all social interactions. There are various ways of linking the transformation of identification to the occurrence of war. The author presents how the framework for studying security presented by the Copenhagen School may be applied to the issue of the outbreak of war. The chapter is mainly about understanding the outbreak of war, not about explaining the causes of war.

Politics and Understanding

Most studies of the role of identity in politics tend to look at the imagery of war, the narrativity of war, the symbolic technologies of war and the like. However, they do not necessarily offer causal explanations which are cast in terms of the outbreak of war as a 'dependent variable' at all, but simply go about the task of theorising the political in other ways. Instead of asking 'why questions' when considering the outbreak of war, as Roxanne Lynn Doty (1996) suggests, the question of 'how' the outbreak is possible may be more enlightening, and is an approach with a long heritage in peace and conflict studies (Wallensteen, 1994).

These two different approaches were infused by two very different views on the concept of the political. If, as mainstream political science tends to take for granted, the political is a question of 'who gets what when', then war becomes one of a number of mechanisms by which a certain distribution of values and goods can be realised. Crucially, the 'who's' that are supposed to get something at a particular point in time are treated as fixed entities. These entities are not themselves changed by the distributional games in which they participate, war being one of them. As Sir Michael Howard (1983, pp. 1, 7) puts it, 'War has been throughout history a normal way of conducting disputes between political groups. [Now,] war is only a category of social groups, sovereign states'. Along this line, Stephen van Evera (1994) provides an example of how questions of identity may be brought to the analysis of war in this spirit: identities are treated as fixed, externalised and hence non-negotiable.

In contemporary international relations literature, identity is perceived as a given attribute which exists prior to human interaction. The attributes derived from a biological essence presume that humans are born into predetermined nations or born into predetermined gender roles. Even when this notion is not acknowledged explicitly, it has survived as an implicit presupposition. For instance, being 'German' in 1800, 1814, 1871, 1900, 1945 and 1990 is 'somehow' considered as the same thing, and it is a fact of immediate political relevance. Once confronted with the absurdity of this presupposition, a common response is to admit that, of course, it is not the same thing, but being German in 1990 nevertheless depends on coming out of a specific German trajectory. This can indeed be so, but that would ignore that (1) different representations of German identity are at any one time clashing and trying to crowd one another out; (2) these clashes have a political character; and (3) what is being said about earlier German identities is, in and of itself, part of the representation of contemporary German identity. Arguments about German identity are related to how specific historical experiences impinge on present-day politics. The discussion about identity is less relevant if they cannot specify how, when, and preferably why these historical experiences are employed in contemporary historical discourse. Put another way, if history is relevant to representations of identity, it is because we insist on it in our own stories about history, and not because 'history' is simply there, outside of contemporary discourse, independent of time and space as an essential quality. The relevance of historical examples must be upheld continuously by keeping those examples alive as reference points for ongoing discourse.

The following approaches, therefore, regard collective identity as always in a state of formation. Collective identity is an ever-lasting negotiation about who an individual is, how the who comes about, how individuals become a party to it, and how it is reproduced over time. If viewed in this 'relational' way, a causal approach is no longer appropriate since it actually excludes the question of identity formation *ipso facto*. Thus, it is not a coincidence that the causal approach to the outbreak of war has neglected the question of identity. The very way in which the question is phrased actually excludes the possibility of reflexive analysis. Identity, after all, is a question of who 'we' are, and if politics is about how 'we' shall live, then identity must be a necessary aspect of all politics.

Instead of seeing the political simply as a question of how already fixed actors decide between themselves 'who gets what when', one may, of course, see it as an ongoing negotiation of who 'we' are. Since a 'we' is unthinkable outside relations to a set of 'theys', the political, understood as the question of who 'we' are, is a question of separating 'us' from 'them'. More specifically, it is a question of separating friend from enemy. Chantal Mouffe's recent identity-inspired elaboration further clarifies this point.

In order to make her argument, Mouffe starts off by evoking a distinction between the political and politics. The political describes the ineradicable and ever-changing antagonism and hostility which characterises human interaction. On the other hand, politics, taking note of the permanent antagonism characterising the political, seeks to establish a certain order and to organise human co-existence. She then lambastes liberal politics for misunderstanding the very nature of the political by not taking the issue of basic antagonism into consideration. Politics is constituted by its outside (its *exterieur constitutif*), and inevitably bears the marks of its own exclusions. That is to say, if politics is a question of who 'we' are, then politics is a question of drawing up boundaries between that 'we' and the rest of the world. In a standard poststructural fashion, Mouffe proceeds to suggest that the way to alleviate the impact of this inevitable exclusion is to recognise that since the 'we' is constituted by its outside, 'we' must also somehow be that outside:

> On a general philosophical level, it is obvious that if the constitutive outside is present inside every objectivity as its always real possibility, then the interior itself is something purely contingent, which reveals the structure of the mere possibility of every objective order. This questions every essentialist conception of identity and forecloses every attempt conclusively to define identity or objectivity, inasmuch as objectivity always depends on

an absent otherness. Identity cannot, therefore, belong to one person alone. No one belongs to a single identity. We would go further and argue that not only are there no 'natural' or 'original' identities, since every identity is the result of a continuing process, but that this process itself must be seen as one of permanent hybridisation and nomadisation. Identity is, in effect, the result of a multitude of interactions that take place inside a space whose outlines are not clearly defined (Mouffe, 1994, pp. 109-10).

Mouffe draws two conclusions for political practice, one about the unwanted and impossible forging of a European self, and the other about democratic politics in general. On the topic of Europe, she insists that a European identity, if conceived as a homogeneous identity which could replace all other identifications and allegiances, would not be able to solve our problems. On the contrary, she argues with reference to Derrida, the whole discourse around European identity should be geared to the question of respect for diversity:

> If we conceive of this European identity as a 'difference to oneself', as one's own culture as someone else's culture, then we are in effect envisaging an identity that accommodates otherness, that demonstrates the porosity of frontiers, and opens up toward that 'exterior' which makes it possible. By accepting that only hybridity creates us as separate entities, it affirms and upholds the nomadic character of every identity (Mouffe, 1994, p. 111).

While Mouffe presents a solid case, one should also add a dimension at the core of Mouffe's earlier work (Laclau and Mouffe, 1985). Precisely because class distinctions (in the old Marxian, not Bourdieuan sense) are evaporating as possible identities, political space is opening up for the plethora of social identities around which social movements have congealed over the last 25 years or so. The mushrooming of the number of available identities cannot be easily brought together in one overarching narrative of self. As a reaction to that, there is a rush to defend the story of self which revolves around the nation. In these circumstances, the permanent antagonism, which characterises human interaction, threatens to trigger the ever-present possibility of violence, rather than transform antagonism.

Linking the literatures on identity and the outbreak of wars, then, must mean reflecting on how war is implicated in establishing friend and enemy relationships. Perhaps the first three tasks to be tackled are (1) going to war as a means of including and excluding subjects of world politics (still a statist concern); (2) the outbreak of war as a way of representing an identity; and (3) how certain symbolic economies work to produce war as an outcome of ever more sharply defined friend/enemy relations. These key questions of identity are overlapping. The first understands war from an intentional angle, the second from a psychoanalytically informed angle, and the third from a functional angle.

Inclusion and Exclusion: Ringmar

First, how war may be used as a way of including and excluding certain human collectivities as recognised players in world politics should be addressed through the study of intended, instrumental war-making. The literature on secession, nation-building, and the expansion of international society are of particular relevance here. Erik Ringmar's book on Sweden's entry into the Thirty Years' War in 1630 deals most directly with the concept of inclusion and exclusion based on identity.

According to Ringmar, explanations which postulate a number of interests and point to a specific outcome -- like the initiation of a specific war -- are somewhat constrained and even alarming. Explanatory work from this perspective becomes essentially a matter of picking out the most relevant interests. Specifically, Ringmar argues that:

> We cannot merely be satisfied with the fact that a certain explanation explains something, but we must also find out how this explanation is achieved. We need to know which causal variables go with which others, why certain factors are brought in and not others, and under what circumstances certain assumptions can be expected to hold. By asking these more basic questions we are, however, no longer engaging in a historical or a scientific investigation of facts, but instead in an investigation of how those interpretations are constructed which the existence of fact presupposes. As I will argue, it is only through an investigation of the preconditions which guided the work of previous scholars that we can criticise those preconceptions and come up with new, alternative ways in which to organise our data. As a pre-empirical investigation of this kind will show, historians and social scientists -- despite their many differences -- generally subscribe to one and the same theory of action: the notion that human beings are 'rational' and that their actions can be explained by reference to the 'interests' of the person or group who perform them (Ringmar, 1996, p, 12).

Having thus taken an anti-foundationalist (no givens) and narrativist (there are only stories) position regarding the possibility of writing history, it comes as no surprise that Ringmar finds fault with social science efforts to explain action, specifically the action of going to war. Ringmar divides in two parts the efforts made by social sciences. First, there are those who take their cue from 'the logic of the situation' -- a general logic regarding the relative power of states which is constructed in order to give a structural explanation. Choucri and North's (1989) lateral pressure model, Gilpin's (1988) theory of hegemonic wars and Doran's (1989) power cycle theory provide an illustration.

The fundamental problem with theories of a situational logic, Ringmar argues, is that they get the entire causal relationship between material factors and humans wrong. These theories imply that we live in a material world which 'presents' us with various more or less constraining options. The theories are found wanting because they attempt to explain specific situations from general conditions without considering the crucial role of the in-between factor of human intentionality. We live in a material world that we interpret, and it is on the basis of these interpretations that we present various options to ourselves. 'Hence it follows that a mere description of material factors will never tell us much about what actions a person will undertake. What an outside observer should study is not material factors, but instead the interpretations given to material factors; the way in which human beings make sense of their world' (Ringmar, 1996, p. 37).

Another major social theory on the reasons for the outbreak of war is derived from the so-called behavioural revolution in the social sciences which culminated in the 1960s. By focusing not on material factors, but on decision making processes, Ringmar acknowledges the 'vast improvement' inherent in the process of actually introducing humans into explanations of war. However, these theories are also deemed insufficient because they tend to concentrate on the background of the actual decision: if the focus is not the logic of the situation, then it is on the logic of the decision making as a process. This, Ringmar insists, is tantamount to ducking the issue:

> The focus is always on the 'hardware' of the decision making process, as it were, not on matters of 'software': it is not what people think about their worlds -- how they go about making decisions. [T]he theory presupposes

the prior existence of a meaningful world, but it remains agnostic regarding how this world was created (Ringmar, 1996, p. 39).

Ringmar concludes that combining historical and social scientific theories may tell us about the general background leading to a decision, and *how* a decision was ultimately reached, but they cannot tell us *why* a decision was more meaningful to decision makers than others.

Significantly, Ringmar introduces a setting to the stories through other story-telling entities. These 'others', about whom the self tells stories and who tells stories about the self, is a *constitutive* part of story-telling. They are the key *audiences* of the stories, and as such they participate actively in the formation of both identity and interests, making both these concepts relational. 'In order to find out whether a particular constitutive story is a valid description of us, it must first be tested in interaction with others'. It is also argued that '[s]ince all stories require audiences, it follows that we cannot formulate notions of interests in isolation from other people -- we simply cannot want things alone' (Ringmar, 1996, pp. 79, 80).

Leaving stories about actions behind and focusing on constitutive stories (where actions still play a crucial part), Ringmar goes further to describe how stories are confirmed. Confirmation cannot be given by just anybody, but only by those others which the self recognises and respects as *being a kind of self*. These sets of others are referred to as 'circles of recognition'. To a state, for example, the circle of major importance will, therefore, be made up of other states.

An instance worthy of particular theoretical attention is, where others deny recognition to the self's constitutive stories. In this case, the storied self has three options: to accept stories told about it by others; to abandon the stories which are not recognised in favour of others; or to stand by the original story and to try to convince the audiences that it does, in fact, apply. 'Thus while the first two options mean that we accept the definitions forced upon us by others, the third option means that we force our own definition upon someone else' (Ringmar 1996, pp. 82, 185). Typically, this is done through action.

The need to obtain recognition for constitutive stories, Ringmar insists, will be greater at so-called 'formative moments', periods of 'symbolic hyper-inflation -- times when new emblems, flags, dress codes, songs, fêtes and rituals are continuously invented'. It will also be greater for social upstarts -- newcomers approaching a circle of recognition -- than for others. Where states are concerned, examples may include Sweden's attempt to be recognised in the 1630s and 1640s, the Soviet Union's in the 1920s and 1930s, and Turkmenistan's or Kazakhstan's ongoing attempts to be taken seriously as fully-fledged members of international society. Thus, '[s]ocial upstarts are likely to be very good rule-followers, not primarily because they fear punishment in accordance with the rule if they fail, but because they want to be identified as members of the group where a particular rule applies' (Ringmar, 1996, p. 86).

Having sketched out his narrative theory, Ringmar then analyses particular actions in terms of stories. The point of the analysis is to look at the story which a certain self, for example, a state, tells about the action. This is done in terms of the meaning that goes into the story. Then that particular action -- the question of why a state goes to war -- will have to be subsumed under the category of either 'stories about interests and actions' or 'constitutive stories about identity and action'. In order to determine this, Ringmar presents a checklist of the following points.

First of all, '[t]raditional explanations phrased in terms of interests should produce ambiguous, highly contested or perverse results'. It must be a formative moment period when new metaphors are launched, when individuals and groups tell new stories about themselves, and when new sets of rules emerge through which identities were classified. Thus, '[t]he particular person or group whose action we want to explain must be engaged in a process of identity creation. It must be someone who tells constitutive stories and tries to establish a presence in both time and space; someone who constructs an affective geography of friends and enemies; someone who pays careful attention to the rules of the social system to which he or she seeks to belong'. We must identify an occasion, or a series of occasions, on which recognition was denied under humiliating circumstances. We need to prove that our people or group suffered as a result, and that the failure of recognition was indeed experienced as a loss of dignity, worth and 'face' (1996, pp. 90-91).

If these criteria are fulfilled, as Ringmar demonstrates in the case of Sweden in 1630, going to war can be more convincingly explained in terms of the desire to be recognised. Ringmar's approach is particularly useful because it is presented as an explanation, and may therefore slide more effortlessly into the literature on the 'causes' of war than most other identity scholarship. His work is particularly angled towards cases where aspiring states already recognise themselves as such. However, we may want to study the outbreak of war more generally, as an outcome of concrete political processes, where one particular 'cause' (such as a king's intention to have himself and his state's status recognised by other kings and other states) is not what we are interested in. In this case, we need a more process-oriented understanding of how the representations of self and other are actually forged.

Different stories of self, with different room allotted to entities such as 'state', 'nation', 'society', 'religious community', 'minorities' and other relevant human collectives, will always be in internal competition for domination. One cannot simply privilege a story, which the state tries to impose about a certain political entity, and bracket all the other stories told about competing selves that it is up against. Different stories of the self may implicate war as a possibility in different degrees and in different ways. The politics of representation is explained by poststructural identity scholarship.

Re-presentation of Identity

A number of interesting studies, on how representations of 'self' and 'other' go hand in hand with the waging of war, are found in identity scholarship, but there is no one book or article which, like Ringmar's, actually applies identity scholarship to the outbreak of war. Typically, however, a poststructural analysis will demonstrate how the construction of self is implicated in the killing of the other. As the Schulte-Sasses puts it, 'a society that uses representations of war as a means of unifying the body politic in an imaginary fashion needs an elaborate network of signs representing Oneness and Otherness' (1991, p. 72).

The Schulte-Sasses further highlights how, for a country such as the US, 'nationalism is part and parcel of a production of signs that can best be described in cultural, historical, and psychoanalytic terms' (1991, p. 94). The explicit reference to psychoanalysis is of the essence here. The Gulf War is interpreted as 'a means of stimulating a unified body politic' (1991, p. 68). The postulate is that there are two contradictory drives in modern society: the first drive (which we have already discussed in connection with Mouffe's elaboration of the political) concerns agonistic politics; the second drive deals with the desire of each individual to imagine the body politic as unified and socially cohesive. Governments, they argue, may try to shift attention away from the agonism of domestic politics towards aesthetic pleasure in the body politic by going to war. This tendency will be even stronger when traditional state strategies for mustering support, such as representations of utopias, have lost much of their lustre:

> Media images become the post-modern heirs to narratively constructed utopias... [W]ars are at least in part propelled by their power to unify the body politic and to instil in the state's subjects the illusion of being masterful agents of history. This illusion of being a historical agent is again an aesthetic representation of substitutes with which we can identify and depends on images that contain nothing messy or confusing, such as dead bodies or a humanised enemy. While experiencing ourselves, collectively and individually, as a unified body, we simultaneously fall prey to the illusion that we can decipher and master the world. The danger is, of course, that in experiencing what 'theory' likes to call the jouissance of mastering the world as text and the text as world, we cover up our actual impotence as agents, which in turn worsens the nation's material situation (economy, infrastructure, education system, etc.) and increases its dependence on images of superiority (Schulte-Sasses, 1991, pp. 70-71).

This psychoanalytic insight is seldom referenced explicitly by most international relations scholarship (Shapiro, 1992). This topic may be ever present in politics and may continue to increase in importance. For this approach to be successful, it must clearly specify how it will vary across time and space, and particularly how outbreaks occur at certain places and times. An unwillingness to be specific enough in asking the questions when it comes to an outbreak of war is a feature of poststructural scholarship which draws less heavily on the psychoanalytical tradition. Among abundant examples (Behnke, 1997; Hansen, 1997; Neumann, 1996), the point is illustrated by casting a glance at David Campbell's book, *Writing Security: The United States Foreign Policy and the Politics of Identity*. In this successful empirical reading of identity in international relations literature, Campbell describes US foreign policy as a seamless web of discourse and political practice playing itself out through a series of engagements with others. The US self is understood as a narrative structure, and it is argued that 'For a state to end its practices of representation would be to expose its lack of prediscursive foundations; stasis would be death' (Campbell, 1992, p. 11). Due to the role played by immigration in its genesis, the

United States is presented as the imagined community par excellence, providing the need to have its representational practices recognised and confirmed.

Campbell advances an ethical consideration relating to the tendency and ability of the human collective to carry out the practices of representation while living in difference; that is, without 'othering' other collectives. This, however, is exactly what the United States is still failing to do. One of the consequences is the perpetual lookout for new collectives to 'other':

> If we understand the Cold War to be a struggle related to the production and reproduction of identity, the popularly heralded belief that we are witnessing the end of the Cold War embodies a misunderstanding: while the objects of established post-1945 strategies of otherness may no longer be plausible candidates for enmity, their transformation has not by itself altered the entailments of identity which they satisfied (Campbell, 1992, p. 195).

Campbell describes in detail how foreign policy, with its focus on border maintenance, is a particularly apposite practice for identity formation, while also stressing internal consequences. His reading of early US Cold War diplomacy and the work of the Washington State Legislative Fact-finding Committee on Un-American Activities, for example, stresses how

> Concomitant with this external expansion was an internal magnification of the modes of existence which were to be interpreted as risks. Danger was being totalised in the external realm in conjunction with its increased individualisation in the internal field, with the result being the performative reconstruction of the borders of the state's identity. In this sense, the Cold War needs to be understood as a disciplinary strategy that was global in scope but national in design (Campbell, 1992, pp. 172-73).

Once again, Campbell's approach demonstrates that while poststructural work reveals interesting general insights, it does not directly engage the question of how the outbreak of specific wars is to be analysed in detail and compared to other cases (and non-cases) of the outbreak of war. More formalism is required in this endeavour, and I suggest that one way of achieving such a goal is to analyse the work done by the Copenhagen School of Security Studies.

Introducing the Concept of 'Violisation' to the Copenhagen School

Certain symbolic economies work to produce war as an outcome of ever more sharply defined friend/enemy relations. If the initial focus is on actor intentions and subsequently on re-presentation, then the area of concern is, first and foremost, with the markers, or diacritica of the boundaries of the actors. In other words, the focus is on what delineates and binds the actors. The most effective way to analyse how these diacritica are bound up with the outbreak of war is to add a small but crucial supplementary factor to the work by Barry Buzan, Ole Wæver and others who constitute the Copenhagen School of Security Studies.

If the exercise undertaken in this chapter is to link the various literatures on identity formation, the innovation would appear to be a rather incestuous one. The work of the Copenhagen School defined by McSweeney (1996, p. 162) and Neumann (1996, p. 162) can be extended to understanding the outbreak of war. More specifically, this means introducing a category of 'violisation' to the concept of 'securitisation'.

As Wæver (1995, p. 67) described in her 1988 paper that launched the concept of securitisation, 'State security has *sovereignty* as its ultimate criterion, and societal security has *identity*. Both usages imply survival. A state that loses its sovereignty does not survive as a state; a society that loses its identity fears that it will no longer be able to live *as itself* (emphasis added). This dichotomisation in identifying the referents of security can cause problems in conceptualising the outbreaks of wars. The declaration of war, after all, is still an activity where states play a crucial role. While societies and society-level groups may continue to be active in a number of ways, both before and after the declaration of war, interesting grey areas emerge where a state collapse introduces questions regarding, for example, whose name the war is fought for, and in the case of the existence of bands operating without clarity, questions regarding what status, if any, the state has conferred on them. The issue of civil war further complicates the picture. The point for our purposes, however, is that the differentiation between state and society which relegates identity to the sphere of society is not only unhelpful, but is downright detrimental to attempts to link the issues of identity and war. De-differentiation is then needed for studying the outbreak of war within a Copenhagen School framework.

In a preview of the next major co-authored book by the school, Barry Buzan (1997, p. 13) writes that, 'the Copenhagen School argues against the view that the core of Security Studies is war and force. Instead, it constructs a more radical view of Security Studies by exploring threats to referent objects, and the securitisation of these threats, that are non-military as well as military.' It would appear that the School has (so far) consciously avoided confronting the issue of the outbreak of war while immediate theorising has taken place elsewhere (see especially Wæver, 1996, p. 113). Where the issue has proved unavoidable, it has tackled the question by drawing up what is referred to as a 'checklist of causal components' rather than attempting fully to integrate the issue into the proposed theoretical framework. Its central work, *Identity Migration and the New Security Agenda in Europe* (Wæver et al., 1993), has a chapter entitled 'Societal Security and the Explosion of Yugoslavia'. The indirect reference to an 'explosion' of Yugoslavia, rather than to the outbreak of war, is illustrative.

This exteriorisation of the concept of outbreak of war from the extant work of the Copenhagen School is relatively easily amended by de-differentiating the concepts of state security and societal security. Identity has pertinence at both the societal and the state level. It can be highlighted as an aspect of sovereignty. After having suggested where the conceptual gap in linking identity and the outbreak of war is located, we need to explore strategies to close it.

The Copenhagen School argues that securitisation can be thought of as an extension of politicisation:

> [I]ssues become securitised when leaders (whether political, societal, or intellectual) begin to talk about them -- and to gain the ear of the public and the state -- in terms of existential threats against some valued referent object. Securitisation can thus be seen as a more extreme version of politicisation. It is the inter-subjective establishment of an existential threat with a saliency sufficient to have substantial political effects. In theory, a public issue can be located on the spectrum ranging from non-politicised (meaning that the state doesn't deal with it, and it is not in any other way made an issue of public debate and decision); through politicised (meaning that the issue is part of public policy, requiring government decision and resource allocation or more rarely some other form of communal governance); to securitised (meaning that the issue is presented as an existential threat requiring emergency measures, and justifying actions outside the normal bounds of political procedure). In principle, the placement of issues on this spectrum is open; depending on circumstances, any issue can end up on any part of the spectrum (Buzan, 1997, p. 14).

In terms of identity, politicisation is a matter of inscribing certain differences between self and other by defining the diacritica of self and other. That is, certain differences which have not been activated as part of the political so far are being politicised. That makes it possible, retrospectively, to talk about them as having been 'non-politicised' before they were 'politicised'.

Securitisation, on the other hand, includes the added burden of defining what constitutes the security politics of a certain human collective in establishing political diacritica. Wæver tends to think about security as existential or ontological politics. The political is understood in terms of distinguishing friend from enemy, defining who 'we' are, and identifying threats to who 'we' are. There exist four respective processes for politicisation, de-politicisation, securitisation, and de-securitisation. An identity, for example, may be securitised by speech which inscribes meaning in terms of security politics. At the same time, it may also be de-securitised by speech unsubscribing such a representation.

By attaching the importance of speech to the process of securitisation, the Copenhagen School highlights the constructed, intra-subjective character of the concept of security and hence also of the *modus operandi* of security politics. The concept of discourse is used to de-differentiate words and action and analyse them separately. The outbreak of war may, of course, also be conceptualised as a speech act. The words 'I hereby declare war' indeed can mean going to war (provided one's institutional station and preparations are appropriate). Actually waging war, however, needs more than declarative speech. It requires the use of force, which can be characterised as a violisation of politics. Thus, waging war is, by definition, not only a question of speech, but also of actions.

A crucial role in war involves the action of killing. More generally, the acts of violence literally inscribe the will of one collective onto the body politic of another human collective. For a good reason, the number of people killed has almost always become the defining trait of what war is -- whether it be '317' suggested in Richardson's research or '1000' used for the Correlates of War Project (Wiberg, 1976).

This view is, of course, in and of itself neither new nor surprising. For example, Wæver quotes Clausewitz to the effect that 'War is an act of violence pushed to its utmost bounds' (Wæver, 1995, p. 53). When war-like activity does not include acts of violence, they are referred to by modifiers as, for example, 'wars of position' and 'cold wars.' In order to link the work of the Copenhagen School to the outbreak of war, it may be useful to examine the concept of securitisation. The concept for those acts of speech which perform the tasks defined by Buzan, Wæver and others is different from a new category for cases where large scale violence actually takes place.

If the issue under consideration is the outbreak of war, we can best apply the Copenhagen School's framework to this question by defining the threshold between securitisation and violisation at the point of the outbreak of war itself (meant by violence on a certain scale) rather than at the point where an individual dies. This is not to deny that a certain identity is already violised in situations such as an asylum centre being arsonised, resulting in death, but simply to acknowledge that the question of scale must be addressed. It is not societal security and the identity/society nexus, but identity and war, which implicates the state very directly. Societal violence is not intended to impinge on the question of whether state borders may be bracketed. Attention is focused on cases where the issue is the re-presentation of states. In this context, Clausewitz's formulation of war as the continuation of politics by other means can be classified, both directly and indirectly, within the Copenhagen School framework of politicisation and securitisation. We can add the category of 'violised' to the two existing concepts of the Copenhagen School such as 'politicised' and 'securitised'. The two corresponding processes of 'violisation' and 'de-violisation' can be examined in the following extended continuum:

Non-politicised — politicised — securitised — violised

The main argument against differentiating the concept of securitisation, as it currently stands, may be that this would detract attention from security speech by pointing to the material factors in cases of large-scale violence. The work of the Copenhagen School has opened up the question of the referent of security by highlighting how identity pertains to states -- and not exclusively to society. Problematically, this proposed shift would take some attention away from societal questions. For a number of reasons, this may indeed be a loss. The mirror image of such a critique would be that reserving violence for actions with a material character actually downplays the violence wrought by structural factors and by speech acts. As already noted, the Copenhagen School argues against the view that the core of Security Studies is war and force. Adding a category of 'violisation' at the extreme end of the continuum does, of course, have the effect of once again highlighting war and force. This would be worthwhile, since security studies must, out of necessity, tackle the issue of outbreaks of war.

As for the question regarding empirical research, an obvious first case to which the proposed extended continuum could be applied would be the outbreak of war in former Yugoslavia (Eide, 1997). We have, in this situation, a number of cases where national identities became not only securitised, but also violised. Serb and Croatian national identities, Bosniak political identity and Muslim religious identity provide suitable examples. By contrast, Macedonian ethnic identities were securitised but not violised. The term 'violised' is applied only when violence takes place on a certain scale. It would be interesting indeed if it can be demonstrated whether the outbreaks and non-outbreaks of war can usefully be analysed in terms of violisation of identity, or if it turns out that the structure of identities was not a crucial factor in the outbreaks of these wars.

Conclusion

Scholarship on identity reveals a number of insights useful for the study of the outbreak of wars. For various reasons, however, most extant scholarship has largely been preoccupied with other forms of social interaction than those which have led to war or have come close to war. This focus is on the action of going to war itself. A plethora of other forms of human interaction are related to war. Between the specific and explanatory focus of Ringmar's narrativist study, and the general and critical focus of dealing with how the self is implicated in war in poststructural studies, I suggest that the formalised and process-oriented framework of the Copenhagen School stands out as a particularly promising starting point from which to launch empirical studies of identity and the outbreak of war. The prerequisite is the adoption of the concept of violisation, understood as the process whereby an already securitised issue such as identity becomes a *casus belli* over which blood must run.

4 War and Globality: The Role and Character of War in the Global Transition

MARTIN SHAW

Globalisation has generally been understood as a set of processes in the economy, culture and society. The literature tends to discuss political changes as consequences of globalisation (Scholte, 1997). The state, it is commonly argued, is undermined by globalisation. War has hardly ever been discussed in the mainstream globalisation literature. In the more specialist literature on war and violence, some linkages have been proposed: trends such as the fragmentation of nation states, transnational linkages of ethnic communities, transnational refugee movements as a result of war, and global markets in weaponry, have been identified as related to globalisation (Kaldor, 1997). The debates on globalisation and war have not impinged very substantially on each other. A systematic attempt to integrate the understanding of war with global theory is missing.

In this chapter I argue, on the one hand, that globalisation cannot be examined without an understanding of the role of war in contemporary history, and on the other, that war cannot be understood today outside the global context. The argument involves, therefore, a double revision: by showing what happens when we write war into globalisation and globality into war, our ideas about both globalisation and war are transformed in the process.

The Meaning of Globality

Although the literal meaning of the word *globalisation* is to make things global, there has been surprisingly little discussion, in the academic literature on globalisation, of what *global* means. The adjective has continued to be widely used synonymously with world, or even international. Although the process of globalisation must surely make things more global, the global as a condition -- the outcome of the process -- has hardly been named, let alone understood. Only recently have writers begun to use the term *globality* to describe the condition of a globalised world (Albrow, 1996).

What does 'global' mean? How might globality be constituted? The simple answer indicated by the literature seems to be that it represents the breaking down of spatial limits. It is defined, in some accounts, as the tendency of social relations to achieve global reach or scope, together with the intensification of such global interconnections due to the compression of relations of time and space (Giddens, 1990; McGrew, 1992, p. 23). These tendencies are also connected to the increased understanding of the world as a common human environment. Ecological globalists represent human life as part of the planetary system of our globular Earth.

In social science, however, our common humanity remains a concept of *social* relations. The fundamental social meaning of globality, we might conclude, is the growing tendency of these relations to develop in a common worldwide framework of meaning (Shaw, 1994, pp. 1-28). Increasingly actors frame their actions with reference to a common world society, rather than in a more restricted framework. This marries the ecological meaning in so far as the physical environment of human society is increasingly understood as both shaped by and shaping this common social context.

What kinds of actions or social relations constitute a global world? Although, in principle, globality is constituted by social relations in general, a particular understanding of social relations has dominated the literature. Globalisation is primarily understood to refer to economic, and secondarily to cultural relations. In global relations, the market rules: the marketisation of cultural relations, through global communication technologies, completes globalism.

Politics is understood, in this dominant account, principally in epiphenomenal terms. Politics does not constitute globalisation, but is affected by it. Political forms, above all, the nation state, are understood as being undermined by globalisation. An academic critique of globalisation will involve showing that economies are not as de-nationalised and nation states as ineffective as globalisers suggest (Hirst and Thompson, 1995). Alternative politics, in many radical versions, is one of resistance to globalisation. War and violence only enter the discussion as instances of what happens when nation states are weakened by globalising forces.

Both the globalisers and resisters have bought the myth of the market: market trends *could* transform the world and weaken states, even if they have not actually done so to the extent that the globalisers posit. This assumption is, however, historically untenable. Market relations have always depended on authority relations and the organisation of violence as much as they have determined political relations (Mann, 1986). State forms have changed partly because changes in patterns of market activity have created new possibilities for mobilising power. But the ways in which states and other actors have mobilised violence have had enormous effects on the capacity of market actors to produce and sell commodities. This historical perspective is missing, for the most part, from globalisation debates. A balanced, historically-sensitive account of contemporary processes will try to grasp the mutually constitutive and contradictory relationships between state and markets, rather than accepting a one-dimensional notion of marketisation.

War in the Constitution of the Global World Order

In the second part of this chapter, a historical account is outlined in which state relations and war play a large part in constituting globality. The emergent global world of the 21st century is as much a political order as a form of market economy or culture. Like previous forms of world order, it involves new state forms, rather than the negation of such forms in general. Indeed we may go so far as to say that it is the development of new state relations, new relations of violence and new state forms which are *defining* globality as a distinct epoch.

Some conceptual clarification is in order. By state relations, I mean not just the relations between states but the social relations in which state institutions are embedded. Relations of violence refer to those social relations in which there is large scale systematic mobilisation of physical force. These are the relations which have historically bounded the centres of state power. Although they also involve actors other than states in the conventional sense, relations of violence typically involve state-like institutions and have been those social relations which have defined both states in general and the boundaries of particular states. By state forms, I mean the institutional forms of state power. These include the structures not just of individual centres of state power, such as nation states, but of inter-state relations.

In the early modern period, the growth of market activity within feudal authority relations did not lead directly or simply to the development of capitalism. Transformations of polity both responded to and facilitated the growth of market relations. The main political form which emerged has been understood conventionally to be the nation state. In fact, the early modern state form was reflected in *the state within the European inter-state system*, the modern character of which was first defined in the Treaty of Westphalia. This system only gradually acquired a modern national (and hence inter-national) character as the state came to be understood as based socially on the nation.

The *international system of nation states* of the first half of the 20th century can be characterised by the high modern state form, the result of a long historical transformation within the European state system. Its development was intertwined with what has been seen as the earlier stages of globalisation. And the modern European state was imperial as much as it was national. Extending the authority of European state centres to non-European territories embedded these states in worldwide social relations. It meant, too, that early forms of world economy were based on forms of world-empire: there were separate imperial worlds, characterised by more or less discrete economic and cultural as well as political relations (Shaw, 1997).

The international system of nation states embedded in a European-dominated world economy and cultural universe prefigured globalisation but it was not, in the contemporary sense, a global world. It is instructive to understand why. It is not because worldwide, transcontinental connections were weak. On the contrary, clearly they were growing, and took the forms of international trade and communication. It is not because boundaries of empires were impermeable. Clearly both commerce and culture partially transcended them. It is because the boundaries of these empires, however permeable, were always potentially, and often actually, *borders of violence*. There were more or less discrete territorial 'monopolies of legitimate violence' (Weber, 1978, p. 54). Empires were 'bordered power containers' (Giddens, 1985). In such a divided world, globality was still a dream.

Critics of the idea of globalisation often argue that the pre-1914 world was characterised by similar levels of international trade, if not cultural interchange, to those of the contemporary world (Hirst and Thompson, 1995). We see now why they miss the point. The fundamental difference between the pre-global and the globalising world is not economic, or even cultural, but political. The pre-global world of the late 19th century was a divided world of competing empires. The emergent global world of the 21st century is a world in which political unification has occurred so that territorial boundaries between state jurisdictions are no longer, in many cases, borders of violence. Instead of the violent competition of empires or blocs, we have an emergent global authority structure in which nation statehood, while more universal, is also largely de-linked from its historical context of war. Fundamental transformations of state relations, relations of violence and state forms have taken place.

How has a global order emerged, historically, during the 20th century? Has there simply been a spontaneous growth of commercial and cultural intercourse, so that borders have shrunk in significance? We have only to state this thesis to see how untenable it is as a summary of 20th century world history. We can then begin to place globalisation in its historical perspective. In order to move from the imperial order of 1900 to the global world of 2000, on the contrary, the world has had to move through a momentous, violent transition, through a century of world war and cold war.

The international system, based on empires, led to total war. This involved the extreme marshalling of economy, society and culture by rival imperial states. As a result, autarky threatened to supplant international commerce and cosmopolitan culture. Total war in turn generated the politics of totalitarianism and the Orwellian spectre of a world completely divided between rival imperial blocs.

Only from this extreme manifestation of the violent world order did the possibility of global order emerge. The worldwide common experience of mass slaughter and victimisation, and the worldwide common determination to avoid experiences of the same kind, led to a widely-shared vision of a new world order in 1945. This vision was based on the cooperation of nation states in the new United Nations system. It was the 'dialectics of war' (Shaw, 1988) which first thrust to the fore the possibility of globality.

The prospective global world of 1945 was stillborn because of Western-Soviet rivalry. Nevertheless, 1945 was the fundamental turning point in the movement towards globality. In a further development of the paradox, the Cold War, for all its danger, was the political structure in which the infrastructure of globality was nourished. The victory of 1945 abolished the structure of competition between empires which was the culmination of the previous world order. Of the rival empires of the first half of the 20th century, Austria-Hungary had disintegrated after 1918. Germany and Japan were fundamentally defeated, and Britain and France, although victorious, were emasculated, and their world systems were transformed into components of a worldwide Western order of independent states. Only the United States and Soviet Russia remained as the new superpower hegemons of a period in which *state-blocs* replaced empires controlled by nation states.

In the bloc order, the state forms of the international system were largely preserved. Blocs were, formally, alliances of national states, and hence of national societies and cultures. In this sense, the bloc order of the Cold War was still based on an international system of nation states. However, while the Soviet bloc was little more than a reconstructed and expanded Russian empire in totalitarian guise, the Western bloc was the incubator of new state relations, relations of violence, and state forms. Within the Western bloc, economy and society were increasingly integrated transnationally. Borders of violence between the major Western states were abolished, and relations of violence were transferred to the borders with the Soviet bloc and other borders within the so-called Third World regions. The state form of the new era was *no longer simply the nation state within the inter-state system*. The nation state now existed only in the context of the panoply of military alliances and international economic institutions which constituted the wider *Western conglomerate of state power*.

This 'Western state' (Shaw, 1997) clearly had semi-global functions during the Cold War period. The United Nations system was only partially able to function as a set of global institutions during the Cold War. But some institutions like the International Monetary Fund and World Bank, which were dominated by the West, had an effective global scope. Institutions of the broad West, such as the Organisation for Economic Cooperation and Development, and institutions of the narrow West, such as the Group of Seven, largely set the perimeters of global economic management. The Western state also dominated the Third World through the postcolonial linkages of large parts of Asia and Africa with Britain, France and other former imperial powers, as well as the continuing dependence of most of Latin America on the United States. In all these ways, the Western state had a genuine worldwide reach its Soviet rival always lacked.

The world in the Cold War period was dominated, therefore, by a very attenuated form of the international order which reached its climax in the Second World War. On the one hand, the results of that war were the emergence of a new bipolar bloc system of military conflict, which can be seen as the final form of the old international order based on nation states. On the other hand, however, the World War and the Cold War itself led to the development of much of the *superstructure* (the UN system) and *infrastructure* (the Western state) of a global order which would fundamentally transcend the inter-state relations.

Two general conclusions can be drawn from this discussion. First, state relations can be seen as *defining* the nature of world order, including the possibility of globality. The old world order was clearly constituted by certain forms of state, the relations of violence and their role in organising national and international society. The world order of the Cold War years could not be seen as a decisive break from the old order because at its centre was the bipolar military conflict of the major state-blocs. Despite all the developments which pushed towards globality, the structures of the Cold War -- in society as well as in state forms -- inhibited global developments.

Second, just as state relations define world orders, so changes in state relations are necessary to *transform* these orders. The military, political and social crisis of 1945 represented the first, most important stage in the transition from internationality to globality in world order. But it was only a beginning. It required a further transformation of state relations to bring globality to fruition. The economic and social movements within Cold War structures could lay the foundations for a global world. Only a further shift in state relations could bring it into existence.

Understanding the Contemporary Global Transition

We have two major images of contemporary world transformation. On the one hand, there is globalisation, understood as the economic and cultural changes which undermine statehood and borders. On the other hand, there is the idea of the post-Cold War period, in which big conflicts of major states are replaced by violent but relatively minor fractures of states and societies. These understandings may sometimes be brought together in *ad hoc* ways, but we have no theoretical framework which enables us to make sense of the entirety of both processes.

This chapter proposes, in the light of the preceding discussion, that we see the current period as one of transformations which complete the major change in world order begun with the Second World War. In short, the bloc-system of the Cold War was a transitional form, between the international order of the first half of the 20th century and the emergent global order of the 21st. The beginning and end of the Cold War transition were marked by the two major military and political crises, that of 1945-47 in which the Cold War emerged from the conclusion of the Second World War, and that of 1989-91 in which global order emerged from the collapse of the Cold War.

It is curious that globalisation discussions are usually only contingently related to the end of the Cold War. And yet the simplest reflection will show their linkages: it is no accident that globalisation became a dominant theme in the 1990s after the Cold War ended. Although the term globalisation, first used in the 1960s, has been in common use since the 1970s and became increasingly connected to the understanding of market liberalisation in the 1980s, it is in the 1990s that it has dominated social-scientific and, to a considerable extent, political debate.

Market liberalisation was not sufficient to bring globalisation to the fore, or enough to define a global order. Economic and cultural liberalisation played their parts in making the end of the Cold War inevitable, undermining the viability of the autonomous economic projects of Soviet-bloc and Third World communist states as well as their insulation against Western political ideas. However, only changes in military-political state relations could allow globality its full scope. It was the collapse of the Soviet bloc -- which threatened in 1989 to bring down with it the Chinese communist state -- that opened the former communist world to full involvement in world markets and communications. Globalisation in its conventional economic and cultural senses *depended* on the military and political transition of the end of Cold War.

So how should we understand the current transition? It is clearly not a change of the fundamental socio-economic relations, but a process in which capitalist market relations are intensified and achieve a universal scope. It is fundamentally *a transition in state relations*, with important implications for economy, society and culture -- especially in those regions which during the Cold War were removed from full participation in world markets. Globalisation is about incorporating more or less the whole world into a single system of authority relations centred on a single set of state institutions. It is, in the terminology of international relations, a unipolar world, in which, however imperfectly, an integrated raft of Western and United Nations state institutions dominates more or less the entire world society. In this sense, globality is constituted by politics, and globalisation is an essentially *political* transition.

The transition to a global world is complete only in a limited sense. With the collapse of the Soviet bloc, there is no longer a potentially equal alternative centre of world authority and power. It is unlikely, therefore, that there will be another world crisis of equal significance to the crisis of 1989-91. In other aspects, however, it is profoundly incomplete: it has a deeply unfinished, contradictory and unstable character. Global authority relations are formally centred on a fundamentally weak set of institutions, in the UN system, with very limited legitimacy in world society, authority over national centres of state power, and resources and capacities to formulate, let alone enforce, global norms or policies. Global authority depends excessively on the Western state, and indeed on the United States, and is mediated overwhelmingly by the inter- and intra-state politics of the West. Many states outside the West are relatively weakly integrated in global and Western state institutions, and some are even weakly embedded in society. Global state relations at the end of the 20th century represent, manifestly, a relatively weak, unstable and variable framework for global society.

The transition to the 21st century is one which remains, therefore, highly problematic. The events of 1989-91 made it possible to envisage a global world in a way which was not fully possible during the Cold War. But these events did not, in themselves, bring a new global world order into anything like full and coherent existence. On the contrary, in this sense the transition has hardly begun. States, it has been suggested, are often 'institutional messes'. The emergent global state relations and forms of the early 21st century are the biggest, but also the messiest set of institutions in world history, and many crises are likely to mark their continued development and consolidation.

The Role of War in the Global Transition

There has been a profound transformation in the role of war in the transition from the international to the global world order. In the international order based on nation states, the dominant form of war was inter-state, *particularly* between the major centres of state power in the world. At the same time, there were important forms of intra-state or civil war: a dialectic of inter-state war, revolution and civil war was part of the overall pattern of state relations during this era.

During the Cold War period, the prime form of war was inter-bloc, but since direct bloc war remained 'cold', the 'hot' secondary forms of war, both inter- and intra-state, were the forms within which bloc conflict was most manifest. Whereas in the early decades of the Cold War period, many important wars were about the dismantling of European empires, later they were more about the rivalries of independent centres of state power and the shape and forms of local states. While most wars had a Cold War aspect, few were simply or predominantly expressions of Cold War rivalries.

The transition to the Cold War thus involved the *suppression* of the major forms of inter-state war which had produced the catastrophic violence of the first half of the 20th century. However, many wars were still connected with the decline of the dominant imperial relations of the previous period, as well as resulting from the new state relations of the post-imperial era. Similarly in the contemporary global transition, the end of the Cold War has removed the major danger of war resulting from inter-bloc or superpower conflict. But while it has removed some of the bases of Third World conflicts which were connected with the Cold War, wars have also arisen from the disintegration of Cold War forms.

It is important to emphasise the significance of the end of inter-bloc conflict, since this major gain is too often taken for granted in contemporary debate. However unlikely intercontinental nuclear war was during most of the Cold War period, even the slightest possibility of such a war (at times there was clearly more than that) imbued the whole world order with the danger of the most catastrophic imaginable war -- a sense which became acute in times of crisis. The removal of this threat has created a powerful presumption of peace as the *normal* basis of global relations. It is also important to emphasise the effects of removing the Cold War underpinnings for wars like that between Iran and Iraq, and in Afghanistan, Cambodia and Angola. Although the end of the Cold War by no means resulted in a simple end to these wars -- in each situation, new violence arose in the early 1990s -- it did reduce some of their supports, and certainly changed their political roles, and may in the longer term be seen as the beginning of pacification.

The 1990s have, however, been far from the decade of peace which the end of the Cold War seemed to herald. On the contrary, they have seen such a rapid spread and transformation of warfare that the term 'new wars' has been used (Kaldor, 1997). The key question for contemporary analysis is how much these wars are short-term effects of the transition of 1989-91, and how much they reflect deeper structural characteristics of state relations in the global era. Clearly the collapse of the Soviet and Yugoslav multi-national states in 1991 has spawned a series of wars in the Caucasus, Central Asia and the Balkans, some of which continue towards the end of the decade.

While these wars have been represented as civil and more precisely inter-ethnic wars, they mostly involve conflicts about which elites shall control which successor states and which territories. They involve exaggerated forms of the general problems of the transition from state-controlled industry to market relations which has occurred throughout the ex-communist regions. They both generate and mobilise extreme forms of the general de-formalisation of the economy in these regions. In the war zones, corruption, the black market, Mafia-type groups and armed criminal gangs, which have grown throughout much of the former Soviet empire, have often become dominant. Even in Sarajevo, the beacon of Western-type pluralistic civilisation in the Balkan quagmire, much of the city's defence fell for a time into the hands of ruthless criminal gangs.

The post-Soviet and post-Yugoslav wars are not the only ones which can be attributed to the post-Cold War transition. Many late Cold War conflicts have mutated into new wars in the 1990s. The financial and political failure of Iraq in the 1980s war with Iran impelled it into the new wars with Kuwait, as well as with its own Shia and Kurdish populations, in 1990-91. The US-led, UN-sponsored coalition which expelled Iraq from Kuwait itself mobilised both the ex-Cold War armoury of the West and a global-era political alliance with post-Soviet leaders. Cold War-sponsored factions like the Mujehaddin in Afghanistan, Khmer Rouge in Cambodia and UNITA in Angola, have fought re-configured wars but have lost out in the new political circumstances, even if the former Soviet-backed regimes in these states have also dissolved or mutated. The withdrawal of Cold War backing has also precipitated regime collapse which has led to new wars as is exemplified in the disintegration of Somalia.

Although these wars of the 1990s can be seen as ramifications of the collapse of the Cold War and the communist system, it is far from certain that they can be overcome once a transitional period is gone through. Many of the new states which emerged from the decline of European empires in the 1950s and 1960s have also proved weak and prone to disintegration. Indeed, it is precisely the acceleration of this trend in the 1990s which has led to so many new wars. The new wars of Yugoslavia and Central Asia have had their counterparts in West Africa, Sierra Leone and Liberia; in Central Africa, Rwanda and the Congo (ex-Zaire); as well as Angola, Mozambique in the Horn of Africa. Even in South Africa, where the post-apartheid transition resembles at the formal political level the more successful post-communist transitions, there has been substantial localised violence.

The global transition is thus accompanied by a widespread collapse of local state forms, notably in Africa and the ex-communist States, which is unlikely to be overcome in the short term. Although the global transition has involved a widespread democratisation not only in ex-communist states but also in Latin America, Asia and Africa as Cold War supports for authoritarian regimes are removed, this process has been problematic. Even if consolidated democratic states are less likely to go to war, transitional democracies, in which elites seek new ethnic-nationalist legitimacy, may often *generate* violent mobilisations.

This is not only a problem of relatively minor states in the Balkans or Africa. The global transition also leaves, at the end of the 20th century, very substantial areas in which strong, more or less classical nation states are relatively weakly embedded both in global and regional integration processes and in stable national social and political structures. Not only in the Middle East, but also throughout Asia, even in huge states like China, India, Pakistan and Indonesia, national political forms and inter-state relations may still interact in ways which have classically produced major wars. Many states in the Middle East and Asia have large military forces and nuclear, chemical or biological weapons, raising the prospect of further major wars -- more like the Iran-Iraq war and the Gulf War than some of the smaller localised conflicts of recent times, and conceivably on an even larger scale.

Instabilities of state forms still pose therefore dangers of war, even major war, in the 21st century. These instabilities arise both from problematic relations of state and society and from crises in relations between states. The Iraqi case is the contemporary paradigm: external war has fed internal war, and vice versa. The difference from the recent past is that whereas local or regional wars were then seen as dangers to the stability of the Cold War system, they are now seen as threats to *global* order.

From wars of state disintegration and genocide to inter-state conflicts, war represents a problem of the viability of globality. The emergent global order assumes a coherence of authority relations from the local and sub-national level, through national authority, to regional and world-level structures. At the centre of the global power structure -- the Western and UN state institutions -- both inter- and intra-state instabilities represent weaknesses in the system of authority relations which render global relations problematic. Both the possibilities of unfettered commercial relations and the global norms of human rights are threatened by the violent breakdown of authority. This breakdown requires, therefore, global responses.

The paradox of the current phase of the global transition is that while the necessity of such responses is increasingly seen as inevitable, there remains enormous uncertainty about them. Western state leaders have not chosen global leadership: it has been thrust upon them by their own relative success, by the succession of crises in which problems have presented themselves, and by the pressures of media and civil society. Western state leaders remain most concerned with their national constituencies. They are reluctant to invest national resources, personnel and authority in any radical way in global institutions. These institutions, moreover, remain based on nation states, and many non-Western states are even more conservative, seeing in extensions of global authority and power threats to their own autonomy and sovereignty in relations with society.

Degenerate War and Global Policing

These changes in the role of war are also related to transformations in the *character* of war. In the era of national and international relations, war was understood primarily as a rational policy-oriented action of states:

the continuation of policy by other means, as Clausewitz (1976) famously defined it. The interpretation of this dictum (in both strategic and Marxist orthodoxies) has often been extremely one-sided, emphasising state rationality and neglecting the implications of the violence of war. It was this logic of the 'other means' which Clausewitz elaborated elsewhere in his volume (Howard, 1981). He wrote in the aftermath of the wars of revolutionary nationalism which marked the emergence of 'the people' as military actors -- indeed he saw them as responsible for the violence of modern warfare. His concept of absolute war anticipated the modern totalisation of violence, but he wrote before the 20th century synthesis of nation state mobilisation and destructive capacity.

War in the international system era could not be understood, therefore, in purely Clausewitzian terms. The new form of war was the synthesis of state, nation and *industrial* society (Shaw, 1988). From the 17th century onwards, military discipline had anticipated industrial discipline. But from the middle of the 19th century, war-preparation harnessed the new industrial technologies of manufacturing, transport and communications. At the same time, the mass conscript army, first seen in revolutionary France, became the norm of nation state mobilisation. In the late 19th century, the industrialisation of war was organised in what were later called military-industrial complexes, industrial sectors underwritten by states and protected from market fluctuations (MacNeill, 1982). At the same time, the emergence of mass politics and mass media led to the classical mass militarism of patriotic mobilisation and propaganda.

The result of these 19th century changes was not merely to remove many earlier constraints on absolute violence -- the 'friction' of which Clausewitz had written -- but to develop a social infrastructure for mass killing which would not merely transform war but engulf society. The new 'mode of warfare' (Kaldor, 1982) was total war -- total not merely in the violence between its protagonists, but in its mobilisation of economy and society and its murderousness toward civilian populations. Total war involved dynamic relationships between state and society (Shaw, 1988). Mobilising economy and society for total war, nation states first transformed them into semi-autarchic war-machines, then made them targets for other states' industrialised violence. In the 1939-45 culmination of the international system of total war, war became doubly genocidal, as an outcome of both strategic choices (Allied area bombing) and political ideology (the Nazi and Soviet extermination of minorities).

This total mode of warfare underwent a double transformation in the Cold War, nuclear age. On the one hand, the refinement of the capacity for instantaneous destruction represented the possibility of and unhampered realisation of the trend toward absolute war. In this sense the totalisation of war was *extended*. On the other hand, the ability of states to develop this capacity without mass mobilisation meant that they increasingly relied on relatively small, professional militaries and technologically sophisticated workforces. On the mobilisation side, totalisation was *diminished*: in line with this trend, major features of the total war era such as state control of economies, political totalitarianism and conscription all went out of fashion. Western society in the Cold War period had a paradoxical relationship to war -- on the one hand, it was absolutely threatened by its awesomely enhanced killing capacity, but on the other, it was demobilised and became in many senses *post-military* (Shaw, 1991).

The paradox of the mode of warfare in the second half of the 20th century is summed up by the fact that the principal form of violence was cold war -- planned but not fought, 'imaginary war' (Kaldor, 1991). The dominant understanding of war as a rational means for states was located within this mental universe, even to the extent that it neglected the hot wars which were actually being fought. These wars, like the wars of the previous era as a whole, were both inter- and intra-state. Although the conventional thought of this era, which continued during the Cold War, maintained that inter-state and civil wars were distinct types of war, warfare throughout the era crossed this boundary. From revolution to civil war to international war, and *vice versa*, was often the circuit of violence. Guerrilla warfare -- in its mid-20th century forms clearly a variant of total war -- was both a form of revolutionary violence and an element of inter-state war. While some major wars, from Korea to Iran-Iraq, resembled the conventional struggles of the total-war period, in others, like Vietnam, unconventional violence played a major part (as, of course, it did in many places in 1939-45). The hot wars of the Cold War period continued the trend of the world wars towards a greater ratio of civilian to military casualties.

Despite many precedents and continuities, the sort of wars which are being fought in the global transition represent further, important shifts from these dominant models of the earlier era. The rational use of war as a means of inter-state conflict was rendered problematic by the advent of weapons of mass destruction, and has now become (more or less) anachronistic. With the near-completion of decolonisation and the collapse of communist politics, wars of national liberation and revolutionary transformation have become less and less viable. Inter-state war is increasingly the resort of rogue states -- typified by Saddam Hussein's Iraq, which has initiated both the most serious wars of the last twenty years and is among the most determined in its development of weapons of mass destruction. However there remain many powerful states with the capacity to wage war on a terrifying scale, and it would be premature to rule out further devastating inter-state wars.

While many wars of the 1990s have had inter-state aspects, there has been an increasing tendency for wars to be *primarily* campaigns of violence against civilians, waged by parties, groups and elements of decomposing state apparatuses, often in the name of ethnic or tribal groups. Nazism is the closest model for the new warfare in the old canon. The definition of the Jews -- a civilian population of city, town and village-dwellers spread across central and eastern Europe -- as an enemy appeared irrational by the then standards of conventional inter-state war. By the standards of contemporary warfare, however, it is almost a rational model -- if only in the sense that like conventional war aims, it was a goal pursued methodically by a large centralised state apparatus.

In the early global era, genocide has become almost universal, but it has been a more localised practice of much more variegated groups -- a do-it-yourself genocide of paramilitaries, bandits and vigilantes as well as regular units, embedded in networks of corruption, black marketeering, protection rackets, arms and drug trafficking. While overall direction and rationalisations have not been lacking -- often high political authorities have initiated mass killings -- implementation has often been more haphazard and decentralised. If participants act rationally, it is often not principally in terms of a centralised master-plan, but in terms of local and individual projects of self-aggrandisement, revenge, etc.

Contemporary warfare therefore involves *degenerate* forms of the models of war which applied in the international system era. States no longer fight each other in all-out conflicts, but support, often indirectly, genocide against civilians in their own or neighbouring territories. States no longer mobilise national economies and societies -- wars arise from the disintegration of such national frameworks, with centralised authorities no longer able to raise taxes and armies. Regular armed forces are in decay, often supplemented by paramilitaries, local self-defence units and foreign mercenaries. Weaponry is small-scale but may be high-tech. This form of warfare borrows from both the guerrilla warfare and the counter-insurgency of the former period, but the warring groups seek population displacement rather than territorial control. Instead of instituting an ideologically conceived programme of social change, they claim 'democratic' legitimacy based on identity by forcibly achieving a homogenous population. The displaced populations swell the growing encampments of refugees in neighbouring territories.

Degenerate warfare does not produce or mobilise so much as trade, loot and steal. As Kaldor (1997, 1998) shows, domestic production typically collapses in zones of war, with some exceptions of particularly lucrative primary products such as drugs or precious metals which are protected. Local asset transfer, in which urban middle classes especially are forced by inflation and shortages to dispose of valuable property and goods at knock-down prices in order to buy necessities, is one legal way in which war is financed. But local requisitions are rarely sufficient. External aid of various kinds -- from remittances from overseas workers and aid from diaspora communities to support from state sponsors and taxing or looting of humanitarian aid -- is essential to the prosecution of degenerate war. The circle is completed by the transformations of military production, now increasingly organised in a competitive global market for weaponry.

Corresponding to the forms of degenerate war are transformations in the forms of military activity originating in the pacified world, especially the West. The main military function of the state becomes what is described as peacekeeping or peace-enforcement, although these are misnomers since often, in the new wars, peace has not been established before UN or Western forces become involved. In reality, what is involved is global policing, or what Kaldor (1998) calls 'cosmopolitan law-enforcement' -- the enforcement of globally legitimate norms in general and international law in particular.

Military institutions in the West and elsewhere have hardly adjusted to these new roles. Mostly they still employ modified versions of the resources and doctrines they developed in the Cold War. To some extent, the exigencies of the emerging global order have reinforced tendencies, like the movement away from conscription, which were established in the Cold War. In other respects, they profoundly challenge the doctrines, priorities and status hierarchies of the military. The emphasis on large scale, sophisticated weapon-systems, epitomised by nuclear weapons, is anachronistic, and can only be justified by an extension of 'imaginary war' thinking even further from reality. The role of air power, in general, although not completely outmoded, is rendered very problematic in responding to often complex localised political situations. An emphasis on politics, negotiation and understanding is at a premium, and has led one military sociologist to see the 'soldier-scholar' as the archetype of the new officer (Moskos, 1993).

In this new kind of soldiering, the historically dominant forms of masculinity are also redundant, and taboos against women and homosexuals are not so easily maintained. The traditional culture of the military already lost its wider social dominance in the West during the Cold War, when 'armament culture' (Luckham, 1984) and 'spectator sport militarism' (Mann, 1987) replaced traditional mass-participation militarism. Now traditional military culture is increasingly questioned within the military, too, as the institution adapts to new roles.

Towards Warless Globality?

The contemporary world is in the early stages of the development of a global order. The old international political order has undergone a fundamental transformation at its core. In the pacified West, national and international state institutions are components of a huge conglomerate of state power, increasingly institutionalised in forms which claim global as well as regional legitimacy. These global state forms are embedded in networks of economic, social and cultural power which partially embrace all areas of the world. At the same time, in some regions outside the Western core of North America, Western Europe and Japan, both interstate war (notably in the Middle East) and genocidal wars of state fragmentation (notably in Africa, the ex-Soviet region and the Balkans) remain major dangers. They threaten not only people in the zones of warfare, but the stability and security of the emerging global order.

Extending pacification from the broad West to the remainder of the non-Western world -- no less a project than the abolition of war -- is essential to a stable globality. Clearly it is a complex and long-term task, and involves extending all the transformations of world order which have been involved in global developments to date. Most fundamentally, it involves the expansion of the density, coherence and legitimacy of global state institutions. The task is to consolidate a robust framework of democratic global authority relations which are accepted by state institutions, social groups of all kinds and individuals across the world. Clearly this goal implies transformations of local state forms, the consolidation of national and local democracy as a corollary of the extension of democracy at regional and global levels.

This transformation in turn requires social and economic changes. As the European Union recognises in its incorporation of new member states, common standards of economic development, political culture and human rights are necessary to embed common authority structures. In order to achieve such standards, common resources must be devoted to economic, social and political reform in the applicant states. In the global political framework, similar considerations apply in principle. Given that this framework is not only larger but looser, with vast discrepancies of economic and social conditions as well as political regime, the task is far more serious. Nevertheless, given that almost all state units are members of the United Nations, and that the Universal Declaration of Human Rights applies to all individuals within these states, the global framework exists in outline form. The task is to extend and deepen this framework, to embed it in a greater commonality of economic, social, cultural and political institutions, and to develop institutions and means of implementing global authority.

Inevitably, this will involve devoting the resources of the wealthier centres of society and state power not only to the problems of the poorer and weaker areas but to the development of global institutions themselves. Among the activities in need of development is that of war-management, in which new institutions and techniques could prevent and control conflict. But overall, it is far more important to the aim of controlling war that global economic, social and above all political institutions should be developed. The massive resources devoted by major states to arms and soldiers should be devoted in part to new forms of global policing, law-enforcement and war-management, but in larger part they need to be diverted to non-military uses -- to global political as well as socio-economic development.

Clearly the major paradox of the emerging global order is the reluctance of its leaders to assume their responsibilities, and to grasp the necessity and possibility of transformation. Global leadership remains embedded in the national politics of small horizons. In the first decade of the global transition, what stands out is the reactive mode of global institutional development and the tardiness and poverty of responses to crises of global authority. It is almost certain that in the coming decades, global transformation will continue to be conditioned by crisis. In all probability, only further major challenges to global order will compel the kinds of radical changes necessary to construct stable authority relations. Only through dealing with the degenerate war of the early global age are we likely to reach a mature globality in which war as a major form of social action is finally overcome.

Part III
Approaches to Peace

5 From Arms to Disarmament Races: Disarmament Dynamics after the Cold War

BJØRN MØLLER

The problem of armament dynamics is one of the classic themes of peace research because of its obvious relevance to the focal point of this field. Not only is war the direct antimony of peace, but preparations for war, such as the production and acquisition of armaments, also appear to be incompatible with peace. The intrinsic importance of the topic aside, the problem of armament dynamics also attracts peace researchers' attention because of its intellectual appeal, especially among scholars and scientists from the natural sciences, economics and mathematics. The topic simply lends itself to mathematical treatment, such as modelling and game theory, more than most other topics related to war and peace (Nicholson, 1989, pp. 147-66; Isard, 1988, pp. 17-85; Gleditsch, 1990; Wiberg, 1990a; Intrilligator and Brito, 1993; Sandler and Hartley, 1995, pp. 73-109).

In this chapter, the author briefly, and without any attempt at 'scientific' sophistication, recapitulates classical arms race theory as well as certain alternative explanatory approaches. The focus is, however, on two questions. First, how could we solve the arms race problem with special attention being paid to alternative defence? Secondly, is the arms race a phenomenon of the past with the implication that the proposed solutions might have become 'answers in search of questions'?

The Armament Dynamics

Classical Arms Race Theory

The classical paradigm of 'arms races', which most people probably have in mind when using the term, is that of the 'Action-Reaction Phenomenon' (ARP), where one state's arms acquisitions are determined by those of its opponent(s), and vice versa (Rathjens, 1973; Kahn, 1983; Buzan, 1987, pp. 76-93; for a qualification, Hammond, 1993).

This is also the classical (textbook) example of the so-called 'security dilemma' (Jervis, 1976, pp. 58-93; Collins, 1996), because it tends to place states in the unfortunate position 'between a rock and a hard place'. The two horns of the security dilemma are, respectively, to do nothing or to respond. If a state does nothing, but the opponent arms, its relative military strength may be weakened to such an extent that it becomes an easy target for aggression, in the form of 'compellence' or outright invasion and conquest. If it responds with an arms build-up, based on incomplete knowledge about the motives driving its opponent to arms acquisitions, it may inadvertently bring about precisely what it intends to avert. Its own arms build-up may be perceived as threatening by the opponent who, in turn, may feel forced to an arms build-up that is regarded as compensatory and reactive. The result may be a spiral of arms acquisitions among states who want nothing more than to live at peace with their neighbours.

It has been rightly pointed out that the security dilemma is not, strictly speaking, an inevitable feature of an international anarchy, but that rather it is 'what states make of it' (Wendt, 1992). However, once one state has been unmasked as a 'predator', all states will be inclined to see each other as potential predators, thereby making the security dilemma an enduring feature of anarchy -- albeit one with exceptions as well as a solution, both of which I shall return to in due course. The fact that some, but not all, states are predators means that we have to distinguish between three different types of ARP-driven arms races:

(1) 'Races to win' between 'predators': both are seeking a superiority that will allow them to defeat the other.

(2) 'Defensive races': one contestant is actually a predator seeking a war-winning superiority while the others are merely trying to prevent this without having any aggressive motives.

(3) 'Red Queen races' where all the 'runners' are defensively motivated, i.e., only determined not to lose the race against the respective other 'runners' under suspicion of being possible predators. In such a race, states behave like the runners in Lewis Carroll's famous novel, *Through the Looking Glass*, who ran 'very fast for a long time' without getting anywhere. As the Red Queen put it, behind the Looking Glass 'it takes all the running you can do, to keep in the same place. If you want to get somewhere else, you must run at least twice as fast as that!' (Carroll, 1962, p. 216)

As it is not particularly surprising that predators as well as their envisaged targets spend large sums on arms, we can instead focus our attention on the more difficult case of defensively motivated states in a setting where there are no predators. Why do such states find difficulty arriving at a stable level of armaments where all of them can feel secure without overspending on their military? In other words, what are the dynamic elements in 'Red Queen arms races?'

One part of the explanation is the determination of 'sufficiency'. If states, for instance, define sufficiency as an approximate numerical balance of strength, they are in trouble, as such a balance is bound to look quite different depending on the angle from which one views it. Prudence dictates that governments should base their planning on worst case assumptions, or at least not on overly optimistic assumptions, because it is, in truth, better to be safe than sorry. Hence, states have to reckon with the possibility that their opponent(s) will enjoy a certain mobilisation lead, as any prospective aggressor inevitably would. By implication, they have to compare their own peacetime strength with what the potential aggressor might have assembled and deployed before launching an attack -- which is only possible by having a peacetime strength superior to that of one's opponent(s). An actual balance will thus tend to be perceived by both sides as an imbalance that needs to be redressed. This may account for some of the dynamism.

A supplementary explanation may be found in the distinction between genuine (or 'reactive') and 'proactive reaction'. 'Reactive reaction' occurs when a state reacts to actions on the part of its opponent(s), not only after the fact, but also after the (often time-consuming and uncertainty-ridden) process of detection, verification, and interpretation of the facts. Because such reaction may often come too late to be adequate, states prudently tend to prefer anticipatory or 'proactive reaction', i.e., to 'react' to the expected next move of one's opponents, rather than to their last actual move.

For all its attractions, however, there is a problem with anticipation when it takes place under conditions of 'limited visibility', namely that states may actually respond to figments of their own imagination rather than to their actual opponents -- who may not even be genuine opponents. The ARP phenomenon thereby becomes increasingly surreal and 'virtual', because the basis for states' expectations about the future behaviour of their respective opponents is usually 'mirror imaging' infected with enemy images. States thus tend to expect or fear from the other side exactly what they might do themselves, were it not for their own inherent goodness -- an attitudinal feature that cannot safely be assumed in the case of one's opponent(s). Typically, the development of a weapon is presumed to spur a quest for countermeasures by the opponent, hence calls for counter-countermeasures, etc. If the other side is only moderately security-minded, and even more so if the other side is actually a mirror image of the first state, the stage is set for a self-perpetuating ARP. Contrary to the 'real' ARP, this is, however, a virtual one, representing an interaction of plans and expectations rather than actual weapons deployments.

In principle, it is thus conceivable that the arms race might come to a 'happy ending', where states cease to deploy weapons against each other and limit themselves to potential weapons and blueprints. Unfortunately, it is at least equally likely that states will feel more comfortable with actual, rather than potential weapons, hence the perpetuation of the arms race without any rational foundation.

Alternative Explanations?

If the happy ending does not become reality, it may be due, in part, to the fact that arms build-ups may have more propellants than the ARP. These factors are occasionally even assumed to be the main, as opposed to merely contributory, causes. Taking the above self-referring arms race theory a step further, certain analysts thus see the arms race as entirely 'autistic,' i.e., as driven almost exclusively by domestic determinants (Senghaas, 1972, 1990. See also Buzan, 1987, pp. 94-113).

One of the most powerful explanations is the theory of the military-industrial complex (MIC) forming an 'iron triangle' -- the armed forces themselves, the arms industry and the defence department officials -- of societal forces which benefit from, and hence have shared vested interests in perpetuating, the arms build-up (Barnett, 1970; Pursell, 1972; Kaldor, 1981; Gottlieb, 1997). One need not be a Marxist, but only partly convinced of the 'bureaucratic politics paradigm' for it to be plausible that such factors as economic interests and/or bureaucratic expansionism and inertia play a role, and that those involved in the arms race will fight for its continuance (Allison and Morris, 1975; Allison, 1983). What the MIC theory does not satisfactorily explain is why the MIC should invariably be more successful in its bureaucratic in-fighting than other 'complexes', such as the 'urban housing complex' or the 'primary education complex' (Sarkesian, 1972). Further complicating the issue, most countries import the majority of their weaponry rather than producing it indigenously. In such cases, the industrial supply-push factor is external rather than domestic, which makes it even harder to account for its alleged relative strength in a competition with powerful domestic interest groups over the distribution of scarce societal resources. While it is quite plausible that the MIC may exert a certain influence, it is counterintuitive that it should always prevail.

A related theory of armament dynamics is that of the technology-driven arms acquisitions (Albrecht, 1990; Thee, 1990). Such theorising may go no further than claiming that the 'scientific community' has its share of responsibility for the continuing arms build-up because scientists tend to succumb to the temptation of plentiful resources and inherently challenging technologies. When analysts proceed to technological determinism, they tend to assume the burden of proof, while generally being unable to actually prove their case.

None of these 'alternative' explanations may be able to stand alone. For instance, it is inconceivable that, say, a decision such as that taken in 1983-86 by the UK, Germany, Italy and Spain to produce the EFA (European Fighter Aircraft, also known as 'Eurofighter 2000') will be taken solely on the basis of appeals to jobs, profits or technological challenges. It can only be justified by reference to a mission, which can hardly be anything but an external threat to national security (Enserink et al., 1992, pp. 101-106; Willett et al., 1994; Albrecht et al., 1994). This need for legitimation takes us back to the aforementioned ARP theory. The latter thus seems to be the basic theory, yet one in need of certain qualifications, for which the 'domestic factors' theorems are obvious candidates.

This also suggests that there may be no watertight barriers between the theories. What is *really* motivated by domestic concerns has to be legitimated with reference to external threats -- which, in reality, decision makers may actually come to believe over time. Furthermore, arms production for the sake of jobs and profits may nevertheless come to represent, or at least be perceived as, a threat to other states. These states may thus respond with counter-measures, which may necessitate compensatory steps. The reverse is also partly true: What may originally have been motivated by a threat may gradually produce its own constituency.

Why Worry?

It is not self-evident that arms races are bad. In fact, one might regard them as 'functional substitutes for war', e.g., as elements of cold wars that are surely preferable to hot ones. Indeed, if the arms race should become increasingly virtual, we might even be approaching a situation where the mere design of weapons would replace their actual use in war. This would definitely represent a civilisational quantum jump -- similar to a substitution of debates or chess games for duels to the death. Nevertheless, there are several reasons to worry about arms races, especially 'Red Queen races'.

First of all, there seems to be a significant correlation between arms races and the outbreak of war (Wiberg, 1990b; Siverson and Diehl, 1993). However, there are several possible causal explanations for this correlation. Either the arms race may somehow directly cause war, even though the precise form of such causality is difficult to account for, or the arms race may be a contributory cause of the subsequent war, for instance in the sense that it produces levels of armament that are (economically and/or otherwise) unsustainable. Hence, countries may, at some point, face the choice between opting out of the race, with all the accruing risks, or 'getting it over with' by starting a war. A reverse causality is, however, also entirely conceivable, where the risk of war is the real cause of the arms race that precedes it, since states that feel threatened (and justifiably, as demonstrated *ex post facto* by the outbreak of war) are inclined, and prudently so, to arm. This alternative explanation, however, cannot satisfactorily explain the aforementioned 'Red Queen races', even though it may be used to reinterpret this phenomenon as something different.

Secondly, military expenditures represent a diversion of societal resources from civilian use. There may, of course, be some 'spill-over' effects, in the sense that military production and R&D (research and development) may generate both demand and productive capacities available for the civilian sector. As a general rule, however, this factor only needs to be taken into account in subtracting from gross expenditures in order to determine the net costs of arming. How much to subtract obviously depends on the degree of import dependence, as arms imports may, at most, generate jobs in the exporting country, at best partly compensated for by offset orders (Martin, 1996). This is particularly a problem for small and 'developing' countries which tend to *not* develop, partly because of excessive military spending (N. Ball, 1988; Büttner and Krause, 1995; Krause, 1992).

Thirdly, and finally, arms racing requires some 'ideological' underpinnings (or superstructure) *inter alia* because the above diversion of resources calls for legitimation. Inflated force comparisons, enemy images, and a generally distorted view of the world are among these immaterial costs that are no less significant even though they are, by their very nature, unquantifiable (Shimko, 1991; Ungar, 1992).

Escape Routes from the Arms Race?

Granting that the arms race is a problem, the question remains about its solution. Several proposals have been made which are briefly described and assessed in the following.

Arms Control

The most modest attempted solution is that of 'classical' arms control philosophy (Schelling and Halperin, 1985; Schelling, 1986; Blechman, 1983; Bull, 1987; Adler, 1992. For a critique see Gray, 1992). Arms control is better understood as an integral part of defence planning as opposed to a mode of disarmament. What sets it apart from 'traditional' defence policy is that it prudently takes anticipated steps by respective opponents into account and seeks security by means of negotiations as well as through other unilateral steps. What matters is not so much to reduce the level of armaments as to make the level more stable, thereby contributing to national security. In some cases, 'stability' may require more arms rather than less -- even though it is, of course, always desirable to achieve security at the minimum level. What matters most, however, is how the resources are spent, which specific types of armaments are produced, and how they are deployed.

The historical track record of arms control has not been impressive (Carter, 1989), a fact that has been attributed to the complexities of negotiations in a competitive, even antagonistic, setting. Arms control may thus become a functional substitute for, or even an integral part of, arms racing, where states seek unilateral advantages at the expense of their opponents. Hence the attraction of somehow 'short-circuiting' the system by means of various forms of informal arms control, such as gradualism. Such strategies presuppose that the parties to the arms race are aware of their entrapment in a 'Red Queen race' without any prospects of winning, and are looking for an escape route. Under such circumstances, unilateral and unconditional small steps may be useful, as they may demonstrate a willingness to go further, should a certain reciprocation be achieved (Johansen, 1993; Ramberg, 1993).

Disarmament

The diametrical opposite of arms control is the slogan of 'General and Complete Disarmament,' (GCD) which one still encounters in such places as UN resolutions.

As 'general and complete' is not tantamount to 'irreversible', GCD has to be acknowledged as incompatible with prudent defence planning as well as with stability, as it would place a high premium on deception and break-out. In a completely disarmed world, the first state to acquire a significant amount of military power would enjoy an overwhelming superiority that none of its neighbours would find acceptable. Hence, everybody would want to guard against such an eventuality, implying that GCD would never be genuine.

What might conceivably salvage the (noble, but probably hopelessly utopian) ideal of GCD might be the aforementioned 'virtuality'. It is, for instance, conceivable that states might relinquish their actual arms holdings and feel secure with the mere demonstrated potentiality. This is, for instance, how Jonathan Schell envisaged the abolition of nuclear weapons to come about: via a substitution of 'blueprints' for actual nuclear weapons, and a replacement of armed with weaponless deterrence (Schell, 1984, p. 119). It is conceivable that the same might work for conventional weapons: nobody actually possessed them while being aware that everybody else might acquire them. While this just might make states content with the mere potential of weapons, such an outcome does not seem at all likely. Moreover, should just one state 'break out', the 'delicate balance of not yet implemented options' would collapse.

Another possible solution with a certain appeal is a very radical version of collective security where a strong United Nations would enjoy a monopoly on military power, while national military establishments would be prohibited. Such a supranational monopoly on the use of military force would provide ample safeguards against any breakout from the 'no-weapons regime'. Hence the arrangement might be quite stable and robust, once in place -- the trouble being that it may well be impossible to establish in the first place. At the very least, the moment does not appear at all ripe for such a radical departure from the anarchical nature of international politics (Bull, 1995, pp. 244-245 and *passim*).

Defensive Restructuring-cum-Disarmament

The idea of defensive restructuring of the armed forces occupies a middle ground between arms control and GCD. It shares with the former the high emphasis on stability (in the dual sense of crisis and arms race stability) as well as the priority assigned to qualitative over quantitative factors. It has the objective of disarmament in common with GCD, although it envisages the retainment of armed forces for a significant period.

The distinguishing characteristic of a 'non-offensive defence' (NOD) -- the aim of defensive restructuring -- is a defence posture that ensures its possessor against military aggression without enabling it to attack others (Møller, 1991, 1992, 1995). In the real world, of course, this is not a question of absolutes, but of enhancing defensive capabilities while simultaneously limiting offensive strength. To do so holds out the promise of an escape from the arms race, as it would resolve (or at least mitigate) the security dilemma -- states could simply make themselves more secure without subsequently making others less vulnerable, wherefore their military measures would not call for reciprocal steps by their adversaries. NOD would thus go a very long way towards making 'Red Queen arms races' between defensively motivated states inconceivable. It might even be possible to reverse such an arms race by transforming spiralling arms build-up into a downward spiral, i.e., a 'disarmament race', via gradualism: A state might take a significant, but limited (hence low-risk) restructuring step towards defensive restructuring of its armed forces as a token of its defensive intentions and an open invitation to reciprocate with similar defensive steps.

As far as the other forms of races are concerned, where one or all 'runners' are out to win, defensive restructuring would not suffice to bring the race to a halt. However, by presenting credible evidence of its own defensive inclination, a defensively motivated state might unmask a 'predator state' as such, thereby making it harder for the latter to justify its arms build-up as 'defensive'. As a general rule, because of the propensity of states to 'balance' against aggression rather than to 'bandwagon' with the aggressor (Walt, 1985), states with defensive postures would also usually have greater access to outside assistance in the case of attack. Defensive restructuring between opposing predators is highly unlikely to occur as this would obviously thwart their aggressive plans. It is not much more likely to affect the domestic determinants of the armament dynamics except in so far as it makes the justification of an arms build-up more difficult. Its main impact is on defensive arms races, the elimination of which would also be a significant accomplishment.

The theory of NOD rests on two presuppositions, namely that distinctions between offence and defence are possible, and that defence enjoys an inherent superiority over attack. This would allow for a reduction (preferably even elimination) of capabilities for attack without critically negative implications for defence. This is not the place to argue these points in any detail. It suffices to underline that it is *not* a question of singling out specific categories of weapons as 'offensive' and 'defensive', respectively, but rather of transforming military postures in their totalities as well as the strategies and operational conceptions that underlie them (Lynn-Jones, 1995). While this will usually involve a change of the 'weapons mix' of the armed forces, it is also a question of logistical support, deployment patterns, etc.

The following formula for 'defensive stability' thus only depicts an ideal situation in abstract terms. While it may be possible to approximate it in real life by using it as a guideline for military policy, to operationalise it is extremely difficult and beyond the scope of the present article:

$$D_A > O_B \text{ and } D_B > O_A$$

The 'formula' simply describes a situation where each state's (i.e., A's and B's) defensive strength (D) surpasses the offensive strength (O) of its respective opponent, i.e., a situation where either one would prevail if attacked by the respective other. If defence is really, by its very nature, less demanding than attack, the margin may be very wide for quantitative and/or qualitative force disparities that will not upset this 'stability through mutual defensive superiority'. Even though numbers would still matter, the criterion of 'balance' could be relaxed considerably, as even the numerically inferior side could feel secure (up to a point, of course), if only its forces are specialised on defence.

After the Cold War, Disarmament?

Optimists might argue that all of the above presumed solutions to the arms race problem have been rendered irrelevant by the apparent 'outbreak of peace' since 1989.

A Disarmament Race?

Generally speaking, the global resources spent on armaments have indeed declined considerably since their all-time peak in 1987, from 1.36 trillion constant 1995 US dollars (USD) to a 'mere' 864.5 billion USD in 1995, according to the figures of the US Arms Control and Disarmament Agency (ACDA) (see Table 1). The London-based International Institute for Strategic Studies (IISS) reports an even lower (and misleadingly precise) figure for 1994, namely 821,578 million USD, whereas the Stockholm International Peace Research Institute (SIPRI) prudently refrains from calculating global military expenditures (ACDA, 1996, *passim*; IISS, 1997, p. 311; George *et al.*, 1997, p. 163). While disagreeing on the details, all three authorities concur that the arms race of the 1980s has definitely come to an end, and that a resumption is highly unlikely.

It is, however, also apparent from Table 1 that the reductions in military spending have primarily taken place in the developed world, while those of the developing countries have been much more modest.

Table 1: Military Expenditures (in millions constant 1995 US$)

	Developed World	Developing World	World
1985	1,101	230	1,331
1986	1,128	231	1,359
1987	1,140	220	1,360
1988	1,138	211	1,349
1989	1,105	200	1,305
1990	1,048	222	1,271
1991	937	221	1,159
1992	829	219	1,048
1993	768	189	957
1994	712	189	902
1995	668	197	865
Reduction	-39%	-14%	-35%

Source: Adapted from US Arms Control and Disarmament Agency (ACDA), 1996, p. 49.

Another piece of bad news that should temper any exhilaration over the 'end of the arms race' is that several small arms races still appear to be in progress, and that others are likely to be set in motion. Moreover, most of these residual arms races are only 'small' in the sense of involving fewer countries than the global arms race of the Cold War era. On the local or regional scale they may be equally intense and prone to lead to war, just as they may consume a comparable amount of societal resources badly needed for other purposes.

In the following section, a brief, and inevitably superficial, overview of the residual arms races is presented, accompanied by a (highly tentative) assessment of the prospects of the aforementioned presumed solutions to the arms race problem with a special focus on defensive restructuring. This presupposes a region-by-region (or even country-specific) evaluation of the nature of the dynamics driving arms acquisitions, as the measures required to halt or prevent arms races differ from those needed to contain domestic pressures (see also Mason 1995).

Residual Arms Races

The resolution of the East-West conflict in Europe has allowed several other, hitherto subdued, conflicts to re-emerge. The only conflict that (until now) seems to assume the form of an arms race, however, is the conflict between Greece and Turkey.

The roots of the conflict are found in the Cyprus issue, disputed territorial rights in the Aegean Sea, and conflicting interests pertaining to the rest of the Balkans (including the former Yugoslavia). The manifestation of the conflict, however, is an arms race (see Table 2) accompanied by military posturing and occasional small armed clashes.

Table 2: Aegean Sea (in millions constant 1995 US$)

	Avg. 85-90	1991	1992	1993	1994	1995
Turkey: MilEx	4612	5388	5849	6406	6322	6606
Arms Imports	1227	1326	1076	1258	1128	700
Greece: MilEx	4940	4625	4882	4845	4932	5056
Arms Imports	772	287	780	891	482	825

Source: Adapted from ACDA, 1996, pp. 72, 94.
(MilEx = Military Expenditures)

Contrary to the bipolar arms race of the Cold War, however, this one is complicated by the multipolar setting, as Turkey's military policies are not merely responses to that of Greece, but to a range of other factors as well, including developments in the Caucasus and Central Asia, the Middle East, and the Persian Gulf region. As Greek and Turkish armament decisions are very likely to be interdependent, defensive restructuring (in the sense of giving priority to the acquisition of weapons strengthening the defence) would appear to hold some prospects for alleviating tensions and slowing down the arms race. However, as a mere stabilisation of the 'Greek front' would allow Turkey to concentrate its strength against Iraq, or others, there seems to be a need for 'embedding' such a solution in a broader framework involving the Middle East and Persian Gulf region.

The arms race in the Middle East has abated significantly through the 1990s, probably reflecting the peace process as well as the changing balance-of-power produced by Iraq's defeat in 1991 (Cordesman, 1993, pp. 177-376). However, the apparent (relative) stability is tenuous and might be upset completely if the peace process loses its momentum as it may well have done already.

A defensive restructuring of military postures throughout the region would undoubtedly help, especially as far as Israel, Egypt and Syria are concerned. The risk of a Syrian attack against Israel (with or without the participation of Egypt and/or Jordan) seems remote as the balance of power has shifted considerably in Israel's favour. Especially in view of its (undeclared, but undisputed) nuclear weapons capability, Israel could thus safely abandon its pre-emptive and/or 'taking the war to the enemy' strategy in favour of a more defensive one, which would allow Syria and Egypt to likewise adopt more defensive postures, particularly as Syria is, for the time being, relieved of worries about Iraq. Such a defensive restructuring should represent a hedge against a resumption of a 'Red Queen race', whilst providing the defensive side with enhanced warning of attack preparations by a prospective aggressor.

The situation around the Persian Gulf appears very unstable, with very massive arms acquisitions on the part of the Gulf Cooperation Council (GCC), that are partly matched by a (slower and much more defensive) Iranian build-up (see Table 3; and Cordesman, 1993, pp. 377-684). We are thus probably witnessing a fully fledged arms race, to which Iraq will undoubtedly become a party, once UN-imposed constraints are lifted. The nature of this arms race is, however, less clear than sometimes assumed, as it seems unlikely that the leading 'runners' (i.e., the GCC) are aiming to win. Rather, they may be trying to over-insure themselves against Iran and Iraq whilst seeking to ensure US support by means of 'burden-sharing' in the form of large purchases from the ailing US arms industry. Be that as it may, set in a context of a 'dual containment' of both Iran and Iraq, such a military build-up is very likely to provoke a response in kind.

Defensive restructuring (as has already occurred, to a limited extent and involuntarily, with Iraq) might help a lot, particularly if the author is right about his assumption of a basically defensive Iranian orientation -- which may not endure, if the Islamic Republic continues to find itself surrounded by hostile and increasingly offensively armed neighbours (Møller, 1997). Even if Iran is actually a predator state, a more defensive orientation by the GCC countries would seem advisable, as this would make it more likely that they (as 'innocent victims' of an impending attack) would be eligible for US or UN support. In either case, a more defensive emphasis in arms purchases would thus help contain the arms race in progress.

Table 3: The Persian Gulf (in millions constant 1995 US$)

	Avg. 85-90	1991	1992	1993	1994	1995
Saudi Arabia: MilEx	22447	39240	37650	21470	17630	17210
Arms Imports	8561	9282	8390	7968	6560	8600
Kuwait: MilEx	4064	17620	20430	3759	3146	3488
Arms Imports	309	320	1049	970	226	900
UAE: MilEx	2272	5415	2256	2228	2178	1880
Arms Imports	600	387	366	482	410	875
Oman: MilEx	2071	1602	1901	1773	1864	1735
Arms Imports	117	55	11	147	297	460
GCC total MilEx	31078	65171	62892	29839	25391	24916
Arms Imports	9836	10132	9977	9640	7575	10925
Iran: MilEx	11295	8654	5410	6333	5586	4191
Arms Imports	2622	1768	914	1153	400	270
Iraq: MilEx	18887	9698	NA	NA	NA	NA
Arms Imports	5969	0	0	0	0	0

Source: Adapted from ACDA 1996, pp. 59, 75, 78, 85, 87, 89, 94, 95.

In South Asia, India and Pakistan have been at loggerheads ever since independence-*cum*-partition in 1947, especially over the Kashmir issue. While the conflict has previously assumed the form of war, its most obvious present manifestation is an arms race, which even has a nuclear aspect (Singh, 1995). Here as well, defensive restructuring would presumably help, even though the 'China factor' complicates matters, as India is obviously not merely arms racing against Pakistan but more significantly against China. Should it nevertheless prove feasible, a halt to the arms race is likely to entail even greater benefits than in most other settings: It would free resources that are badly needed for economic development, thereby reducing poverty. This would tend to stabilise (in the long run, at least) the political situation, thus providing both India and Pakistan with a wider margin for (what might be depicted as) concessions to the respective other side that might help 'break the ice', i.e., facilitate a resolution of the political conflict.

Northeast Asia features at least one actual and several potential (interlocking) arms races (see Table 4; Ball, 1993; Wattanayagorn and Ball, 1995).

Table 4: Northeast Asia (in millions constant 1995 US$)

	Avg. 85-90	1991	1992	1993	1994	1995
ROK: MilEx	10267	11950	12740	13050	14280	14410
Arms Imports	767	1216	527	1153	1435	1100
DPRK: MilEx	7180	6525	5916	5556	5638	6000
Arms Imports	637	99	32	5	92	100
Japan: MilEx	42262	48430	49510	50070	50540	50240
Arms Imports	1432	1216	1291	603	718	625
China: MilEx	53198	53270	55390	56390	58470	63510
Arms Imports	664	332	1398	603	267	725

Source: Adapted from ACDA 1996, pp. 65, 76, 77, 78.

First of all, the conflict between the two Koreas has been extremely tense ever since the 1953 cease-fire that has yet to be replaced by an actual peace treaty. Both North and South are heavily armed, with the latter, moreover, supported by a strong US military presence. The arms build-up has all the characterising features of an arms race, even though its nature is a matter of dispute. The South undoubtedly sees the Democratic Peoples Republic of Korea (DPRK) as inherently aggressive, i.e., as racing to win, in sharp contrast to (the self-image of) the Republic of Korea (ROK) as defensive. The North may, however, also feel endangered, not only because of the perceptual distortions felt by most authoritarian regimes, but also because it has been consistently outspent by the South. As the Korean arms race may thus actually be a 'Red

Queen race', defensive restructuring holds some promise of mitigating the situation, especially in the setting of the deep crisis of the North Korean economy (Møller, 1996).

A by-product of the disastrous situation in the DPRK may be a breakthrough in inter-Korean relations that may lead to unification, either gradually or in a swift 'German style'. Korean unification might conceivably trigger another arms race, as it would significantly alter the balance of power in the region. Not only would the armed forces of a unified Korea be merged, they would now also become available for 'external use', which might spur either a Chinese or a Japanese reaction. Whichever would come first, the respective other would be likely to reciprocate. This situation might ensure a particularly dangerous arms race between the Northeast Asian giants that might also come to involve the United States and/or Russia. In order to forestall this risk it would be imperative that Korean unification be accompanied by a defensive restructuring of the armed forces. It will, likewise, be important for Japan to maintain its (until now) predominantly defensive military posture, and for China to acquire power projection capabilities with great circumspection -- as it might otherwise come to find itself involved in two simultaneous arms races: one with the other powers in Northeast Asia and the United States, and one with the Association of Southeast Asian Nations (ASEAN) group and Taiwan.

Even though arms acquisitions in Southeast Asia have been massive, it would probably be premature to proclaim an arms race to be in progress (Acharya, 1994). Rather, the ASEAN states have probably been engaged in an 'innocent' modernisation of their armed forces (made possible by their, until the crisis beginning in 1997/98, impressive economic growth) combined with a strategic reorientation from domestic conflicts to conventional national defence. Neither are the arms purchases of the states in the region thus directed against their respective neighbours, nor probably against any other state (yet). Regardless of the innocent motivation, however, states may inadvertently come to be regarded as threats by their neighbours, especially in a context of souring political relations. It is, for instance, conceivable that the recent economic crisis might weaken ASEAN as an institution and lead to intensified rivalry in which case there are plenty of 'dormant' territorial and other issues that might ultimately lead to armed conflict. In order to prevent this from happening, a defensive orientation will be of some importance.

Table 5: Southeast Asia (in millions constant 1995 US$)

	Avg. 85-90	1991	1992	1993	1994	1995
Thailand:MilEx	2649	3008	3392	3988	4069	4014
Arms Imports	406	635	398	147	400	1100
Indonesia:MilEx	2015	2058	2110	2192	2423	3398
Arms Imports	286	33	54	94	51	170
Malaysia:MilEx	1459	2021	1996	2161	2303	2444
Arms Imports	166	122	140	283	871	750
Singapore:MilEx	2367	2961	3213	3274	3386	3970
Arms Imports	317	420	237	136	236	200
Philippines:MilEx	1141	1360	1275	1494	1402	1151
Arms Imports	97	155	151	63	92	90
Brunei:MilEx	471	NA	469	NA	348	269
Arms Imports	5	0	0	0	0	5
Vietnam:MilEx	2021	738	NA	NA	446	544
Arms Imports	2002	221	11	10	82	200
Myanmar:MilEx	1151	1500	1775	1594	1741	1833
Arms Imports	52	431	161	136	103	140
China:MilEx	53198	53270	55390	56390	58470	63510
Arms Imports	664	332	1398	603	267	725
India:MilEx	7539	7061	6991	7872	8502	7831
Arms Imports	3542	1022	699	283	236	410

Source: Adapted from ACDA 1996, pp. 62, 63, 65, 74, 81, 87, 90, 93, 97.

The Arms Trade

At first glance, the peaceful and 'disarmamentalist' post-Cold War world features a number of potentially dangerous localised arms races. As it happens, most states rely on arms imports for the majority of their build-up. The arms races are thus directly (and almost exhaustively) reflected in the arms trade statistics that do not warrant complacency. Even though the global arms trade has declined substantially since Cold War intra-block sales, it seems to have reached a plateau around 1992 from which it shows no indication of coming down (see Table 6). Because of the import-dependency of the above residual arms races, a curtailment of the international arms trade (in the form of supplier constraints) holds some promise of slowing down or perhaps even stopping arms races, simply by barring access to weaponry. Unfortunately, however, the track record of arms trade regulations is far from impressive (Krause, 1993; Anthony, 1991). Among other factors, attempts at supplier constraints on the arms trade have, so far, largely failed. This may be due to what one might call the 'arms exports prisoner's dilemma'.

Table 6: Imports of Major Conventional Weapons (in millions of constant 1990 US$)

	1990	1991	1992	1993	1994	1995	1996
World total	30,899	26,494	24,840	26,444	21,820	23,189	22,980
Industrial	12,226	12,348	13,237	12,563	8,855	6,236	5,554
Developing	18,673	14,147	11,603	13,881	12,966	16,953	17,425
Africa	1,661	779	492	294	634	571	427
Americas	1,684	2,619	1,994	1,485	2,323	1,898	1,220
Asia		629	13,274	10	493	8,591	6,843	753
Europe	10,078	8,469	9,473	9,061	6,458	4,299	4,107
Middle East	6,585	5,774	5,597	7,532	5,567	6,001	5,603
Oceania	399	262	441	535	455	66	559
ASEAN	1,187	1,043	1,103	741	2,252	2,841	1,170
NATO	5,630	8,491	9,390	7,500	6,701	3,934	2,922

Source: Anthony, 1997, p. 292.

If a state bans its arms exports to an unstable region, while other supplier(s) do not, the ban will have no significant effect on stability. The other(s), however, will be able to take over the market shares of the state showing restraint, leaving the latter at an economic disadvantage. As all exporters will tend to reason along these lines, a supplier ban is unlikely to be effective -- and the more loopholes it is believed to have, the less effective it will actually be.

Even if everybody were to agree on, and actually comply with, a ban on exports, the outcome would be uncertain. The vulnerability to arms embargoes differs considerably between the states in the region: Countries with easy access to hard currency and/or indigenous skills

(Iran, Iraq, Saudi Arabia) are generally less vulnerable than countries lacking these assets. Furthermore, in some regions there are large indigenous production capabilities which would undoubtedly be strengthened by supplier-imposed embargoes. This would not necessarily improve stability significantly, indeed it might even damage it by a resultant proliferation of 'dirty bombs' and various unsafe technologies. Moreover, the former suppliers would clearly lose lucrative foreign sales, without much prospect of making up for this in terms of civilian exports, since militarisation would continue. Since everyone would stand to lose, and no one to gain, such a supplier-imposed arms export ban is probably a non-starter.

The payoff structure would, however, be significantly different in a long-term supplier-plus-recipient arms trade control regime, i.e., a regime regulating not merely exports (the supply side), but also imports (the demand side). Everybody (but more than anybody else the regional states) would stand to gain from the improved stability. The former suppliers would, of course, lose their arms exports, but they would not have to worry about losing shares in a no longer existent market. Moreover, a replacement of the revenues from arms sales with those from civilian exports for development purposes would be a distinct possibility.

Even in the context of a combined supplier and recipient regime, arms trade regulations must be based on a consensus about what to limit and to what extent. Here, the desirability of limiting arms transfers has to be weighed against respect for the legitimate need of states to defend themselves. Logically, there are two main approaches to arms transfer regulations: the discriminatory and the non-discriminatory.

Discriminatory arms trade regulations might, for instance, consist of a ban on the trade in weapons of mass destruction, such as already implied by the Non-Proliferation Treaty (NPT) and the Australia Group's regulations. The Missile Technology Control Regime (MTCR) regulates the transfer of long-range and high payload surface-to-surface missiles and technologies to produce them. This might be extended to an integrated 'transfer regime' covering both ballistic missiles and advanced strike aircraft. It has also been suggested to use the Conventional Armed Forces in Europe (CFE) Treaty's categorisation of tanks, artillery, APCs, combat aircraft and helicopters as the matrix for arms trade regulations. The curtailment of the trade in such especially destabilising weapons might be combined with unconstrained supplies of more defensive types of armaments, such as anti-tank and sea mines, anti-tank missiles, air defence weapons and the like.

Pessimists have questioned the practicality of such regulations, and recommended more 'blunt instruments', such as an across-the-board moratorium on arms transfers to entire regions. There are, however, certain precedents for discriminatory regulations, and there seems to be a growing recognition among the major suppliers of, first of all, the need for curtailing the arms trade and, secondly, for giving first priority to such weapons as contribute to offensive capabilities. This was reflected, *inter alia*, in the 'P5 Initiative' of 1991, wherein it was stated that

> ... the transfer of conventional weapons, conducted in a responsible manner, should contribute to the ability of states to meet their legitimate defence, security and national sovereignty requirements... They recognised that indiscriminate transfers of military weapons and technology contribute to regional instability... They also recognise that a long-term solution to this problem should be found in close consultation with the recipient countries.

There remains, however, the (alleged) problem of the 'rogue channel', i.e., exports by (what the West regards as) 'rogue suppliers' (e.g., China, North Korea, Russia, other former Soviet republics, and South Africa) and imports by 'rogue recipients' (states such as Iran, Iraq, Libya, Cuba and the DPRK) who are placed in the category by being subjected to embargoes. Even though the problem cannot be ignored, the way it is presented by the United States appears exaggerated, as the total volume of 'rogue transfers' is dwarfed by that between 'respectable' exporters and importers. The best way of dealing with it may be to abolish the 'rogue' label entirely and acknowledge that there is nothing wrong with, for example, North Korea supplying Iran with such weaponry as merely serves national defence purposes, while there may be something wrong with the trade between respectable countries if it consists of such weapons that constitute a latent threat to the neighbours of the recipients.

Conclusion

We have thus seen that the 'arms race problem' persists, albeit 'only' on a regional scale, in parts of Europe and Asia, including the Persian Gulf region. In most cases, action-reaction dynamics seem to be at work, implying that whatever may resolve or mitigate the security dilemma may help, such as a defensive restructuring of the armed forces and the application of 'defence only' criteria to arms purchases. While supplier-imposed limitations would help, the most promising avenue appears to be the creation of combined supplier and recipient regimes to the effect of limiting offensive capabilities region-wide.

6 Conflict Resolution Roles in International Peacekeeping Missions

DANIEL DRUCKMAN, JAMES A. WALL and PAUL F. DIEHL

With the end of the Soviet-US rivalry ushering in what may be termed a new world disorder, international peacekeeping has climbed to the top of the agenda of the United Nations and many national governments. Yet, despite the increasing resort to peacekeeping, there is little systematic understanding of its appropriate application. Progress depends on advances in conceptualisation and analysis. To improve the conceptualisation, we provide a three-dimensional taxonomy for framing the various peacekeeping missions. To strengthen the analysis, we link the literature on mediation (and related forms of conflict management) to recent developments in the theory and practice of peacekeeping.

As we think about mediation in the context of peacekeeping operations, we are drawn by the earlier literature to a conception that emphasises the control of conflict.[1] Traditional peacekeeping consists of the stationing of neutral, lightly armed troops, usually with the permission of the host state, as an interposition force following a cease-fire to separate the combatants. Examples are the deployment of UN peacekeeping troops to Cyprus beginning in 1964 and to southern Lebanon in 1978 (Diehl, 1994). Control in these situations consists of relying on leverage to coerce settlements. However, as Fetherston notes, a shift in perception from control to management is needed 'because it not only legitimises (conflict management) activities but shows that peacekeeping without peacemaking and peacebuilding, especially in protracted social conflict situations, will be ineffective in the long term, and possibly also in the short term' (1994, p. 157). By management, we refer to activities intended to deal with the sources of conflict in order to create the conditions for conflict resolution. The challenging question is whether peacekeeping can contribute to the long-term resolution of conflicts. By placing peacekeeping in a conflict resolution framework, we can improve our understanding of how this might be accomplished.

Dimensions of Peacekeeping

The term *peacekeeping* has been used to designate a wide range of activities, often improperly referring to any international effort involving operations intended to terminate armed conflict or to resolve long-standing disputes. Concerned primarily with the military functions of peacekeeping, we emphasise the various functions served by operations. These functions are described in our earlier work in the form of a taxonomy that includes and expands on the definition of traditional peacekeeping (Diehl, Druckman and Wall, 1998). We distinguished among twelve types of military peace operations in terms of twelve general characteristics.[2]

(1) Traditional peacekeeping: Stationing troops in an area after the cease-fire so as to keep combatants separate
(2) Observation: Collecting information and monitoring activities
(3) Collective enforcement (e.g., Kuwait): A large scale operation to defeat an aggressor
(4) Election supervision: Monitoring an election after a peace agreement
(5) Humanitarian assistance during conflict: Transportation and distribution of life-sustaining food and medical supplies
(6) State/nation building: Restoration of law and order in the absence of government authority (i.e., failed states)
(7) Pacification: Quelling civil disturbances and defeating local armed groups
(8) Preventive deployment: Stationing tripwire troops between two combatants to deter the onset or prevent the spread of war
(9) Arms control verification: Inspection of military facilities, supervision of troop withdrawals, etc. as part of an arms control agreement
(10) Protective services: Establishment of safe havens, 'no fly' zones, etc.
(11) Intervention in support of democracy: Overthrowing existing leaders and supporting freely elected government officials.

(Supporting democratic norms can also be considered as collective security.)
(12) Sanctions enforcement: Use of military troops to enforce sanctions (e.g., banned arms trading) defined by the international community

As noted in the list above, examples of operations are collective enforcement, preventive deployment, humanitarian assistance, and intervention in support of democracy. Among the characteristics of the peace operations that we considered are: the clarity of relationships with the host country; the clarity of procedures, goals, and desired outcomes; the extent of control over the conflict; the ease of exit from the mission; the possibility of mission creep; and the extent to which various constituencies are tolerant of the costs borne by the mission.

The results of a scaling exercise show that the twelve operations could be organised in terms of three dimensions, including the role of the peacekeeper (as primary or third party) and the conflict management process (as distributive or integrative). We also noted that the peacekeeper's operations can vary in terms of the ratio of 'combat' (fighting) activities to those of 'contact' (communicating, negotiating, etc.) These dimensions are represented in Figure 1.

Briefly consider each of the dimensions: First, with regard to the primary/third party axis, peacekeepers do not always function in third party roles. In some situations they are actually part of the conflict, invited by (or choosing to align with) one party or another as a member of a coalition in which they are a combatant or a negotiating party with clear interests in the outcome. In other situations, they are invited by a host country as a third party to deal with a crisis or resolve an ongoing dispute. The primary/third party distinction refers generally to differences in the extent to which peacekeepers are relatively neutral with respect to outcomes. When peacekeepers are primary parties to the conflict, they prefer an outcome that favours their own interests. When they function as third parties, they are not a principal party in the conflict and prefer outcomes that satisfy the interests of the principals or primary parties. In addition, peacekeepers may not retain the same role throughout their deployment. In some situations, the peacekeeper's third-party role shifts to that of a primary party in the conflict. In Somalia, for example, as a result of deaths to their peacekeepers, the US switched from a third-party humanitarian role to that of primary-party combatant before exiting from the situation.

It is important to realise that peacekeepers at times generate the conditions for mediation. For example, when two groups are physically fighting or are shooting at each other, mediation is difficult, if not impossible. To set the stage for mediation, peacekeepers in these cases must first separate the disputing parties and identify their leaders. Likewise, in a primary-party role, peacekeepers frequently must generate the conditions for negotiations. For example, while on a mission, peacekeepers might find that hostile forces refuse to withdraw from an occupied area and are in no mood to negotiate over the issue. However, when the peacekeepers increase their power position (with air strikes, circling helicopters, or ground reinforcements) so that they are militarily superior to the hostile forces, negotiation will probably be viewed as an acceptable option.

With regard to the distributive/integrative dimension, the distinction between the two processes was originally made by Walton and McKersie (1965) in labour-management negotiations. Distributive interactions are those in which the parties attempt to increase their own outcomes

Figure 1: Three Dimensions of Peacekeeping Operations

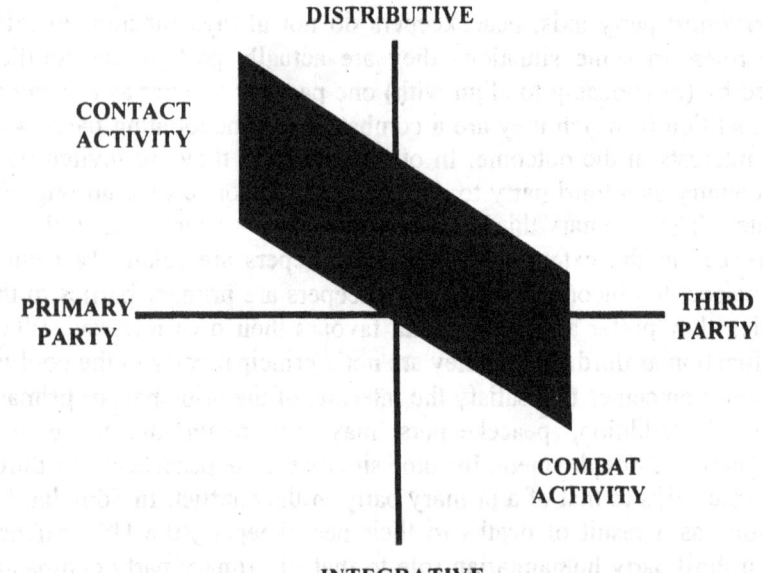

(usually money, territory, positions, or power) at the other's expense. In integrative interactions, the parties attempt to achieve mutually beneficial (win-win) solutions to a problem. Usually parties in an integrative interaction also seek to improve their relationship and to hammer out enduring solutions. In making this distinction, we do not narrowly refer to calculations of gains and losses. Rather, we refer to the way situations are defined as relative (differences in gains), absolute (joint gains), or a combination of these approaches. This dimension refers to the orientation taken by peacekeepers as defined by their function or task.[3]

Finally, as for the third dimension, peacekeepers find that their visions vary in terms of the ratio of combat (fighting) to contact (communicating) activities. For example, contrast collective enforcement (higher combat than contact activities) with election supervision (higher contact than combat activities). This ratio has been shown to have implications for the likelihood of mediator effectiveness in the sense of settling or resolving the conflict. Mediators are more likely to be effective in missions involving contact or communication activities, or those that are less intense in terms of number of fatalities (Bercovitch and Langley, 1993; see also Bercovitch et al., 1991, Kressel and Pruitt, 1989). They are also more likely to be effective in less complex conflicts of relatively short duration (Bercovitch and Langley, 1993).

How are the various missions arranged on these three-dimensional axes? In the primary party and distribution arena, peacekeepers find themselves in missions such as collective enforcement and interventions in support of democracy. They are third parties in such distributive conflicts as preventive deployment and humanitarian assistance during conflict. Operations involving disaster relief or sanctions enforcement cast the peacekeeper in a primary-party role confronted by a situation that can be regarded as being integrative in the sense of searching for joint gains through problem solving. They are third parties in such integrative situations as election supervision, observation, and arms control verification.

Turning to the final dimension, we find that restoration, emergency, and monitoring interventions are examples of missions involving more contact than combat activities whereas the collective enforcement mission usually entails a high level of combat activity. In this chapter, we are primarily concerned with the implementation of peacekeeping missions. Thus, we focus attention on the day-to-day activities of peacekeepers rather than on the resolution of the major issues dividing the conflicting parties. Evidence from field surveys conducted by Lester B. Pearson Canadian International Peacekeeping Training Centre indicates that peacekeepers are engaged in a variety of contact activities. One hundred and ninety-seven Canadian soldiers in the Bosnian and one-hundred and eighty-five soldiers in the Croatian United Nations operations were asked a number of questions about their experiences during the time period November 1993 to April 1994. Almost all of the officers surveyed reported having negotiating experiences; about half of them indicated that they experienced mediation or conciliation. Further, the preponderance of contact relative to combat activities reported by these peacekeepers (three times as many contact activities as compared to combat activities in the Croatian operation) suggests that contact skills are increasingly important (Last and Eyre, 1995).

The following discussion is organised in terms of strategic decision making and is divided into several sections. Building on findings from studies of mediation, we discuss, first, how mediators choose tactics and implement a plan. Second, we focus on the negotiation role and discuss how goals are set and plans are developed. Following a discussion of the cultural environment for peacekeeping, we offer advice to peacekeepers based on our decision making framework. The chapter concludes with some implications for civilian negotiation and mediation.

The Peacekeeper as a Third Party

The peacekeeper, as a third party, targets and attempts to improve the relationship between the disputing parties. Doing so requires the peacekeeper to develop and implement a strategy or plan. Figure 2 (see page 112) gives a concise representation of strategy development. Initially, the peacekeeper sets goals, analyses the situation, and develops/chooses the appropriate strategy and tactics that will move him toward the goal. Once this is done, the peacekeeper manoeuvres and implements the strategies.

The feedback arrows in Figure 2 simply indicate that the goal-setting and strategy-development sequence is an ongoing interactive process in which the peacekeeper modifies her behaviour based on experience. For example, goals are lowered if the strategy is put into effect and fails; likewise tactics are modified as the peacekeeper discovers new approaches. The paragraphs that follow develop the various parts of the framework for the third-party role while the next section deals with the peacekeeper as negotiator.

Goal Setting

In setting goals, the peacekeeper must consider the goals of all parties. He might seek to maximise the joint payoffs to all parties, or he can opt for maximisation of the disputants' payoffs, at a major sacrifice to his own. For example, US peacekeepers were sacrificing the morale of their troops -- and some argue, their combat effectiveness -- in Bosnia for the benefit of the Muslims, Serbs, and Croats in that region (Hedges, 1997).

Theoretically, but not practically, the peacekeeper can set a goal of maximising her own outcomes and those accruing to her constituency. Or she can ignore the concrete, short-term outcomes to concentrate upon improvement of the relationships among the parties. For example, this seems to be the goal of the peacekeepers in Cyprus. With the relationship between the Greek and Turkish inhabitants rather stabilised, the peacekeepers choose activities, such as jointly installing a sewage system (a superordinate task), not so much for the outcomes they yield but for the improvement of the relationships between the communities.

Situation Analysis

When analysing the situation, the peacekeeper must first determine if there is a conflict between the disputing parties. Typically there is, and the peacekeeper must develop skills in analysing the causes and issues of the conflict.

Causes are often distinct from the issues, and many of the causes lie within the parties themselves (Augsburger, 1992), in their perceptions of each other, their communications, past interactions, and structural relationships (Putnam and Wilson, 1982). A disputing party may have the goal of hurting the other party or may simply be angry. Such feelings will generate conflict. With regard to perceptions, conflict is likely to occur whenever one party perceives the other side's actions to be harmful or unfair. Interpersonal communication leads to conflict (Putnam and Poole, 1987) when it contains insults or intentions to harm the other. Structured interdependence between parties who have opposite goals will quickly engender conflict. Because conflict has so many causes, the peacekeeper must become adept at identifying the genesis of the current dispute and determining how they can be best addressed.

Figure 2: Strategy Development

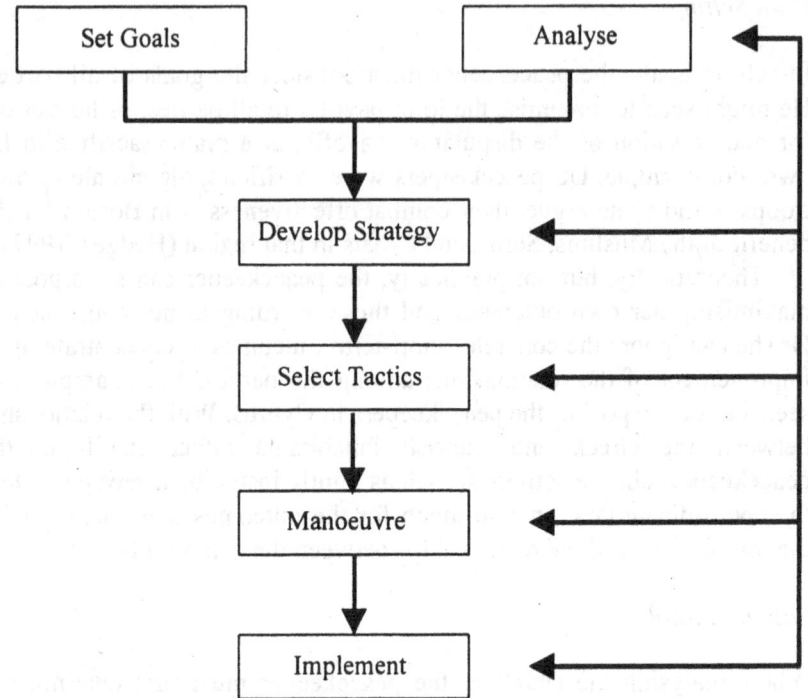

Peacekeepers must also understand the issues that are generating problems. When parties interact and come into conflict, it is usually over issues that are either large or small, simple or complex, emotional or substantive (Walton, 1987). Certain issue characteristics have been shown to generate conflict and thereby merit the third party's attention. One is complexity. Complex issues are more apt to lead to conflict than simple ones. Likewise, multiple issues, as opposed to a few, more often spawn conflict. The explanation in both cases is rather clear: complex and multiple issues are more likely to generate misunderstanding, tap divergent interests, and unearth dissimilar goals. Issues of principle or nonnegotiable needs also generate conflicts (Fisher, 1994; Rouhana and Kelman, 1994). On these types of issues, parties become emotionally bonded to their positions and find that trades involving reciprocal give-and-take are quite difficult. Broad or intangible issues are another source of conflict and are less amenable to conflict resolution (Vasquez, 1983; Diehl, 1992). Because such issues entail high stakes and are often indivisible, the parties hold strongly to their positions and move toward conflict (Albin, 1993). Once in the conflict, the all-or-nothing characteristic of the issue makes palatable, face-saving, and piecemeal trades quite difficult to arrange (Zechmeister and Druckman, 1973).

The peacekeeper should address issues and causes that are of low cost to deal with and about which she has some knowledge. She should work with the disputing parties to solve complex, multiple issues, and issues of principle. Issues and causes that are intractable should be ignored as long as possible. Also, the agenda should be arranged so that early agreement on simple issues and successful elimination of minor causes of conflict produce momentum for improved relations (Fisher, 1994; Pruitt and Rubin, 1986).

Tactics

Having defined the overall goals for the mission and analysed the situation, the peacekeeper begins to develop a strategy and to select tactics. The literature on third-party processes reveals that the line between strategy and tactics is blurred (Carnevale and Pruitt, 1992) and that third parties (even when placed in primary party roles), for the most part, rely on sets of tactics rather than on major strategies to improve the disputing parties' interactions. This being the case, we discuss tactics first, then strategies.

When managing the conflict, the peacekeeper has three targets for tactical behaviour: (1) the disputing parties themselves, (2) the interparty relationship, and (3) the peacekeeper-party relationship (Wall, 1981). Each will be discussed in turn.

Disputing Parties

In general, a peacekeeper can take steps to move the parties off their current positions and to nudge them toward positions that are more agreeable to the other side. The research literature suggests several tactical approaches. In order to encourage concession-making, peacekeepers should be sensitive to face-saving concerns as well as devise incentives that increase the motivation to reach an agreement. Experiments have shown that bargainers are willing to forfeit material gains in favour of saving face (Podell and Knapp, 1969; Pruitt and Johnson, 1970). However, concessions may not be sufficient to produce agreements. Additional incentives are often needed to seal the deal. These may require a balancing of threats (negative sanctions) and promises (positive sanctions) (Kissinger, 1979). But, opportunities may exist for agreements that limit the amount of compromise needed. In their third party role, peacekeepers may identify solutions not recognised by any of the disputants (Douglas, 1972). They may expand or reframe the agenda to alter the perceived balance of rewards and costs to all sides (Pruitt and Rubin, 1986; Lall, 1966). By so doing, they increase the possibilities for optimal or integrative agreements.

Disputants may represent complex factions and constituencies. In this case, peacekeepers should take into account internal divisions by empowering moderates or by recognising, sometimes tacitly, the disputants' accountability to both their own group and its constituencies. A variety of tactics for reducing these pressures were suggested by Walton and McKersie (1965) and elaborated in more recent work (Lim and Carnevale, 1990; Wall, 1981). Many of these tactics involve balancing the advantages of private (excluding other members) and public (including constituents) negotiation.

Interparty Relationship

As the peacekeeper targets the parties, her primary concerns must be on the interparty relationship and the agreement that will be implemented. In seeking these goals, the peacekeeper may follow many routes. One is setting up the interaction. The peacekeeper often discovers that the parties are fighting but not talking. There might be a stalemate in which there is neither talking nor fighting. There could be an absence of interaction because some other third party has separated the parties and prevented their interaction (as in the case of traditional peacekeeping). In such situations, the peacekeeper must often establish a negotiation relationship between the parties and stabilise the process. Doing so may require that the third party identify the leadership of the opposing groups and then bring them to the bargaining table.

Having established the interaction and identified the disputing parties, the peacekeeper next faces the task of enticing them to negotiate. Often this is a difficult task because the parties do not like the negotiation format; they feel, especially after open fighting, that negotiating is a sign of weakness; they believe negotiation gives some legitimacy to the opponent; or they believe negotiation puts them at risk in some way (Pruitt and Rubin, 1986). To overcome these obstacles, the peacekeeper must discover the parties' objections, and then discount or reduce them. Also, the outcomes from negotiating or interacting peacefully may be increased just as the costs for refusing to negotiate are raised. Furthermore, at times the peacekeeper may need to protect some of the negotiators.

After initiating interactions, the peacekeeper can establish the protocol for the negotiation process by suggesting and enforcing mechanisms through which the interaction will be conducted. These can be formal and specific agendas or somewhat more informal ones. In addition, she can inform each party as to what behaviours can be expected from the other side and advise each one on its own initial and responsive actions.

When establishing protocol, the peacekeeper can provide evaluations of the situation. In joint or separate meetings she can enumerate and describe the important issues, interpret their complexity (or simplicity), note how similar problems have been handled, and provide data as to the costs of continued disputing (Lim and Carnevale, 1990).

Once the interaction is under way, the peacekeeper should channel the initial discussion toward an area in which she believes the parties can agree (Maggiolo, 1971). As both sides discuss this arena, the mediator needs to expand the agenda to bring in additional issues. In doing so, she should set up trades in which one disputant gives in on issues that are of low value but of high value to the opposing side. As she facilitates such trades, the peacekeeper must maintain the integrity of the interaction channel, enforce the protocol rules, and proscribe such behaviours as retracting offers previously made or threatening the other side.

At times, the peacekeeper will find it necessary to separate the disputing parties (Pruitt, 1971). This separation allows her to sever, relay, or modify communications for the sake of productive negotiations. She might reopen the channels and bring the parties together if this is useful, forbid their interaction if it seems likely to incite antagonism, or create a formal schedule of meetings if such a mechanism proves helpful.

As the peacekeeper severs and reconstructs the interactions, she can manage the parties' power relationship. This relationship is of great importance to both the peacekeeper and the parties. Typically, the mediator should strike a balance between the parties' total power positions. Doing so lowers the probability that the stronger side will attempt to exploit the weaker and that the weaker will break off the relationship or seek to undermine the stronger's position (Thibaut, 1968). If the power relationship cannot be balanced, the peacekeeper must bargain with or use force against the stronger side to constrain the exercise of its power. As an example, NATO forces in the fall of 1995 carried out intensive artillery bombardments and air strikes against the Serbs in Bosnia. These strikes seriously reduced the power of the Serbs and constrained them from using it in future hostilities (Wall and Stark, 1996).

Peacekeeper-Party Relationship

To be successful in interactions with the parties, the peacekeeper must gain their trust and confidence. Tactics with these goals are typically labelled 'reflexive' (Kressel and Pruitt, 1985, 1989). They include appearing neutral, not taking sides on important issues, letting the parties blow off steam, using humour to lighten the atmosphere, attempting to speak the parties' language, expressing pleasure at progress in the negotiation or conflict resolution, keeping the parties focused on the issues, offering new points of view, bringing in relevant information, and correcting any party's misperceptions.

When utilising these tactics -- as well as many of the preceding ones -- the peacekeeper may find that she sacrifices the image of neutrality. This is not a major obstacle if she demonstrates trustworthiness and effectiveness or if the parties feel that the intervention provides more benefits than costs.

Strategy

Currently the literature does not provide adequate descriptions or prescriptions for mediation strategies. A strategy, in mediation as well as in warfare, football, chess, bridge, and organisational policy, is a broad plan of action for attaining some goal. For example, in a retreat-and-flank battle strategy, an army retreats when the enemy attacks in force. Once the enemy has extended itself, the army flanks the enemy, striking at one or more vulnerable points. Or, in a simpler strategy, the football team might initially establish a running attack and then shift to a mix of running and passing. Note the ingredients in each of these strategies:

goals, actions, and timing. The literature deals adequately with the goals and action components of third-party strategies, but ignores the importance of timing.

One group of researchers (e.g., Carnevale, 1986; Carnevale and Henry, 1989; Kressel, 1972; Kressel and Pruitt, 1985, 1989; van de Vliert, 1985) describe third-party strategies as techniques that are oriented toward a similar goal. Specifically, Kressel and Pruitt (1985, 1989) hold that a reflexive strategy consists of techniques that orient the third party to the dispute and establish the groundwork for later activities. A substantive strategy includes techniques that deal directly with the issues and actively promote settlement, whereas contextual tactics alter the climate or conditions between the disputants.

A second group of scholars (e.g., Carnevale and Pruitt, 1992; Kolb, 1987; McLaughlin, Carnevale and Lim, 1991; Silbey and Merry, 1986; Touval and Zartman, 1985) has taken a different tack, combining techniques that share conceptual or operational similarities (other than goal). For example, Silbey and Merry's (1986) typology contains four principal categories: (1) the third party's presentation of self and programme, (2) its control of the mediation process, (3) its control over the substantive issues, and (4) its activation of commitments and norms. In a similar fashion, Kolb (1987), after in-depth interviews, laid out alternative strategies or postures that the third party assumed. She distinguished between helping and fact-finding corporate ombudsman roles. The helper invents individualised solutions to the problems people present, whereas the fact-finder investigates whether proper procedures were followed and if there are plausible explanations for a complaint.

A third group of researchers (Elangovan, 1995; Lewicki and Sheppard, 1985) classify the third party's techniques into strategies according to the target for control. Sheppard (1984) maintains that third-party strategic behaviours differ along two principal lines: decision control and process control. A third party's decision control is the management of the outcomes of the dispute. By contrast, process control entails management of the presentation and interpretation of evidence in the dispute. Elangovan (1995), relying heavily on Sheppard's concepts, generates five strategies. The third party influences the outcomes in ends control strategy. Means control strategy involves the third party's influence in the process of resolution. Full control strategy requires the third party's role in both. The third party affects neither outcomes nor process in low control. Part control strategy requires the third party to share both controls with the disputants.

Finally, another group of investigators (e.g., Lim and Carnevale, 1990; Karambayya and Brett, 1989; Kim *et al.*, 1993; Wall and Blum, 1991; Wall and Rude, 1985) has defined strategies as techniques that are used together by third parties when they deal with disputes. For example, in their factor analytic study, Kim *et al.* (1993) discovered techniques used together in four strategic combinations: reconciliation, dependence, data gathering, and analysis. In attempting to reconcile the disputants, the peacekeeper nudges the parties together, lubricates the exchange with a drink, and argues for mutual compromise which may include emphasising the moral imperative for reconciling. The dependency strategy emphasises the disputants' interdependence as well as pointing out that the conflict is disrupting the highly-valued harmony between them. To regain the harmony, the peacekeeper obtains an apology from one or all sides. The other two strategies are more procedural. Gathering information is a separate strategy but may also be a first step in a larger analytical approach where third parties diagnose the situation, take account of the historical relationships among the disputing parties, and, then, support the plausibility of certain agreements on logical grounds.

The above four approaches deal quite adequately with the goals and action components of third-party strategies. Furthermore, some of the literature (Elangovan, 1995) deals creatively with the contingencies under which the various strategies are or should be applied. However, none of the approaches deals with the timing aspect of strategies. This omission is unfortunate because timing is an essential element in any strategy. In a retreat-and-flank battle strategy, for example, *when* the army flanks and attacks is essential. If it is either too early or too late, the strategy would fail. Likewise, *when* a third party uses various sets of techniques is quite important.

Manoeuvring

The peacekeeper's options for manoeuvring are manifold. Specifically, he can increase his own strength, reducing that of the parties, or leveraging them. If the peacekeeper attempts to weaken either or both parties, perhaps by closing off some of their options or by preventing them from forming coalitions, he risks generating resentment. Possibly one or both parties' retaliation may convert the initial third-party relationship into an adversarial primary-party affair.

Under some circumstances, the peacekeeper might try leveraging the parties, that is, bringing her own strength to bear at a time or place that is advantageous. For example, Secretary of State Henry Kissinger in the Yom Kippur war of 1973 delayed munitions shipments to the Israelis until they had only a one-day supply. Nevertheless, this approach also risks the resentment of the parties and encourages retaliation.

Implementation

We propose a simple contingency approach for implementing peacekeeping tactics and strategies. Such an approach is based on two observations. The effectiveness of most tactics is contingent on the situation, and we know more about what a peacekeeper can do than we do about what is effective, at least given the current state of research findings.

The first observation dictates that the peacekeeper should choose tactics that fit the situation. To date, we know that the following behaviours are likely to be effective in a wide range of situations. These include (1) separating aggressive opponents (Pruitt, 1971); (2) controlling the agenda and helping the sides to establish priorities among the issues (Lim and Carnevale, 1990); (3) adding control to the process (Prein, 1984); and (4) being friendly to both sides (Ross et al., 1990).

Other behaviours or tactics are more likely to be effective in some situations. Humour might be used when the peacekeeper detects hostility (Harbottle, 1992). If there are many issues, the peacekeeper should simplify the agenda and suggest trade-offs. When the disputing parties lack bargaining experience, the peacekeeper should educate them or note procedures that have been used in the past. When the parties are able to resolve their own problems, the third party for the most part should not intrude (Lederach, 1995).

The second observation suggests that peacekeepers should adopt a pragmatic approach. They should first try techniques that seem reasonable. If none of these work, then they should try a different set. Again, if there is failure, a new set should be put in place and the failure noted. This approach should be continued until the relationship between the parties as well as the outcomes improve. Most important, the peacekeeper, in this process, must be diagnostic, remembering what failed and what was successful for each episode. This is consistent with the experiential learning model discussed above. In addition, the peacekeeper should also use feedback in the process of evaluating and modifying the goals, tactics, and manoeuvres.

Feedback

As noted earlier, the feedback arrows in Figure 2 indicate that goals, tactics, and strategies are modified as the peacekeeper/mediator gains experience. For example, goals are usually lowered when a strategy fails. Likewise, tactics are modified as the peacekeeper discovers new approaches. While the feedback adjustments are manifold in any mediation, the most important ones for peacekeepers are those involving goals. When establishing and adjusting her goals, the mediator must continually make trade-offs between micro-level effectiveness (the effective performance of specific military duties) and macro-level effectiveness (the overall success of the mission). A very specific example is that of a peacekeeper who refrains from killing snipers -- a choice not to pursue the micro goal of self defence -- so as to improve the chances that the leaders from the two sides will meet and make concessions at the bargaining table, a sign of success at the macro level. On the other hand, a peacekeeper might violate the macro goal of neutrality in order to pursue the micro goal of protecting civilians in a 'safe haven' under her command.

The Peacekeeper as a Primary, Negotiating Party

Here we need to reiterate two points made earlier. First, some missions require peacekeepers to act more as a primary party than as a third party. Second, on occasion, peacekeepers may shift roles -- from a third party to a primary party -- within a specified mission. For example, even under the assignment of a traditional peacekeeping mission (stationed in an area after the cease-fire so as to keep combatants separate), peacekeepers can find themselves moving from a third party to a primary party role when they are attacked by one side. In a primary party role -- initially or as the result of a shift, the peacekeeper finds that the required skills are quite different from those needed in a third party role. Most importantly, the necessary skills are more related to negotiation than mediation.

Goal Setting

In primary party missions, for example, intervention in support of democracy and sanctions enforcement, the soldier must control or modify other parties' behaviour in some fashion. A simple example is having individuals line up to receive water allocations. A complex example is having a hostile army withdraw from occupied territory (Abizaid, 1993).

When attempting to control other parties, the soldier has limited power and, consequently, cannot prescribe their behaviour, while ignoring their preferences, goals, ideas, values, etc. Instead, he must negotiate and plan to operate from a limited power base. Specifically, the soldier must define his aspirations, which are the net outcomes (benefits minus costs) that are expected or sought from the interaction or mission (for example, 200,000 people fed for 3 months with no loss of soldiers' lives at a cost of $10 million, using 1 battalion of troops).

Such goal setting also consists of developing the limits of fallback positions beyond which the soldier will not budge. The soldier could possibly seek to maximise his own payoffs without concern for those received by the other parties. Other possibilities exist; for example, the soldier could attempt to maximise the others' payoffs or the joint payoffs. Alternatively, he could simply improve the relationship with the parties, rather than raising anyone's outcomes.

Even though goal setting is the first step in a strategy, it must, at times, be quite fluid. On occasion, the available information is insufficient for establishing a goal. Other times the original goal may be incorrect. In addition, the situation, as well as the behaviours of the various parties, may change radically. Finally, the mission or demands of superiors may be altered. It is also possible for these latter determinants -- mission and superiors' orders -- to require that the goal be very rigid. In such a case, the soldier has the advantage of a stable goal but the disadvantage of inflexibility -- not being able to revise goals as the situation dictates.

Situation Analysis

When choosing a goal and reflecting on the proper strategy, the soldier needs to perform an analysis of the situation, examining (1) his own position, (2) the other party's position, (3) the relationship between them,

(4) the interaction process, and (5) the broader context within which those interactions occur.

When focusing on his own position, the soldier must determine which issues are more or less important: Does an issue have high payoffs or costs? Is it a matter of principle that the solder feels should be important? Do the constituencies hold the issue to be of importance (Walton and McKersie, 1965)? Which issues can be traded (Pruitt and Rubin, 1986)?

While considering the issues, the soldier judges his aspirations as well as the initial offer and limit for each issue. This includes developing a rationale for the choices, assessing possible trade-offs between issues, and determining the value to be placed on the relationship with the other parties. In weighing trades, a soldier may consider making compromises on issues that result in increased trust and improved relationships with the other parties.

When making such judgements, the soldier must remember that a settlement is unlikely to occur if he fails to consider the others' reactions or the opponents' positions on the issues. Such reflections often require adopting the other's perspective (Neale and Bazerman, 1983). Although this has been shown to be a difficult challenge (Johnson, 1967; Summers *et al.*, 1970), it is worth the attempt. It includes deciding which issues are more or less important, getting an idea of the other's aspirations and limits, as well as determining their evaluation of relationships. For example, if the opponent has attractive alternatives and places a low value on the relationship, she is likely to be a tough bargainer. An opponent with limited alternatives and low aspirations will probably be more cooperative (Pinkley, 1995). Gathering information through monitoring the other's statements and proposals is an important part of the bargaining process (Druckman, 1977, 1978). It leads to the kinds of changes in expectations and adjustments of moves that can produce agreements (Coddington, 1968; Snyder and Diesing, 1977).

Strategy

With an initial goal and situation analysis in mind, the soldier develops or selects a strategy. This is the general plan for dealing with the other party, whereas the tactics are the specific steps that will be followed (Wall, 1995). A strategy can range from simple to complex. A simple strategy could be one of consistent force wherein the soldier brings in many troops, places them in strong positions, and then demands that the others withdraw (Abizaid, 1993). A second simple strategy could be one of reciprocity -- that is, making a concession (Esser *et al.*, 1990). If the others reciprocate, the soldier makes another concession, then awaits a reciprocal concession. If the other party plays tough, making no concessions, then the soldier does likewise. A third strategy is to place the burden of concession making on the other party by refusing to compromise. Some implications of these exchanges have been demonstrated in experimental studies (e.g., Axelrod, 1984).

A more complex strategy is the bluff-twist (Wall, 1995). Here the soldier begins the bargaining with a bluff that she knows the other party will call. As the other party calls the bluff and overextends itself, the soldier cuts its line of retreat, as well as alternatives, and then exploits any vulnerabilities that result.

Strategies, simple or complex, can be intended to raise the outcomes for both sides. For example, the soldier can attempt to expand the resources or negotiation scope so that all parties involved get more of what they want. The soldier can exchange concessions on different issues with the other party, having each yield on an issue that has high payoffs for the other but low payoffs for him (Pruitt and Rubin, 1986). Or the soldier can consider the underlying interests of all parties and develop ways to satisfy those interests.

Tactics

Strategies are developed and pursued by piecing together different tactics which represent the specific steps or actions. A large number of tactics are available to the soldier, falling into the broad categories of threatening, coercive, conciliatory, rewarding, posturing, debating, and irrational tactics (Wall, 1995). The negative tactics of threats and coercion are attempts to reduce the other's outcomes. These can be used early in an encounter, to reduce the others' aspirations, or later, in the encounter as a last resort (Tedeschi and Bonoma, 1977). The positive tactics of conciliation and reward are attempts to improve the relationship and reinforce desired behaviour (e.g., Tedeschi and Bonoma, 1977).

Posturing tactics are used primarily to alter the other's perception of the soldier's role and behaviour. Debate tactics consist of problem-solving discussions and exchanges of information (Walcott *et al.*, 1977).

For example, the soldier notes the issues and tasks she would like to avoid (e.g., to whom God gave the disputed land) or uses logical arguments to convince the other of the merits of the approach. The irrational tactics are those that seem to give the soldier low outcomes or outcomes lower than those likely to result from alternative actions. As the adage 'crazy like a fox' suggests, sometimes these tactics can produce fine results.

Manoeuvres

Manoeuvres are steps to improve the soldier's position. Just as an infantry lieutenant moves his platoon to high ground prior to battle, the soldier can take steps to improve his position in personal interactions. These include steps to increase his own strength, to decrease that of the other, or to leverage the opponent. Efforts to increase one's own strength include stockpiling resources, building adequate hard force, and creating alliances. Efforts to decrease the other's strength include closing off the opponent's alternatives, preventing the opponent from forming alliances, and reducing his stockpile of resources. The soldier can also leverage the other by attacking his weaknesses or by opening a discussion with a more pliant member of the opponent's team whenever one of the others is obdurate.

Implementation

When implementing the strategy, the soldier puts the plan into action with tactics. The keys here are timing and feedback. With regard to timing, some tactics must be used simultaneously and others in selected sequences. With regard to feedback, the soldier must observe the other's responses to his tactics and manoeuvres. If the other is reacting as expected, the soldier can hold a steady course. If this is not the case, she must reconsider and perhaps modify the goals, strategy, tactics, and manoeuvres.

The Cultural Environment

When engaging in mediation by setting goals, analysing the situation, developing and implementing strategies, peacekeepers interface with two cultures, a civilian culture and that of the nation to which they are posted.

Civilian Culture

The first, perhaps alien, culture is that of civilians. Peacekeepers usually are soldiers who have operated for an extensive period within a military culture, and, therefore, are accustomed to taking orders and conforming to them. They are healthy, well fed, well clothed, and regularly well paid. In short, they exist in a protective, orderly environment that has a great deal of structure. The civilian culture, especially that to which the peacekeeper is likely to be posted, is quite different. It is frequently disorderly, and life for many civilians is very tentative. They are often sick, ill clothed, and paid erratically. Furthermore, civilians, for the most part, do not like being ordered about, especially by military personnel.

The impact of the military-civilian divide is multifaceted, with one critical aspect being differences in goals. The peacekeeper's goal (in Figure 2) of keeping the peace differs from the civilian's goal of staying alive and earning a living. The simultaneous pursuit of these may generate conflict rather than peace. For example, roadblocks might be set up to keep one militant faction from having access to and attacking the other. The goal from a traditional peacekeeper's perspective is to minimise conflicts which could result in civilian, as well as military, casualties. This is a legitimate goal, but the farmer's goals might be more pragmatic. Examples include getting to his fields without waiting and gaining access to markets on the other side of the dividing line.

Civilians often tend to dislike or distrust soldiers. Therefore, peacekeepers must vigilantly monitor civilians' reactions to their presence and behaviour. Often the most straightforward, non-assertive tactics can be misunderstood and resented. For example, asking a civilian family to get out of a car is many times seen as a prelude to looting it.

Indigenous Culture

The second culture encountered is that endemic to the disputing parties. Seldom is the peacekeeper given a mission within his own country. Rather, he is often posted to areas which (1) perceive conflict differently, (2) have different social structures, and (3) have different norms concerning interpersonal relations.

Consider first the perception of conflict. People from many non-industrialised cultures think of conflict as the normal way of interacting. From childhood, they are taught to settle differences by fighting (Merry,

1989). Therefore these people tend to accept and rely on conflict (somewhat as an alcoholic relies on alcohol for life-sustaining calories). That is, conflict has a 'win-win' appeal. In most Western cultures (i.e., the peacekeeper's culture), conflict is often viewed as one person opposing or negatively affecting another person's interests. In other words, conflict is perceived as having a 'win-lose' effect on the parties (Donohue and Kolt, 1992; Pruitt and Rubin, 1986; Putnam and Poole, 1987; Thomas, 1992).

From a different perspective, Polynesians and several other agricultural-based societies view conflict as a mutual entanglement that is detrimental to both parties. In this perspective, the situation is 'lose-lose'. For Koreans and residents of other Asian countries with a strong Confucian underpinning, conflict is viewed as a mutual disruption of society's harmony (Augsburger, 1992; Hahn, 1986). These societies feel that the character and impact of conflict on the disputants is irrelevant. The major negative impact is the disruption of the larger community and the violation of its norms.

The second cultural factor is the structure of society and the resultant perceptions. Cultures in the West, for the most part, are rather egalitarian and do not have a strong ingroup-outgroup orientation. Other cultures, such as the Muslims and the Japanese, do have this orientation. Also consider that within many cultures, including mid-African and Polynesian, family and clan structures prevail (Wall and Callister, 1995).

Norms

Finally, a major cultural impact comes from the society's norms. Even casual observations reveal that these vary from culture to culture. One widely-accepted norm is reciprocity (Gouldner, 1960). In Western societies (Homans, 1961) and in Japan (Goldman, 1994), people feel that an outcome given to one individual or group obligates that party, in return, to give a similar outcome (repayment) to the original party. Similarly, a cost imposed on a party permits, or even obligates, them to retaliate against the party imposing that cost. Although many cultures abide by this norm, others do not. Rather, they perceive that an outcome given by one party to another is a sign of weakness or deference. Thereby, it does not obligate any type of reciprocation. Instead, it raises the expectation that the original party should deliver an additional outcome.

Because the reciprocity norm has a strong impact on an individual's behaviour, the peacekeeper needs to know if that norm exists in the culture to which she is posted. For example, in cultures with strong hierarchical structures, reciprocity is not a societal norm. There will be some reciprocity within levels, but not between them. Typically, a higher-level person does not initially make a concession to a lower-level person, because that would be incongruous with her status. When receiving a concession from a lower-level person, the higher-level person does not reciprocate because the concession is considered a gift to which a high-level person is entitled (Augsburger, 1992).

Advice for Peacekeepers

Two of our primary goals in this chapter were to improve the conceptualisation of peacekeeping and to enhance its analysis. By delineating the twelve peacekeeping missions and framing them with a three-dimensional paradigm (Figure 1), we have addressed our first goal. By utilising a simple decision model to link the peacekeeping and mediation/conflict management literature, we have provided some insight into our second goal. In addition to these contributions, our paradigms enable us to tender some prescriptions for peacekeepers and, at the same time, to present some novel insights into mediation research.

Distributive Versus Integrative Processes

The distinction between integrative and distributive encounters has a major relevance for peacekeeping roles. Most importantly, different tactics are suited for the two types of situations. In an integrative situation, the peacekeeper should adopt a problem-solving approach (Kressel *et al.*, 1994). This approach is characterised by persistent question-asking intended to achieve an understanding of the causes of the conflict. The peacekeeper should be willing to depart from strict neutrality, especially when the conflict is being fuelled by one of the parties. By doing so, however, the peacekeeper runs the risk of becoming a primary party in the conflict. This makes it a more demanding challenge than a settlement-oriented approach discussed below. Its effectiveness depends on the extent to which the peacekeeper is flexible. It also relies on the eagerness of the disputing parties to find quick settlements. The disputants are less likely to reach an agreement when time pressures are low and alternatives are attractive.

By contrast, distributive conflicts are often approached with a settlement orientation (Kressel *et al.*, 1994). That is, peacekeepers are primarily concerned with getting a settlement. They remain neutral and do not question the disputing parties about the underlying issues in their conflict. This approach is efficient and may be beneficial if the parties are strongly motivated to end their dispute as when, for example, they are faced with time pressure or have unattractive alternatives. The settlements may, however, be less durable, and the approach can produce unfavourable attitudes toward the peacekeeper.

Several other tactics discussed earlier can also be used in distributive situations. They support or enhance the peacekeeper's leverage over the disputants in order to attain a settlement that works for the parties and is also acceptable to the peacekeeper and his constituents. Examples are managing the parties' power relationship, managing the interaction through a schedule or agenda, channelling the discussion, separating the parties when necessary, and closing off some options. While appearing neutral with regard to desired outcomes, the peacekeeper attempts to exert considerable control over the process referred to above as a *means control strategy*. This has the advantage of providing a structure for discussing and settling contentious issues. However, it has the disadvantage of creating resentment toward the peacekeeper as well as jeopardising future interactions between the parties.

The tactics used by peacekeepers to settle distributive conflicts are not unlike those used by the bargainers themselves. They focus somewhat narrowly on interests, compete with each other for control over the process, and attempt to win in the sense of maximising relative gains in the outcome. This kind of competitive bargaining is typical in the antagonistic relationships that exist between parties in conflict zones (Druckman, 1980). It has been shown to perpetuate or hinder future relations (Druckman *et al.*, 1988). Therefore, a major challenge for peacekeepers in distributive settings is to change the way the parties perceive their conflict.

In order to change distributive perceptions, the mediator must, first, persuade the parties that their conflict is fuelled by misunderstandings that may polarise the differences between them in regards to interests or values. Second, she must offer the possibility that solutions can be found that do not require concessions from either party. The parties' orientations must be changed from maximising relative gains to seeking joint gains. Third, the parties must be encouraged to engage in a strenuous process that includes the sharing of information about interests and needs. Developing trust in the peacekeeper is essential; the parties must believe that the peacekeeper is committed to searching for the best possible solution. Fourth, the peacekeeper must help the parties develop an understanding of the implications of any agreement for their long-term relationship. Exposing them to arguments about the importance of relationships in negotiation (Fisher and Brown, 1988) and in post-Cold War international relations (Saunders, 1991; Stern and Druckman, 1995) may contribute to the necessary changes of perspectives.

Contact and Combat Activities

Having offered some prescriptions for distributive versus integrative disputes, we now shift focus to the contact/combat facet. Here the bottom line is unequivocal. Peacekeepers need to be trained for both contact and combat activities. In the highly-charged conflict situations that they often face, they at times must resort to using coercive tactics in order to prevent further escalations in the interactions or simply to protect themselves against attacks launched by one or the other party.

Even though there has been a change in the purpose of peacekeeping operations from conflict control to management, there is still a large amount of combat-related activity in many types of missions. Based on the Canadian survey mentioned earlier, Last and Eyre (1995) reported that an average of about 25 percent of peacekeepers' time is spent in combat-related work.[4] The most frequent combat experiences reported were being a target for rocks thrown, encountering mines, coming under small arms fire, being restrained, and being held at gun point. The most frequent contact experiences were working with interpreters, negotiating with civilian police and belligerent factions, and interacting with local civilians.

Instructive results were obtained when the data were broken down by ranks. Combat activities occurred with roughly equal frequency at all levels -- enlisted, senior non-commissioned officers (NCOs), officers, but contact activities were considerably more frequent among officers. In fact, the officers reported about twice as many contact (about 40 percent) as combat (about 20 percent) activities in the Bosnian operation, and almost three times as many contact (about 40 percent) as combat (about

15 percent) activities in the Croatian operation.

With regard to activities involving negotiation, almost all officers and many senior NCOs reported having had these experiences with a soldier or officer of one of the warring factions while only 29 percent of the enlisted group reported having these experiences. Similarly, more officers (60 percent) reported negotiating with civilian leaders of one of the factions than the enlisted group (about 15 percent). With regard to mediation or conciliation, about 50 percent of the officers and NCOs reported that they had these experiences while only about 10 percent of the enlisted officers had performed mediation functions.

These findings support the observation that modern military peacekeepers are involved in managing or resolving conflicts (i.e., contact activity), particularly at the level of officers. For this reason it is important that they be trained to develop negotiation and mediation skills. This is also the case for junior officers and enlisted personnel who are often, even if less frequently, confronted by situations in which they must deal directly with interpersonal or inter-group conflicts. However, the extent to which these skills are needed depends, to a large degree, on the type of mission in question. The Canadian survey documents soldiers' activities in one type of operation, which they refer to as 'limiting damage'. This type of mission may consist of more combat activities than monitoring missions but more contact activities than missions involving collective enforcement. Contact skills are also less important when peacekeepers are stationed as part of an interposition force in an area of low population density such as the Sinai Desert than when they are assigned to such missions as election supervision or humanitarian assistance where they must interact on a daily basis with the local population.

Clearly, peacekeepers must learn to move between roles, sometimes being combat-ready and at other times being sensitive to the sources of conflict and issues in the role of a third party. To do this effectively, they need to be trained in a variety of relevant skills so that they can handle the changes that occur within missions as well as assignments to different types of missions. This is best done through practice exercises that anticipate the variability that exists in the setting where they must perform (Druckman and Bjork, 1994). We have proposed elsewhere a confidence-building approach to mediation skills acquisition which is based on this principle and takes into account the possible incompatibilities of skills needed for different activities and missions.[5]

Primary and Third Party Roles

As noted above, peacekeepers must learn to shift roles, sometimes using combat skills and at other times relying upon contact proficiencies. Such flexibility is also necessary for their primary and third party roles.

In theory, the distinction between primary and third party roles is rather clear. For primary-party missions (e.g., disaster relief, collective enforcement), the peacekeeper must control or modify the other parties' behaviour in some fashion. A simple example is having civilians in a disaster relief mission line up for water allocations. A more complex example is forcing a hostile army to withdraw from occupied territory (Abizaid, 1993).

By contrast, in third party missions, the peacekeeper, for the most part, controls the relationship between disputants. The activities and skills are quite different from those needed in the primary party role. Namely, they are more likened to mediation and arbitration activities than to negotiation and one-on-one confrontation activities of the primary party.

In practice, however, the distinction between the two roles blurs as the peacekeepers play them concomitantly. They may be perceived as playing a role that is different from the one intended, or they shift roles in or between missions. Perhaps simultaneous role fulfilment is the most prevalent of these obfuscations. In Somalia, for example, the Indian peacekeepers were officially on a humanitarian assistance (primary party) mission to deliver life-sustaining food to the population. Since rival factions and clans vied for control of many areas in which the food was to be delivered, however, the peacekeepers frequently had to broker peace between the factions as they were delivering the aid.

This blurring and shifting of roles spawn a prescription somewhat analogous to that proffered in the contact/combat activities: the peacekeeper must be trained for both primary- and third-party activities. In addition, she must learn when and when not to shift from one role to another.

Implications for Civilian Conflict Resolution Roles

Having drawn prescriptions for peacekeepers from this analysis, we now shift our focus to draw insights from our peacekeeping observations that could prove useful for negotiation and mediation in other settings. The first step in our extrapolations is to emphasise that peacekeeping entails the management of intense conflicts. Therefore, our observations are most relevant to the mediation of other intense conflicts.

One insight is spawned by the primary/third party axis in Figure 1. This axis, in tandem with our earlier discussion, reveals that a mediator may become a primary party in an intensive dispute even though she intended to play, or previously served in, a third-party role. For example, such a shift was reported recently in a Chinese community mediation. Initially, the street committee mediator served as a third party, mediating between two neighbours over the punishment for one son's vandalism. When she was threatened by the son, with some family backing, and consequently had him jailed by the police, she shifted to a primary party role.

This example indicates that mediators outside of the peacekeeping arena can shift from contact to combat roles. Admittedly the shifts to more forceful techniques made by hostage negotiators, industrial mediators, community mediators, or marriage counsellors are not as drastic or potent as those taken by peacekeepers. Yet they do entail a progression from contact to combat tactics. Such a movement is seen in an example of a strong-arm mediation by two Malaysian policemen. A citizen had reported to them that he had been swindled by a local con-man. When the police brought the victim and con-man together to settle the problem, charges and counter charges followed. Knowing the reputation of the con-man, the police beat him, returned the money to its rightful owner, and wrote up the case as 'unsolvable'.

Having considered the axes in Figure 1 separately, we now turn to considering them together, noting that a mediator's adoption of more forceful techniques and a movement toward the combat end of the contact-combat axis is often accompanied by a shift to a primary party, as opposed to a third party, role. Such a shift is noted in peacekeeping. When a Dutch peacekeeper comes under fire while he maintains a roadblock, it is very difficult for him to act as a third party, to feel like a third party, or to be perceived as a third party when he returns fire. Likewise, it is quite difficult for a mediator in a labour-management dispute to remain perceived as a third party when she threatens one side or points out illegal activities. The threatening labour-management mediator must realise, like the Dutch peacekeeper who is returning fire, that she has shifted to the 'combat-primary party' arena and must adjust her strategy and tactics accordingly.

The final implication is spawned by the culture factor. For the most part, peacekeepers realise they are interacting with parties from a different culture. Typically the distance from home as well as the language barrier drive this point home, as do the parties'/disputants' clothing, skin colour, stature, food, emotional displays and religious icons. Because the cultural differences are so striking, peacekeepers generally consider these in mediating or negotiating. As a result, peacekeepers are cautious. They strive to maintain emotional self control and develop strategies. Moreover, the peacekeepers are open to feedback. They attempt to empathise with the parties and to understand how the others view the issues, the disputes, and the peacekeepers' behaviour.

Such steps enhance the peacekeeper's effectiveness. Consequently, we feel it would be useful for civilian mediators and negotiators to assume that the disputants come from a culture other than their own. Such an assumption would motivate civilians to develop strategies and to focus on better communication. Likewise, this framing would foster better self control, empathy for others, and a general caution in their approach.

We have seen this 'alien culture' perspective adopted by civilian hostage negotiators. Readily, they admit that the hostage taker comes from a culture quite different from their own. Negotiators are used to a culture that typically has rules and education levels; where people are well-fed; where fairness is respected, and violence is not rewarded; and where people are generally trustworthy. Therefore, the hostage negotiators plan, focus on communication, empathise, and seek rapid accurate feedback. Given that the 'alien culture' assumption seems useful for hostage negotiators, as well as for peacekeepers, its application to labour negotiations, environmental mediations, civil court settlement mediations might also be warranted.

We close with a conclusion about which we have mixed feelings. In the mediation of intense conflict by peacekeepers as well as by civilians, we are able to evaluate the mediation when it fails. However, it is very difficult to evaluate the effort when it is not a failure. Seldom is any intense conflict totally resolved by mediation. Rather, it tends to improve or does not escalate. It may diminish over the long run. We are pleased to be able to extrapolate confidently from one setting to another. Yet, we are dissatisfied that giving third or primary party conflict resolution roles 'two thumbs up' is as difficult in civilian settings as it is in peacekeeping.

Notes

[1] See Fetherston, 1994, for a review of this literature.

[2] These missions are limited to those that national militaries have performed, those on the UN agenda of possible peacekeeping mission, and those that have received serious consideration in international policy-making circles. Four missions, considered in an earlier analysis (see Druckman, Singer and Van Cott, 1998, ch. 6), are excluded here because they are primarily domestic: drug eradication, anti-terrorism, disaster relief, and aid to domestic civilian populations. The former were shown to resemble the more enforcement-oriented operations; the latter two missions formed a cluster of missions that deal with domestic emergencies (see Diehl, Druckman and Wall, 1998 for a further discussion).

[3] A meta analysis conducted by Druckman (1994) showed that orientation toward the bargaining situation strongly influences the process and outcome of negotiation.

[4] The survey consisted of ninety-six questions asked of sampled respondents in each of three ranks: enlisted soldiers, noncommissioned officers (NCOs), and officers. Of these, 50 questions were relevant to the combat-contact distinction: 32 dealt with combat activities, 18 with contact activities. From the answers, profiles were constructed for each of the two operations (Bosnia and Croatia). These profiles show the relative balance of combat and contact experiences for the operations and how these experiences vary by rank.

[5] The details are discussed in ch. 7 in Druckman, Singer and Van Cott (1997).

7 From Conflict Resolution to Conflict Transformation: A Critical Review

RAIMO VÄYRYNEN[1]

The New Context of Conflict Resolution

The world system is becoming polarised. It is divided into a centre where the majority of the ageing population benefits from rising living standards and a periphery where most often young people experience stagnant or declining social conditions. The income distribution is becoming increasingly unequal, especially in the periphery where, by United Nations Development Programme (UNDP) criteria, 1.3 billion people live in abject poverty. The world economy is becoming globalised, but the process is selective and uneven, spreading both new wealth and poverty. It is difficult to imagine how a world system in which several gaps divide people in entirely different worlds can be stable in the long run.

How can we best make sense of this new diversity and complexity in the international system? A simple distinction between the centre and the periphery based on capabilities is outdated. A more nuanced approach focuses either on major international processes or the nature of actors involved. The former approach has been adopted by Immanuel Wallerstein (1980, pp. 114-19, 284-89) who argues that there are core and peripheral economic processes which give rise to corresponding zones of the world economy, while the semi-periphery combines these two types of processes. The latter approach has been pursued by Kalevi J. Holsti (1996) who distinguishes between strong and weak states, defined by their degree of vertical and horizontal legitimacy.

Wallerstein argues that core economic processes are associated with a strong state, while the peripheral processes are linked with a weak and fragmented state. A strong state does not need to be intrusive and oppressive; to the contrary, capital-intensive, high value-added production in the core may require less market intervention. On the other hand, a peripheral state which is weak in relation to the world market can be quite oppressive internally. Holsti seems to agree with this analysis, although he does not link the strength of the state as strongly with the core-periphery structure as Wallerstein does.

Obviously, conflicts and their control are quite different in peripheral economic zones and weak states than in core zones and strong states. In particular, restraints on violent conflicts differ between these two categories of zones/actors. In the centre, restraints are due either to the democratic control of decision making, integrative effects of the market mechanism, or the spread of peaceful culture. Peace and stability thus result either from democracy, capitalism, civilisation, or all of them. These three tenets of peace are derived from liberal thinking.

The civilisational perspective relies on the view that in the course of history, stricter limits on 'uncivil' behaviour are established through strengthening and democratising the state. As a result, peaceful social spaces are enlarged at the expense of violence and crudeness, first within nations and then across the borders. In its most recent version, the civilisational approach tries to integrate various explanations -- such as the state monopoly of force, social equality and welfare, and democratic participation -- into a comprehensive account for peace civilisation and constructive conflict culture (Senghaas, 1995).[2]

The civilisational view maintains that a pluralistic civil society, as opposed to a coercive state, is the main source of peace and civility. It is also consistent with the parallel argument that states with strong internal and external legitimacy tend to be stable and predictable in their actions. Such a view overlooks, however, the possibility that a precondition for increasing 'civility', i.e., the consolidation of state power, may come at a high price as wars have been waged to consolidate state structure. Moreover, if things go wrong, a strong state has more capabilities to turn both against its own citizens and start wars with other states. In that sense, 'the modern state is too civil by half' (Keane, 1996, p. 27).[3]

In today's world, the political structures of core states and zones face several challenges ranging from subnational ethnic mobilisation through political alienation to economic pressures of globalisation. However, their political and social structures are robust and flexible enough to cope with most of these challenges without a major erosion of the restraints on violence and the capacity of peaceful conflict resolution. Democracy plays a major role here; in addition to being internally peaceful and avoiding war in their mutual relations, democratic countries are more capable of defusing potentially destructive conflicts and settling them without a recourse to force (Dixon, 1994). In the core, the risk of a civil war is almost non-existent and even the danger of interstate war has been receding to the background.

In the peripheral zone and weak states the situation is quite the opposite. The postcolonial state is weak and is often fragmented along political or ethnic lines. The state's monopoly of force may be challenged by competing centres of power which claim their share of the society's resources. A state may become so weak at the interface of global and subnational pressures that it collapses entirely. The decline of foreign aid and the reduction of public budgets due to structural adjustment programmes have reduced the funds available to rulers to maintain their clientele relations and, thus, the stability of the political system.

A paradigm competing with the democracy thesis stresses the 'coming anarchy' imagery, initiated by Robert Kaplan (1994, 1996). He sees societies moving from an organised national system to a more fragmented polity in which primordial sentiments, profit motives, and military ideologies dominate the political processes. Societies are governed from below by warlords, criminal gangs, smugglers, and populist movements. As societal institutions crumble, the country becomes parcelled into political and economic turfs where private gains are pursued by coercive means. The national economy disintegrates into enclaves which have direct, often informal links with the world market.

Kaplan suggests that Turkey and West Africa, especially Liberia and Sierra Leone, are areas in which social anarchy is already reigning. He predicts that Egypt is one of the main candidates to turn chaotic in the near future (Kaplan, 1996). In a more solid conceptual and empirical way, William Reno has documented the rise of warlord politics, the disintegration of the economy, and the fragmentation of the political system in the Democratic Republic of Congo, Liberia, Nigeria, and Sierra Leone. He does not see the current situation as anarchy, but a rational way for the warlords, in the absence of state structures, to accumulate power and wealth. The rulers of weak states both draw upon the principle of sovereignty and mimic warlords in efforts to compete with them and insert the country to the global economy (Reno, 1995; 1998).

Of course, not all peripheral states have failed or collapsed. Some of them have robust bureaucratic structures (e.g., Senegal), others have a coherent, growing economy (e.g., Botswana), and yet others are experiencing a democratic transition (e.g., Mali). However, the disintegration of the postcolonial, neo-patrimonial states is such a pervasive trend in Africa and several parts of Asia that it cannot go unnoticed (Clapham, 1996). The trend is especially pertinent as it has both caused and been followed by large scale violence which has, in turn, paved the way to major humanitarian crises in Afghanistan, Mozambique, Somalia, Sudan, and elsewhere.

The brief outline of the situation prevailing in the core and peripheral areas indicates that both collective violence and its absence in today's world are linked primarily with their internal conditions. Obviously, external factors play a role in shaping the internal structures of societies, but they can hardly provide an adequate explanation of why they remain peaceful or turn violent. Liberalism is able to account for at least a part of the civility in the core. However, neither the realist nor the liberal variant of traditional international relations theory has been able to offer a satisfactory explanation of the changing nature of violence in the periphery (Holsti, 1998, pp. 104-109).

These considerations lead to a two-zone model of the world system. Such a model is, of course, simplified, but it underlines correctly the divided nature of the world; the centre is quite stable and peaceful, while instability and violence prevail in the periphery. A key assertion in this model is that the core and periphery are increasingly de-coupled from each other (Goldgeier and McFaul, 1992, pp. 486-88). A similar proposition is captured by the distinction between the 'zone of peace' and the 'zone of turmoil'. In the former, democracy helps to transform conflicts into 'ordinary problems'. In the latter, conflicts are pervasive, though not necessarily permanent, due to poverty, militarism, and a lack of democracy (Singer and Wildawsky, 1993).

Both of these models seem to assume that even though relations between the core and the periphery matter, their internal conditions are even more decisive. This view is shared by Mohammed Ayoob (1998, pp. 45-47) who coins the term 'subaltern realism' to stress the primacy of domestic factors, especially the process of state-making, in shaping the patterns of order and violence. In 'subaltern realism', the international structure does not determine political processes within societies, as neorealism suggests, but it rather directs and constrains them in a selective way. Neorealists have not been able to argue convincingly that their approach can adequately account for the causes and cures of civil wars (David, 1997).

This paper suggests that most approaches to conflict resolution have not adequately taken into account the important differences between the core and peripheral conflicts. They may help to manage the former, but fail to address the causes and the nature of the latter. To regain its validity, research on the resolution of conflicts must take their transformation much more seriously, especially in the periphery. International intervention continues to fuel violence in the periphery. However, more common is the effort to mitigate it by the involvement of third parties. This goal is often unattainable, though, and intervention may even worsen the situation. Intervention succeeds only if the domestic conflicts in the periphery are restructured in a manner that at least some of their root causes are eliminated.

Criticising Negotiations and Conflict Resolution

The distinction between the political conditions in the core and the periphery should have major implications for the feasibility of conflict resolution and approaches to it. One can assume that conflict resolution would be organised and instrumental in the core, but messy and difficult in the periphery. In fact, this assumption is not new and radical at all. However, many practitioners of conflict resolution seem to have failed to integrate this fundamental insight in their work.

Much of the literature on conflict resolution tends to assume that disagreements between parties are resolvable once appropriate methods have been identified and applied to the practical problem. The main method to solve a conflict is obviously negotiation which, to be effective, should focus on mutual gains rather than fixed interests of a zero-sum nature. This can be done by conducting 'principled negotiations' in which people are separated from problems, a variety of possible outcomes are generated, the outcome is based on an objective standard, and the focus is on interests instead of positions (Fisher, Ury and Patton, 1991, pp. 9-14). Thus, conflict resolution is a combination of art and science.

The purpose of negotiations is to identify one or more possible equilibria in a zone of agreement where all parties perceive their interests to be better served than in the absence of an agreement. Often, the initial positions of actors are not located in the zone of possible compromise, and it is the task of negotiations and mediation to find that zone. Typical advice to negotiators stresses the importance of creating a condition for reaching an agreement. This can happen, for instance, by cultivating shared interests, exploiting the scale economies of the agreement, and utilising the existing differences in creating new value. Obviously, the negotiators have also to agree on how this newly created value is apportioned between them (Sebenius, 1992, pp. 28-31; Rubin, 1994, pp. 35-37).

An explicit objective of the negotiation analysis is to help a party to realise its interests in cooperation with others. By looking at the situation from the perspective of one party and taking its preferences as sovereign, the negotiation analysis is 'asymmetrically prescriptive' and 'radically subjective' (Sebenius, 1992, pp. 20-21). Conflict resolution, especially if it is pursued by mediation, differs from this approach by making an effort to identify and understand the interests and values of all parties involved and provide a symmetrically prescriptive solution. While both negotiation and dispute resolution aim at a commonly acceptable solution and overlap each other as instruments, they differ in the underlying philosophy; the former focuses on actors and the latter more on the situation and the potential consequences of the failure.

However, both the advocates of negotiations and conflict resolution tend to emphasise the necessity of a systematic and professional approach to them. In their view, negotiation and conflict resolution require advice, training, and possibly intervention by third parties to mitigate tensions, identify common interests and the range of possible outcomes, and help the parties to achieve a compromise. Like in medicine, remedial action in conflict resolution requires professional specialisation which can be achieved by appropriate research and training.

This thinking is spelled out by Mitchell and Banks (1996, pp. 1-2) who point out that 'there is no good reason to tolerate the high level of conflict that exists in the world, because the knowledge exists to enable something to be done about it'. They urge the adoption of a practical, instead of a theoretical approach which would 'consist of a set of procedures for dealing with deep-rooted and frequently violent conflict.

The procedures are explicit, strictly so, and they call for a high level of expertise on the part of those of who seek to apply them'.

In the instrumental approach, conflict resolution is a mode of prescriptive, but also disinterested managerial action, conducted by a 'guild' of professional practitioners. 'Getting to Yes' amounts to a problem-solving approach which, to be effective, can be mastered only by those who have adequate professional training, experience, and prestige. True practitioners of conflict resolution develop their own techniques to solve disputes to the mutual satisfaction of the parties. These techniques may even be commodified and be sold in the political or commercial markets.

The instrumental approach is premised on the manageability of conflicts. Expert methods and professional training help to find an appropriate solution to most, though not all, conflicts. The commercialisation of conflict resolution leads to (over)stress the manageability of crises. To receive a commission, the conflict manager has to convince potential customers that their problems can be solved and their 'troubled partnerships' remedied.

To be able to develop a credible model for the solution of a conflict, the manager should limit the range of issues and focus attention on disputes 'within the domain of the responsible governing body(ies)' (Dukes, 1993, pp. 46-47). In other words, the conflict has to be simplified to render it manageable. Most of the instrumental approaches, whether a problem-solving workshop or third-party mediation, assume a homology between different levels of conflict. They consider an individual, acting in small groups, to be the vantage point for conflict resolution. The participants, whether communal actors or public decision makers, are advised to be 'behaviour units only, entities which are capable of acting' (Mitchell and Banks, 1996, p. 32).

The instrumental approach has been criticised on two counts. The 'soft' criticism argues that this approach focuses too exclusively on the conflicts of finite interest which can be more easily divided, rearranged, and enhanced than values and identities. Due to their divisibility, conflicts over resources are more manageable and solvable. In identity conflicts, the issues are more abstract, complex, and serious as the physical existence of the communities involved may be at stake. Therefore, it is suggested that the efforts to resolve the conflict should be preceded by an interactive dialogue. A rush to the solution may even deteriorate the conflict (Rothman, 1997, pp. 12-17).

The 'hard' criticism of the instrumental approach argues that it comes close to 'technological fixes' and provides 'pseudo-solutions' to problems. Anatol Rapoport (1989, pp. 545-46) suggests that such fixes are, in effect, a method of exercising power from outside, while true conflict resolution relies on the 'search for self-knowledge' as a way out of the spiral of violence. Such an approach turns the table from the external intervention to the internal change that can be fostered by forgiveness and mutual reconciliation. In this view, conflict resolution becomes ultimately a way to reshape and control one's own social life and relate it to that of others by creating a 'third reality' in which the past grievances and disagreements are downplayed.

The instrumental emphasis is most visible in the legal methods to settle disputes. The 'objectivity' of law can also provide a solid basis for solutions, especially in business conflicts. Although legal methods are most common in intra-state conflicts, they can also be applied to inter-state conflicts provided that they are divisible in terms of money, territory, or some other finite resources. In that case, a technical approach can be used to apportion costs and benefits as an element of the solution. Thus, the generalisability of norms and means, and the divisibility of issues seem to be the main conditions for an effective technical, instrumental settlement of disputes.

Invariances in the effectiveness of conflict resolution are, thus, due to the universalism of the method rather than the similarity of actors, issues, or situations. In the most recent literature on conflict resolution, the new multiplicity and heterogeneity of these factors are occasionally admitted. However, this recognition does not seem to lead to any new conceptual or theoretical breakthroughs (Rasmussen, 1997).

This chapter argues that the disjuncture between the nature of current conflicts and the prevailing theories and methods of conflict resolution is too big, and may even be widening, in particular, in the zone of turmoil. This trend may make conflict resolution theories increasingly irrelevant and, in the worst case, counterproductive. They promise that professional conflict resolution techniques can help to solve vexed social conflicts, while in reality they are quite helpless to deal with deep political and economic problems. They may delay the resort to other remedial measures, such as mutual reconciliation and the empowerment of marginalised people, or more forceful external intervention.

It is argued below that method cannot be separated from substance. A critical distinction runs between violent and nonviolent conflicts. The method, whether it is based on mutual negotiations or third-party mediation, cannot be the great unifier in the theory of conflict resolution. Instead, effective conflict resolution can be developed only by obtaining an adequate understanding of the basic categories of conflict structures, actors, issues, and situations.

These categories are inherently dissimilar. For example, a humanitarian emergency in Somalia can be compared with neither the Indo-Pakistani conflict over Kashmir nor with the political-religious conflict in Algeria. The dissimilarity of cases means, in turn, that the method is subordinate to substance and must be calibrated to the special traits of the conflict. As to substance, power -- its nature, distribution, and use -- is a key factor in any conflict and cannot be omitted in efforts to control and mitigate it.

New Directions

Culture and Complexity

The development of conflict resolution techniques has made much progress in recent years and mitigated some of the most obvious problems of the technical approaches. For instance, cultural obstacles to productive negotiations and communications -- manifest by differences in values, norms of acceptable behaviour, and linguistic conventions -- are increasingly recognised. The exchange of information in negotiations does not necessarily lead to a shared understanding of problems. Moreover, the concepts and their meanings may have quite different political implications in different cultures.

Raymond Cohen (1997) has shown that there are two quite different approaches to negotiations. The 'Western' style, pretending to be universal, is individualistic, relies on explicit communications, and strives for solving specific problems. The 'Oriental' style is more collectivistic, uses non-verbal communication and declines to isolate a specific issue from its larger context. The latter style pays more attention to status and symbols, such as honour and integrity, and tries to avoid confrontation. Also the conception of time is different in these two styles; in the West, short-term thinking prevails, while the East thinks more in historical terms.

The complexity of the negotiation process is, of course, due also to other factors than cultural differences, including the continued expansion of the issue areas and the increasing linkages between different levels of organisation. Instead of considering the conflict a unidimensional cycle of events in which different phases and mutually stimulated moves by the parties follow each other, its complexity should be recognised. Conflict moves ahead simultaneously on different trajectories, pushed by a complex interaction of actors, issues, and interests. Often contradictions develop between these trajectories and lead to unexpected and even perverse results (Zartman, 1991).

As conflict resolution practitioners have no way to make the environment constant, they cannot but try to manage the ensuing complexity. Such a complexity is particularly characteristic of multilateral negotiations which tend to have cross-cutting instead of reinforcing cleavages which are more common in bilateral negotiations. If the actors and issues are linked and separated by multiple lines of division, the management of negotiations may become more difficult. At the same time they may open up new opportunities for integrative bargaining and flexible coalition formation (Hopmann, 1996, pp. 254-58).

Overlooking this complexity, conflict resolution literature continues to be based too much on an overtly simplified picture of reality. For instance, the existing works pay inadequate attention to environmental constraints or opportunities for conflict resolution, rely on a static analysis of actors and their mutual relations, and believe rather uncritically that there is a solution to every conflict. All these assumptions can be challenged by arguing that conflicts can neither be isolated from their environment nor regarded as static phenomena. Moreover, the belief in the manageability of all conflicts is unrealistic and potentially dangerous.

Much of this criticism pertains to conflict resolution that is informed either by game theory or other formal approaches. True, game theory has made progress over the decades; for instance, it has shed part of its static and mechanical image by developing a theory of moves and inserting the concept of power into the preference structures of actors (Brams, 1990). Game theory tends to exclude, however, the context outside the actor preferences and strategies. Much of it pretends that preferences are generated internally rather than by the interaction of players with each other and the environment.

Psychological and organisational approaches to conflict resolution do not suffer so much from the exclusion of the environment or the static bias as from an excessive belief in the manageability of conflicts. Elaborated strategies are developed and justified by experimental knowledge to bring the parties closer to each other, redefine their values and interests, use threats and promises to persuade the recalcitrant actors to cooperate, and ultimately eliminate negative relationships. A firm belief in the effectiveness of various conflict resolution techniques characterises, for instance, the work of Fisher, Ury and Patton (1991); Pruitt and Carnevale (1994); Rubin, Pruit and Kim (1994) and Schellenberger (1996). While often elaborate and interesting, many of the solutions recommended by this approach do not sufficiently consider the unpredictability and unmanageability of today's social conflicts.

An interim conclusion from this discussion is that many a conflict resolution approach is derived from a rather narrow reading of the social reality. They have grown out of the liberal democratic model of society in which interests and actions are, as a rule, characterised by individuality and rationality. Such principles are integrated, for instance, in game theory and rational choice methods which predominantly reflect the ideals of the liberal market society. They also suggest, as elaborated by Michael Nicholson (1992) that a formal statement of problems will help to clarify the underlying dynamics of conflict and thus resolve it by social engineering.

The rational approach may, of course, work as conflicts are seldom so irrational that they are not at all open to formal procedures to mitigate or resolve them. These procedures fail, however, to address arational motives of human behaviour and thus discuss meaningfully the identitive aspects of conflicts which include ethnicity and religion, and the relations between the individual and the group (for a more comprehensive approach, see Hardin, 1995).

Another problem in standard conflict resolution theory is the assumption of the existence of homology between different levels of society. This assumption justifies the transfer of lessons and techniques of conflict resolution from one level to another; for instance, from small groups to national or international systems. However, this is often unwarranted, because *getting to yes* has a very different meaning in small groups and complex organisations. In fact, the bigger and more complex the actor, the more likely it is that problems are never resolved. Instead, they are subject to 'endless negotiations', which, in Cohen's (1997, pp. 202-207) view, characterise China's relations with other countries.

John A. Vasquez (1996, pp. 132-37) has suggested that the main conceptual problem in conflict resolution lies between individual and group levels of analysis. In other words, knowledge and experience on group processes, but not on individual behaviour, should provide lessons for the resolution of interstate conflicts. The fact that this transfer of knowledge has not taken place is, in his view, primarily due to the reluctance of political realists to use the experiences of stable domestic societies to solve conflicts in 'anarchic' interstate relations.

Vasquez is right that the domestic 'zones of peace' can expand into regional security communities and thus help to enhance the stability of international relations. It is, however, doubtful how relevant empirical generalisations on individual behaviour in small groups are for conflict resolution. Moreover, the point made by Vasquez should be expanded from the international core to its periphery where the dividing line between intra- and interstate relations has largely been broken down. Both of those relations in the periphery are often characterised by semi-anarchical conditions. Thus, the real faultline may not be between domestic and international spheres, but between the core and the periphery.

The Role of Power

The success of a professional conflict manager requires that s/he must be able to control simultaneously several factors in the conflict system itself and its environment. For this purpose, the manager must wield adequate power in the situation. It is surprising that the centrality of power in conflict resolution is not always recognised. For instance, in considering the effectiveness of mediation, a widely used text is content to state that it may require the 'modification' of social and issue structures and the 'encouragement' of momentum, trust, and face saving (Rubin, Pruitt and Kim, 1994, pp. 202-15). This is a very limited and 'soft' understanding of power and its uses.

The issue of power appears differently in bargaining and problem-solving approaches to negotiations. The former is anchored in realism and the latter in liberal institutionalism.[4] Bargaining uses both negative and positive means of power, while problem solving tries to develop creative and consensual solutions to a common problem. The role of power in conflict resolution has to be understood in a nuanced way, not only as the utilisation of existing asymmetries to compel or induce the adversary to accept a particular outcome, but also as appeals to normative standards. In conflict resolution, one possibility is to consider both power-based and normative relationships among actors and then assess which of them can be more easily influenced to bring about a positive change (Greenhalgh and Kramer, 1990).

Technical approaches tend to underrate the relevance of power and overrate the importance of negotiating techniques. Thus, Fisher, Ury and Patton (1991, pp. 177-87) conclude that 'how you negotiate (and how you prepare to negotiate) can make an *enormous* difference, whatever the relative strengths of each party'. They even instruct the readers not to ask 'who is more powerful'? For the sake of fairness, one has to add, however, that they provide some useful ideas on how negotiation power can be enhanced by using constructive forms of power, such as the importance of understanding interests and using external standards of assessment.

P. Terrence Hopmann (1996, pp. 99-119) makes a serious effort to explore the impact of power asymmetries on interstate bargaining. He observes, among other things, that asymmetries create an incentive, especially for weaker parties, to identify other than negotiated alternatives, because they are able to obtain, by bargaining, a proportionally smaller share of the outcome. On the other hand, one can argue that negotiations create an institutionalised relationship which better protects the interests of smaller actors who do not have resources to pursue their goals effectively outside institutions.

The tendency to overlook power imposes unnecessary limits on the theory and practice of conflict resolution. Power is vital both in integrative and distributive solutions to conflict, although the nature and role of power differ in these two solutions. In complex and/or fragmented conflict systems, the nature of power resources possessed by the actors may not always be relevant. For instance, standard distributive techniques of bargaining are not necessarily effective in complex conflicts as they are unable to embrace the diversity of actors, issues, and interests. Neither may the power resources of bargainers be relevant for the task they are facing.

In an asymmetric conflict, impartial mediation is seldom able to remove the root causes of the conflict. It may even serve the interests of the stronger party and thus exacerbate the conflict. In such a situation, 'principal' rather than 'neutral' mediation is needed to rectify the imbalances (Princen, 1992). On the other hand, there is no assurance that principal, 'muscular' mediation will really serve the needs of the marginalised parties to the conflict. Moreover, the reliance on asymmetric power in controlling the conflict may elicit direct or indirect counter-strategies to escalate rather than contain it (Jabri, 1996, pp. 83-84).

Going beyond the bargaining framework and developing various unconventional, 'non-agenda' solutions are sometimes considered a remedy, but they can also complicate the conflict. The response of Bosniaks to acquire money and weapons from Iran and other Islamic countries to circumvent the asymmetric effects of the UN arms embargo provides a relevant example. It is clear that the arms embargo was not only discriminatory of the Bosniak government, but it did not serve well its stated purposes; i.e., the prevention of conflict escalation and the protection of peacekeepers (Cigar, 1995, pp. 166-80). On the other hand, in 1996-97 the alliance of the Sarajevo government with Muslim countries weakened its political position, at least in Western capitals.

One needs both a critical analysis of asymmetric social relations in conflict and a strategy to empower the weaker parties as an element of a comprehensive approach to peacebuilding. In other words, both the analysis and resolution of conflicts have to be placed in a larger structural context to make it relevant and just. Indeed, justice should be a key element in conflict resolution, although different ideas of justice may become reasons for the continuation and escalation of the conflict.

Therefore, justice as a goal of conflict resolution cannot mean that the outcome should be exactly the same for all parties. The justness of the outcome can be assessed only by combining several principles of justice. The outcome may even be unequal provided that all parties are satisfied with the fairness of the process by which the negotiated result has been achieved. Thus, to be helpful in conflict resolution, the principle of justice needs to be disaggregated and pursued by acceptable means (Zartman, Druckman, Jensen, Pruitt and Young, 1996). Justice might be a medium in what Dieter Senghaas (1995a) calls 'provocative mediation' which makes an effort to awaken the parties to see the commonality of their long-term interests and thus prepare ground for the use of more standard practices of mediation.

Much of the recent conflict resolution literature can be challenged as it is based on the unwarranted premise that the conflict situations are well structured, predictable, and manageable. These assumptions lead to stressing the importance of techniques by which conflicting values and interests of the parties can be potentially reconciled. A parallel point is that while the decision making approach may be useful in studying conflicts between small groups and governments, it is less useful in accounting for turmoil, war, and humanitarian crises within nations. Much of today's world is inherently unstructured, volatile, and unpredictable, calling for more profound social adjustments than what the standard conflict resolution can provide.

Resolution Versus Transformation

Complexity and Conflict Resolution

There are at least two obstacles to a successful application of the handbook theories of conflict resolution: structural complexity of conflict situations and deep-seated incompatibilities of interests and values among the actors. These impediments tend to slow down and complicate efforts at resolution even if the parties would have the necessary 'political will' needed to solve the conflict. Robert Jervis (1997, pp. 29-39) has analysed, in a general vein, how interactions and interconnections produce effects which are indirect, unintended, mediated, and delayed. Therefore, many events cannot be understood if the focus is on local, linear processes and their immediate outcomes.

Thus, the outcomes of external intervention, whether aiming at mediation or enforcement, cannot be predicted from the actions themselves. A conflict manager can only hope that the intervention has a desired outcome and, in the best of the cases, try to create a self-reinforcing process in which the parties to conflict come to accept the arguments and advice of the third party. That is why the traditional approach is right in stressing the relevance of psychological aspects and images in conflict resolution.

Complexity creates a situation in which the requirements of solving the conflict easily overwhelm the actors involved. For instance, issues are so numerous and inter-linked across levels and problem areas that their negotiated solution often becomes protracted, or even impossible.

The preferences of actors can also be so numerous and cross-cutting that there is no obvious solution to the conflict (Hopmann, 1995, pp. 44-45). Links between levels are, in part, produced by their leaders with whom mediators have to deal. Negotiation styles with top, middle-range, and grassroots leaders have to be different, yet each of these styles and levels of leaderships interact with each other (Lederach, 1997, pp. 38-43).

In a complex conflict, transformation rather than resolution is often a more feasible option. One reason for this is that the conflict transformation approach can be more easily linked with social and political theories, and thus new insights are gained. Technical conflict resolution is more likely to be stimulated by limited psychological and organisational theories. It may even be that the application of these theories to conflict resolution has come to a point of diminishing returns due to major changes in the conflict environment.

Conflict Transformation

Conflict transformation can be understood in several different ways. The normative understanding stresses the need to create constructive, nonviolent solutions to violent conflicts or threats. In the best of the cases, conflict transformation can encourage the establishment of cooperative and just societies. This approach is most explicitly represented by John Paul Lederach (1995, pp. 8-9, 12-15) who calls for a transformative practice in which unpeaceful relations are restructured over a long term by education, advocacy (nonviolent activism), and mediation.

In a similar vein, Frank Dukes (1993, pp. 47-49) points out that a 'transformative practice' in conflict resolution has to be based on a critical assessment of the society and its ills, including disintegration and alienation. He suggests that ideas derived from participatory democracy, feminism, and environmentalism can provide guidelines for a transformative practice which should nurture 'an engaged community', 'a responsive government', and 'a capacity for problem solving and conflict resolution'. Thus, the ultimate purpose of conflict transformation is social change.

An important difference is whether conflict transformation is supposed to have a specific end-state or whether it is an open-ended process. Both versions of conflict transformation reject the idea that the purpose of conflict resolution is the restoration of the *status quo ante* as it gave rise to war in the first place. Therefore, conflict transformation aims at the promotion of a more peaceful reality embodying new social relations, institutions, and visions. In that sense, conflict transformation and education have a strategic element; the goal of peace is sought through the redefinition and restructuring of a conflict situation (Lederach,1997, pp. 107-23).

The normative approach to conflict transformation runs a risk of becoming a movement for the general improvement of society rather than just mitigating and redefining the conflict. If the normative view adopted is too long term, the focus on the mitigation of violence and its effects may have to take a back seat. Therefore, one needs an intermediate approach between the 'technical' conflict resolution and the 'normative' transformation of conflict. For the sake of brevity, I call such an approach the 'social' transformation of violent conflicts. In fact, Lederach's ideas (1995, 1997) are not far removed from such an approach.

A key issue in the social transformation of violent conflicts concerns the definition of their root causes and their malleability. In theory at least, conflict transformation should focus on those root causes of violence that are malleable. This line of thinking runs, however, the risk of deteriorating into social engineering in which causes of violence are 'removed' to attain the goal of peace. Such an approach is based on a linear, mechanical image of society instead of discontinuity and complexity. Therefore, a more proper methodological perspective to conflict transformation is provided by social constructionism in which reality is restructured by human actions. Transformation draws upon various resources of social power which help to create and expand political spaces for peace (Fetherston, 1998).

'Social' transformation of conflicts departs from the assumption that collective violence in society tends to be instrumental. In other words, it is used either to defend existing entitlements or acquire new ones. If the goal is to reduce the amount of violence in society, either the entitlements or the permissible means, or both, should be redefined. Conflict transformation is more focused on entitlements than instruments. It may aim at a thorough structural change in society, but usually its objectives are more modest. Conflict transformation aims to redefine and rearrange key parties and their coalitions, issues, rules, and interests in a manner that the conflict becomes less violent and destructive (the idea of conflict transformation has been developed in Väyrynen 1991 and 1994, pp. 389-99).

The main challenge to the problem-solving approach is the mutual incompatibility of interests and values among parties to a conflict. It can drastically curtail the zones of bargaining and compromise. Patriotism, as opposed to civic nationalism, is one source of such an incompatibility as it fosters the myth of belonging rather than law or reason. Patriotic national or ethno-national identities are based on common ethnic and linguistic roots which can, in turn, encourage authoritarian, intolerant, and divisive political practices (Ignatieff, 1994, pp. 5-11).

There are means to deal with identity conflicts by relying on critical introspection and resonance (Rothman, 1997). However, the prevalence of patriotism or other strong identities makes it difficult to separate 'people' from 'problems' as technical conflict resolution tends to do. It also tends to overlook intra-group differences between individuals and thus attribute to them various stereotypical features and attitudes. Large scale violence is justified by the de-humanisation and even demonisation of the opposed group.

Leaders who are unwilling to compromise integrate strong identities with authoritarian politics to strengthen their power base. The primacy given to power and its perks by various 'pathological leaders' obviously undermines efforts at conflict resolution. African experiences suggest bluntly that 'negotiated settlements are possible only if such leaders are marginalised' (Ohlson and Stedman, 1994, p. 124; see also Stedman, 1996, pp. 347-49). On the other hand, even bad leaders can have enough popular support so that they are needed to implement a peace agreement.

Obviously, in the analysis of identities, one has to strike a fine balance between their historical roots and political construction. Neither a pure primordial nor instrumental account of identities is correct. Instead, one can speak of the construction of identities which can be both traced back to their history and adopted by political leaders for their own purposes. In that sense politically relevant identities are created by the decisions and interactions of the parties. Identities are constructed to distinguish one group from another and establish a new system of power both within and between groups. The creation of Sinhala identity, to distinguish Buddhists from Tamils, is a good example of an 'invented enmity' that complicates the resolution of the Sri Lankan conflict (Little, 1994).

I am pessimistic on the possibility of conflict resolution approaches to curtail the current wave of violence in the world's peripheries. This criticism can be obviously countered by saying, firstly, that conflict resolution has never been intended to provide total answers and, secondly, that it seems to work after all. More conflicts have been mitigated in the 1990s than at any time after World War II: South Africa, Angola, Bosnia, Mozambique, Uganda, Liberia, Northern Ireland, Guatemala, and El Salvador.

However, except for Bosnia, Northern Ireland and the Israel-Palestine crisis, traditional conflict resolution theories, especially those pertaining to third-party mediation, seem to have contributed only little to the understanding and resolution of these conflicts. In other words, negotiations have not been conducted according to the conflict resolution manuals; they have often broken down or their results have not lasted; and the mediators have not always served the intended purposes.

A lesson seems to be that conflict resolution should be more contingent and transformatory and less mechanical. The contingency model of conflict resolution stresses the need to match intervention strategies with the key characteristics of the conflict. It also emphasises the importance of correct timing of intervention to de-escalate tensions. Finally, the contingency approach pays attention to the close interaction between objective and subjective features of conflict and notes that the impact of subjective factors tends to increase with the escalation of conflict (Keashley and Fisher, 1996; Fisher, 1997, pp. 163-84).

In other words, the contingency model relaxes the omnipotence of the method and contextualises the choice between different means of intervention. While the model's link with conflict transformation is helpful, its view on the stages of conflict is simplified. The model assumes that all conflicts proceed from discussion through polarisation and segregation to destruction. This model is also based on the assumption of linearity which does not hold in practice as conflict often moves back and forth between cycles and may well return to violence (Fisher, 1997).

The idea of conflict transformation stresses the dynamic and discontinuous nature of conflicts instead of treating its basic features as linear and constant. It also recognises that for many conflicts there is no easy and obvious solution, especially if their asymmetries are embedded in national and international inequities. Therefore, it is often more realistic to try to mitigate the violent aspects of the conflict by limited external interventions without trying to resolve it once and for all. In the best of the cases, the redefinition of issues, actors, rules, and interests may transform the nature of the conflict so that resolution becomes possible.

Two Worlds of Conflict Resolution

The 'zone of peace' among the liberal industrialised countries is becoming a historical fact. They have created a 'pluralistic security community' in which war is highly unlikely. It seems that this zone is expanding from the Atlantic area, where it is underpinned by economic and technological interdependence, to much of Europe and potentially even to Russia. On the other hand, serious sources of violence remain at its edges -- in the Balkans, the Transcaucasus, and Central Asia. These areas can only be pacified by integrating them in a more close and equitable manner in the world economy. The area in which instrumental models of conflict resolution can potentially work may thus be growing.

The spread of democracy and free market economy will help, but it cannot be a panacea. It has been argued on empirical grounds that while democracy is usually peaceful, transitions to it can be violent. Democratising states are more likely to fight wars than either autocratic or democratic states. Potential explanations of this fact include the tendency of democratisation to fuel nationalism, the lack of effective governance in a transitory society, and ensuing uncertainty and short attention span. The instabilities of countries in democratic transition may in specific circumstances contribute to the use of violence (Mansfield and Snyder, 1996).

It seems that a crucial precondition for the successful democratic transition is the adequate economic progress and social protection of people. Otherwise nascent political institutions will be under too strong a strain. For this reason, democratisation requires investment in the strength of the state and power-sharing arrangements between diverse political forces to manage the transition (Przeworski *et al.*, 1995, pp. 182-84). Various mechanisms of conflict resolution cannot compensate for institutional weaknesses in the transition. They can be potentially useful, though, in later phases when the system gains capacity to solve problems.

In the liberal, industrial core of the world, the interstate war is highly unlikely. Internally, these countries have rather well-organised societies in which conflict regulation has become institutionalised. Sure, there are domestic economic and political tensions, but they seldom escalate to major threats to life and death. If they do, means for peaceful settlement are available or state coercion is used to suppress terrorist or other anti-governmental forms of violence.

In a sense, life in the 'peace zone' is a dream world of conflict resolution specialists as problems are largely predictable and manageable. As this zone is knit together by common interests and social practices, the problem-solving and consultation methods elaborated in the psychological, organisational, and legal approaches to conflict resolution are appropriate tools to manage non-antagonistic conflicts.

The mother of all pragmatic theories of conflict resolution was developed by Ralf Dahrendorf. He suggested in the 1950s that the parties to the dispute must admit that the social conflict is real and genuine, and cannot be eliminated by simple appeals to national unity and common interests. The parties must also become organised and recognise each other in order to be able to deal effectively with the conflict. They must also agree on the rules of the game in their mutual efforts to regulate the conflict by means of bargaining and negotiation. If these guidelines are applied, even antagonistic conflicts can be resolved (Dahrendorf, 1957).

Dahrendorf's reason to emphasise the resolution of industrial conflicts was made possible by the class character of post-industrial society. He feared that if they are permitted to escalate, a social revolution may follow. Today, such fears are no longer widespread as the traditional class struggle has all but disappeared in industrialised societies and the problem of violence has a different face. Dahrendorf (1988, pp. 149-58) has himself noted this change and analysed the paradox that the emergence of the new social underclass, cultural segmentation, and other dividing lines have not given rise to new organised struggles and violence, though they probably should have.

Dahrendorf points out that new scourge is 'anomie' which refers to the lack of individual stakes in society and the violation of social norms which the state cannot or does not want to punish. Alienation has gone so far that the state has decided to exclude certain groups and areas from the implementation of law. As conflicts appear as anomie, they tend to be unstructured and fragmented. Dahrendorf (1988, p. 161) calls these conflicts 'situational'; they are 'disconnected acts of public violence which achieve little apart from the aches of participants and the fears of the bystanders'.

It is obvious that these types of anomistic, situational conflicts are much harder to resolve than organised conflicts of interest. In such conflicts, the manifestations of violence are subjective and 'disconnected'. Due to anomie, the underlying incentive structures are poorly defined and those people affected have not been organised. The practitioners of conflict resolution have little to offer to alleviate social exclusion and anomie, and their consequences. Therefore, it is no wonder that this time Dahrendorf (1988) refuses to offer any practical strategies to deal with the new types of conflict and of violence.

Another German thinker, Hans Magnus Enzensberger follows in Dahrendorf's footsteps. He pays particular attention to the rise of urban violence and notes how it is less organised than violence used in civil wars. Therefore, Enzensberger (1994, pp. 19-31) speaks of the 'molecular civil wars' in the urban centres, such as Sao Paulo, Karachi, Los Angeles, Johannesburg, and Moscow. In urban wars, 'violence has freed itself from ideology' and 'have-nots are shooting each other'. Thus, violence becomes scattered and privatised, while the number and type of its participants multiply (Keane, 1996, pp. 146-52).

Indeed, the spread of urban violence both in the decaying cities of the industrialised north and the growing cities of the south is a problem whose control over which gains little from, say, models of bargaining and mediation. Inner-city violence is rampant, though declining, in many US cities and it is not unknown in Europe, either. The rapid rate of urbanisation in the south is creating internally segregated mega-cities. In the urban ghettos, access to public services and gainful, legal employment is limited, but so are opportunities for the state to discipline people. In major cities, homicides have become a leading cause of death and a major public health problem, especially for the young male.

However, ideas of 'molecular wars' and public-health models create a problem. They do not take into account the fact that violence is not neutral, but an instrument of power which is used by individuals and groups to gain political domination and material wealth (Väyrynen, 1994, pp. 389-99). This is also the case with urban violence in which gang leaders, mobilising streetfighters by promises of money and status, instigate the use of force to defend and expand their turfs. Not infrequently, violent clashes occur between gangs of established city dwellers and migrants from the rural areas. The migrant groups often have different ethnic or religious identities than the established groups with the intention to carve a niche for themselves in the urban slums.

The control of urban violence calls for a new tack in urban planning, desegregation of suburbs, reorganisation of the city police, and other comparable policy reforms. It is interesting that novel approaches to law enforcement take new types of conflict in the multicultural nature of the urban environment more seriously than traditional methods of policing (Shusta et al., 1995). It is important to bring violence to daylight from the bottom layers of urban society. It has been suggested that violence can be better controlled by cultivating 'public spheres of controversy', where violence is made visible and monitored nonviolently by citizens (Keane, 1996, pp. 165-77).

Another type of violence which is difficult to manage by mediation and other traditional techniques concerns the hate crimes committed against immigrants. The proportion of the immigrant population in industrialised countries is growing, although more slowly in recent years than before. Immigrants often live together in separate, easily identifiable communities where they retain their cultural values and everyday habits standing in contrast to those of the local population. Cultural tensions are visible in countries such as Austria, France, Sweden, and Germany (in which there were 200 xenophobic offences in 1995, and as many as 382 in 1994).

The propensity for violence is further increased by the activities of extremist groups (racists, fascists, skinheads, etc.) against which immigrant youth may organise themselves for protection. Tensions behind anti-immigrant violence are not only ideological and cultural, but also economic. Although immigrants capture far fewer jobs from the local people than often thought, the slow economic growth of the 1990s in the industrial core and associated middle-class anxieties fuel opposition and violence (for further analysis, see Witte 1996). It is clear that established approaches to conflict resolution cannot provide a solution to this type of violence. One reason is the asymmetric political nature of the conflict; immigrants may be considered intruders to the country by the others and thus should not receive fair treatment.

The limited value of established conflict resolution is obvious also in the efforts to resolve humanitarian emergencies in which violence triggers large scale hunger, disease, and displacement of people. The number and seriousness of humanitarian disasters have both increased in the 1990s. In many areas they have become a regional rather than merely a national problem. The escalation of emergencies seems to have resulted both from international political and economic changes and the growing vulnerability of societies, including the failure of states and the collapse of economies. In the international system the bottom appears to be falling out and there is nobody to catch all those people who are either killed, suffering, or deported to refugee camps (Väyrynen, 1996).

Humanitarian emergencies pose such massive political and social problems that they can be managed and solved only by a fully fledged commitment from the international community. Such a comprehensive international response has, however, in most disasters been slow to come and inadequately coordinated. Moreover, the local political conditions can make a humanitarian mission very strenuous. Research needs, in turn, to be focused more on the economic, political, and cultural causes of emergencies, their escalation, and strategies of termination rather than on abstract general models of conflicts.

In summary, theories and methods of conflict resolution provide few remedies to mitigate, for example, urban violence or large scale humanitarian disasters. These forms of violence have such deep roots in global and local changes, which are often inter-linked, that the rational adjustment of interests or values by closer contacts and better adjudication may not help much. As societies become more deeply divided, their potential for violence can ultimately be curbed only by institutional and economic reforms, not by workshops and mediating teams. Such reforms must encourage assimilation and distribute entitlements and political influence in a fairer manner.

However, such a policy is possible only if public authorities are able and willing to act in an impartial manner in arbitrating differences and redistributing resources. In many cases this is an unrealistic assumption as public powers are firmly on the side of one party. The distribution of public positions between groups in a crisis-ridden society, where resources and opportunities are more limited than in a stable society, amounts in reality to the struggle for political power and economic advantage (Hardin, 1995).

The struggle for power and resources also means that the criss-crossing ties between ethnic and religious communities are limited. These communities also tend to maintain parallel organisations to which individual members are committed. Therefore, according to Milton J. Esman (1994, pp. 243-44), 'strategies of conflict management that seek to capitalise common interests across ethnic boundaries and cross-cutting memberships usually fail'. This conclusion is contradicted by those who argue that either because of institutional arrangements or civic associations, inter-ethnic relations do not need to be conflictual and, in fact, cooperation in such relations is more frequent than generally assumed (Fearon and Laitin, 1996).

Conclusion

Increasing chaos and turmoil means that future conflicts will be more complex and intractable. They are not organised in the manner expected by prevailing models of conflict resolution. For instance, the relations both within and between identity groups are far more complex than assumed in most conflict theories. There may be more rivalry within a dominant group for public positions than between groups whose leaders may even collaborate for mutual advantage. Violence and cooperation are not polar alternatives, but they may be intertwined between groups.

Standard models of conflict resolution specify sets of factors such as the subject matter of conflicts (interests, understanding, and ideology), conflict processes (debating, bargaining, and fighting), influences on conflict (individual, role, and situational factors), and the contexts of conflicts (domestic, regional, and international) (Druckman, 1993). Such categories may be helpful in conceptualising conflicts in well-structured societies where actors have specific positions and roles and their behaviour and relations are regulated by a set of mutually recognised rules.

In an organised society, conflict resolution can be a rational exercise. Research questions then revolve around the problem of effectiveness; the relations between the parties and the interests and issues at stake, the kind of a mediator who can produce the best effect, and how the third-party intervention should be timed. The bottom line is that we 'need to study what mediators do, how they do it, and the consequences of their actions' (Bercovitch and Houston, 1996, p. 30).

Much of the violence in today's world, however, is not structured this way, it is more fragmented, complex, and unmanageable. Control and reduction requires a reorientation of conflict theory towards a greater emphasis on contingency approaches and the transformation of conflicts. More attention must also be paid to various institutional methods to mitigate violence. They include a better integration of communities, power-sharing between contending groups, decentralisation of political power to the regional level, and redistribution of economic resources.[5]

This new tack in conflict resolution theory and practice would bring to light the issue of how society should be structured to make and keep it peaceful. Somewhat paradoxically, techniques of conflict resolution can be more effectively applied in a society in which deep divisions and intense confrontations have disappeared and a constructive culture of conflict resolution has been established.

Notes

[1] I am grateful for comments on an earlier version of the paper to A.B. Fetherston and Janie Leatherman who both were at the time of this drafting Visiting Fellows of the Joan B. Kroc Institute for International Peace Studies at the University of Notre Dame. I would also extend my thanks to Mohammed Ayoob.

[2] Peace cultures tend to be cumulative as they tend to avoid all kinds of violence and resovile conflict communally as soon as they occur (Bonta, 1996).

[3] In a similar fashion, Cohen, Brown and Organski (1981) argue that state power has been accumulated through military struggles in which competing centres of power has been succumbed. Over time, state expansion stimulates economic growth which becomes, in turn, an antidote to violence.

[4] This comparison is further developed in Hopmann (1995).It should be noted, however, that even though game theory is closer to bargaining than problem solving, it does not usually take the nature and distribution of power seriously: see Brams and Taylor (1996).

[5] On various institutional solutions to conflicts, see O'Leary (1994) and Sisk (1996).

8 Preventing Conflict Escalation: Uncertainty and Knowledge

DAN SMITH[1]

Introduction

In the 1980s and 1990s, the idea of conflict prevention has become increasingly attractive to many of those concerned by issues of peace and conflict -- regardless of whether they work as reseachers, in non-governmental humanitarian organisations, within the United Nations system, in other inter-governmental organisations, or in governments. This is not surprising. The case for preventing conflicts from escalating into violence, war, massacre, mass flight and genocide hardly needs to be rehearsed. The argument that prevention is better than cure -- prevention is preferable in human, moral, strategic and economic terms -- is intuitive to the point of cliché. It can be regarded as axiomatic that the safest system of international security is one in which lethal armed conflict does not occur. It follows that a major task for security policy is to design a viable general framework for preventing conflict escalation. This should include long-term strategies of peaceful economic and social development, as well as short- to medium-term policies that can be used to prevent specific conflicts from escalating into violence (Boutros-Ghali, 1992; Lund, 1996; Carnegie Commission, 1997; Swedish MFA, 1997; Wallensteen, 1998).

Long-term preventive policies are strategic approaches to social, economic and political development designed to build mechanisms that handle conflict with a minimum of violence. They aim at 'management of social and political conflict through good governance' (Nathan, 1998, p. 27). The other category of preventive policies -- short- to medium-term policy instruments -- is almost always discussed in the context of intervention. That is, when the perspective is imminent escalation, the discussion of prevention focuses on the situation in which a country's government is unable or unwilling to prevent conflict escalation. For escalation prevention, action by external forces is then a necessity. Depending on the case, intervention will be more or less unwelcome to the government in question and will be more or less forceful in terms of policy instruments used. There is some disagreement in the prevention literature about whether military action can be included under the heading of prevention. Lund (1996) argues that the great advantage of prevention is to make military intervention unnecessary, which means that prevention is by definition non-military. The Carnegie Commission (1997) is among those arguing that military action in the early stages of escalation can be regarded as preventive.

A commitment to being ready for short-term preventive intervention creates the need for understanding the processes of escalation and the roots of the conflict. This is necessary in order to know that, without remedial action, escalation would ensue. It is the basis of early warning, which is (or should be) itself the basis of the risk assessment underpinning a decision on preventive intervention. Though the importance of early warning is accepted everywhere, it is also increasingly argued that the obstacles to prevention reside primarily in the domain of politics. One such obstacle, it is argued, is the tendency of political decision makers to focus on short-term issues. Another is that pragmatic politicians will consider the popularity of any major action with their political constituency. It is hard to gain public support for decisive action until massive human tragedy hits the TV screens. It is equally hard to show that preventing conflict escalation in another country ever got a politician re-elected. Above all, criticism is focused on a lack of political will in what is conventionally but loosely referred to as the international community. This line of argument offers a good object of criticism and a clear alternative. Though there remains a wide range of views in the heated debate about intervention, especially with armed force, there has been very little dissent from the view that preventing escalation is in principle both desirable and feasible. Stedman (1995) is virtually alone in raising difficult questions.

A considerable degree of impatience has begun to permeate the prevention debate. So clear is the case for early action, it seems, that only the mulish short-sightedness of politicians can explain why conflicts are allowed to escalate. The argument that the real obstacles to preventive policies are to be found in a lack of political will implies at least two things. First, it suggests that reluctance to intervene preventively is not based on reason. Second, and relatedly, it suggests that there is no special difficulty about early warning. This in turn implies that there is enough knowledge of conflict causation to offer a reliable system of predicting conflict escalation. This chapter, while premised on the desirability of preventive action, offers a critical exploration of these two connected elements of the case for preventive policies. It begins by reviewing the terrain of uncertainty in which preventive policies are necessarily shaped. The key issues here are the distinction between willingness and will, the fear of hubris and the problem of making policy choices. The author then looks at the degree to which the terrain of uncertainty can be narrowed by the deployment of knowledge.

The Terrain of Uncertainty

In the debate on intervention, including preventive intervention, commentators, researchers, and policy advocates often pay remarkably little attention to the possibility of doubt. It is all too often implicit in the arguments in favour of urgent, decisive intervention that uncertainty is a moral issue, rather than an intellectual one. Implicitly, to be uncertain is either to lack sympathy for the victims or else to lack the will to act on that sympathy. A presumed moral clarity then becomes a means of urging the international community into action, or criticising it for a lack of will to act, whether over Bosnia-Hercegovina (Gow, 1994, 1997; Rieff, 1994), Rwanda (Destexhe, 1994), or in more general terms (Reisman, 1990; Pastor, 1993; Plant, 1993). This mode of argument is an effective polemical device for staking out a position, but does not always lead to the clearest analysis, let alone to a clear discussion. In the intervention debate in the 1990s, there were not only disagreements but also arguments that were incommensurate with each other. The debate was marred because the participants often talked past each other (Hoffman, 1995; Smith, 1997a).

There are two particular problems in this attack on the lack of will. First, while a claim that the situation is characterised by uncertainty can be used as a rhetorical device to fend off the case for intervention, it is also true that situations often are characterised by uncertainty. Rieff (1995) strongly criticises the failure of the West and the United Nations to protect the ordinary people of Bosnia-Hercegovina from 1992 to 1995, yet he remarks that neither he nor his press colleagues at the time knew what it was that the West and the UN should do. That is an unintended concession that the situation in Bosnia-Hercegovina was genuinely uncertain. In consequence, moral clarity was not matched by prescriptive clarity. In such a situation, the response of critics should be to reduce the breadth of uncertainty by generating more knowledge. Trying to drown the uncertainty by turning up the moral volume is not a responsible strategy.

The second problem of focusing on a lack of will is that it may lead the critics astray. They could be right that the reason for decisive action not being undertaken has nothing to do with uncertainty. They could still be wrong in their focus on will: the real reason might be not a lack of will but a lack of willingness. Whereas a lack of will implies that the actor is not capable of carrying out a desired action, a lack of willingness means the actor does not desire to carry out the action. Sharp's (1997) study of British policy in Bosnia-Hercegovina indicates that British and French policy from 1992 to 1995 should not be assessed simply as a lack of will to protect Bosnia. In her analysis, given US reluctance to intervene with force until late summer 1995, the British and French governments actively pursued limited goals based on regional stability. They did not lack the will to do what the critics of their policies thought proper; rather, they disagreed with their critics. This disagreement could not usually be expressed openly because it was based on somewhat cynical, *realpolitik*-type considerations that were not likely to sell well to public opinion. In these circumstances, it was relatively easy for the critics to make convincing accusations that the governments lacked will. The critics' moral polemic could usually win the public argument, but could not persuade the British and French governments to change their policies. To the extent that a dialogue on policy is regarded as important -- especially before positions become entrenched in polar opposition -- it is worth the time it costs for advocates of this or that policy to understand the reasons why their proposals are not being adopted.

The case of Kosovo illustrates some of the dilemmas. Since the early 1990s, many commentators have warned of massive conflict escalation if no action were taken to meet both the needs of the Albanian majority and the fears of the Serb minority. In March 1998, Serbian police actions raised concern that massive escalation was imminent. Belatedly, the western press began to discuss a second Bosnia, high-powered diplomats visited Belgrade, and a specially convened meeting of the six-power

Bosnia Contact Group threatened renewed sanctions and other action against Yugoslavia. At the same time, there were conflicting press reports about whether NATO and the US were planning to deploy additional NATO forces on the Kosovo border and surrounding areas. So clear has the foreknowledge of escalation been that this could be a textbook case of the lack of will to act early and, when escalation happens as forewarned, a lack of will to act decisively. This argument, however, assumes that the Contact Group has a unified position on Kosovo and a clear view of what could be done, if only it had the will. In fact, the Contact Group did not have a unified position, because the Russian government disagreed with the Western reading of the rights and wrongs of the conflict. It did, however, agree with the West that the appropriate objective was greater autonomy for Kosovo within the existing Federal Republic of Yugoslavia. But this objective was not accepted in March 1998 by either the government of Yugoslavia or by the leaders of the Albanian opposition. There was moreover a striking lack of clarity about the means by which the objective could be achieved. Sanctions are an extremely dubious instrument, more likely to punish ordinary people than political leaders, and often encouraging patriotic support for the leaders and their policies. Threats to use armed force also raise serious problems. Some of these problems reside in international law, because state sovereignty is a central feature of the international legal and political system. In addition, there is the question of the US attitude. The US sent armed forces to Bosnia-Hercegovina only reluctantly, late in the day, on the basis of promises that the deployment would last only a year, and when the fighting had stopped. This approach to the use of force appeared to be backed by the US public whose dominant opinion seemed to be cautious and realist (Kohut and Toth, 1994). In short, the politics surrounding potential intervention in Kosovo were complex, both in the Federal Republic of Yugoslavia and among the states that might intervene. There was every reason for uncertainty, despite the fact that the leading Western powers were clear that they wished to prevent conflict escalation.

In this, Kosovo is not unique. Or, rather, the uniqueness of the situation in Kosovo does not lie in the fact that the politics of intervention are complex. Almost all situations into which intervention may be justified are similarly complex, each in its own way. Indeed, it is a prime characteristic of contemporary conflict that it is not neat. It tends to lack shape, to have no clear beginning and no clear end. Open declarations of war are rare, while cease-fire or peace agreements that do not work are common. Examples in the 1990s include Angola, Burundi, Cambodia, Chechnya, Colombia, Croatia, Ethiopia, Israel, Liberia, the Philippines, Sierra Leone, Somalia, and Sri Lanka. There are numerous reasons why wars continue after agreement has been reached to end them. Stedman (1997) considers the role of 'spoilers' in the peace process. There may not be enough commitment to the process, or a change of mind when the scale of risks and costs becomes apparent. Change in the balance of power within internally divided parties may be more important than changes in the balance between them. New parties may join the conflict (or existing groups become stronger) on the basis of rejecting the terms of peace and compromise. Whatever the specifics, the underlying problem in wars that return after peace is that the basic terms of the conflict are unresolved. When the issues and terms of division remain politically cogent, especially in the absence of a new set of rules for peaceful pursuit of goals, there is a permanent risk of renewed violence.

The implications of this for policy-makers considering intervention -- preventive or otherwise -- are profound, and potentially profoundly inhibiting. How are they to know what they are getting into if they authorise intervention, especially using armed force, but even if confining themselves to a combination of economic and diplomatic actions? Whatever instruments are used, intervention involves an investment of both finance and prestige. The time-line of intervention is also not clear. In *An Agenda for Peace,* Boutros-Ghali (1992) presented a sequenced conceptualisation of peace operations: *preventive diplomacy* (a term that has since been replaced by *preventive intervention* or *preventive action*), *peace-making* (including *peace enforcement*), *peacebuilding* and *peacekeeping*. These policy categories have structured many of the terms of debate since, but Nathan (1998) challenges their neatly sequential nature. The truth that is emphasised by considering the record of wars which return is that the process of conflict and peace is often cyclical rather than linear. Preventing escalation is not easy. It may not be successful and, if not, it is very likely that it will have to be tried again after a peace agreement. If preventive intervention fails, it will pave the way toward war-time intervention, which will commit the intervening powers to post-war intervention, which is itself an effort at preventing renewed escalation. For escalation prevention is as much to do with what happens after war as before it, and peacebuilding is a preventive as much as a post-war strategy.

As has been pointed out in the case of Bosnia-Hercegovina, perhaps most effectively by Gow (1997), decisive action is impossible without a clear objective. The difficulty is that the objective ought to encompass not just a short-term goal such as mitigating a humanitarian crisis. It must also look beyond the cease-fire and beyond emergency aid. Moore (1996) argues that the longer term objective of humanitarian intervention -- and, other things being equal, this should be as true of preventive as of war-time intervention -- should be achieving a social rehabilitation adequate to prevent a return to violence. This goal means a long-term commitment to sustaining social engineering. This is a task of enormous dimensions and of dubious viability. In such tasks, hubris beckons. Roberts (1994, p. 109) warns against the temptation of trying to do too much, arguing, 'There is sometimes a case for deciding not to tackle a problem, even if it is serious'. Stedman (1992, pp. 9-10) argues that most civil wars 'become amenable to settlement only after they have played themselves out with ferocity'. Ignoring this, he warns, means that 'humanitarian assistance may extend war and anarchy rather then end it'. It is not surprising that some observers conclude that in the case of ethnic conflict, it is impracticable to engineer peace. Taking this as his starting point, Kaufman (1996) argues that the objective of intervention should be the physical separation of warring communities, achieved by an enforced removal of populations. This also goes by the name of ethnic cleansing, a solution advocated for Bosnia-Hercegovina not only by ethno-nationalists, but also by outside observers who despair of peaceful reunification and refugee return in that divided country (Jenkins, 1997).

When European Union mediation in Yugoslavia began in June 1991, according to Little and Silber (1996, p. 159), the diplomats and politicians involved 'behaved as though the war had no underlying structural causes at all'. Typically, the task of mediating peace negotiations was treated as if it consisted of talking to the leaders in Yugoslavia and, in a much used phrase, 'banging their heads together' (Little and Silber, 1996, p. 159). This incoherent and ignorant analysis of the conflict causes was one reason why efforts at intervention and mediation got bogged down during the second half of 1991. It was the product of an institutionalised intellectual laziness among the powers that sought, by one means or another, to intervene in Balkan politics in the early 1990s. It stands as a reminder of the importance of knowledge and understanding as the basis for intervention. Improved knowledge and analysis cannot resolve all the problems of intervention; not least, fears of hubris may be well founded, and the international states system is still based on respect for state sovereignty. Not all the problems can be solved -- but perhaps some can.

The Limits of Theoretical Knowledge

It is easy to warn that there is a risk of violent conflict in any given country. To be on the safe side, and make sure that some predictions are borne out by events, one can put together a very long list of risk countries. But it is not very useful. Policy makers must decide how to deploy available resources. They cannot address all possible cases of conflict escalation, so they need to know which cases are probable and which ones to rule out. This raises a challenge of negative prediction -- to state which conflicts will not escalate in the near future. This is the toughest challenge for those who would make policy-relevant predictions of conflict escalation. Useful prediction is not the same as an across-the-board warning.

Armed conflict is a complex social and political process. It involves multiple decisions by multiple actors. Studying the history of a war's outbreak is usually complicated, with subtle choices about which factors to stress and what evidence to trust. Attempting to develop general causal explanations of armed conflict multiplies the challenges. For general theoretical explanation, a particular source of complexity is that of a large number of variables that may be relevant, few are relevant in any one case. There are two necessary conditions for war, and very many sufficient conditions (Welch, 1993, p. 8). War is possible if weapons are available and if there is a dispute between two or more parties. What makes war probable is subject to enormous variation.

The effort to sort out the processes by which wars come about has focused until recently on international conflict. Only in the 1990s has the global importance of internal or civil conflicts been widely recognised, even though civil or internal conflicts have been more common than international or inter-state conflicts at least since 1945 (Singer, 1996, p. 35). This reflects a narrow focus within the academic discipline of international relations, concentrating on relations between states, rather than exploring the international system as a whole (Goldstein, 1994, p. 1). It is true that, before the 1990s, scholars such as Gurr (1970),

Horowitz (1985) and Rapoport (1989) had attempted to take the study of armed conflict out of that narrow focus. But the volume of literature on the causes of international wars is much greater than the volume of literature on civil or internal conflicts. In it, Levy (1989) found, there is not much agreement, except on the finding that democratic states virtually never go to war with each other. This is 'as close as anything we have to an empirical law in international relations' (Levy, 1989, p. 270). Chan (1997) and Starr (1997), however, show that considerable theoretical work is still required in order to explain the democratic peace. Apart from this empirical finding, the results of much research are somewhat meagre. There is little that commands consensus. While it is widely accepted that war cannot be explained by a single cause, 'even this view is sometimes challenged' (Levy 1989, p. 210). The literature on causes of international armed conflict, then, does not give great grounds for optimism about finding reliable general explanations of internal armed conflict.

Social science theories of the causes of armed conflict are most likely to concentrate on background conditions and long-range causes in order to develop general explanatory power. For example, 'group entitlement' theory (Horowitz, 1985) pulls ethnic and economic factors together. 'Relative deprivation' theory (Gurr, 1970) incorporates economic and political forms of deprivation into a less specified social and anthropological background. Research on the democratic peace is considering whether democracies are as peaceable with others as among themselves. Rummel (1995) argues that they are, while Risse-Kappen (1995) represents the sceptical view. All these approaches raise questions about the relationship between political system, social harmony and economic prosperity. These elements are placed in a causal chain linking environmental pressure to conflict in the theoretical approach first developed by Homer-Dixon (1994).

Poor economic conditions for the majority of citizens appear to be the most important long-term causes of internal armed conflicts in the 1980s and the 1990s; degradation of renewable resources -- specifically soil erosion, deforestation and water scarcity -- are also significant (Hauge, 1997). There is also a strong association between armed conflict and extreme abuse of human rights in the form of extra-judicial executions, disappearances and active death squads (Smith, 1997a, pp. 18-19). Repression is not an alternative to war: they walk hand in hand. Auvinen (1997) also finds this combination of economic and political injustice underlying conflict for the 1980s. The statistical associations do not appear to be so clear in the case of ethnic difference. In a large proportion of conflicts in the 1990s, the opposing parties appear in part to be defined by ethnicity, but it is not the most ethnically diverse countries that are, as a group, the most war-prone (Smith, 1997b, p. 30).

An initial, broad-brush conclusion from this is that armed conflict is concentrated among the poorest and most repressive countries of the world and is often between parties that are, to differing degrees, defined by their ethnic identities. There are, however, many armed conflicts in countries that are not among the poorest and most repressive of the world. Likewise, there are countries that are extremely poor and repressed but do not have a war. In the same vein, in many of the most ethnically diverse countries, there is no violent conflict, and there are many wars between groups that are not divided by ethnicity, and many between groups that share important features of their ethnic identity with each other.

Methodological Openings

The conclusion above is not very extensive or ambitious. It does, however, have the useful effect of highlighting the importance of a research strategy that embraces the null case, the one(s) for which a starting hypothesis or generalisation does not work -- in our context, the cases in which armed conflict does not happen. The null case is especially important when considering how it could be possible to give a useful early warning of imminent conflict escalation. The ability to recognise cases where escalation is unlikely is dependent on an understanding of null cases. This is not because the null case carries more weight in itself; the fact that armed conflicts occur in countries that are not the poorest and most repressive countries does not make poverty and repression unimportant. But the null case does encourage us to look for other factors that may have to be present for poverty and repression to lead to conflict. It might be worth seeking the co-factors in other long-term conditions. History might be a relevant place to look, assessing the impact of colonialism, for example (Ajayi, 1997), or the effect of a war-torn past on the present. However, it is also necessary to look at more short-term issues. The summary case studies of contemporary conflicts by Brogan (1992) repeatedly illustrate the value of going into more detail than large number studies permit. An attempt to understand the evolution of individual conflicts must focus attention on politics and on the actions of specific organisations and individuals. Thus, as well as the social, cultural, economic and environmental background, we must also pay attention to the political foreground. Without that, an explanation of causes is far from complete.

Alongside long-term structural explanations, therefore, we also need Clausewitz (1976). The great Prussian military philosopher defined war as 'an act of force to compel our enemy to do our will' and 'the continuation of policy by other means'. Keegan (1994, pp. 3-12) shows that this is deficient as a definition of war because it ignores the way that culture shapes both why and how people go to war. To let Clausewitz dominate the exploration of causes would be a clear error, yet the background factors influence events in the direction of armed conflict only via politics. Wars are conscious and consciously decided affairs. Explanation of their causes must embrace the background alongside the foreground, both the structural causes and the factors that lie within the decision making power of political actors.

One way to meet the challenge of maintaining an analytical balance between the different types of factors involved in the onset of war is to opt for a methodology based on exactly that typology. Dessler (1994) offers a good opening in this direction. In the multiplicity of causes of armed conflicts, Dessler sees not just different causes but different types of causes. He presents a four part typology in which to organise them. In his terminology, *channels* are fundamental lines of 'political, social, economic, or national cleavage... found at the level of the group, rather than the individual'. These may be constituted by the exclusion of some groups from power, the systematic favouring of others, and regional economic differences. Channels are, in short, the basic elements of the social and political structure. To explore them is to illuminate the background causes and underlying conditions of conflict. Dessler's second category is the *targets*, or objectives of a political actor: 'The target is what the conflict is about'. Researching targets means looking at the causes for which people fight. This also means looking at the short-term means by which the causes are pursued as well as how they are depicted. In other words, it is political behaviour in general that we look at under this heading. If channels are background causes, Dessler's third category, *triggers*, consists of the factors that affect the timing; referring to them explains not why a conflict started but why it started *then*. They are often events or actions by significant actors, which narrow the choice of the players, making peaceful approaches less attractive and violent options more. Lastly, *catalysts* are factors that affect the intensity and duration of the conflict; they may be internal, such as the military balance between the opposing sides, or external, such as UN intervention. They may be within the control of either party, such as their tactics (whether they avoid attacking civilian areas, for example), or outside their control, such as terrain and, in some conflicts, the cycle of seasons and the weather. This typology switches the focus from background conditions to actors and back again. It does not provide a theory of causation but a way of organising theory.

Preventing conflict escalation in the short-term means preventing the action of the third of Dessler's category of causes -- the triggers. Short-term crisis response is the most obvious way to do this -- convening high-powered international meetings, appointing special representatives and envoys, offering balanced incentives and sanctions for cooperative and uncooperative behaviour respectively. This activity is complex and demanding. It is most likely to be successful when it is well prepared. But the triggers of armed conflict are, almost by definition, hard to predict, often seemingly random factors that can have their effect very fast. The classic example, of course, is the assassination in Sarajevo that triggered World War I. Thus, diplomatic action to block the triggers has to be based on an understanding of the longer-term factors. This is the importance for escalation prevention theories explaining the causes of armed conflict through background factors, such as those scholars referred to above (Gurr, 1970; Horowitz, 1985; Rapoport, 1989; Homer-Dixon, 1994; Risse-Kappen, 1995; Rummel, 1995; Auvinen, 1997; Hauge, 1997). However, it is also clear from this discussion that this theoretical work focuses on one type of cause, one aspect of causation. To use Dessler's terminology, it addresses the channels. Important as it is, it is inherently incomplete. It has to be complemented by an approach that sheds some light on the targets -- on the objectives and behaviour of the major political actors.

Political Mobilisation

It is convenient to explore this by reference to those numerous armed conflicts that are discussed in both scholarly literature and more popular commentaries on ethnic conflicts. It is usual to understand this term as meaning not only that the parties involved are ethnically different, but also that their ethnic differentiation is no coincidence. In general, referring to an ethnic conflict implies not only a description of at least one of the parties, but an ascription of at least one cause (if not *the* cause) of conflict as ethnic difference. In Dessler's (1994) terminology, this approach sees ethnic difference as a channel, a basic underlying condition of violent conflict. More often than not, the term 'ancient' will crop up somewhere, as in former US Secretary of State Warren Christopher's argument that war in Bosnia-Hercegovina was caused by 'ancient ethnic hatreds' (Calhoun, 1997, p. 61). In the Balkans in the 1990s, the diplomats and politicians of the external powers first erred by seeing the violence of Yugoslavia's break-up as easily amenable to treatment by stern diplomacy -- just a matter of banging a few heads together (Little and Silber, 1996, p. 159). When that failed, they erred in a different direction by depicting the problem as a product of the hot-blooded nature of the Balkan people (International Commission on the Balkans, 1996, pp. 13-14). It is implicit in such arguments (though not always in the use of the term 'ethnic conflict') that not much can be done to resolve such conflicts or help such people.

Some of the problems in this way of depicting the causes of conflicts can be best understood through the abstract categories of Dessler's typology. Seen through that optic, it is evident that the 'ancient hatreds' explanation of wars in the Balkans makes three errors: it understands ethnicity exclusively as a channel; it understands it to be the only channel; it does not consider any other type of cause.

The error is not in regarding ethnic difference as one of the underlying social divisions -- i.e., as a channel. That is realistic. But the question is how that channel functions -- how it feeds the conditions of war. It is clear from case study after case study that ethnic difference is often embroiled in conflict, and that people in those conflicts often believe that the fundamental issue over which they are fighting is ethnic difference. That perception is important, but by no means enough. The fact that the most ethnically diverse countries in the world are not the most prone to violent conflict should give us enough of a hint that it is inadequate to look at ethnicity alone. The results of quantitative research cited above indicate the importance of economic conditions and political system in determining propensity for violent conflict. The crucial change of focus that is required in order to move away from the 'ancient hatreds' explanation, however, is to shift the weight of explanation from channels to targets -- from the underlying social conditions to the objectives and behaviour of the main political actors. In particular, it is worth focusing on political mobilisation. Findings from quantitative research direct our attention toward the double injustice of harsh economic conditions and the denial of political rights (Auvinen, 1997; Hauge, 1997). Translated into the language of political mobilisation, the issue is not just injustice but an exploitable perception of injustice -- a sense of relative deprivation in Gurr's (1970) terms, or of a group's entitlement to certain benefits in Horowitz's (1985).

In explaining the break-up of former Yugoslavia, and more specifically explaining why it was accomplished amid such violence, it is important not simply that Yugoslavia was a multi-ethnic state, but that there was a more than 100 year history of ethno-nationalism. In the Socialist Federal Republic of Yugoslavia, constitutional and political power was distributed on an ethno-national basis. This shaped the organs of both state and party. Thus, when in 1987, nationalism started to be the strongest political currency in then Yugoslavia, it did not come out of thin air, nor out of hot blood. It came straight out of the political system. Its renewed salience began in Serbia and the first response from another republic came from Slovenia. As soon as nationalist rivalries started to be expressed between the leaderships of the different republics, there was a momentum toward break-up, because of the system of rotating presidency. When the founder of SFR Yugoslavia, Tito, died in 1980, the mechanism that had been created for choosing the Federal president was a simple system of rotation between the six republics and two provinces. Thus, even before nationalist rivalries between republics, effective political power was draining out of the Federal State apparatus and into the republic apparatuses.

Nationalist politics had never completely died out in Tito's Yugoslavia. But the first time the nationalist card was played by a post-Tito communist leader was in 1987 by Slobodan Milosevic. It was part of a strategy for gaining control of the Serbian party (Little and Silber, 1996). Because ethnic difference is often central in group identity and common prejudice, it is easy material for mobilisation by political leaders. The conflict that led to Yugoslavia's break-up began as rivalry over the distribution of power within a political elite. It became explosive because major political players found that the best way to pursue their objectives was by appealing to national identity and pride and to a sense of injustice. The fear that Serbs were being discriminated against in the southern province of Kosovo was a real one, even for Serbs who never visited the region and had no interest in it because of its economic backwardness. Political mobilisation was accomplished by appealing to that fear and the perception of injustice. Similarly, when a nationalist response came in Slovenia and later in other republics, it was a political strategy that was effective in part because of a genuine fear of Serb domination, as well as a belief that the road to prosperity lay through secession.

Though there were and are many genuine Serb and Slovene nationalists, neither the Serb leader Slobodan Milosevic nor the Slovene leader Milan Kucan had any nationalist record before 1987 (Little and Silber, 1996). They were successful party men from the late Tito era, who equally successfully put on the clothes of nationalism, and thus extended their hold on power. This does not mean that all nationalist leaders are non-nationalists at heart. In the Balkans, such an inference would be quite inaccurate in the cases of Croatian President Franjo Tudjman and Bosnian President Alia Izetbegovic. Both can be regarded as principled nationalists. Yet in explaining why nationalism suddenly grew in appeal and strength in Croatia in the autumn of 1989, having been silent since 1972, and why politics in Bosnia-Hercegovina divided along ethnic lines in 1990, the same concepts of power politics are relevant as those that help explain the earlier recrudescence of nationalism in Serbia and Slovenia (Little and Silber, 1996).

The contention for power between new and old political elites is a significant part of the explanation of the build-up to the war between Chechnya and Russia in 1994-96. It is crucial in the seizure of power in Chechnya by General Dzhokhar Dudayev and his allies in August and September 1991 (Tishkov, 1997, pp. 200-206). The leaders of both Chechnya and Russia seemed unable to avoid escalating their disputes into full-scale war during the second half of 1994. This was also in part the product of rivals manoeuvring for power in both Chechnya (Tishkov, 1997, pp. 216-18) and Moscow (Shapiro, 1995).

What are called ethnic conflicts, then, are conflicts over power or for access to economic resources (including environmental resources in other cases not explored in this essay), which come to wear an ethnic mask. Ethnic difference is of central importance not as a sole cause (or explanation) of armed conflict, but rather as an instrument of mobilisation for political leaders. Using the metaphor of ethnic mask is by no means intended to downplay the reality of a sense of identity, in or out of violent conflict. Rather, it is intended to focus attention on the strategies of political mobilisation that are a critical element of conflict escalation. The problem and the tragedy of ethnic mobilisation is that, once the ethnic mask has been donned, it can be very difficult to remove. When a revived sense of group identity coheres around resentment and grievance, especially in time of crisis and war, it can lead to apparently irreconcilable hatred in protracted and often cyclical conflicts. The prime contemporary example is in the Hutu-Tutsi rivalries of Burundi and Rwanda. These do not date from time immemorial; there is no sign that they pre-date the work of the colonial administrators who defined the groups as different and proceeded to favour one at the expense of the other. It was in this that the resentment grew. From the moment of independence, political leaders systematically exploited that group grievance in order to maintain (or challenge) power, producing forty years of wars and massacres (Copson, 1994). Singhalese-Tamil conflict in Sri Lanka unfolded in a similar way in the years after independence, leading to prolonged civil war (Uyangoda, 1996). Here, in Dessler's (1994) terminology, we come to the category of catalysts -- the factors that affect the intensity and duration of the war. In many armed conflicts today, both the tactics and strategy of one party or both involve direct attack on civilians -- ethnic cleansing, massacre and systematic rape in Bosnia-Hercegovina and Rwanda, bombing civilian areas in Chechnya. The memory of these horrors perpetuates a bitter sense of group identity.

Conclusion

We begin with the problem of making knowledge useful. To know how to prevent war, or to bring it to an end as soon as possible if it breaks out, and then to prevent it from returning after a hiatus, we must know why and how it occurs. The theoretical study of the causes of armed conflict is therefore closely linked to the practicalities of mitigating violence. Using a four-part typology of causes, this essay has focused on two categories of channels and targets -- the underlying social conditions and the behaviour of key political actors. The reason for focusing there rather than on the triggers of escalation -- the immediate events that precipitate large scale violence -- is to identify factors that come early enough in the path to violence for preventive action to be feasible. The action of triggers is often too sudden. Two key words emerge from this exploration of the problem: injustice and mobilisation. Some social conditions give rise to a perception of injustice -- economic deprivation, political repression, a sense of group grievance. That perception can be exploited and large numbers of ordinary people mobilised by shrewd political leaders. As practical policies of preventing conflict escalation become more feasible, it will be because we are developing a fuller understanding of the combination of social conditions and political action encompassed by those two key concepts.

Warning of conflict escalation needs to be early enough that preventive action can be taken, specific enough that resource choices can be made, and reliable enough that political leaders will give it credence. It is, of course, possible, that even with such warning, action will not be taken until it is too late to prevent tragedy, if at all. To the extent that preventing escalation is discussed in the context of intervention by outside powers, there could be many grounds for hesitation and reluctance. There could be reluctance to undertake an open-ended commitment that will lead to major investment in social engineering. There could be reluctance to intrude into other states' sovereignty. Or there could be the widely diagnosed deficiency of will power. Improved theoretical understanding of the causes and dynamics of conflict escalation cannot, therefore, make it inevitable that successful preventive action will be undertaken.

It is not very likely that will power can be generated by scholarly knowledge. But it is distinctly possible that improved knowledge of escalation dynamics will help encourage states to overcome some of the inhibitions of sovereignty. In the 1990s, the sovereignty objection has been selectively set aside when disaster has already arrived and the state has stopped 'fulfilling the basic responsibilities and functions that go along with sovereignty' (Nicolaïdis, 1996, p. 24). There are several necessary conditions to be met if the sovereignty barrier to preventive intervention is to be overcome (Semb, 1992). Perhaps the most important is to ensure that setting aside sovereignty in the name of preventing conflict escalation does not become a cover for setting aside sovereignty to prevent a small state following policies a big state does not like (Chopra and Weiss, 1992). In each case in which arguments are made for preventive intervention despite sovereignty, preventive policies are more likely to be endorsed if it is possible to rely on predictions of large scale humanitarian crises. The research that makes that possible is also the basis for understanding both the extent and limits of a proposed intervention, so that if there is reluctance to accept over-long and over-heavy commitments, the discussion can at least be conducted on the basis of analytical understanding.

Given the depth and breadth of uncertainty at present about conflict escalation and prevention, it would be remarkably premature at best and hopelessly complacent at worst to claim that all the problems of knowledge had been solved and the research community could now offer reliable predictions. Certainly, the claim that there is no problem of knowledge and no reason for political decision makers to be uncertain about conflict prevention is not warranted by the scholarly literature on conflict causes. Basic research, therefore, has a significant role in reducing the terrain of uncertainty.

Note

[1] The author is grateful for the Ford Foundation's support for research at the International Institute for Peace Research (PRIO), on which this chapter is based.

9 Self-Determination and Minority Rights

JENNIFER JACKSON PREECE

> If every ethnic, religious or linguistic group claimed statehood, there would be no limit to fragmentation, and peace, security and economic well-being would become ever more difficult to achieve... The sovereignty, territorial integrity and independence of States within the established international system, and the principle of self-determination of people's, both of great value and importance, must not be permitted to work against each other in the period ahead....[S]olutions to these problems should enhance the situation of minorities as well as the stability of States.
>
> Boutros Boutros-Ghali,
> *An Agenda for Peace*

Introduction

This essay addresses the following question: why should ethnonational minorities be a subject of international relations when this field is concerned, in the main, with states and not groups or individuals within a state's domestic jurisdiction? If international actors demonstrated no concern for such groups, then ethnonational minorities certainly would not be an appropriate subject for international politics though it would still be suitable for domestic governance or constitutional law or political sociology among others. However, international interest in ethnonational minorities does exist: international organisations both today and in the past have been concerned with such groups.

The reason for such interest is that in the contemporary practice of self-determination, there is often little, if any, fit between international boundaries and ethnonational identities. International minority rights guarantees are an attempt to limit the potentially destabilising self-determination claims of those ethnonational groups who exist as minorities within states. Such minority rights practices thus disclose a prior consideration for the territorial status quo: the principle of self-determination is set in the context of respect for existing territorial boundaries.

Since the end of World War I, the nation state has emerged as the uncontested normative grounding for political independence. The international system is justified by the doctrine of self-determination, which asserts that every nation has a right to independent political control over a given territory and its people. Yet despite this avowed doctrine, ethnonational minorities do not possess political independence and thus are living proof that the practice of state sovereignty and the actual borders of states often do not conform to the principle that legitimates them. Moreover, this political independence is not easily obtainable -- and in many instances will never be achieved -- because of inherent difficulties in the territorial redistribution that it requires.

As a result, the political aspirations of many minorities will not only remain unfulfilled but -- as the history of the 20th century illustrates -- may become serious sources of international instability and even conflict. Given an international system that is normatively based upon a nation state ethos, the problems of ethnonational minorities cannot be easily ignored by international actors since they are potential threats to international peace and stability. Some kind of international policy on this question is thus required by international organisations -- be it stipulations guaranteeing territorial integrity as in the OAU Charter or ethnonational minority rights as in Organisation for Security and Cooperation (OSCE) documents. International relations scholars should therefore examine these problems and policies.

In the discussion that follows, European developments feature prominently. That is because following the end of the Cold War, the interwar practice of internationally guaranteed minority rights has been resurrected by the OSCE and Council of Europe (COE). The settlement of 1919 made minority rights a prerequisite for international recognition of new or enlarged states in Central and Eastern Europe and placed these provisions under international guarantee by the League of Nations. Significantly, the League Minority Rights System did not apply outside Europe -- with the exception of Iraq, which was required to make minority guarantees regarding its Kurdish population as a condition of admission into the League of Nations. Significantly, both the interwar and post-Cold War experience with international minority rights guarantees fundamentally distinguishes Europe from other regions in the world.

Although ethnonational diversity within states is a global experience, the practice of internationally guaranteed minority rights is not. The international world outside Europe, apart from North America and Latin America, is a post-1945 world, and its norms and institutions are a creature of the post-war settlement and decolonisation, neither of which institutionalised international minority rights provisions. Existing boundaries were sacrosanct in the 1945 settlement such that self-determination after 1945 concerned only pre-existing juridical entities (colonies, federal units, etc.), and individual human rights guarantees did not recognise ethnonational groups.

After decolonisation, the Latin American practice of *uti possiditis juris* or territorial inviolability was taken up by the new states of Africa and Asia because they have a similar problem; given their ethnographic complexity, there is the real fear that existing states formed out of prior colonial units may fall apart along ethnonational lines. For example, most African states are composed of a variety of ethnic groups, many of which straddle boundaries with neighbouring states. There are consequently sociological pressures for territorial revisionism in many parts of the continent, and thus African states have found it politically expedient to avoid all consideration of sub-state ethnonational groups and their rights. Territorial integrity is accorded priority in the OAU Charter, Article 3 which stipulates 'respect for the sovereignty and territorial integrity of each state'.

In Asia, too, the inherited colonial borders have generally been respected. Moreover, when the colonial borders occasionally have been challenged successfully on ethnonationalist grounds, this has usually led to partition rather than ethnonational minority rights guarantees -- India/Pakistan being the classic example. Thus, minority rights have been, by and large, excluded as a subject of international relations by the post-1945 settlement in most parts of the world.

Nations, States and Self-Determination

Self-determination is a highly indeterminate concept in the international system. The nation itself has been variously interpreted in accordance with both civic and ethnic criteria.[1] For example, West European nation states are supposedly based on civic identities whereas Central and East European states allegedly rest upon ethnic identities. This difference, it is often conjectured, accounts for the political stability of Western Europe as opposed to the instability and unrest of Central and Eastern Europe. More importantly, these contradictory interpretations of which social groups constitute a nation ultimately rendered the idea of national self-determination equally ambivalent: should self-determination be understood as the right of ethnic nations? Or should self-determination be understood as the right of political nations defined by pre-existing juridical units? There is no straightforward answer to this question; evidence can be found to support either interpretation (Jackson Preece, 1997, pp. 75-92).

In 1919, distinct linguistic and cultural characteristics were widely accepted as proof of nationhood. If the peoples inhabiting a particular territory had a unique language and culture, then they could legitimately claim a right to national self-determination. For example, Thomas Masaryk, the founding President of Czechoslovakia, argued that Czech and Slovak were simply two dialects of the same language and therefore the Czech and Slovak peoples were one ethnic nation and should be incorporated in one political unit -- i.e., Czechoslovakia. Linguistic arguments of this kind were also made in favour of a common South Slav kingdom consisting of Serbs, Croats and Slovenes, among others.

Similarly, if an ethnic nation was unable to form its own independent political unit and instead was forced to exist as a minority within another state, then this minority was entitled to preserve its own distinct ethnonational identity as reflected in its language and culture. This philosophy gave rise to the League of Nations System of Minority Guarantees, which sought to protect the rights of minorities through a combination of collective decision making and the moral approbation of international public opinion.

In practice, however, this consensual conflict-resolution formula for the preservation of minority rights broke down not least because the international goodwill it relied upon was not forthcoming. Consequently, continued demands for ethnonational self-determination on the part of minorities became a source of international rivalry and discontent within the interwar state system. These principles were ultimately used by the Third Reich to justify the dismemberment of Czechoslovakia in 1938, the transfer of Southern Slovakia and half of Transylvania to Hungary in 1940, and the creation of fascist Slovak and Croat puppet states.

After 1945, the United Nations was reluctant to adopt the interwar rhetoric of national self-determination and its concomitant language of minority rights. Inis Claude contends that the UN Charter was formulated 'without consideration of the questions of principle' which arise from the existence of ethnonational minorities in a 'world dominated by the concept of the national state as the... unit of political organisation' (Claude, 1955, p. 113). More than this, however, there was a deliberate move to discredit the idea of self-determination understood in ethnonational terms. This was, in large measure, a reaction against the failure of the League experiment and, indeed, the weakness of the 1919 system of nation states and national self-determination that underscored it. Understandably in the aftermath of World War II, national self-determination -- and the secession and irredentism it could provoke -- were viewed as serious would-be threats to the new international order. The prospect of widespread decolonisation and creation of new, and potentially weak, states in Asia and Africa only heightened such fears.

As a result, the UN Charter incorporated the vague phrase 'self-determination of peoples' as distinct from the more familiar and discredited 'national self-determination' in the hope of avoiding that sort of ethnonational minority controversy which had plagued the League of Nations system. Articles 73 and 76 further define such 'peoples' in terms of the pre-existing colonial territory and not according to ethnonational criteria. The motivation behind this 1945 adoption of political as opposed to ethnic criteria in assessing claims to self-determination was clearly a desire to preserve the colonial territorial status quo and in so doing international peace and stability.

This overarching post-1945 concern was specifically expressed and affirmed in the 1960 UN Declaration on Granting Independence to Colonial Territories and Countries which clearly states that 'any attempt aimed at the partial or total disruption of the national unity or territorial integrity of a country is incompatible with the purposes and principles of the United Nations Charter'. For similar reasons, the UN Charter (1945) made no specific mention of ethnonational minorities but instead endorsed the principle of universal human rights. There was also the implicit connection made within the Charter, and specifically elaborated in later UN documents, that its approach to the problem was a general one: it sought to protect individuals belonging to ethnonational minorities against discrimination, rather than to ensure satisfaction of the separate interests of minorities, which conceivably might become pretexts for secession or irredentism.

This view was reinforced as increasing numbers of new states in Asia and Africa became members of the United Nations. Once these Asian and African states had acquired independence, they were very reluctant to address any questions of ethnonational minority rights or national self-determination that remained because that would put in doubt the territorial integrity of the new states (Mayall, 1990, chs. 7, 8). Third World states have generally and prudently viewed the problem of self-determination as primarily directed against colonial powers and the avoidance of rule by European minorities. Once colonial rule has been overcome and the non-white majority has gained power, questions of self-determination are no longer considered to apply. Thus it is argued that any non-white minorities which may remain in postcolonial states can not legitimately claim ethnonational minority rights. The ex-colonial territory and its borders are sacrosanct.

The only United Nations human rights instrument adopted between 1945 and 1989 which even incorporated a specific minorities clause is the 1966 International Covenant on Civil and Political Rights (ICCPR). Article 27 stipulates that 'in those states in which ethnic, religious or linguistic minorities exist, persons belonging to such... minorities in community with other members of their group shall not be denied the right to enjoy their own culture, to profess and practice their own religion, or to use their own language'. This provision, however, gives state signatories the freedom to determine whether or not ethnic groups in their jurisdictions constitute minorities. Needless to say, many states that possessed ethnonational minorities effectively avoided their international obligations in this regard by redefining these groups under a different rubric, be it 'immigrant', 'aboriginal' or whatever. Meanwhile, the UN Sub-commission on the Prevention of Discrimination and Protection of Minorities, the only UN body specifically charged with examining minority questions, tended to ignore the second part of its mandate (protection of minorities) in favour of the first (prevention of discrimination), presumably because it was more conducive to the territorial integrity of existing states.

Moments of State Creation

Membership in the existing club of nation states is only revised at moments of far-reaching international change wherein it is practically and normatively possible to challenge and overcome the previous territorial status quo. As already intimated, the membership of nations in the international club of states was redefined on three occasions in the 20th century: after the First World War, after the Second World War, and after the Cold War. On each of these occasions, new states were formed out of defeated, discredited or disintegrated multinational empires whose lands were comparatively easy to parcel out to new or reborn states because existing borders failed to satisfy the normative criterion of self-determination.

Even under these circumstances, a prior concern for international order as reflected in the territorial integrity of existing states meant that such claims for independence were only successful in a limited range of cases: highest level constituent units of empires or federal states which were dissolved in keeping with the principle of *uti posseditis juris* or respect for frontiers existing at the moment of independence; territories where self-determination was applied by plebiscite; mandated or trust territories; and formerly independent territories that reasserted their independence with at least the tacit consent of the state affected (Kingsbury, 1992, p. 487).

From 1919 to 1920, new states were created in Central and Eastern Europe out of the defeated Austro-Hungarian Empire, Ottoman Empire, and Prussian Kingdom. There emerged a dozen new or enlarged states all of which claimed legitimacy on grounds of ethnonational identity, often as determined by plebiscite: Poland, Czechoslovakia, Austria, Hungary, Yugoslavia, Romania, Bulgaria, and Albania. Added to these were Finland and the Baltic States, which emerged out of the disintegrating Russian Empire: Estonia, Latvia, and Lithuania. Significantly, however, the principle of national self-determination was, in practice, confined to Europe. Although the victorious Entente Powers (particularly Britain and France) were grudgingly prepared to accept the notion that European peoples had a right to self-determination -- though here, too, a certain hesitation was evident as in Britain's unwillingness to grant full self-determination to the Irish -- they were unwilling to extend this right to their colonial subjects and territories.

It was not until after the Second World War that new, often multi-ethnic states were created out of the European colonies in Asia and Africa, the majority of which followed pre-existing colonial frontiers. The post-1945 determination to preclude secession and irredentism was by and large successful. Some successor states did manage to expand their post-independence borders beyond the pre-existing colonial frontiers -- e.g., India annexed Goa (which was still a colony at the time); Indonesia annexed West Irian and East Timor (the latter, of course, is not widely recognised); and China annexed Tibet (which had an historic dependent relationship with China). But most irredentist claims -- e.g., Spain to Gibraltar, the Philippines to Sabah, Morocco to Mauritania, the Republic of Ireland to Ulster, the Argentine to the Falklands, and Taiwan to the Chinese Mainland -- remained unsuccessful (Mayall, 1998, pp. 9-10). Similarly, of the three major Cold War secessionist crises -- those involving Katanga, Biafra, and Bangladesh -- only the latter succeeded. By and large, the territorial status quo held and this territorial stability is, of course, a major feature of the Cold War period.

The international legitimisation of pre-existing territorial units remained a fundamental practice of the international system after the Cold War. In keeping with long established practice dating back to the League of Nations and the 1878 Berlin Congress convened to resolve Serbian, Montenegrin, Romanian and Bulgarian demands for independence from the Ottoman Empire, the various bodies charged with determining the criteria for international recognition of new states in Central and Eastern Europe and the former Soviet Union again acknowledged minority provisions as essential prerequisites with the aim of controlling the rate and extent of state disintegration.

In December 1991, the European Union (EU) Council of Ministers established general guidelines concerning the recognition of new states in the former communist block. The policy established that new states would only be recognised if they were democratic and had committed themselves to proceed toward independence peacefully and by negotiation in good faith. New states would be required to respect the provisions of the United Nations Charter, the Helsinki Final Act and the OSCE Charter of Paris for a New Europe, particularly those concerning the rule of law, democracy and human rights. In addition, they were expected to guarantee the rights of ethnic and national groups and minorities in accordance with developing OSCE commitments (Kingsbury, 1992, p. 487). These guidelines also called upon the

Conference on Yugoslavia, with the advice of the Badinter Arbitration Commission (both created by the Europe Union in August 1991 in the hope of ensuring a peaceful and orderly transition in former Yugoslavia), to consider specific requests for recognition from Yugoslav Republics. This commission further identified the guarantee of minority rights as a fundamental requirement that would have to be satisfied before recognition could take place.

Just as with decolonisation in Latin America, Asia and Africa, pre-existing internal boundaries were inherited without regard to ethnonational demographics. Thus previously recognised autonomous areas within Yugoslav federal republics (for example, Albanian majority Kosovo or Hungarian majority Vojvodina in Serbia) were not entitled to independence and nor were other regions within the successor states in which a rival ethnic group predominated -- as in the Serbian enclave of Krajina within Croatia. Such an interpretation was directly aimed at preventing further fragmentation and the additional political instability that would unleash. Territorial integrity determined which claims to independence would take priority, and therefore order trumped ethnonational self-determination except where the states involved so agreed. Thus while multinational states in Central and Eastern Europe (Czechoslovakia, Yugoslavia and the Soviet Union) were replaced by new, ostensibly ethnic nation states, their boundaries followed those of the pre-existing federal units. Slovakia and the Czech Republic replaced Czechoslovakia; Slovenia, Croatia, Bosnia, Macedonia, and a rump Yugoslavia consisting of Serbia-Montenegro replaced former Yugoslavia; and Estonia, Latvia, Lithuania, Belarus, Moldova, Ukraine, the Russian Republic, Georgia, Azerbaijan, Armenia, Kazakhstan, Uzbekistan, Turkmenistan, Tadzikistan, and Kyrgyzstan replaced the USSR.[2] Yet, regardless of how borders are drawn, in most cases, there will remain 'entrapped' ethnonational minorities -- hence the problem.

Such redistributions of sovereign statehood often awaken the political aspirations of ethnonational minorities whose desire for their own ethnic nation state is as yet unfulfilled. And when it is not forthcoming, those minorities inevitably feel themselves victims of that international order which does not (and cannot) give every nation self-determination defined in ethnic terms. For example, the redistribution of sovereignty to ethnonational minorities in multinational Czechoslovakia, Yugoslavia and the Soviet Union which immediately followed the end of the Cold War, by no means, removed the problem of ethnonational minorities in Central and Eastern Europe. There remain many Central and East European states whose jurisdiction encompasses regionally concentrated ethnonational minorities that might come to demand their own, independent political units. Romania, Bulgaria, Hungary, Slovakia, Serbia and the Ukraine are but a few examples. Consequently, ethnonational minority demands that continue to be ignored or unanswered still constitute potential threats to international peace and stability in post-Cold War Europe.

These frustrated national ambitions are not without international significance since they can and in fact have historically become the impetus for ethnonational minorities to engage in internationally disruptive behaviour, for example, secessionist movements such as that attempted by Krajina Serbs in Croatia during the early 1990s; irredentist movements such as Armenia's claim to Nagorno-Karabakh in neighbouring Azerbaijan; wars of national liberation such as General Dudaev's attempt to wrest Chechnya free of political control from Moscow in 1994/95; acts of international terrorism such as the highly publicised bombings carried out by the Irish Republican Army (IRA) in the United Kingdom; the Kosovo Liberation Army (KLA) in Serbia or the Kurdistan Workers' Party (PKK) in Turkey, among other actions, all in order to achieve the ultimate goal of independent statehood. Such actions may disrupt international peace and stability (and are often committed with this goal in mind so as to encourage the redistribution of statehood in a given nation's favour) either directly or by their potential to draw in neighbouring states or to create mass refugee flows across borders or to inspire similar movements of national liberation elsewhere.

International Responses to the Problem of Minorities

Historically, the existence of minorities in an international system that purports to be based upon a norm of self-determination has evoked three international responses: (1) an individual human rights regime, (2) the physical elimination of ethnonational minorities either by adjusting peoples to match borders or borders to match peoples, or (3) a regime of ethnonational minority rights that falls short of sovereign statehood.

Firstly, the problem of ethnonational minorities can be addressed by redefining it in terms of individual discrimination and equality, thereby provoking international requirements for existing states to remove any legal or political barriers of individual membership in a minority by guaranteeing equality of civil and political rights to all its citizens regardless of their ethnonational identity. Such international stipulations would be compatible with domestic programmes aimed at assimilating individual members of minorities into the dominant cultural group within existing states, thereby removing any future threat of demands for special treatment within the state or secession from it. This particular course of action was supported by the United States and other major powers after the Second World War both because of the failure of the League minority system to prevent interwar ethnic conflict in the new states of Central and Eastern Europe, and the prospect of decolonisation in Asia and Africa where ethnonational diversity was even greater and thus potentially even more destabilising. Consequently, the new international order established after 1945 included a regime of universal individual human rights but not one of minority rights.

Secondly, ethnonational minorities can be physically eliminated by removing peoples to fit existing state boundaries or by adjusting boundaries to fit existing ethnonational demographics. Minorities can be physically transferred to another state in which their ethnonational group already forms the majority. Such potentially large movements of people raise a number of moral and practical problems not least of which is the issue of force. If each and every person in question were desirous of such a transfer, the procedure would not be overly contentious. However, it is reasonable to assume that in every such community at least some individuals, and perhaps many, will not consent freely to such a transfer. Should such individuals be forced to leave against their will? What of the economic and social costs such a mass migration would create for the country that received this large group of people? Indeed, given the costs associated with absorbing large numbers of migrants, a potential recipient state might, in fact, refuse to accept some or all of the people concerned. What then? Moreover, what is to be done about those minorities that have no state in which their ethnonational group already forms the majority? Transferring such minorities will shift but never remove problems arising from their existence. More practically, even assuming every minority could and was willing to be transferred, who would oversee not only the movement of peoples but the disposition of their property? How should homes, businesses and other nonmoveable goods be compensated? These are only a few of the difficult questions that population transfer can provoke.

The process of removing peoples can take one of two forms -- though certainly one and possibly both are morally suspect. Population transfers sanctioned by international agreement have occurred on several occasions during the 20th century. For example, minority exchanges between Greece and Turkey and, to a lesser extent, also between Greece and Bulgaria following the First World War were provided for in the Treaty of Lausanne and the Treaty of Neuilly. Similarly, the transfer of ethnic Germans back to Germany from across Central and Eastern Europe after World War II was authorised by the Potsdam Protocol.[3] But -- far from providing reassuring evidence that population transfers are a practical and legitimate response to the problem of ethnonational minorities -- these historic examples are usually subjects of international controversy because of the human suffering they entailed.

Even more controversially, minorities may be forcibly dispersed from their homelands without international sanction and with no attempt at fair procedure or compensation for lost properties. 'Ethnic cleansing' has become a term of abuse comparable to 'genocide'. Such methods were applied in Bosnia during 1992/93 and met with widespread international condemnation. This was not the first time forced population transfers had been imposed on the peoples of Central and Eastern Europe. Both Hitler and Stalin had also forcibly moved peoples en masse during the Second World War. Indeed, the transfer of German minorities back to Germany after 1945 was, in part, a retaliation for Hitler's race resettlement policies in Central and Eastern Europe. Worse still, the ethnonational minority in question can be methodically annihilated as Nazi Germans attempted to exterminate European Jewry in the name of Hitler's so-called 'Final Solution'. The United Nations and other international organisations prohibit ethnic cleansing and genocide as crimes against humanity. Sadly, such normative considerations are often not enough to prevent their use by domestic forces. Nor are they sufficient to guarantee international action in all cases. Thus in 1994 the UN Security Council refused to invoke the Genocide Convention with regard to Rwanda and reduced the size of the UN peacekeeping force at exactly the moment when according to the UN Commander on the ground, a stronger force might have been able to limit the killings (Mayall, 1998, pp. 9-10).

Instead of removing peoples, the problem of ethnonational minorities could -- again at least in theory -- also be resolved by adjusting borders to match existing ethnonational demographics. The victorious great powers of 1919 attempted to put this ideal into practice. Yet such an endeavour assumes there is some optimal division of territory that will succeed in giving every ethnic nation its own homogeneous state. As the so-called Committee on New States charged with the task of fixing the post-1919 boundaries of Central and Eastern Europe was quick to discover, it was virtually impossible to create homogeneous ethnic states in the region. Ultimately, any solution to the problem of ethnonational minorities that attempts to secure a perfect fit between ethnonational groups and boundaries (population transfers, ethnic cleansing, genocide or border revision) is, in reality, no solution at all because it fails to recognise that ethnonational self-determination (i.e., every ethnic nation in its own homogeneous state) is, in practice, unobtainable given that many if not most ethnic groups are inextricably intermingled in the same territory.

Finally, the problem of ethnonational minorities may be recognised for what it is: a condition of 'collectives' who may reasonably claim to possess that indeterminate trait which is the current normative underpinning of states, namely nationhood, and yet, for practical purposes, cannot enjoy outright political independence. Minority rights are an attempt to limit the potential destabilising effects of such ethnonational exceptions to the prevailing rule of international legitimacy. Because minorities have these normatively significant characteristics, they may be deemed to have legitimate international claims to certain special rights even if these fall short of statehood. For example, the members of minorities may be recognised to possess certain rights in addition to equal citizenship that would enable them to preserve and promote their ethnonational identities in existing states. Such rights might be the freedom to speak a minority language in certain circumstances, the right to be educated in this language, the right to use minority language, the right to form minority associations, build minority schools and community centres and so forth. Provisions of this kind were partially incorporated into the League of Nations minority system. More than this, minorities themselves may be recognised to have certain rights as 'collectives'. Ethnonational minorities *per se* might, for example, be recognised to possess rights to self-government in those regions where they predominate, or to an appropriate share of public revenues in order to build and maintain schools, churches, and other community institutions.

Behind these ethnonational minority guarantees is the assumption that granting special concessions to ethnonational minorities will make them less inclined to challenge the existing territorial status quo. Yet although this rationale may be logically sound and morally justified, pursuing it internationally raises serious problems with regard to state sovereignty. It is unproblematic for international law to recognise alongside state rights those individual rights of equal citizenship within the state, because these have no effect upon the formation or survival of rival national 'collectives' and therefore are not a serious threat to any existing state's sovereignty.

But internationally recognising ethnonational minorities unavoidably strengthens another potential national claimant to the existing state's territory. An international system of minority rights would not only limit state sovereignty by imposing international requirements on a state's treatment of its citizens, but even more controversially, it would grant international status of some kind, whether directly or through their members, to ethnonational units that could come to rival the power or authority of the states affected. Or, at the very least, they would fit awkwardly into the state system and so create tensions and conflicts. It is because of such possible repercussions that most statesmen and stateswomen have been extremely hesitant to adopt ethnonational minority rights. Indeed, they have until very recently found it politically expedient to rephrase the problem in the language of individual human rights consistent with a civic interpretation of self-determination which recognises only pre-existing juridical units, and seeks to protect their borders from secession and irredentism.

Ethnonational Minority Rights after the Cold War

Since 1989, international willingness to consider ethnonational minority rights has noticeably increased, particularly in European regional organisations. This abrupt shift in attitude was necessitated by the collapse of communism in Central and Eastern Europe and the former Soviet Union, which aroused ethnonational aspirations for political independence throughout the region. Moreover, this ethnonational reawakening on the part of both minorities and majorities produced varying degrees of conflict between certain ethnic groups and the fear that it will spread.

In its most extreme form, these tensions escalated into vicious military confrontations: between Serbs, Croats, and Bosnians in the former Yugoslavia; Armenians and Azerbaijanis over the disputed enclave of Nagorno-Karabakh as well as Kelbajar and Fizuli; Georgians and Azeris over Abkhazia, South Ossetia, and the Marneuli District; and the Russian military and pro-independence Chechen forces in Chechnya. Elsewhere in Europe, serious political disputes between ethnic groups have occurred. Relations between the Hungarian minority and the Romanian majority in Transylvania have been strained since 1989. In March 1990, ethnic Hungarians and their representatives in Tirgu Mures were attacked by supporters of the Romanian ultranationalist party *Vatra Romaneasca*. In the ensuing three days of violence, two people were killed and two hundred and sixty nine were injured. In Slovakia, too, the Hungarian community's claims for ethnonational minority guarantees have met with hostility from certain political factions in the larger national community -- particularly Meciar and his Slovak National Party. Meanwhile, all three of the Baltic States have instituted measures to assert their cultural dominance over Russian minorities. By October 1992, all three had instituted citizenship laws, which required residency and language proficiency tests that few Russians would be able to pass, at least in the short term. Similar examples of ethnonational minority/majority conflict could be cited with reference to Ukraine, Hungary, Bulgaria, Serbia, Croatia, Turkey, Russia, and so on.

At the same time, a new-found freedom of mobility after 1989 made it possible for members of ethnonational minority groups to join their ethnic kin in those states where they already formed the majority. Many thousands chose to make this move, and consequently the early 1990s saw the greatest movement of peoples in Europe since the end of the Second World War. Germany, Hungary and Turkey received the largest numbers of ethnic migrants but significant numbers also fled to Austria. The conflicts in Croatia and Bosnia dispersed huge numbers of ethnically cleansed refugees throughout the former Yugoslavia and beyond. These mass migrations were themselves identified as possible sources of political instability in both the states of emigration and of immigration. Thus were ethnonational minority questions an important subject of international discourse and action after the Cold War, particularly, although not exclusively, within European regional organisations.

In 1992, the UN General Assembly approved the Declaration on the Rights of Persons Belonging to National or Ethnic, Religious and

Linguistic Minorities. This declaration significantly improved upon earlier UN efforts to internationally protect ethnonational minorities. By adding to the general cultural, religious and linguistic minority provisions of ICCPR Article 27, the further political provisions to 'participate in relevant national and regional decisions, to establish and maintain associations, and to have contact both within and across international frontiers' constituted a floor for post-Cold War thinking on minority questions. Other regional organisations might agree on something better than this basic code but they could not go beneath it.

The initial European regional response to the re-emergent minority problem evident in the Badinter Commission report and other EU rulings regarding the recognition of new states in Central and Eastern Europe and the former Soviet Union discloses an immediate recognition of its significance to post-Cold War order and stability. Clearly something had to be done to address the issue. A particular response directed at those states of the former communist bloc where the potential for ethnic conflict was greatest must have seemed the most obvious and easily implemented course of action. And that is precisely what the European Union did in its relations with the successor states of Yugoslavia and the former Soviet Union.

Nevertheless, this response was criticised on a number of counts. It was argued, for example, that norms of minority protection were being invented in the heat of the moment, not fully spelled out, applied on a case by case basis to new states by existing states which were not otherwise committed to their application, and implemented without adequate systems of international monitoring and enforcement (Kingsbury, 1992, p. 493). If the post-Cold War European response to the problem of ethnonational minorities was to be something other than piecemeal, more detailed normative standards with systematic procedures for implementation and enforcement would have to be developed. This daunting task was undertaken by the Organisation for Security and Cooperation in Europe (OSCE) -- previously the Conference on Security and Cooperation in Europe (CSCE) -- and the Council of Europe (COE), both of which, by the late 1990s, included as members virtually all the states of Europe and the former Soviet Union.

The OSCE was concerned with formulating codes of state conduct towards minorities both as a way of minimising ethnic conflicts and as a way of preventing the oppression of individual members of ethnonational minority communities. The OSCE therefore incorporated statements of minority rights in all of those official documents that formed the basis of the organisation's activities at that time. These included the main OSCE human rights standard-setting text of this period, the Copenhagen Document (1990), as well as the Charter of Paris for a New Europe (1990), the Geneva Report on National Minorities (1991), the Moscow Document (1991), the Helsinki Document (1992), and the Budapest Document (1994). Moreover, in December 1992, the OSCE created the office of High Commissioner for National Minorities (HCNM) to assist in member states' implementation of ethnonational minority standards and to help resolve ethnic conflicts.

At the same time, the condition of ethnonational minorities was also examined by the COE as a potential obstacle to the democratic transformation of former communist states in the region and as an economic and social problem in those states that were on the receiving end of minority migrations. Various COE bodies, including the Parliamentary Assembly, the European Commission for Democracy Through Law, the Steering Committee of Human Rights and the Committee of Ministers, examined ethnonational minority rights proposals between 1990-1995. The member states of the COE decided, at their Vienna Summit Meeting on 9 October 1993, to adopt both a minorities protocol to the European Convention on Human Rights (ECHR) that would be open to ECHR signatories, and a separate convention on minorities which would be open to both members and non-members of the COE. The decision to adopt a Convention on National Minorities was implemented in 1995, but little progress has been made with regard to the additional protocol. This failure results from both ideological differences amongst member states as regards the suitability of individual versus collective minority rights formulations, and a widespread fear that transferring minority responsibility to the European Court of Human Rights in Strasbourg would judicialise an issue over which many European states are determined to retain domestic political control (Jackson Preece 1997, pp. 351-55).

While most OSCE and COE provisions for minority rights augment the post-1945 human rights regime and the global minimum standard outlined in the 1992 UN Declaration on Minorities, the 1990s European regional response to this problem also reveals both an important reappraisal of League of Nations' linguistic and cultural guarantees, and the nascent formulation of rules with no clear precedent in international agreements. This recent standard-setting experience further distinguishes

Europe from the rest of the world as regards ethnonational minority rights guarantees. The extensive provision made for minority language use and cultural development, particularly as regards the COE's 1992 Charter for Regional and Minority Languages, represents an important continuation of interwar thinking on this subject which had been largely ignored or forgotten during the Cold War. Even more importantly, the recent prohibitions against assimilation and forced population transfer and suggestions for various forms of minority autonomy evident in the Copenhagen Document and the 1995 Minorities Convention embody innovative responses to the demands of ethnonational minorities in former Yugoslavia and indeed elsewhere in post-communist Eastern Europe.

Significantly, the various minority rights standard-setting texts adopted by these two organisations in stages during the mid 1990s were eventually reaffirmed in the provisions of the North Atlantic Treaty Organisation's (NATO) Partnership for Peace (1994) programme with former states of the Soviet block, the EU's Pact on Stability in Europe (1995) and various EU provisions stipulating accession criteria. There thus came about a thorough interweaving of COE, OSCE, NATO and EU provisions regarding security and minority rights. All of these major European organisations appeared to be operating in tandem using common minority rights terminology based upon the standard-setting activities of the OSCE and COE. In this sense, then, one can reasonably speak of an emerging post-Cold War European minority rights regime.

The 'Strategic Concept' adopted by NATO Heads of State and Government in 1991 outlined a 'broad approach' to security 'based on dialogue, cooperation and the maintenance of a collective defence capability' (NATO, 1995, p. 22). It sought to integrate political and military elements of NATO's security policy into a coherent whole that would establish cooperation with relevant European institutions (EU, OSCE, COE) and new partners in Central and Eastern Europe in order to create a 'common European security and defence identity'. *The North Atlantic Cooperation Council's Work Plan for Dialogue, Partnership and Cooperation* (1994) which outlined the aims of the Partnership for Peace programme with Central and East European states specifically identified 'conflicts and issues arising from ethnic and minority problems affecting security in a changing Europe' as an important 'political and security-related matter' of 'particular interest' (NATO, 1995, p. 261). Following this, *The Partnership For Peace Framework Document*

(1994) required NATO member states and other states subscribing to it to reaffirm their commitment to the Helsinki Final Act and all subsequent OSCE documents, including those specifying ethnonational minority obligations (NATO, 1995, pp. 266-67).

At about the same time, a pact to promote stability and peace in Europe by tackling the problem of minorities, strengthening the inviolability of frontiers, and reinforcing the democratic process and regional cooperation in Central and Eastern Europe was proposed by French Prime Minister Edouard Balladur and endorsed by the European Council (of 29 October 1993). The Pact (signed in Paris in 1995) sought to create a new set of international commitments and a new framework within which signatory states (broadly the same as the states participating in the OSCE) could create a climate of confidence favourable to the strengthening of democracy, respect for human and minority rights, and economic progress and peace. Two regional roundtables, one for the Baltic states and another for Central and Eastern Europe, were established with the aim of encouraging neighbouring signatory states to resolve disputes bilaterally and explore new forms of cooperation. Several of these bilateral cooperation agreements were relevant to ethnonational minority questions and specifically reaffirmed minority rights commitments undertaken by the OSCE and COE. The OSCE was given responsibility for monitoring implementation of the Pact and for initiating follow-up procedures.

Moreover, by 1993 minority rights provisions were recognised as a criterion for membership in the European Union. The tripartite Council-Commission-European Parliament Declaration of 1977 on Human Rights already required EU applicant states to be parties to the European Convention on Human Rights (ECHR) and to accept the right of individual petition under the ECHR. The European Convention itself is only open to Council of Europe Members, and thus Council of Europe membership criterion has been a tacit precondition for EU membership since 1977. Prior to admitting a new member state in the 1990s, the Council of Europe conducted an intensive examination of an applicant's constitution and laws as well as the conduct of its various officials to determine whether or not these gave due regard to minority rights.

In this way, there emerged indirect minority rights criteria for EU membership. From this policy, the EU's 1993 European Council meeting in Copenhagen specifically ruled that Central and East European states would only be permitted to join the European Union once they had satisfied stipulated standards concerning the stability of institutions guaranteeing democracy, the rule of law, human rights and respect for and protection of minorities. This fundamental component of the *acquis communautaire* (i.e., existing European Union law) was later reaffirmed in the various Europe Agreements concluded with Central and East European states in the 1990s -- which also reiterated OSCE and COE minority obligations -- and in the landmark Maastricht Treaty (signed in 1992 and entered into force in 1993).

The international consideration of minority questions that was so clearly a major focus for European regional organisations after the Cold War immediately raised the problem of preserving international stability (which usually comes down to preserving the territorial status quo of existing states) while also maintaining some semblance of international legitimacy or at least normative justification of the international system. The main diplomatic challenge confronting international bodies such as the OSCE and COE in the early 1990s was to formulate a response to ethnonational minority demands that was, on the one hand, strong enough to afford the possibility of genuine protection for minorities, while at the same time reassuring those states possessing such communities that their sovereign powers and territorial integrity were not being challenged.

Minority Rights Implementation and Enforcement

There is an entire spectrum of potential options ranging from state self-reporting to outright military intervention which, in theory, could be used to enforce state compliance with international obligations regarding minority rights. These possibilities may include voluntary rapporteur missions, mediation, international review of a state's performance, public criticism, mandatory rapporteur missions or mediation missions, judicial review, withdrawal of membership in international organisations, trade sanctions and humanitarian intervention. Different examples will almost certainly yield equally different responses as to what constitutes generally acceptable and unacceptable enforcement. This fact accounts for the necessity in any enforcement exercise of balancing competing claims of the sort outlined by Boutros-Ghali in the quotation cited at the beginning of this essay. There is nevertheless an emerging history of international practices concerning human rights and now also ethnonational minority rights enforcement mechanisms in the post-1945 UN nation states system.

The 1992 United Nations Declaration on the Rights of Persons Belonging to National or Ethnic, Religious or Linguistic Minorities -- which constitutes the global minimum standard of state conduct towards ethnonational minorities -- did not itself contain any specific enforcement measures despite initial proposals to do so because agreement on these was not forthcoming due to a widespread fear that this might encourage secession and irredentism. Instead, Article 9 indicated that the UN system as a whole was expected to contribute to the fulfilment of the minority provisions.

There were several pre-existing UN bodies whose monitoring activities with regard to other human rights treaties already gave them some role to play in scrutinising the condition of ethnonational minorities. These included the Human Rights Committee, the Committee on Economic, Social and Cultural Rights, the Committee on the Elimination of Racial Discrimination (CERD), and the Committee on the Elimination of Discrimination Against Women (CEDAW). Similarly, the ongoing activities of the Subcommittee on the Prevention of Discrimination and Protection of Minorities were, of course, directly relevant. During the Cold War this body chose to ignore its second mandate (protection of minorities) in favour of the first (prevention of discrimination) since it was more compatible with the territorial integrity of existing states. Following 1989, however, the subcommittee's activities showed renewed interest in the situation of ethnonational minorities.

In addition to these UN monitoring bodies and the self-reporting activities they encouraged, the Optional Protocol to the International Covenant on Civil and Political Rights (which entered into force in 1976) provided a quasi-judicial mechanism for alleged minority rights violations. It gave the Human Rights Committee competence to examine individual complaints and issue final decisions on their merits. It should, however, be pointed out that although these decisions read like judgements, they are *not* legally binding. The committee examined a number of ethnonational minority cases between 1976-1995 both from the perspective of non-discrimination and the right to identity. These cases included Sandra Lovelace v. Canada (1977), Chief Ominayak v. Canada (1984), A. Yilmaz-Dogan v. The Netherlands (1984), Ivan Kitok

v. Sweden (1985), Dominique Guesdon v. France (1986), Bhinder v. Canada (1986), and Demba Talibe Diop v. France (1989).

During the Cold War, the CSCE and the COE also made use of certain mechanisms to enforce human rights standards. However, the methods of enforcement favoured by these two institutions differed fundamentally. The CSCE -- as a Cold War diplomatic conference -- employed an ad hoc method of internal review of member states' conformity to their human rights commitments coupled with external criticism designed to encourage compliance through the moral approbation of public opinion. In contrast, the COE -- as an early embodiment of European federalist ideals -- utilised a quasi-judicial system of enforcement.

Until the CSCE began its metamorphosis into the OSCE at the Paris Summit of 1990, it proceeded from conference to conference (Helsinki 1973-1975, Belgrade 1977-1978, Vienna 1986-1989) with no other institutional structures. These conferences covered the full range of CSCE commitments and were supplemented by specialised meetings, i.e., the Expert Meeting on Human Rights (Ottawa, 1985), and the Expert Meeting on Human Contacts (Bern, 1986). The main activity of such meetings was the discussion of member states' compliance with their undertakings in the human and other dimensions.

The discussion of human rights records proved useful in publicising violations and thus in providing political pressure for reform. This pressure was, of course, increased by the voluntary monitoring activities of non-state actors such as Helsinki Watch, the American based Commission on Security and Cooperation in Europe and the British based Helsinki Committee of the All-Party Parliamentary Human Rights Group. Unfortunately, during the Cold War there was no recognised procedure of following through on questions raised during the follow-up meetings or by the various human rights organisations committed to increasing public awareness of the Helsinki Final Act's (1975) human dimension. This perceived shortcoming was a major impetus for the institutionalisation of the CSCE following 1989 and its ultimate transformation into the OSCE.

In contrast to the CSCE's ad hoc review of participating states' human rights commitments, the COE possessed a quasi-judicial system of enforcing its main human rights standard-setting text, the European Convention on Human Rights (ECHR). The ECHR contained an elaborate formula for the arbitration and, if necessary, judicial review of disputes regarding the enforcement of human rights. It should be pointed out, however, that the Court of Human Rights itself had no direct powers of enforcement and that responsibility for implementing its judicial decisions ultimately rested with the Council of Ministers of the COE. If a political resolution between the parties concerned could not be reached, there remained one final enforcement mechanism at the ministers' disposal: expulsion from the organisation. History has proven that expulsion from the COE is not an idle threat, as both Greece and Turkey were in previous years suspended from the council for human rights violations. But it is an extreme measure that is not taken lightly.

Following 1989, there was increased activity by international organisations regarding the enforcement of human rights. This was perhaps most strikingly evident in the number of UN interventions between 1989-1995 most notably with regard to the Kurds in Iraq, the wars in Croatia and Bosnia, and the anarchy in Somalia, which were authorised at least partly on humanitarian grounds. At the same time, however, a growing realisation of the problems involved in intervening in ethnic conflicts, made clear by the Yugoslav case, also encouraged these organisations to make wider use of their activities in other areas, particularly with regard to preventative diplomacy and confidence building measures aimed at encouraging a climate of compliance.

Because the minorities problem resurfaced in European politics at precisely that moment at which the OSCE was itself undergoing rapid and far-reaching institutional change, the OSCE came to possess many more mechanisms for minority rights enforcement between 1990-1995 than did the COE. The piecemeal nature of the structural transformation meant that each new adaptation incorporated certain elements designed to address the minorities question in Europe. It was not until the December 1992 Helsinki Document, however, that a specific instrument for minorities -- the High Commissioner for National Minorities (HCNM) -- was created. The HCNM was intended to assist in member states' implementation of minority standards and to help resolve ethnic conflicts. Significantly, however, the HCNM's involvement is limited to nonviolent situations presumably because it is feared that such activity might be misinterpreted as international support for or at least sanction of secession and irredentism. In Europe, too, the integrity of existing states and their borders is clearly of paramount value.

However, because the COE was an established international organisation (dating back to 1948), its response to the increasing number of ethnic conflicts in East Central Europe during the early 1990s was generally to amend pre-existing institutional structures rather than create an entirely new enforcement apparatus. Both COE minority rights texts contain specific enforcement machinery consisting of state self-reporting, the international review of states' performance and potentially also public criticism. Obviously, this minorities machinery was nowhere near as stringent as that required by the European Convention on Human Rights which was enforced by the European Court of Human Rights. The proposed minorities protocol to the ECHR would have utilised this more experienced and rigorous system. However, as already indicated, no such protocol has as yet (1998) been adopted by the COE.

The European Charter for Regional or Minority Languages requires state signatories to present reports detailing the measures they have taken with regard to their minority language commitments. These reports are submitted to the Secretary General of the COE once every three years. The reports themselves were both to be made public and examined by a committee of experts. Any legally established body or association within the state in question is permitted to draw the attention of the examining committee to matters it considered relevant to the charter's effectiveness. After consulting the state concerned, the committee then decides whether or not to take such information into account when preparing its own report. The experts' opinion is then submitted to the Committee of Ministers along with the state's own comments. The expert's report can be made public at the discretion of the ministers. Finally, the Secretary General makes a two-yearly detailed report on the application of the charter to the Parliamentary Assembly.

The Convention for the Protection of National Minorities contains similar measures for the scrutiny of states' performance of minority rights. The Committee of Ministers has responsibility for monitoring the implementation of the convention. Each signatory is required to submit reports on its implementation to the Secretary General both on a periodic basis and at the Committee of Ministers' request. In evaluating the adequacy of the measures taken by the various signatory states, the Committee of Ministers is assisted by experts in the field of minority protection.

In addition to these measures, various ongoing activities of the COE also contribute to the implementation and enforcement of standards of state conduct toward ethnonational minorities. Minority rights standards are regularly discussed in both the COE Council of Ministers and the

COE Parliamentary Assembly. The latter also commissions reports both on ethnonational minority rights in general and on the circumstances of particular minority communities in Central and Eastern Europe. Activities sponsored under the auspices of the European Cultural Convention with regard to culture, education, architectural heritage and athletics specifically aim at, among other things, ameliorating tensions within multicultural societies. The COE currently also sponsors several pilot projects designed to improve the circumstances of ethnonational minorities and ease tensions between ethnic groups. Similarly, the COE's Standing Conference of Local and Regional Authorities of Europe aims to create conditions in which ethnic communities that straddle international frontiers might form Euro-regions to bridge these jurisdictional divides on matters of common interest such as education, culture, science and the environment. For example, the Carpathian Euro-region, which included parts of Poland, Ukraine, Slovakia, Hungary and Romania, has been established to help these countries rediscover their common heritage.

Moreover, by 1993 the condition of minorities had formally become a determining factor in COE membership. Prior to admitting a new member state, the COE conducts an intensive examination of an applicant's constitution and laws as well as the conduct of its various officials to ensure that all of these gave due regard to minority rights. Unfortunately, the COE's decision to admit first Russia (in February, 1996) and then Croatia (in November, 1996) is an important reminder that *realpolitik* considerations can be expected to take precedence over minority rights enforcement when the two come into conflict. The 1990s minority rights record of Russia and Croatia left much to be desired. In both states ethnic conflicts escalated into armed confrontation -- between Russians and Chechens over the secession of Chechnya and between Croats and Serbs over the secession of Krajina -- and both had been less than keen on international calls for improved minority rights protection to help quell the unrest. Nevertheless, the view that Russia and Croatia should be integrated into European institutions prevailed over the view that they should be excluded: in the interests of European order and stability it was judged necessary to overlook their minority infractions and admit them to the Council of Europe regardless of formal membership requirements to the contrary.

Success or Failure?

As is apparent from the preceding discussion, the UN, OSCE and COE generally sought to bring about compliance with ethnonational minority rights standards through conflict prevention rather than more direct means of economic sanctions or military enforcement (the UN's involvement in Iraq, former Yugoslavia, Somalia and Rwanda and the OSCE's involvement in former Yugoslavia and Chechnya being obvious exceptions). Instead of imposing economic sanctions or sending in peacekeeping forces (which would have required a degree of financial and military involvement few member states were willing to accept) these organisations aimed to prevent potential conflicts from reaching the point at which such drastic measures might become necessary. Their goal therefore was to *encourage* democratisation and respect for human and minority rights within states by providing both timely expert advice and external mediation to help resolve ethnonational minority/majority conflicts at the earliest possible stage and before they began to present any threat to the international system.

This sort of enforcement policy has both its critics and its advocates. Some analysts have argued that international organisations lack credibility so long as they do not have the capacity to militarily impose compliance (Posen, 1993, pp. 103-21). Others retort that regardless of an initiative's actual success or failure, its very existence is indicative of the priority accorded to international standards of state conduct: the mere presence of international monitors ensures the continued awareness of the conflict and facilitates political pressure (Walker, 1993, pp. 165-68). Given the serious instrumental and normative difficulties associated with international enforcement, the latter conclusion seems more plausible.

Let us briefly examine the 1990s record of European regional organisations as a case in point. As a general rule, it is difficult for researchers and other outsiders to evaluate the relative effectiveness of mediation and other diplomatic activities, which by their very nature occur behind closed doors. There is nevertheless evidence of a certain, limited degree of success defined in terms of armed conflict prevention for OSCE and COE involvement in national majority/minority disputes.

For example, in order to ensure COE membership, Bulgaria adopted measures that demonstrated a newly found willingness to comply with ethnonational minority standards in the treatment of its Turkish minority. The HCNM was capable of defusing several potential ethnonational minority/majority conflicts: between Russians and Latvians in Latvia, Russians and Estonians in Estonia, Russians and Lithuanians in Lithuania, Russians and Ukrainians in the Ukraine, Hungarians and Romanians in Romania, Hungarians and Slovaks in Slovakia and Slovaks and Hungarians in Hungary. The ongoing diplomatic efforts of both the OSCE and COE to resolve international tensions between Central and East European states arising over minority questions led to a number of bilateral treaties on good-neighbourliness and friendship signed under the auspices of the EU sponsored 1995 Stability Pact. These included agreements between Bulgaria and Turkey, Latvia and Russia, Lithuania and Russia, and Hungary and Slovakia.

The most significant evidence -- albeit speculative and based on counterfactual reasoning -- for the benefits of this kind of preventative enforcement is the fact that most ethnonational minority/majority disputes in Europe and the former Soviet Union did not escalate into violent conflicts between 1990-1998. In most cases, the parties concerned confined their actions to those forms of opposition permissible within a democratic system. This observation, even though it is counterfactual, *should* be taken seriously. Why? Because as Andreas Osiander demonstrates, the code of international conduct 'is not concerned with *promoting* certain types of action, but with *preventing* behaviour that would disrupt the system'. In other words, 'structural principles' such as minority rights 'operate successfully if nothing is seen to happen' (Osiander, 1995, pp. 6-7).

In those situations where rival ethnic groups employed armed force, little was accomplished with regard to ending hostilities. For example, the OSCE -- which involved itself in 'hot' conflicts such as Yugoslavia, Georgia, Nagorno-Karabakh, Tajikistan and Chechnya during the early 1990s -- had little if any success in bringing peace to the various warring factions. Nevertheless, as Adam Roberts has made clear 'the historical record suggests that the management of communal conflicts is inherently difficult' and so 'international institutions should not be judged harshly merely for running into difficulties' (Roberts, 1995, p. 407).

Certain characteristic features of ethnic conflicts make them particularly difficult to resolve once fighting has begun. First, a large number of combatants are usually involved and political control over them tends to be haphazard. Second, since ethnic populations tend to be intermingled within the same territory, there are usually numerous points of friction between opposing groups rather than a clear line of battle.

Third, also as a result of intermingled populations, the involvement of civilians -- who may be attacked or ethnically cleansed -- is almost unavoidable. Fourth, regardless of the logistics involved, once communal leaders embark upon a militant course of action and commit the human, military and economic resources of their group to such an endeavour, changing course becomes fraught with political difficulty, particularly once soldiers and civilians have been killed, property destroyed, children orphaned and refugees forced to relocate to other areas. In these circumstances, a cease-fire may appear to imply surrender unless at least some strategic gains are seen to justify the great human and other sacrifices made. So, it is all the more important to prevent such conflicts from developing, which arguably the OSCE and COE have done within Europe and the former Soviet Union.

But this brings us to the thorny problem of resolving ethnic conflicts that have deteriorated into violence. In the end, outsiders cannot resolve such conflicts: they can only encourage the insiders to do so. The willingness to respect ethnonational minority rights, uphold cease-fires, enter negotiations and accept a peace settlement must come from the parties directly involved. As Jack Donnelly has noted, stable regimes that protect human and minority rights over the long run almost always have arisen, and must arise, from sustained national political vigilance (Donnelly, 1995, p. 70). This conclusion is normative as well as instrumental. Just as one cannot 'force' an individual to be free -- for such an imposition would not only be practically problematic to carry out but would itself constitute a denial of freedom -- neither can one 'force' a nation to be democratic or to respect minority rights.

Final responsibility for success or failure in the protection of ethnonational minorities rests with domestic rather than international actors. This instrumental and normative reality fundamentally limits all *international* action to enforce human and minority rights; ultimately, minority rights are matters of *domestic* political practices and international organisations can do little more than encourage these. One should perhaps add that research suggests domestic minority rights regimes, voluntarily assumed and sustained, can be very effective at ameliorating ethnonational tensions within states and, since they are domestic in origin, do not raise the same sort of problems regarding state sovereignty that are associated with international guarantees (Lijphart, 1977, 1984).

Conclusion

The frustrated political ambitions of ethnonational minorities are significant for international relations because of their potential to create disruption and disorder within the international system. Minority efforts to achieve self-determination may put international stability at risk by creating violence within states, by drawing in neighbouring states, by inspiring similar secessionist or irredentist movements elsewhere or by precipitating mass refugee flows across frontiers. Indeed, such nationalist acts are often committed in the hope of creating as much international disorder as possible so as to encourage the redistribution of state sovereignty: this dynamic brings ethnonational minorities on to the international agenda and makes minority questions subjects of international as well as domestic politics. Within international relations, minority rights are an attempt to limit the potential destabilising effects of self-determination, the exception to the prevailing rule of state legitimacy. Behind these international guarantees is the assumption that granting special concessions to minorities will make them less inclined to challenge existing state borders.

This is because the underlying ethos of the contemporary state system is the territorial status quo established in the post-war settlement and decolonisation. The UN Charter of 1945 entrenched existing boundaries. The principle of self-determination was affirmed, but it was set in the context of respect for existing borders. The right of self-defence thus became the right of existing UN member states to defend not only their territory but also their citizens and thus preserve the inviolability of the state. Secession and irredentism were severely curtailed. New states were recognised on the basis of *uti possedítis juris* and not ethnonationalism. Consequently, minority rights as international rather than domestic guarantees are fundamentally limited by the right of existing states to territorial integrity.

Recognising the proper limits of international action is not, however, a prescription for inaction. To conclude that the requirements of international order and stability must have priority over the rights of ethnonational minorities does not imply that international actors should ignore the problem. On the contrary, in circumstances similar to those existing in Central and Eastern Europe and the former Soviet Union during the 1990s, it would be unwise, indeed risky, to do so. The international system does accord rights to non-state actors even though these obviously have less priority than the rights of the constituent sovereign units which make up that system and the territorial settlement that underscores it.

Consequently, states have a duty -- arising from their international commitments -- to promote a respect for human and minority rights both within and beyond their own sovereign territories. In as much as principled domestic conduct elevates the 'floor' of international conduct further away from the 'jungle' of pure survival and the struggle of all against all -- thereby strengthening international peace -- it is in the interest of international organisations and their member states to promote it. The greater the ethical conduct of its constituent units, the more 'cosmopolitan' the international community becomes, correspondingly increasing the general security of states and indeed the groups and individuals that comprise them -- thereby encouraging the circumstances in which freedom and democracy can be realised.

Notes

[1] The distinction between ethnic and civic nationalism can be traced back to the works of Hans Kohn (Kohn, 1944; Kohn, 1955). Following the end of the Cold War, this distinction was popularised by Michael Ignatieff in his BBC television series Blood and Belonging and its accompanying publication (Ignatieff, 1993).

[2] Obviously, certain of these successor states -- most notably Bosnia and Russia -- are 'fudged' nation states that possess national minorities -- e.g., Serbs in the former and Chechens in the latter -- who are dissatisfied with the present territorial status quo and indeed have made claims for independence.

[3] The post-WWII movement of German minorities began as an attack of 'ethnic cleansing' and was only formalised at Potsdam, when the Allied Powers tried (without much success) to humanise the process (Marrus, 1985).

[4] These were general treaties of friendship and cooperation which included, among others, statements that reiterated the parties' continued willingness to comply with OSCE and COE minority rights standards.

10 Linking Conflict to Environmental Security

HO-WON JEONG and JYRKI KÄKÖNEN

Environmental problems have been recognised as a threat to human survival over the last several decades. The human impact on the environment in a modern society is ten to 100 times greater than it was in an agrarian society (Lassonde, 1997, p. 60). The need for access to natural resources has increased as more people make greater demands upon them. Given that world resources are finite, nature's ability to recover from the harm done by human activities is limited.

The environment is now considered a significant security issue. Environmental security is affected by a variety of activities made at different levels of a social system. Human well-being can be threatened by transboundary air pollution and insufficient water resources. Environmental issues have moved from the margin to the legitimate area of security policies, particularly since the end of the Cold War. The traditional security establishment such as NATO now promotes cooperative ventures with Russia in environmental issues. There was even discussion about the role of the military in protecting the ozone layer.

Along with changes in the perception of security in the policy making circle, environmental concerns have been brought into security studies. A number of researchers have focused on the linkage between the environment and national security (Renner, 1989; Romm, 1993). Threats to human security can be attributed to environmental degradation.

In most literature, however, only violent conflict has become a major concern, although nonviolent and violent environmental conflicts may have the same root problems (Homer-Dixon, 1994). There are some conceptual advantages in linking violent conflict to environmental security since it helps to broaden notions of security. On the other hand, the linkages between environmental degradation and violent conflict are indirect: conflict has to be understood in terms of larger patterns of social interactions between groups.

Understanding environmental security can be promoted by focusing on the processes and structural conditions underlying the emergence of incompatible interests and values. This analytical framework will help us find strategies for resolving environmentally induced conflict. Overall, security is enhanced by finding ways in which values and interests can be negotiated to accommodate competing needs and bring about structural changes.

Environmental conflict belongs to the core of peace research through its efforts to understand the sources of violence and conflict. While the existing research has been attempting to examine the relationships between scarce resources and violent conflict, there is little focus on how to resolve and prevent environmental conflict. The connections between the environment and peace can be discussed in terms of how to deal with the sources of violent conflict and promote social justice. The solution to environmental problems could not adequately be considered without examining the conditions for social and economic development.

After reviewing past efforts to connect the environment to a national security agenda, the authors suggest ways in which environmental issues can be securitised. Environmental security is re-conceptualised in terms of the sources of environmental threats, the object to be secured and the agents for change. This chapter also examines the structural conditions of environmental threats generated by modern political economy, as well as the impact of competition for scarce resources on inter-group relations. After discussion about how environmental conflict can be managed to prevent violence, the last section investigates obstacles to environmental conflict resolution.

National Security and the Environment

Concerns with violent environmental conflict have expanded the debate of national security. Strategies for promoting national security have to be redefined by natural resource shortages and environmental degradation (Brown, 1977). Environmental changes can have an impact on the material and physical foundations needed for the survival of a state. Threats to national well-being can be associated with environmental damage. For those who advocate a broad definition of national security, environmental well-being becomes part of a state's comprehensive strategy for survival.

Overall, national security will not be guaranteed without the protection of sovereignty and territorial integrity. National security can be defined in terms of the capacity to control those domestic and foreign factors that influence autonomy and prosperity. Not only military but also non-military threats degrade the quality of life for the inhabitants of a state. Elimination of the sources of threats to the environment becomes as important as the absence of military threat.

In a broad notion of national security, environmental issues have also been linked to the causes of violent conflict which require outside military intervention. Degradation of nature leads to a decline in the national economy, which in turn brings about social instability. Long before the Cold War was over, declines in world food production caused by abnormal weather patterns were studied for their implications for US national security interests. Economic difficulties may lead to political instability which would eventually result in US intervention. Violent conflict in resource-stricken Third World countries is directly related to security policies through vested economic and military interests of foreign powers.

The efforts to link national security to the environment, in part, reflect an attempt to widen the scope of the traditional state-centric discourse on security. Introducing ecological security may challenge a military notion of security. Discussion of environmental issues in national security perspectives would easily grab the attention of policy makers.

On the other hand, the attempt to connect environmental problems to traditional security can dilute the original concerns over environmental issues. Large scale environmental degradation draws attention only when it threatens to undermine political stability. Conflict over the environment has significance only if it leads to violence.

Environmental concerns are, in essence, not easily linked to national security. The means for achieving national security in a traditional sense are different from those needed to protect nature and human beings. Vulnerability has been related to external threats, and responses were prepared largely in military terms. The goals of national security are not always compatible with human and common security. Borders have been protected to remove a physical threat from another state, and human sacrifices have been justified in terms of state protection.

States are major actors which compete for resources in the modern international system. A threat to a society is understood in terms of protecting one's own territories. Environmental degradation is an unconventional form of threat not necessarily leading to interstate war. Military tools are not of much value in eliminating environmental threats. The pursuit of national interests in an anarchic international system can be, in fact, detrimental to global security based on cooperation.

National security is more concerned about resource protection than resource conservation. Environmental issues can even be militarised through the need to protect vital natural resources. One state can invade another for acquiring additional resources. Military forces were used to promote economic interests. Strategic interests in Persian Gulf oil have been transformed into a national security issue, especially for states depending on oil imports.

Environmental concerns have not replaced strategies for the use of force or the threat of using force, since 'the fundamental nature of national security strategy is still premised on military power to resolve conflict' (Zebich-Knos, 1998, p. 31). States may still try to solve environmental problems by resorting to force. Some suggested that armed force could be used against a state which is a source of pollution or toxic waste. Since the outcome of war leads to environmental degradation, military solutions to environmental problems are unlikely to make security issues green.

The aim of many military operations has been to destroy not only preconditions for human life, but also living space for other species (Westing, 1986). This was clearly the case in Vietnam where the US army used several different polluting chemicals against nature. In order to achieve national objectives, armies can claim a right to destroy the environment.

In an armed national security model, the military contributed to environmental degradation through its use of resources. States attempt to appropriate natural resources to facilitate the industrial production of the military system. In addition, the military creates hazardous waste in producing and testing nuclear, biological, and chemical weapons.

The price of an F-15 fighter could be more effectively used to protect farmland soil and push back deserts to guarantee food security in politically unstable regions (Myers, 1996, p. ix). The resources used for armed security would not be reinvested to deal with environmental sources of threats. An armed national security model is poorly equipped with handling long term economic threats to human security.

> National defence establishments are useless against these new threats. Neither bloated military budgets nor sophisticated weapons' systems can halt the deforestation... Blocking external aggression may be a relatively simple matter compared with arresting the deforestation of local environments (Brown, 1977, p. 37).

Global environmental issues may find relevance to national security if an understanding is made that the survival of a state will not eventually be guaranteed in a deteriorating natural environment. The traditional scope of security, however, cannot be easily applied beyond its national reach. The nature of global environmental security reflects the common interests of the international community.

Securitisation of the Environment

As distinguished from political, economic, and social systems, the environment includes physical and biological systems (Levy, 1995, p. 38). The environment as a material space has always been closely related to human and social security. Ecological feedback is important to the subsistence of human life. Nature is a material externality to the international system.

The construction of a security agenda requires an understanding of types of threats to the referent objects and the process of perceiving these threats. In the state-centric formulations, major attention is paid to the spill-over effects of environmental problems between states. However, issues invisible in the dominant narrative emerge as a security concern. Environmental threats can come from outside the formal political structure.

The concept of security can be examined in terms of the core values to be protected. The core values can be individual well-being or the survival of a state. Many problems related to environmental changes can affect the social systems. In order to understand the impact of environmental degradation on human well-being, the security agenda has to be broadened to include many different types of threat beyond war and force. The nature of environmental security can be differently interpreted, depending on whose security matters -- a group, a state, an international system, or humanity.

Securitisation of the environment is related to the questions of what needs to be protected as well as who defines security for the environment. Depending on the object to be secured, there are different understandings about environmental security. Given that environmental security has to be broadly defined, it becomes more difficult to identify the specific referent object to be protected than is the case with national security.

In general, the referent object for environmental security can be identified as human lives and well-being. If one widens concerns to include the relationship between the human species and the rest of the biosphere, the possible referent objects of environmental security are large, ranging from the survival of endangered species, the preservation of habitat, to the maintenance of biosphere (Buzan, 1997, p. 17). The goal of security can then be defined in terms of maintaining the ecological balance by controlling human activities.

If humans are considered as a dominant controller of nature, the primary concerns would be sustainability of resource bases which allows continued exploitation of nature. Material satisfaction on a sustainable basis is considered the ultimate security value. Thus environmental security can be achieved by satisfying communities' needs without diminishing its natural stock.

Securitisation of the environment is qualitatively different from controlling military threats. The threats to the environment are complex with the deteriorating relationship between humans and the earth's biological system. If the threats to the planet's future survival result from a growth-oriented development model, alternative development strategies need to be adopted. Since environmental threats can be felt by their social significance of an unsustainable situation, the solutions should be economic and political rather than military. Politics to change the socio-economic system becomes a security agenda. The appropriate level and form of remedy are influenced by the interests and values of the agents (Levy, 1995, p. 43).

Nature is seen as an entity comprised of the relationships between living organisms and their physical environment. The challenge remains to find consensus on an appropriate relationship between physical space and population both at global and local levels (Bradshaw and Wallace, 1996). If the status of humans has to be adapted to the new relationship, this would require a shift in social values.

Understanding Environmental Conflict

One dimension of conflict over the environment is related to competition between societies over resources. Conflict between various social groups can be intensified by threats from a rapidly changing relationship between humanity and the earth's natural systems. If environmental problems are combined with identity issues, they can be a source of intractable conflict. However, environmental problems are an indirect source of conflict in the sense that economic stresses caused by environmental degradation have to be converted into social unrest and political instability.

Environmental conflict can emerge at inter- and intra-state levels as well as an international system level. The direct effect of competition over water and oil at a regional level is more easily observed as a cause of conflict. Given its wide scope and magnitude, however, environmental conflict is diffuse especially at a global level. The nature of conflict over the use of global commons is more general. Tensions arise from the failure of negotiations to find the measures needed to stop atmospheric changes such as global warming and ozone depletion.

In general, environmental conflict is caused by severe degradation of an ecosystem. Resources traditionally regarded as plentiful and naturally renewable can become scarce because of the failure of human beings to adopt sustainable methods of their management. Population growth brings increasing demands for resources while supply decreases with the degradation, depletion and maldistribution of renewable resources. Resource scarcities are translated into economic stresses such as inflation, unemployment, and monetary instability (Brown, 1977, p. 37). Altered resource availability generates changes in local or regional relationships.

Types of scarcity determine the nature of conflict. Environmental conflict can be characterised by the lack of available resources, unequal distribution of resources, or both. Simple scarcity is caused by the insufficient quantity of resources needed for the satisfaction of basic needs. Competition for single renewable resources such as fish, water and land can be a source of conflict (Homer-Dixon, 1991). Demographic and environmental stress causes economic marginalisation defined in terms of chronic poverty and increasing landlessness. Competition for more resources leads to the concentration of resources into the hands of a few. Subjecting the majority others to scarcity may result in relative deprivation. Thus unequal access to minerals, food and water can cause political disputes and aggression.

Social and psychological processes of conflict are influenced by the quantity and quality of resources available to competing social groups. Competition over scarce natural resources and pressure for population movements can generate rising inter-state tensions. The decline in farmland fertility and consequent migration of peasants led to ethnic conflict between Ethiopia and Somalia.

While the decline in economic and social conditions caused by environmental degradation can be a necessary condition for communal conflict, the emergence of manifest conflict is more likely to be influenced by such factors as social cleavages and repressive political mechanisms. In order for latent conflict to become manifest, general social discontent caused by unequal distribution of resources and relative deprivation felt by specific groups have to lead to political mobilisation. If old ethnic rivalries exist, identity may become a more important element even though the conflict was triggered by sudden environmental degradation or disasters. The existence of a repressive political process is more likely to contribute to the transformation of a nonviolent conflict into a violent one. The weakness of political institutions is associated with a lack of capacity to maintain order in response to anti-state violence.

Deforestation, desertification, loss of biodiversity and greenhouse gases are destabilisers to societies. However, there are multiple paths between environmental problems and the occurrence of manifest conflict. Intervening variables are inefficient economies, unjust social systems and inflexible political systems. Some economic and social systems handle stress induced by environmental problems better than others.

Third World countries are more prone to conflict not only because resource scarcities are more severe, but also because social integration is fragile. These countries also do not have reliable mechanisms to deal with conflict. Key social groups are excluded from the institutional decision making process. Disruption of social relations and denial of government legitimacy are common.

Most researchers have associated violence with the dynamics of environmental change (Homer-Dixon, 1994). In linking the environment to social conflict, the existing research has not properly explained the main questions: when and how environmental changes are translated into a social phenomenon.[1] Since not all the conflicts are violent, many levels and forms of conflict have to be considered in understanding environmental sources of conflict.

Behavioural factors often play an important role in determining the outcome of conflict. The process of conflict can be influenced by the existing relationships between groups as well as the availability of social, political and cultural institutions to deal with social discontent. The main function of violence can be more equated with social and political factors than environmental degradation. For instance, institutional weaknesses associated with fragile and heterogeneous states make African countries far more vulnerable to violent conflict than other societies.

Early warning systems may be developed to recognise environmental threats. Environmental degradation can be reported as an underlying cause of conflict (Matthew, 1997, p. 79). Key intervention points could be found to control the behaviour of conflict groups to prevent the outbreak of violence. However, the mere control of violence would not prevent the emergence of future conflict. Value differences and economic interests play an important role in determining the types of environmental conflict. Long term strategies are needed to alter the causal processes leading environmental degradation to conflict by regulating human economic activities.

Political Economy of Environmental Conflict

In the discussion about environmental security, social injustice and inequality have not drawn much attention as a source of conflict. Compared with resource scarcity at a communal level, the conflict between the poor and the rich at both regional and international levels is related to determining responsibility for pollution and prescribing remedies needed to reverse environmental degradation.

In the political ecology of modern history, organised violence was used to bring about large scale environmental changes. Economic growth is based on the overexploitation of natural resources. Due to industrial necessities, control over resources has expanded beyond national territories since the 16th century. As a result, indigenous populations were decimated, and transformation of landscapes led to global environmental changes.

The process of industrial development has often been influenced by changes in the resource bases. In the existing modernisation paradigm, the imbalance between resources and population can be resolved by broadening resource bases as well as developing new technologies. The relation between the territory as a space and population in an organised society has been further imbalanced by the division of ecosystems into separate parcels.

The current environmental crisis has its roots in the geopolitics of industrial capitalism which has been supported by European colonial expansion. People are not equally exposed to environmental problems. Consumption in rich countries causes degradation in the Third World. Forests were cut down in the South to produce the commodities needed for the North. The physical space for developing countries is polluted by multinational corporations (Redclift, 1996). A growth oriented economy in industrialised countries is inter-linked to poverty and environmental degradation (McMichael, 1996). However, the biggest burdens are put on the most marginalised people since they do not have resources to take care of these problems.

Global environmental problems are shared by the whole of humanity and call for global solutions. Since extreme poverty and overconsumption contribute to environmental degradation, solutions to global environmental problems have to address international debt, trade and population growth. However, the management of ecological problems within an existing system would not solve the problems caused by the harm done for the past two hundred years. The dominant paradigm is still based on the idea of unlimited progress. In recent years, for example, economic growth in China has further contributed to a rapid increase in the emission of greenhouse gases.

In a traditional model, environmental security would be enhanced by the major redistribution of income to alleviate poverty and improve quality of life worldwide. It has been widely accepted in the international community that threats to the environment can be handled within the current pattern of an economic growth model. For instance, the World Commission on Environment and Development report suggests that global economic output in a free trade environment must continue to grow rapidly to meet the needs of the poor (Brundtland, 1987). However, traditional free market economic approaches would not reduce the burden of the fragile ecosystem.

Radical changes in economic organisation as well as lifestyles are needed to reduce stress on the environment. Discussion about how to prevent global warming and overexploitation of resources can be conducted at multilateral fora. The negotiation of environmental values and interests can be based on the adoption of broad reference frames. Given the failure of agreement at an intergovernmental level, environmental policy changes at a global level may depend on initiatives taken by global civil society to change public opinion.

Conclusion

The traditional concept of national security has largely stemmed from the experiences of modernisation and state-building. Growth-oriented models are related to state centric security. Since environmental security involves local societies and a global ecosystem beyond national boundaries, traditional security policy does not offer a means to deal with environmental threats (Käkönen, 1992). It is important to have a broad notion of security for resolving environmental conflict since environmental threats faced by people are different from threats to a state. Environmental conflict needs to be resolved in such a way that the relationship between nature and organised modern society can be balanced.

Note

[1] Critiques of the existing research can be made from several different perspectives. Ecological and demographic stress can be partly responsible for political agitation on the part of indigenous groups (Gurr, 1994). Group rights and identity issues are more important in most inter-group conflicts. In addition, the process of economic modernisation explains such social and psychological variables as the existence of relative deprivation better than environmental degradation. For a more comprehensive critique of the methodological and conceptual problems of a model for violent environmental conflict, see Gleditsch (1998) and Rønnfeldt (1997).

11 Postdevelopment: Beyond the Critique of Development

ARTURO ESCOBAR and HO-WON JEONG

Modern expert knowledge and policy making apparatus have not been able to improve social, economic, and environmental situations in Asia, Africa and Latin America. The experiences of people living in the Third World indicate that the modern constructs on which explanation and prescription for development are based have not been appropriate epistemological tools to raise crucial questions relevant to the survival of the marginalised. They fail to guide us in finding solutions to continuing poverty and marginalisation.

Some recent work tries to move beyond this paradox by working through some of the epistemological traps that constrain theories of modernisation and globalisation (Ferguson, 1990; Sachs, 1992; Escobar, 1995). Thinking beyond development defined in terms of modernisation theories can be provided by efforts to conceptualise postdevelopment. The creation of new types of language, understanding and action is a major element in promoting postdevelopment. Noncapitalism is posited against the dominance of capitalism. The meanings of economy and place need to be revisited if local place is asserted against the dominance of space as conceived by globalisation.

Given that the interests of ruling groups dominate the discourse on modernity, visions for an alternative world would not emerge from existing epistemological foundations. Postdevelopment explains today's world in ways that do not reproduce the centrality of Western ways of creating the world. It helps reinvent the world according to the logic of place-based cultures. Postdevelopment seeks to understand other experiences by offering a heuristic device for reassessing the reality of indigenous communities in Asia, Africa and Latin America. Thus, postdevelopment is seen as a research programme for both deepening the deconstruction of the economy and suggesting steps to alternative explanations.

This chapter discusses strategies for conceptualising development issues, examines the domains of problems, and explores alternative possibilities to overcome a modernist paradigm of development. The critique of development strategies based on liberal economic logic is assessed to open conceptual avenues for postdevelopment. Place and culture are utilised as useful notions to understand challenges generated by movements from below.

Deconstruction of Development

Certain notions of individual, society and economy are entrenched in Western social science paradigms. Reality is constructed in the guise of neoliberalism. Emerging theories of globalisation extend modernist frameworks of capital, culture and society. On the other hand, neoliberalism's impact on the Third World is hardly noticed in the discussion of globalisation (Slater, 1995).

Development has long been considered to be solid and material. From market-friendly development to sustainable development, the qualifiers of the term have multiplied. In the development discourse, however, a certain core of elements and relations have remained intact throughout the decades. Changes in the priorities on development have been made possible by the incorporation of new domains, but the basic orientation of existing paradigms went unchallenged.

The concepts of development are transformed in their modes of operations once they are posited in a Third World locality. Depending on political and epistemological orientations, it has been put to different ends. However, the question of development was posed in the ways in which the Third World was constituted as a reality in the West. Development has been viewed as the product of identifiable historical processes in the sense that it reflects a historically singular experience.

The very basic ideas of development have been a central organising principle imposed on social life. The discursive regime of development is based on the apparatus of expert knowledge and institutions. It constructs the world in a manner that everything is seen as self-evident. As the term development has been accepted uncritically, expert language colonised social reality in most Third World countries. Development generates hegemonic relationships by subordinating all aspects of society and economy to its overarching principle.

The production of knowledge is associated with specific forms of power. Expert knowledge is central to the exercise of power with the exclusion of others. The work of knowledge apparatus is precisely intended to achieve the goal of de-politicising issues and transforming the cultural fabric of communities along the lines of modern principles of rationality. Dominant social practices have been successful in keeping established orders in place by continuously renewing themselves. Discursive practice can help identify the processes of seeing and transforming social relations.

Discourse analysis of power questions the regimes of accepted knowledge and truth. Critiques of the dominance of Western knowledge systems provide alternative ways of understanding development. Discursive analysis of development has revealed new ways of looking at what development is and does (Crush, 1995, p. 4). Development exists not only as a value, but also as a dominant problematic or 'interpretative grid through which the impoverished regions of the world are known to the West. Within this interpretative grid, a host of everyday observations are rendered intelligible and meaningful' (Ferguson, 1990, p. xiii). The order of knowledge is based on the regime of representation.

The view of development as invention can be undone or re-created in multiple ways. The task can be achieved by examining the very grounds on which development could emerge as an object of thought and practice. In destabilising those grounds, poststructuralism provides tools for de-familiarising familiar concepts. The primary intention of discursive analysis is to make self-evident knowledge problematic.

The deconstruction of development is aimed at demonstrating the contingent nature of reality. Poststructuralist analysis has de-familiarised development descriptions. The sites and mechanisms of knowledge production and domination are unveiled. Efforts were made to search for the value of alternative experiences and ways of knowing.

The poststructuralist critique of development provides a basis for the emergence of postdevelopment as a heuristic device for opening possibilities for new perceptions. The entrenched concepts of modernity and space continue to construct capitalism as the central referent of development, globalisation and the economy. The notions of space, economy and culture in the globalisation discourse have to be re-examined in order to construct theories for locations and to bring out voices already emerging from the marginalised position.

Postdevelopment is a hopeful arena for introducing the idea of manifold forms of economy in discussions of globalisation. It celebrates cultural and social differences, resistances to hegemony, local power, dynamism, and subjectivity. Reconceived in this fashion, postdevelopment facilitates the incorporation of place-based practices, modes of knowledge, and models of the social and the economic into the process of outlining alternative orders.

Place and Noncapitalism

In conventional understanding, the ontological base of class is determined by capitalism. Economic activities are defined by liberal economic logic. Since capitalism is supposedly superior to traditional economies, noncapitalist forms are seen as primitive, marginal or complementary to capitalism. Noncapitalist development has been marginalised in capitalocentrism, which situates capitalism at the centre of development narratives (Gibson-Graham, 1996, p. 41).

The representation of globalisation is made in the context of the subordination of noncapitalist sites. The globalisation script stresses capitalism's presumed capacity to universalise the market for commodities. Capitalism is inherently spatial through its ability to invade and subordinate all other forms of economic forms. All types of noncapitalism are unavoidably violated, conquered, and subjugated to capitalism. It has been asserted that globalisation will eventually bring about the death of noncapitalist forms of economy.

Though global processes transform social relations at the local level (Pred and Watts, 1992), not all economic forms can be defined in terms of capitalist identity. The development of capitalism in some sites did not wipe out various forms of noncapitalism existing in others. In addition, the demise of older forms has been only partial. Elements of difference are not reducible to the constructs of capitalism that have evolved for centuries. What we do not know is local social reality created after centuries of capitalist development.

The call of Marxism to transform capitalism turns out to be an impossible task. If capitalism is conceived not as something large and embracing, but as something partial, then capitalism may be considered as a set of different practices influenced by subjectivity. Place-based consciousness does not emerge from a traditional economic structure that determines the process of modern class formation. A crisis of individual and social identity can be translated into radical rethinking about capitalism. The anti-essentialist critique of capitalocentric discourses reveals that capitalist practices are contingent and specific, rather than necessary.

Transcending capitalocentrism starts from the recognition of alternative practices in and of themselves. The space for a discourse on economic difference can be created by reintroducing a principle of multiplicity as well as resisting the reduction of every aspect of social reality to a single principle of capitalist determination. A strategy to find alternatives to capitalism would be to displace the economy from the centre of social life.

A different view of economy emerges by focusing on how the marginalised appropriate means for their survival individually or collectively. The sources of noncapitalist class formation are diverse. Class can be redefined in terms of the processes of producing and distributing goods and resources in the subsistence economy at a local level. Understanding class along anti-essential lines challenges the inevitability of capitalist penetration (Resnick and Wolffs, 1987; Gibson-Graham, 1996).

Resistance to globalisation is located in informal sectors comprised of independent commodity production, family support networks, reproduction of community resources, and other types of economic practices of impoverished regions. These forms of arrangements emerge in response to external economic pressure. Economic activities in informal sectors are important sources of living. The effectiveness of wage earners and peasants to disrupt exploitation can be examined in terms of a variety of household practices and community structures.

Communal kitchens, self-help organisations, collective household structures, and various types of rural and urban cooperatives represent noncapitalist ways of organising production. Redundancy and cooperative activities in informal sector economies allow for the survival of surplus labour which cannot find employment in a formal sector. Economic activities as survival means in a large social space are not explained by neoliberal economic logic.

The question of alternatives to capitalism and modernity could be considered in the conceptualisation of place as 'the other' of globalisation. Debates on globalisation and alternatives to capitalism can be re-politicised by the reassertion of place. If place is not a purely empirical and external entity, it needs to be conceived of as a form of lived space endowed with meaning. Networks of various kinds are not associated with a fixed location. Placed-based consciousness is inextricably linked to the conceptions of locality, and this is especially clear in ecological notions of territories.

Defence of lived space can be seen as the essential feature of politics by attempting to answer such questions as who speaks for place. Place is essential to thinking about the construction of identity since it is central to issues of culture and social relations. Thus it is part of any radical political agenda against spaceless and timeless globalisation.

Noncapitalism and local culture can be reasserted against the dominance of space, capital, and modernity that are central to the globalisation discourse. The theory of postdevelopment creates viable possibilities for reconceiving and reconstructing the world from the perspective of place-based culture and economic practices. The world is reconstructed as being embodied in manifold localities.

Cultural Politics

Development imposed from outside can be actively resisted in numerous ways. Far from passively accepting external conditions, local groups may actively shape the process of constructing identities, social relations, and economic practice. Place is the location of a multiplicity of forms of cultural politics. Practices of cultural difference could serve as the basis for noncapitalist alternatives.

Societies are fluid entities stretched on all sides by migrations, border crossings and transnational economic forces. While there is no boundary to the economy, cultures are de-territorialised and subjected to multiple hybridisations. Nature can no longer be seen as an essential principle and foundational category.

Alternative social and economic projects offer empirical evidence for noncapitalism and place-based consciousness. The defence of territory by indigenous social movements illustrates possibilities for rearranging the relationship between place and culture. Their struggle provides important lessons for thinking about alternatives.

The native mapping of a biological world and society cannot be interpreted in terms of Western social science concepts (Strathern, 1980).

Culture does not provide a distinctive set of objects with which one manipulates nature. Contrary to modern constructions, many tribal groups do not have a strict separation between biophysical, human and spiritual worlds. The construction of nature is predicated on links of continuity between the three spheres. This continuity is culturally established through symbols, rituals and practices embedded in particular social relations.

Indigenous knowledge is nested in practices of nature. While systematic classification of animals, plants and spirits may exist, they may not spell out the same modern boundaries between humans and non-humans. The entire universe may be conceived of as a living being. In considering that order and balance are maintained in the biophysical, human, and spiritual circuits, all beings are embraced in the universe by similar principles. In many indigenous cultures, views of time and the relationship between biological and social life are not linear but circular. Cognition reflects experience which embodies 'unbroken coincidence of our being, our doing, and our knowing' (Maturana and Varela, 1987, p. 25).

Since the natural world is integral to the social world, an image of social life is not necessarily opposed to that of nature. Social life has a particular attachment to a territory conceived of as a multidimensional entity. Local practices and relations are based on ensembles of meanings. Relations between cultural systems and productive relations can be highly complex.

Production in indigenous life incorporates cultural, ecological, and techno-economic factors into a strategy that is culturally sustainable. Productivity is understood in terms of particular cultural constructions, social relations, and ecological practices. This process is not subordinated to the economised production of commodities for profit and the rationality of managers and planners.

The struggle for survival in the rainforests is not oriented toward development or the satisfaction of needs even when economic and material improvements are an important issue. The right to exist is a cultural, political, and ecological question. Resistance is waged to preserve cultural and ecological attachment to a territory. Indigenous people may be open to certain forms of market exchange and engage with transnational movements in support of biodiversity conservation. However, they resist capitalist and scientific valorisation of nature. Resistance against capitalist intrusion is seen as a political strategy for survival. They are forced to raise a voice to defend themselves.

Place and culture become a source of political fact. A local model of maintaining a relationship with nature can be reinterpreted as a noncapitalist practice. Thus the politics for survival may be understood in terms of place and noncapitalism. Consciousness of place helps re-centre people in an integrated framework of humans and non-humans. The notion of place rebuilds a relationship between culture and nature.

In globalisation, culture is de-territorialised with the negation or disappearance of difference. The survival of place-based cultures can be ensured by a symmetrical relationship between the local and the global. The globalisation of the local has to be balanced with the localisation of the global. By moving away from bounded definitions of culture, the local can be reasserted to overcome asymmetric discourses of globalisation. In cultural politics based on the representation of reality, forms of opposition and resistance can embody a means of cultural affirmation.

Experimentation is indeed taking place in many localities through exploring the relationship between knowledge and practice. Production of cultures and identities in many communities around the world is linked to economic and ecological practices. The articulation of alternative identity is linked to places and their defence. By allowing manifold ways of constructing culture and identity, place-based practices can create alternative structures that give marginalised groups a chance to survive. Hybridisation might provide a new space not only for the dynamic elaboration of tradition but also for renegotiating forms of power predicated on class, gender and race difference. Constructing political strategies geared to the reassertion of difference can be based on the space created by hybridisation.

Local cultures and forms of noncapitalism can be used to overcome power differentials (Jacobs, 1996, p. 15). Knowledge of localities and identity contributes to the production of different meanings about economy and nature and helps generate alternative discourse within the conditions of capitalism and modernity. Projects of social transformation need to be associated with local processes of cultural reconstruction and invention. Noncapitalist imaginaries need to be projected into the constitution of economic structures.

The challenge remains how local knowledge is to be translated into power and whether this process can lead to the emergence of concrete projects and programmes. The defence of local cultures is not an easy political project, nor is there a guarantee for success. Global market integration brought about by capitalism controls a historical process and spatial practice. Local knowledge may not be free from domination in the sense that it is connected to the wider world through relations of power. Some social relations are determined by dominant external power relations and can be exploitative.

The extent to which local knowledge and practices of nature are sustainable is an empirical question. Not all local practices of nature are environmentally benign. Romanticisation of local knowledge and practice would do more harm than good (Jeong, 1995, p. 333). However, the vision of postdevelopment remains a hopeful sign if we accept the position that 'the future of local knowledge is contextually dependent on its globalistic potential to generate new sources of knowledge from within' (Karim, 1996, p. 128). The defence of local knowledge proposed here is both political and epistemological due to the fact that it arises out of the commitment to a discourse of difference.

Conclusion

Social totality consists of multiple and various relations (Gibson-Graham, 1996, p. 29). The existence of social, cultural and economic differences can be discovered by an anti-essentialist critique of capitalism. The critique of the privilege of space over place, of capitalism over noncapitalism, of global cultures over local ones provides political strategies of those who exist on the side of place, noncapitalism and local knowledge. The question of who defines place, culture and economy needs to be raised against the main thesis of globalisation which renders place-based practices inferior.

Local actors, old and new, play various roles in creating the networks in response to the multiple manifestations of the global. The forms of the global can be resisted by multiple local perspectives. Postdevelopment is under constant construction in the sense that the social history of cultures, economies and ecologies is rewritten by the emergence of new political and economic configurations. A hopeful turn for indigenous movements for survival may be found by the re-articulations of an ontological ground for existence.

12 What is Peace Culture?

MICHAEL N. NAGLER

> The most naive fallacy in the field (of peace research) is not only to believe in global architectonics, that the structure can be constructed and filled with any kind of actors; equally naive is to believe that structure is independent of culture. (Galtung, 1986, p. 259)

The other week I took my grandson and one of his friends, both ten-year-olds, to an event called 'Dinosphere' at Marine World Africa USA, a popular wildlife park in San Rafael, California. There was a long line waiting to get in to this particular part of Marine World, and we wound slowly round a large, rather featureless building, while a mechanical 'T-Rex' periodically came to 'life' and roared at us over the palisade. Next we were made to file through a series of corridors, all very uncomfortable, with hardly any human contact -- only occasional directions barked at us through loudspeakers. If the purpose was to create a sense of disorientation, it occurred to me, even of dehumanisation, the designers succeeded brilliantly, with their dimly lit corridors and almost nothing but a hard concrete floor and an iron pipe railing.

In the next to last holding tank before we entered the theatre -- for that was where we were going, I began to realise, Dinosphere was a show of some kind -- we were divided into groups and after a brief introduction by an actual person we were shown a short video that set the scene for what we were about to experience. Young men and women dressed up as 'scientists' in blue-green jump suits were shown swooping into various places around the planet and 'collecting data', but for the most part looking and acting more like some kind of military swat team. These data, the narrator explained, 'gave governments valuable information -- allowed them to monitor dangerous pollution'. In the last scene the narrator reported with some alarm that a new island had made its volcanic appearance somewhere off the coast of California. A platoon of scientists were shown sweeping out of their helicopter and racing into an official-looking office building. This was 'their most dangerous assignment' (it was not said why, and apparently didn't matter).

With this meagre orientation we were let inside the vast, dark theatre, and were soon strapping ourselves into huge seats resembling those in space-travelling rockets. When the show began, so did the seats; we jostled, jolted and spun about while the fantastic terrain on the screen raced toward and past us. Many near misses. Suddenly we were amidst a herd of huge dinosaurs who lumbered past us unconcernedly as we nearly crashed into their legs. We shot into a cave (virtually, of course) and aroused a fierce T-Rex who lumbered after our all-terrain 'vehicle' as it shot backwards at drastic speed. A few more encounters with huge pterodactyls, and we were safe: an enormous, fantastic helicopter ('Airborne, where are you?') came to whisk us 'home'.

I had huge fun at this thing. Since I have never owned a television set in the six decades of my life, and see very few movies, the experience was as affecting for me as my ten-year-olds. Unlike them, however, on the way home I reflected, what did all this mean? Was it not a text-book case of how deeply violence is embedded in the present culture? Dinosphere conveys a strong message about the prevailing paradigm of our culture, the worldview of the industrial age, which began roughly in the 17th century in Europe. This worldview sees man pitted against nature for survival. In this alienating universe, man needs high technology and (para-) military operations to rescue himself from threatening nature. During the show there was no attempt whatsoever even to imitate contact with nature; on the contrary we sped through the virtual landscape in hermetically sealed machines, enjoying our own thrills and chills. Nature kills, machines save: all this is a perfectly 'normal' message in a perfectly normal entertainment form today -- except that this particular entertainment was being offered in a park dedicated to preserving nature!

To be sure, a text about preserving nature had been delivered by the narrator of the preview (the scientists' mission is to help governments monitor pollution), but it was hastily dropped as soon as the dinosaurs started roaring. The 'sub-text' of Dinosphere, its real message in other words, is diametrically opposed to its superficial pretext about *preserving* nature (which happens to be the purpose of Marine World). It is a basic fact of communication science, that a sub-text communicates more powerfully than a surface text. Dinosphere thus amounts to a powerful anti-nature message embedded in a theme park about the protection of endangered species. I assume it draws people to the park and brings in needed entrance fees; but even on that assumption, its contribution to the cause of environmentalism is far outweighed by its dis-educational message about the dangers of savage nature which has to be warded off by high-technology combat missions carried out by governments.

Even in the narrator's pretext for the adventure of Dinosphere, be it noted (the one pro-nature message of the experience), we are told that 'governments' collect information and monitor dangerous pollution, though in real life it is individuals and non-governmental organisations that carry out most of the environmental action -- more often than not actually fighting against governments to do so. When you stop to think about it, the imaginary governments in the preview don't really do anything: they *monitor* dangerous pollution, which is meant to be somehow reassuring. Passivity and helplessness, precisely what has got us into the environmental crisis in the first place, is another major subtext of the popular Dinosphere show.

Violence against nature (and the violence *of* nature) is only one aspect of the violence inherent in the prevailing paradigm. Based as it is on a fundamental assumption of separateness, even alienation, it is in a very real sense a paradigm of violence itself. Not surprisingly, then, the violence of tyrannosaurs and pterodactyls is only one subtext of violence in Dinosphere. Alongside the thinly disguised military model of 'science', as the tool of industrial people in their fight for wealth and power, their fight against nature and against others, there were subtler, or at least more gut-level messages: how thrilling to race about uncontrollably, (almost) crashing into things, dazed by the loud noise, the disorientation, and above all the dehumanised way one has been treated -- all these are violent and violence-inducing typical features of modern 'entertainment'. So is the fragmented nature of the experience, the sheer speed and disconnectedness of the show's fictional events, which isolates physical, gut feelings (and negative ones at that) in the absence of any coherent meaning. It is interesting to remember in this connection that at the very beginning of cinematography, when D.W. Griffith created the notorious silent film glorifying the Ku Klux Klan, *Birth of a Nation* (1915), he also drastically chopped up the typical one-reeler of the day, which had about a dozen separate shots, to sometimes sixty-eight (Rogin, 1987, p. 192). Dinosphere, like MTV, would have been violent even if it had depicted 'scientists' getting out of their vehicle to smell the flowers -- such is the sensationalistic, mind-jarring texture of the genre. If 'war is made in the minds of men', then surely 'entertainment' forms that make our minds agitated and broken away from reality are laying the groundwork for that birth.[1]

We live in a culture saturated with, and in a way founded on violence. This chapter explores some subtle aspects of the way pro-violent messages are embedded in contemporary culture, and argues that the way to create a better culture is through 'principled' nonviolence; specifically, through concrete actions that build a nonviolent consciousness. At the present time, the nonviolent confrontation of large scale conflict by 'peace-teams' is seen as an outstanding example of behaviour that must be much better understood and supported as the cornerstone of such a new culture and consciousness. Today it is not primarily by operating on cultural forms themselves but by bringing to being a new consciousness based on nonviolent actions that we can re-establish culture on a new basis. Culture is a code we have no access to directly; we can only change it through the things encoded. While all other attempts to escape certain *kinds* of violence, such as crime or war, end up re-invoking the critical elements of the very violence they are trying to escape, the only approach to conflict that avoids them is the approach of principled nonviolence, of which Gandhi is the most articulate and complete representative. Gandhi, master of both the content (nonviolence) and the most effective form (concrete, especially constructive action) of a peace culture, is proposed as the 'culture hero' of the next millennium.

Culture of Nonviolence

A good person today cannot help agonising why, when peace is such a native good in the desires of every human being, a 'treasure that one cannot overpraise', when, as Augustine said, 'nothing that we can talk about, long for, or finally get is so desirable, so welcome, so good as peace', when even a young addict in California says 'I want quiet peace to inject my soul with forever', we seem to do nothing but push it further away from us?[2] There is a peace movement at the political margins of society; there is even a broader-gauge historical swell that Kenneth Boulding called 'the movement toward peace' (e.g., Boulding, 1975, p. 387). Why have they failed? It is not that they have not done some good -- God knows where we would be without them -- but why can they not prevail? Why has the 'movement toward peace' failed to do anything about the Cold War or the catastrophes of Yugoslavia, Rwanda, Cambodia, Chechnya, Sri Lanka, and Algeria, that rose in its wake, or, for that matter, the inner cities of the industrial states?

Dinosphere, silly as it is, shows us part of the answer. We live in a culture saturated with, and almost founded on violence. Even when we try to put out a different message, since we are constrained to use familiar forms of communication in order to be understood, the very medium can convert our message back into a statement about violence without our knowing it. What happened with Dinosphere all too often happens to the peace movement, as some scholars have begun to realise: in order to make ourselves heard, we enter the discourse of the mainstream; we enter its cultural assumptions, which undermine the very things we are trying to say.[3] That is why, as I believe Sisela Bok once said, peace researchers have often 'reflected back, as in a mirror, the priorities of their opponents'. The people who created Dinosphere may well have really believed they were creating a cultural form with a message about protecting the environment; but in order to get the attention of youngsters they gave them what they want, and what they want has been conditioned by completely violence-accepting commercial interests for five decades. Dinosphere shows, finally, that while we must change our culture, it is extremely difficult to do so by working within culture itself.

The fact that the commercial mass media, particularly television, stimulate people to violence has been thoroughly documented, but ignored. Given the depth and subtlety of the mind-shaping that is going on, we have to rank the 'V-chip' approach and the sporadic legislative gestures as utterly superficial. Perhaps we may get further, theoretically and practically if we were to concentrate on the complementary aspect of the problem: not so much how the media make violence seem acceptable as how they make nonviolence *invisible*. There is a very general principle involved here; namely, that we do tend to see the negativity in the world and not see the points of light which could reconstitute it. Violence is perhaps the most concrete and practical negative, for violence can be understood very broadly to encompass, in Johan Galtung's suggestive definition, the avoidable compromise of human needs (Galtung, 1969, pp. 168-74). Conversely, the single most important positive for us to be aware of is nonviolence.[4] A small increase in our general awareness of nonviolence -- what it is, what it has done and can yet do -- might just have an extremely salutary effect on the prevailing paradigm, probably far more than additional exposure or analysis of our ongoing violence. This simple shift of emphasis could have a revolutionary effect on peacebuilding. Most of the movement toward peace, it is fair to say, is reactive and becomes absorbed in fighting wrongs. If they turned that emphasis around, even if it meant or seemed to mean ignoring wrongs for a time being, progress toward peace would leap forward. One is reminded of Toynbee's famous formula: 'Apathy can only be overcome by enthusiasm, and enthusiasm can only be aroused by two things: first, an ideal which takes the imagination by storm, and second, a definite intelligible plan for carrying that ideal into practice' (Carlson and Comstock, 1986, p. 307).

Implicit in this argument is the assumption that nonviolence is, as it were, a better keyword than peace itself to focus our thinking and efforts on achieving peace. In fact, that assumption has been steadily gaining ground for the last quarter-century, so that recently when twenty Nobel Peace Prize Laureates issued an appeal for a new campaign for peace, it contained the following language: 'I sign and support the Appeal of The Nobel Peace Prize Laureates, so that the year 2000 be declared "The Year for the Education of Nonviolence", the years 2000 to 2010 be declared "A Decade for the Culture of Nonviolence", so that nonviolence be taught'.[5]

There are thus three steps to the argument I will be developing here, of which the first two are not particularly controversial. First, the way to revive the movement toward peace is by conscious attention to *culture* -- rather than politics. This is not because politics is not crucial but because culture is prior: our cultural assumptions determine our political decisions. Second, the key single element to focus on in the present culture is *nonviolence*.

To these two assumptions I am going to add a third, which may indeed be controversial or unsettling. Culture, defined as the encoding of a people's values and their way of interpreting the world, has traditionally been the preserve of privileged spokespersons, whom we may call artisans of the word, and it is perfectly natural to think that the way to create a better culture is to get artists and writers involved in creating an alternative voice.

For various reasons, however, today it is no longer possible to alter the prevailing culture through art or fiction; such change can only come from something concrete. 'Concrete' doesn't necessarily mean 'material'. It does mean something that produces a real improvement in how we collectively view things, what the media report and what schools teach. While many scholars from quite various disciplines have come to recognise the importance of narrative in how we view the world, and even how we learn from our experiences, it does not necessarily follow that writing or telling better stories will, by itself change things deeply enough to create a peace culture. Culture is a code to which we have no direct access. We can only change it through the things encoded.

One of the best quips about the invisibility of nonviolence comes from historian Theodore Roszak, who said, 'people try nonviolence for a week, and then when it doesn't "work" they go back to violence, which hasn't worked for centuries'.[6] A form of nonviolence now called Civilian-based Defence worked astoundingly well in Czechoslovakia in 1968, when the Czechs held off Soviet armies for eight months. Soviet military planners had expected, and by all standard military logic had a right to expect, that the country would fall into their hands in four *days*. Virtually no one took note of this astounding achievement which, activists perennially observe, had it been achieved by conventional means at the cost of much bloodshed, would have been world-celebrated. India wrested her freedom from the world-dominating British Empire through the greatest campaign of nonviolence known to human history, but then rapidly armed to protect itself from Pakistan, which was orders of magnitude weaker than Britain. Nonviolence has worked very well, and it is working very well to protect individuals threatened by extremely repressive regimes in Central America (Mahoney, 1997), to unseat dictators (Parkman, 1988) and otherwise check the excesses of their power (Zunes, 1994), to restore peace and to head off war. In one particularly stunning example a single, spontaneous demonstration by totally untrained women thwarted Hitler's policy of extermination with regard to 'half-breed' Jewish-Aryans, saving thousands from the very jaws of the holocaust (Stoltzfus, 1996).

Roszak told only the half of it: people try nonviolence and even if it *works* they go back to violence. They do this not because of a political bias but because they have no cultural framework in which to understand what they've just seen. No one would be fool enough to choose war who could 'see' peace, or use violence who could 'see' nonviolence, but because our culture does not allow our minds to register nonviolence when we see it we are effectively unaware that we have a choice. As any activist knows, the news media stonewall virtually every reference to nonviolence that comes across their desk; and we are doomed to keep on trying to make violence work rather than moving forward.[7] The tragic result of this default reaction is to intensify itself by vicious circles; in criminal justice (where we are really sliding into barbarism), race relations, and defence we resort to more and more forms of violence in order to control the threats caused by that very violence.

Writing a New Story

What behavioural scientists have learned about culture in the last few decades has moved us away from the simple 'nature/culture' dichotomy that dominated much earlier thinking to the realisation that culture-building is an extremely deep process which reaches back into biological evolution itself; as biologist and new-paradigm thinker Mary Clark has recently written, 'The transmission of the socially shared world view, is for human existence equally important as mating and the physical reproduction of offspring'.[8] Attitudes and behaviours surrounding violence, or its opposite, are no exception to this fact. It is the 'sacred narratives' of our culture (for the term, see Dundes 1984) that enable us to understand, or prevent us from understanding, what we're seeing. Often this only becomes clear during a sudden breakthrough, as when ethologist Frans de Waal suddenly realised that he was seeing chimps reconcile after a conflict: 'When the word "reconciliation" popped into my mind, it immediately illuminated the connection... The phenomenon became so obvious that it was hard to imagine that it had been overlooked for so long by me and by scores of other ethologists' (de Waal, 1989, p. 5). We live subject to Roszak's law because we do not yet have the narratives that enable us to understand nonviolent potentials in our own experience. It is in this sense that culture -- the controlling images and metaphors by which we construct the narratives of who we are and what we're doing here -- is the leverage point for any effort that can successfully change the 'minds of men' toward peace.

As the Dinosphere example shows (especially on the charitable assumption that its creators really thought they were sensitising children to the needs of the environment), it is extraordinarily difficult to understand, much less change the worldview in which one is embedded. Sometimes the only way to become remotely aware of it is through the eyes of someone standing outside the culture; for example, this ten-year-old Hopi girl struggling to understand our attitude toward the land and environment: 'Our people spoke to the Anglos, but they don't listen to us; they listen to hear themselves. My grandmother says they live to conquer the sky, and we live to pray to it, and you can't explain yourself to people who live to conquer -- just pray for them, too' (Coles, 1990, p. 25).

Normally, it is not a bad thing that cultural assumptions operate in the background or that the authoritative control over culture is concealed. The rules that peoples live by need protection against manipulation by selfish interests, not unlike the way our DNA needs to be hidden deep within structures of the body for its continuity across many generations. So in normal times even a certain amount of benign self-deception about the sources of our culture doesn't do too much harm, and on the other hand, sustains the norms that allow us to live together and stay reasonably close to at least a negative kind of peace.[9]

However, these are not normal times. Whatever social system we had in place to shape norms and culture through sacred narratives in the past has been overwhelmed by the mass media, which as we know are driven by special interests indeed -- money and power interests, which are not at all the interests of public health, individual well-being or peace. The results of all this have been contradictory, and thus not without hope. As Clark puts it, 'We may begin to suspect we are living in a world view whose jumbled narrative increasingly contradicts itself, while failing to fulfil our most fundamental needs for *belonging*, for *autonomy* and for *meaning*'.[10] We have begun to suspect this. The industrial-age message of Dinosphere, we note, had to be disguised (albeit thinly) behind a more acceptable message about the protection of the environment. That was certainly not the case a century and a half ago, when wildly popular Buffalo Bill programmes communicated their mass message about taming savages-and-nature (Slotkin, 1973, p. 565); it was not even true when William James wrote his famous essay on the 'Moral Equivalent of War'.[11] It is a sign of some progress that the still prevailing paradigm's ideology of conquest now has to be disguised, at least in regard to our relationship to our environment, so that a programme like Dinosphere has to include the recognition that nature has to be protected -- but 'include' is the rub: as we have seen, you cannot 'include' a message about the fragility of nature in a medium shaped by the conception that nature has to be conquered. The subtext, by now part of the medium itself, will undermine the text.

Yet we can take a certain comfort from the fact that the message is now 'jumbled' by contradictory elements instead of being just plain wrong; we can take comfort from the fact that cognitive dissonance is reaching discomforting proportions, because this 'paradigm breakdown' always has to come before a 'paradigm shift'. Without discomfort there will be no change (though most efforts to escape discomfort do not result in progressive or long-term change). We can also take comfort from the fact that awareness of culture and the importance of our narrative is becoming more widespread. The digest, *Utne Reader*, for September-October 1997, was titled 'Story Hysteria'. We may be able to harness some of that hysteria to create a healthier and less jumbled narrative.

Trivial as it may seem, let me go back to Dinosphere one last time. It is a disguised message about technology and violence. Disguised from whom? By whom? That is the first question we are tempted to ask. It is an elusive one. Scholars have known for some time that there is no such thing as neutral 'entertainment' without a subtext (Jewett and Lawrence, 1977, among others, for popular media in particular). That subtexts outweigh surface texts (and can contradict them) is very commonly the case, especially in periods like our own when an old worldview was ceding to some unclear alternative, and this is again pretty well known to parties interested in such things. But the question of *qui bono* (or should we say, *qui malo*), who is doing this to whom, is not so simple. Who is victimising whom in the Dinosphere story?

This brings us to the heart of the prevailing paradigm insofar as that paradigm determines how we address conflicts. In a strictly political approach, once we realise that the mass media are playing such an enormous and irresponsible role in obfuscating manifestations of nonviolence, and thus keeping the world so violent, our reaction is naturally -- but not always helpfully -- anger. When we think politically (in the accepted sense of the term), we look for victimisers and victims, and often no further. Find out who's doing this and make them stop: as Christopher Lasch used to say of this approach, we are always shifting the balance of power but not doing anything to redefine politics as something other than a struggle for power. But the new paradigm begins precisely when, along with a growing number of people, we become uncomfortable with this approach. We feel, in fact, that such a view is part of the problem instead of a solution. While not denying for a moment that people victimise people, setting up such a polarity can oversimplify and almost inevitably creates enmities and even hatreds just when we are trying to resolve them. After all, there is no clear 'them' and 'us' when we think about how people pull cultural wool over their own and one another's eyes. Network executives and newspaper editors respond to 'what the public wants'. Though they also help shape what the public learns to want (so their protestations are partly hypocritical), they would not serve up the prevailing fare for one minute if the public no longer patronised it. Years ago I heard a TV executive, who had been challenged to explain what kind of thinking went into his network's programming that year, shoot back indignantly, 'There was absolutely no thinking involved'. A few weeks after my visit to Marine World I took my grandson and his twelve-year-old sister to a real nature park called Safari West, where we drove right up to herds of zebra and other free-roaming exotic animals. I tried, without much hope, to say something about how much better this experience was than Dinosphere, but Abe, trying to be polite, only said, 'well...'.

Establishing fault and pointing fingers of blame is almost useless as a way of correcting things. Polarisation has become almost as automatic as breathing, and it does nothing but create rivalries and worsen the situation. Much of the controversial and often brilliant work of René Girard has highlighted the nearly universal tendency to apportion blame and ultimately reject 'others' as a precondition for peace: 'The creation of the perfect city, entry into paradise on earth, are always represented as depending on the prior elimination or forcible conversion of those in the "guilty" category' (Girard, 1987, p. 151). I cannot help juxtaposing with this theoretical principle the words of President Clinton before the UN General Assembly on September 22, 1997: 'Nations are now setting the international ground rules for the 21st century, laying the foundation for security and prosperity for all those who live within them, while isolating those who challenge them from the outside' (*New York Times*, 9/23/1997, A3).

One who understands the dynamics of conflict cannot but flinch at these words; if not irony, they evoke such poignancy as they repeat the endless logic of violence in this very context of a hopeful, upbeat vision of the future placed before the world's premier peacemaking body by the world's most powerful statesman. And let us not be lulled by the euphemism, 'isolating', in this pointed reference to Iraq, whose 'isolation' by the 'new world order' has resulted in the death by starvation and disease of an estimated half a million people, very largely children -- one of the greatest humanitarian disasters of the century.

Sacrificial logic may be cloaked in the rhetoric of righteousness, but it is decidedly the 'old law' of retribution and vengeance.

There is only one approach to conflict that avoids this polarisation and scapegoating, and that is the approach of principled nonviolence of which Gandhi is the most articulate and complete representative. This issue is of the first importance, not only because in a new paradigm people will resolve conflicts differently, but because I believe it is by beginning to solve conflicts differently that we act most effectively to bring into focus a new paradigm. Every conflict is an opportunity to invoke a new paradigm, and principled nonviolence is the name for that newness.

'Principled' nonviolence is meant to distinguish what Gandhi and Martin Luther King set out to do from what is called 'strategic' nonviolence. In strategic nonviolence, one simply acts without being violent, regardless of one's state of mind. While overt violence is absent, active concern for the well-being of the other is not necessarily present.[12] To be sure, strategic nonviolence has a role to play in taking the edge off intense conflicts and sometimes breaking the deadlocks of intolerable situations. In a world of intense and spreading conflict that we live in, there is often no time to wait until we have become saints (apparently a very time-consuming process) before we intervene. The beauty of strategic nonviolence is that it does not require the sometimes anguishing (but always, in the end, liberating) conversion of our 'natural' responses but can be done by anyone so inclined. When Bosnia exploded, for example, three thousand people were mobilised by an *ad hoc* project called *Mir Sada* (Seeds of Peace) for emergency intervention. But to lurch from one emergency to the next is not progress toward a new paradigm; to see the dawn of a new culture we need a new value system and worldview, and these can only come from the nonviolence that is based on active, self-sacrificing love, or 'soul-force'. A new culture, in other words, one that does not generate so much abrasive conflict in the first place, must take root from a new cultural idea -- specifically, a new idea of the person and the kind of power and influence persons can exert on each other. In this sense, strategic nonviolence -- whether merely provisional, whether the 'nonviolence of the weak' who might use force if they felt they could -- is not *radically* different from the general matrix of the industrial-colonial worldview. While it may shift power dramatically toward the previously disenfranchised, in the spirit of Christopher Lasch's observation, we would have to admit the ultimate definition of power remains 'power over' (the 'lust to dominate' to which Augustine traced the cause of all war) rather than 'power with'; the ultimate definition of the person remains that of a locus of self-interest. Most proponents of strategic nonviolence would *like* enemies to be reconciled, but they don't *provide* for it.

In principled nonviolence, on the other hand, reconciliation is built in; the reconciliatory outcome is contained in the very method. For these activists, reconciliation is more important than winning; reconciliation *is* winning. This kind of nonviolence does indeed arise from a different worldview which transcends dichotomization and scapegoating. The nonviolence invoked by persons like Gandhi and King -- and there have not been many like them -- was much more than a way to behave. It was a force generated by personal struggle, which Gandhi described vividly in 1920: 'I have learnt through bitter experience the one supreme lesson to conserve my anger, and as heat conserved is transmuted into energy, even so our anger controlled can be transmuted into a power which can move the world' (Prabhu and Rao, 1960, p. 16). Martin Luther King echoes this when he explains that during the campaigns of the Civil Rights Movement: 'nonviolent resistance caused no explosions of anger -- it instigated no riots -- it *controlled anger and released it under discipline for maximum effect*' (King, 1967, p. 17, italics added).

Largely strategic nonviolence has been used, since Gandhi's passing, to lubricate the transition from communist rule to democracy in Czechoslovakia and Poland (compare Yugoslavia or Romania), create a political space for dissent in the repressive regimes of Central America, and in other ways mentioned above. Such movements are essential to the maintenance of a semblance of justice in the industrial age; but to create a true culture of peace, we need something a bit more mind-boggling, more radically different. As King says, '[i]t is not enough to say, "we must not wage war". It is necessary to love peace and sacrifice for it ... the absence of brutal violence is not the presence of justice' (King, 1967, p. 185). While strategic nonviolent practitioners state, quite correctly, that a roused populace can neutralise the power of an illegitimate regime by withdrawing their consent from it (Sharp, 1973, p. 17), those who wield the weapon of Satyagraha put forward their own kind of power. We have mentioned that it arises from a different locus, namely a personal struggle for self-conquest. Likewise the way it restructures the relationship between disputants is entirely different: 'What Satyagraha does in such cases is not to suppress reason but to free it from inertia and to establish its sovereignty over prejudice, hatred, and other baser passions. In other words, if one may paradoxically put it, it does not enslave, it compels reason to be free' (Pyarelal, 1932, p. 35).

There is, without exaggeration, an entirely new energy involved in this transformative process, and from this new energy or new 'drive' comes a new regime.[13]

Life as Message

In his fine study of Jesse Jackson, serialised in the *New Yorker,* Marshall Frady gave a particularly beautiful description of how King conceived nonviolent power:

> King started from the essentially religious persuasion that in each human being, black or white, whether deputy sheriff or manual labourer or governor, there exists, however tenuously, a certain natural identification with every other human being -- that, in the overarching design of the universe which ultimately connects us all together, we tend to feel that what happens to our fellow human beings in some way also happens to us, so that no man can continue to debase or abuse another human being without eventually feeling in himself at least some dull answering hurt and stir of shame. Therefore, in the catharsis of a live confrontation with wrong, when an oppressor's violence is met with a forgiving love, he can be vitally touched, and even, at least momentarily, reborn as a human being, while the society witnessing such a confrontation will be quickened in conscience toward compassion and justice (Frady, 1992, p. 70).

Frady, capturing King's mind very well, invokes succinctly the key elements of a nonviolent worldview: the universe has an overarching design (which cannot be negative in character), every human consciousness without exception is a part of, is linked to this design; therefore in a 'cathartic' moment when right and wrong are suddenly thrown into relief there is something in human nature which cannot but respond humanely; right cannot but be notched up one step higher as 'the society witnessing such a confrontation [is] quickened in conscience toward compassion and justice'.

This is a beautiful description of what one scholar has called the 'nonviolent moment' (Mirsky, 1996, p. 23). History is dotted with such moments, when an oppressor's violence is unexpectedly 'met with a forgiving love' – and iron determination not to submit to his evil designs; and human consciousness is momentarily lifted from the darkness of selfish passion. Why do these moments not become hours and years; why do these numerous flashes -- the successful resistance to Caligula's statue in the Jewish Temple in 39-40CE (Crossan, 1991, pp. 131-36), the wives' rescue of their Jewish husbands from the jaws of the Gestapo in 1943 (Stoltzfus, 1996), the overthrow of Jorge Ubico in 1948 (Parkman, 1988), the Civil Rights marcher's breakthrough of a police and firemen barricade in Birmingham in 1964 (Lynd and Lynd, 1995, p. 401), Aung San Suu Kyi's similar defiance of a rifle squad in Burma a few years later (Kyi, 1991, pp. 120-26) -- never become a flood of light that dispels the darkness?[14] We have already offered a general explanation that we fail to 'connect the dots' which are these points of light, because we are culturally conditioned to see darkness instead. Gandhi himself has well described how 'history', for example, records lapses between moments of truth, not the moments themselves: 'Hundreds of nations live in peace. History does not and cannot take note of this fact. History is really a record of the interruption of the even working of the force of love or the soul... History, then, is a record of the interruptions of the course of nature. Soul-force, being natural, is not noted in history' (Gandhi, 1938, p. 70).

Pondering Frady's superb evocation of such moments, however, we can add something to our understanding of this bizarre situation. Frady is clearly not unsympathetic to what he is describing, so it is the more revealing that he speaks of moments 'when an oppressor's violence is met with a forgiving love...' There is nothing the least inaccurate in this language. The question is, is it complete? Does not even this description, sensitive and well-meant as it is, perpetuate a common misunderstanding about nonviolence? We tend to think of nonviolence as always, or at least primarily, a *reaction*. It can be, but more fundamentally it is a creative, ordering force, as Gandhi says, a part of nature. When we think of it as a reaction to evil, and specifically the humanly organised evil of social oppression, we are only seeing one small part, and a misleading part of its creative potential. Nonviolence is not limited in its effects to that kind of evil, in fact it cannot be limited by any kind, because nonviolence is primarily the mobilisation of good, which exists independently. Indeed, in Gandhi's view (and really that of anyone who is not a Manichean) it is *only* the positive that exists independently. Evil, as Augustine discovered with so much labour, is but good's distorting reflection -- distorted through the medium of human self will.

Clearly, anything that would allow a new cultural paradigm to emerge would have to be not 'deconstructive' only, but also constructive and ultimately, creative. And few people realise, whether they consider themselves in the 'movement' or not, that this is exactly what principled nonviolence is.

In 1651 George Fox was invited out of prison and offered his famous 'preferment' of being captain of a troop of horses instead of languishing in the dank, 17th century cell; but he rose to the occasion by giving in reply what has become a famous testimony of nonviolence: '[b]ut I told them I lived in the virtue of that life and power *that took away the occasion of all wars*... I [am] come into covenant of peace which was before wars and strife were' (Nickalls, 1952, p. 64).

Gandhi's political awakening began in his first confrontation with undisguised racism -- his rude ejection from the Durban train at Pietermaritzburg on May 13, 1893. Yet he seems to have shared from the first Fox's great insight that nonviolence does not come in moments or even in sustained campaigns but rather from a way of life, that it primarily exists to pre-empt violence rather than wait for opportunities to react against it, for he launched his resistance, one year after Maritzburg, on parallel tracks: one track was pressuring the Government to relent in its persecutions of the Indian community; the other was uplifting that community itself. As he quietly put it in an often-overlooked observation in *Satyagraha in South Africa*, already in 1894, 'the question of internal improvement was also taken up' (Gandhi, 1950, p. 43).

This attention to one's own weaknesses rather than, or at least alongside of attention to the opponent's offences is close to the heart of principled nonviolence and its regenerative potential. It seems only natural, and yet it still bears emphasis, that nonviolence eschews the posture of blaming others for one's difficulties. Even if they are in fact exploiting you, you must have weaknesses that give them the handle to do so. Thus, while he knew only too well the ruthlessness and arrogance of the Europeans by the time Gandhi wrote his great manifesto *Hind Swarāj, or Indian Home Rule* in November of 1909, he had to advise his fellow Indians that the British did not 'take' India by the sword and could not hold her by the sword; they could never have come in without her cooperation (Gandhi, 1938, p. 36).

This being true, it stands to reason that correcting one's own weaknesses is not only necessary in itself, it is a powerful way to resist exploitation by others. In the course of time, Gandhi came to feel it was the only way. Though his began, like almost all popular movements, as a reaction, where most movements stay fixed in that posture of 'getting *them* off our back' he added a different string to the community's bow: 'getting *us* up off our backs'. This process seems to have begun about a year after the shock of Pietermaritzburg had worn off, or rather had sunk in, and he fully realised that this 'evil' confronting him and the community would not go away overnight. As Satyagraha matured, so did the emphasis on self-purification. By the 1920s, back in India, it flowered as 'Constructive Programme', a roster of eighteen projects ranging from new education to healthcare, prohibition to cottage industry, designed to rebuild India from the ground up. It was no longer *also* the community's agenda but had steadily become their main agenda. As he put it in a letter to his colleagues in 1942, 'my real politics [is] constructive work' (Pyarelal and Nayar, 1991, p. 268).

In a world that is so negative, any positive movement or innovation will surely clash with the established order of things, but a proactive movement will do so from its own strength. For all these reasons, Gandhi came to feel that the primary emphasis of the freedom struggle must be on Constructive Programme. And so it was. The stunning 'nonviolent moments' which stand out for us as the history of the freedom struggle -- the 'Great March' in South Africa, the March to the Sea in 1930 and consequent 'raid' of the salt pans at Dharasana, the 'epic fast' against the attempt to create a separate electorate for different communities -- punctuated, but did not constitute that struggle. What constituted the struggle was undramatic, non-confrontational, dogged, constructive work. Once in 1940 when an impatient Indian asked him, what will it really take to get the British out, he said 'phenomenal progress in spinning'.

Gandhi: Culture Hero for the Third Millennium

There is an anecdote, doubtless apocryphal, about a savant who came to Napoleon when he was in the prime of his power. The savant pointed out that the emperor would need a new religion to go along with the new world order he was establishing, and offered that he, the savant, had anticipated that need by designing such a religion for him. 'That is excellent', Napoleon is said to have replied, 'Now go out and get crucified for it'. The point of the story is that we cannot change culture just for the asking. In order for culture to encode acts that have certain meanings, those acts have to take place. After all, when the industrial paradigm started in good earnest in the 17th century, old myths that were inconvenient to the new industrial enterprise were thrown out in favour of new ones as Carolyn Merchant has shown in her brilliant study of that fateful transition. 'The change in controlling imagery (from Earth as mother to earth as unruly female) was directly related to changes in human attitudes and behaviour toward the earth. ... Society needed these new images (of mastery and domination) as it continued the process of commercialism and industrialisation' (Merchant, 1980, p. 2). The symbols followed the practice; and so they must again, as we try, as we must, to reverse that mistake and reawaken a sense of reverence for life and nature.

The most dynamic activity in the peace movement now has the potential to do exactly that: this is the effort to provide volunteer nonviolent intervention in key areas of global conflict, part of a dream for world peace which has gathered momentum since the collapse of the Cold War and is now beginning to be documented by a handful of writers (Weber, 1993; Nagler, 1997; Mahoney and Eguren, 1997). Ranging in size and focus from the several-thousand-person interventions in former Yugoslavia to the exiguously small teams of Peace Brigades International or Witness for Peace volunteers who protect threatened human rights workers in Sri Lanka, Central America, Columbia, Israel-Palestine and elsewhere, these visionaries are providing the concrete material of a new peace culture.

Nonviolent volunteers who have risked their lives to interpose themselves between helpless individuals or groups and otherwise unstoppable paramilitary forces have saved many lives and created a political space for resistance in Latin America, Haiti, Sri Lanka and elsewhere. On a larger scale, such groups, when they have worked well, have even prevented war. If anything could break through the cloak of invisibility surrounding the potential of nonviolence, many feel that it will be nonviolent intervention.

Probably four things will have to happen in order for peace-teams' work to become 'visible'. First, all these actions grow out of Gandhi's concept that was originally more 'pre-emptive', more long-term and less interventionary in character (Weber 1996). I feel they will have to return to the Gandhian legacy in the course of time by growing from *ad hoc* emergency interventions into something like the standing peace armies he envisioned.

Second, they will have to take up many forms of constructive work when they are free from the urgency of an immediate conflict, and this implies that they will have to phase away *third-party* interventionary teams, which I believe have a definite role to play in emergencies, to indigenous-based standing volunteer groups whose track record has been considerably brighter, for understandable reasons.

Third, the great majority of us, who are not prepared to drop part of our lives and risk all in the chaos of a Columbia or a Sri Lanka, will have to find our role in supporting and publicising nonviolent interventions.

Fourth, in addition, we all have to bring to life other parts of the grand drama such interventions represent -- the entire project of nonviolent action against war -- in such a way that the general public begins to grasp that there is a larger picture they have scarcely suspected. Given these four parallel developments, peace teams and nonviolence in general could escape the fate of invisibility that has kept nonviolent action under a bushel for all these years.

Both in this particular thrust and in the larger 'movement toward peace' I have been emphasising the importance of Gandhi, and now would like to enlist some other reasons for that emphasis. We moderns like to think of ourselves as pragmatic people. Of course, we gush and sentimentalise, we are falling prey to appalling superstitions as our educational systems break down, but at heart we believe in very concrete, even material realities. In history we ask, 'what really happened'; in science we suspend judgement on anything that cannot be measured. Science is what Willis Harman used to call the 'knowledge-validating system' of our civilisation.

Gandhi is a perfect model for modern nonviolence in this regard. Being Hindu to the core, the divorce of science from religion -- in a word from spirituality and values -- had simply never happened. Nonviolence was not religion (in our sense of the word), but the science of learning to move with those laws. This allowed him to make the statements that can thrill modern listeners:

> This is no appeal made by a man who does not know his business. I have been practising with scientific precision nonviolence and its possibilities for an unbroken period of over fifty years. I have applied it in every walk of life -- domestic, institutional, economic and political. I know of no single case

in which it has failed. Where it has seemed sometimes to have failed, I have ascribed it to my imperfections (Prabhu and Rao, 1960, p. 130).

What is more, he seems to have been aware that in this day and age concrete actions speak to us in a way that signs and symbols do not. We make a fuss about symbols, we even can kill each other for things that turn out to be only symbolic, but our 'bottom line' is things we consider to be concrete: land, money, medicine, numbers and bodies. This also suited perfectly Gandhi's own persuasion; for all his spirituality he had little to do with rituals, for all his superb political showmanship he almost never relied upon *mere* symbols, but rather on the symbolic power of deeds that were practical and concrete. It can be easy to miss this point. For example, on November 6, 1913, 5,000 men, women and children, striking indentured labourers and their families, set out on what is now known as the 'Great March' from the mining town of New Castle in Pretoria to the Transvaal border. While this has been the model for many a 'peace march', most modern marchers overlook the telling difference between the prototype and their own imitation: why were the labourers marching? The Indian miners went on strike, and as a consequence had been thrown out of their living quarters, which were at the mine heads. What was Gandhi to do with them? He resolved on marching them thirty-six miles into the Transvaal. If arrested, he reasoned, they would fill the jails; if not, they would make it to Tolstoy Farm and continue the strike, either way pressuring the Government to respond. He did *not*, in other words, organise a march as a symbolic protest or a demonstration; he led them on a march because they had to get somewhere -- and on the way they could violate an unjust regulation by way of civil disobedience.

If the non-cooperation aspect of nonviolence, the great Satyagraha campaigns, advanced by concrete, and not merely symbolic steps, that was even more true of Constructive Programme. By manufacturing real salt (which was illegal) and real cloth (which happened not to be), he created the infrastructure of freedom in a way that gave immeasurable strength to the acts of defiance he predicted would be increasingly less frequent. Cooperation with good (to paraphrase Martin Luther King) steadily overtook in importance non-cooperating with evil; both required concrete acts for their power. Of course, the spinning wheel is *also* a symbol; it's a very ancient symbol in India, a symbol of the world-process, the 'wheel of existence, of life and death'; in Buddhism the 'wheel of the law'. But what brought that ancient symbol back to political life were real wooden wheels spinning real cloth to answer an immediate economic need. *Charkha,* meaning both the spinning wheel and the campaign to set it back in motion, created economic sufficiency in the hands of idled, often starving people, hundreds of local networks for getting raw material to spinners, get their products to its market, provide and repair the capital equipment of wheels, carding bows, etc., an ethos of simplicity and solidarity with the poorest of the poor, and last but not least, freedom. A picture of a spinning wheel on a billboard or a flag (where it resides today) could have done none of those things.

I believe Gandhi felt that to do something that was only symbolic would send the message either that there was nothing practical to do, or that they were largely helpless -- both very wrong. It is true that an occasional novel like *Silent Spring* or *The Fate of the Earth* can fire people's imagination, but thousands of novels do not, while Mother Teresa created waves of peace by helping the destitute on the Calcutta streets. A well-aimed concrete act has a great deal of symbolic power. Gandhi felt it was unnecessary and even wrong to go for the symbol itself; a movement for today must draw upon the symbolism of the real, not the reality of symbols.[15]

Constructive Programme

The 'jumbled narrative' of our culture is leading us into disaster, and in various ways some people are becoming aware of that. Rarely in history has there been a culture more ripe for change. In order for change to be lasting and positive, however, I am convinced that it will have to arise from events that reveal the power of principled nonviolence. There is both overt and concealed, or 'structural' violence in the present world; both can be reversed by changes that awaken, conscience, by Satyagraha. It does not particularly matter in what sector of society we begin.

In criminal justice, for example, what has been called 'peacemaking criminology' would replace the prevalent 'warmaking criminology' that is based on retribution, the 'old law' back to which we are rapidly regressing in our ignorance of the alternative (Pepinsky and Quinney, 1991). Peacemaking criminology currently exists in isolated, non-governmental programmes virtually ignored by the media and the general public. If it spread beyond this margin, it would work a deep change in our mindset. I have argued, however, that an even more dramatic change would take place if we could see nonviolence replacing war. I have deliberately said 'if we could *see* nonviolence replacing war', because to a degree it is already happening. Where unarmed volunteers are facing down soldiers and paramilitaries, they are demonstrating the potential of nonviolence to replace armed interventions as the way to contain deadly conflict.

If enough people would see and understand this, we would be much closer to peace culture. There are existing alternatives in many other fields that demonstrate the same principle: in healthcare, the environment, social welfare and education, and many such areas. Sometimes the pioneers working such changes do not very well understand themselves what principles are involved; if they did -- or when they do -- these people will be able to articulate their vision so that, given other favourable conditions, starting sporadically but becoming more systematic, the different force being invoked would bring in its wake totally different assumptions about who we are and what we should be doing on this planet.

Of course this is a vast picture. It can be bewildering, but it does have an inner coherence. Hence Gandhi's emphasis on the spinning wheel -- *Charkha*. *Charkha*, the most constructive of the constructive programmes, as well as the most concrete and the most readily doable by everyone without prior organisation (though it led to a superb set of organisations in time) was the flagship project, or as he put it, the 'sun of the solar system' that was Constructive Programme. It could be grasped by anyone -- and, more to the point, done by anyone -- and held in itself the meaning of Constructive Programme as a whole. We, too, should think in terms of a total programme addressing every aspect of needed change *and* a model programme embodying the principles of change. We need both. Some years ago, after a talk on peace at the Berkeley campus, the speaker was asked, 'As an activist, I find it frustrating that we're trying to stop a war here, stop genocide there, stop the arms race all over, and the minute we prevent one thing, there are three more. What we're not stopping is what's causing all these things. And I'm wondering if you have any sense of what that is'. She didn't. We can't afford to 'fix' criminal justice while turning our back helplessly (or uncaringly) on carnage in Kosovo, Tibet, Rwanda or wherever else it next happens, because the principle of not caring will come back to dampen our attempts to put care to work somewhere else. At the same time, though, we as individuals can't do everything. What, then, should be our flagship project?

America is not a materially poor country, like Gandhi's India. We have poverty, increasingly, but it is not due to the lack of things to go around. Therefore 'constructive', in our context, needn't quite mean 'productive' in the same sense that *Charkha* produced real cloth. Producing more is not what America needs to do. I propose, indeed urge, that the flagship project that everyone can get involved in starting now is to put sanity in control of the media. Absolutely everyone can extricate him or herself from the web of violent imagery that the prevailing media have become, and let the networks know they are doing so. It's very effective. Some can also be directly involved in creating alternative programmes, but I lay the greatest stress here on boycotting the prevailing media because that will lay the groundwork for the new nonviolent culture where it's most important, right in our own consciousness.

Every other issue will be beneficially affected. Take that of criminology, once again. When the carnage in Yugoslavia began, very few people seem to have noticed an analysis that explained perfectly what had happened, unlike the incoherent media message about 'the weight of history' and so forth (as though everyone whose ancestors were enemies in 1389 would naturally start killing each other in 1991). I refer to two journalists whose interview was reported in the *Washington Spectator*:

> After all these centuries, why are they killing one another? Volumes have been filled with political analysis... But in all this one banal factor has been overlooked: the poisonous power of propaganda.
>
> The Slav populations of the other formerly communist East European countries just to the north, in Hungary and Romania, developed a hearty scepticism about what they saw on state television or read in government-run newspapers. For some reason, that kind of doubt died in Yugoslavia, if it ever existed. People here have always believed, and still believe, what they see and hear on TV.[16]

We can apply this insight to the rise of criminal violence in America: 'criminals' are people who believed what they saw on television -- that other people are objects, that in order to be fulfilled we need to exploit others and possess as much as possible. We all believe it to some degree. They were unfortunate enough to believe it to a larger degree. Unlike in Yugoslavia, a particular ethnic group is not being set against another, and unlike that situation (or Rwanda's) the message involved is subtext rather than out on the surface, but these differences are not critical. The mass media are causing the upsurge of crime (and misrepresenting, by mythologising, the 'war on crime' which is our unfortunate response). If we bear this in mind, it will help us not only put our attention where it belongs, on the culture of violence that caused the criminalisation rather than on its first victims, those unusually affected by that culture's message, it will also help us give the right *kind* of attention. Non-cooperation with evil must never shade over into animosity toward evildoers -- not even into labelling them as such. In that vein, a realistic response to offenders, a response that is neither sentimental nor vindictive, must begin by accepting them mentally into the world of the salvageable, so we can reintegrate them socially into the world of the law-abiding.

In conclusion, I have argued that the way to create a peace culture is not by operating directly on cultural forms, though that can help, but through actions that embody a different cultural principle, and that can only be through acts of principled nonviolence, including, in fact privileging, what Gandhi called Constructive Programme. Finally, I suggest that in our adaptation of the constructive programme here in the West the 'sun' should be the complete overhaul of the mass media, a boycott of the media as they now are, which can be begun effectively by every one of us, and a judicious new use of their technologies for truth. The rest of the 'solar system' would be made up of various applications of Satyagraha to today's structural and overt problems of conflict.

The only thing that can replace a jumbled narrative is a coherent one -- and in today's world, a real one. Constructive programmes wherever possible, and nonviolent resistance wherever necessary, thus becomes the pattern we are seeking for from which to create a culture of enduring peace. More and more, Gandhi's work and struggle emerge as the key narrative.

Notes

[1] It is interesting in this connection that important words for 'destructive wrath' in early Indo-European languages derive from a root meaning 'activate the mind'. Refer to Muellner (1996, p. 177).

[2] See Augustine, *City of God, pp.* XIX.xi; Teenage heroin addict, in YO, Jan/Feb '97, p.7. Inaugurating a Buddhist temple in Oahu the Rev. Dae-Won Ki said, 'The word "peace" is a banner of our human tribe, and so much have we disgraced and corrupted the word that we feel ashamed to utter it. We continue to employ violence in order to end violence, drawing ourselves ever deeper into disaster' (*Peace and Justice* newsletter, Nov. 1982).

[3] See Ivie (1954) and Cohn (1987), and for a recent roundtable, contributors to *Peace and Change*, vol. 22, no. 3 (1997).

[4] For further definitions of violence and non-violence, refer to my recent article in *ReVision* (Nagler, 1997).

[5] Cedex 2 - France, September, 1997. See earlier the growing consensus in peace research that the opposite of peace is not war, but violence (Schneider, 1973, p.149).

[6] At the moment, neither I nor Professor Roszak can locate where he said this.

[7] And not just activists. While writing this chapter I faxed information to the AP about an impending nonviolent re-possession of their university by Albanian students and professors in Kosovo. When I called the next day to see if my fax had got through I was blandly told 'they tossed it'. The next day's news was about airline crashes and earthquakes.

[8] Mary Clark, *Human Nature Revised* (unpublished ms. kindly made available by the author). Clark goes on, 'although you would be unlikely to appreciate this if you paid attention only to sociobiologists and evolutionary psychologists'. See also Carolyn Merchant (1980, p. 43), who explains that in a holistic view '[i]nstead of dichotomising nature and culture as a structural dualism, ...sees natural and cultural subsystems in dynamic interaction'.

[9] I think in this connection of the scientific 'dereconstruction' of our historical knowledge of the life of Jesus that has been done by the Jesus Seminar (e.g., Borg, 1987; Crossan, 1991). This work, with its unimpeachable scientific and historical credentials, may hurt people whose only basis for faith, and in turn for an ethical life, was what they thought they knew about that life. Good science, in a vacuum like ours, may not be such good sense.

[10] Mary Clark, *Human Nature Revised*, p. 38. I believe that Clark means 'diversity' by the word 'autonomy' in this definition.

[11] If instead of military conscription, the youth, James proposed, would serve in the 'army enlisted against *Nature*' (1911, pp. 290-91): 'They would have paid their blood-tax, done their part in the immemorial human warfare against nature; they would tread the earth more proudly, the women would value them more highly, they would be better fathers and teachers of the following generation'. No comment.

[12] Gandhi's classic definition of the difference between principle and strategic violence is given in Chapter Thirteen of *Satyagraha in South Africa*.

[13] I am thinking of Augustine's refrain in the *City of God*: *duo amores faciunt duas civitates*, 'the two human drives create two world orders'.

[14] Another is recorded in the classic study of Richard Gregg (1935, p. 28) when a British policeman beat a Sikh protestor to the ground but when the man got slowly back on his feet and kept on coming toward him he found he couldn't hit him any more: 'You just can't go on hitting a blighter when he stands up to you like that'.

[15] The attempt to create peace or protest rituals often backfires; a striking example is the pouring of blood on draft files and the like. The protestors think that they are marking the offensive objects as radically other (MacQueen, 1992, p. 67); but that is the opposite of what anointing with blood means in our unconscious reservoir of cultural symbols: note that the English word 'bless' comes from Gothic *blodi sijian*, 'sprinkle with blood'. Like Dinosphere, the well-meaning protestors were reversing their message with its far more powerful subtext. For another example of rituals backfiring see Jack Zipes, 'Tales Worth Telling', reprinted in *Utne Reader* (September-October, 1997, p. 42).

[16] Washington Spectator, Feb. 1, 1994, p. 2.

Part IV

Transformation of Global Order

13 Human Needs and the State

DOV RONEN

This chapter is anchored on the premise that, as the Cold War ended, much of the repression and restraint directly associated with ideological confrontation waned, creating behavioural manifestations aimed at the satisfaction of human needs. The pursuit of vaguely defined national interests by governments and the financial success of economic entrepreneurs are not likely to lead to the creation of a global order that satisfies human needs. While various forms of repression could still change behavioural manifestations designed to satisfy needs, the pressure for the satisfaction of human needs can neither be altered nor repressed. Human needs prove to be truly universal, since all human beings are the same organism. This implies that alterable institutions and policies have to fit unalterable human beings, never *vice versa*.

The human being is not only a social animal or *Homo Economicus*, but also a living organism. It is the realisation of this fact that led me to look at human needs from a cross-disciplinary perspective and, over the years, to the conviction that, without understanding at least some aspects of the functioning of the human organism, including the role of the human brain, we cannot possibly understand human needs.[1] Human needs are related to the requirements of the human organism, so human needs theory must be cross-disciplinary.

A cross-disciplinary analysis of human behaviour, society, and institutions in general is long overdue. It is the artificial separation between the social and natural sciences, and the resulting shying away from a cross-disciplinary approach, that has enabled social scientists to be concerned with 'flourishing economies' and 'improving political climates,' instead of being directly concerned with human beings. There is no true assessment of whether or not human beings are indeed the beneficiaries of 'flourishing economies' and 'improving political climates'.[2] Such a cross-disciplinary analysis is necessary in order to understand the complex issues that pertain to various facets of human behaviour, including conflict.[3] Understanding ongoing political, social, and economic changes, as well as the evolving future global order, requires analysis reaching beyond social science paradigms.

This chapter is based on a synoptic introduction of the cross-disciplinary approach and its utility for the analysis of human behaviour and institutions. It consists of two parts. The first part explains the nature of human needs and finds the connection between our brains and needs satisfaction. The second part focuses on the community as the 'natural' human aggregation; on the state, where most human beings attempt to pursue the satisfaction of their needs; and finally on the government which is supposed to be occupied with satisfying the needs of the governed. The chapter will also suggest that needs-propelled human behaviour is causing the state to fade away and is now shaping a future global order that can be more responsive to the needs of human beings.

The Human Being

Human Needs

The issue of human needs has been explored by a number of scholars over the years (Murray, 1938; Maslow, 1943; Quigley, 1961; Davies, 1977; Galtung, 1980; Burton, 1990b). Each of them has recognised that human needs should be distinguished from a want, a wish, a desire, or a demand (Galtung, 1980, p. 59). However, there have only been superficial references to human needs in terms of the needs of the human organism.[4] If human needs are not met, the mature human being would either not survive, or would not be able to function physically or psychologically.[5]

Human needs are not acquired through socialisation. Food is a human need not because mothers inculcate in their new-borns an interest in eating, not because it is customary to eat, or not because one thinks eating is a good idea, but because the organism requires food. The need for freedom from repression is not learned, nor is it merely a moral principle. What we may learn from various sources, including moral principles, is about our *right* to freedom as well as about our *right* to eat. We may also learn from our social environment about the various *ways* to satisfy our needs.

Needs are not synonymous with wants, desires, demands and interests. Since we *want* to satisfy our needs, we may have an *interest* in satisfying them, but, above all, our organism *must* satisfy them. The frequent use of the term 'needs' in a wide variety of contexts is primarily responsible for its misuse. One does not *need* a fur coat for protection from cold, but may merely *want* one; the human need of protection from cold weather may be satisfied by any warm piece of clothing. Saying that 'the state needs a strong army to defend against its neighbour' is no more than an expression of an opinion that a state *should* have an army. Having an army is not a need for two reasons. First, states do not have intrinsic needs as human beings do. Second, a human need for security may not require an army, but merely good neighbourly relations.

Human needs can be divided into a set of *physical* or *material* needs, and a set of *psychological or psychic* needs.[6] The set of *physical* needs includes, among others, food, water, shelter, sex, and medical care for our bodies. In the set of *psychological* needs we might list, among others, love, respect, trust, appreciation, friendship, and a sense of belonging as opposed to hatred, disrespect, alienation, fear, threat, repression and isolation.[7] Whereas various specific needs in one set may need to be combined with specific needs in the other set, each of the two sets of needs should be regarded as an analytically distinct category.[8]

Each human organism has its own personal needs. Human needs do not refer to socially, politically, or economically defined *groups*, such as voters, consumers, workers, heads of households, populations, investors, or entrepreneurs. Specific human beings can be hungry and homeless. Attributing needs to groups or to categories of human beings may be useful for specific purposes, such as submitting collective demands for a pay-raise. However, for *understanding* the meaning of needs, we have to focus on the personal needs of each human organism.

Human needs are common denominators for all members of humanity at any given time and place since human needs are universal.[9] However, given his or her own genetic makeup and potentialities, each human being is different from any other.[10] Needs are not different because of cultural settings. Individualism, a behavioural pattern specific to Western culture, has no relevance to the needs of the human organism. Needs are identical from person to person and from culture to culture. What *is* different is human *behaviour* and activities. Behaviour aimed at satisfying one's own needs is also affected and shaped by culture. Physical and psychological needs, on the other hand, are shared by all of us.

I prefer the word 'resources' to the satisfiers of needs proposed by Galtung (1980, p. 60). Resources that can satisfy *physical* needs are usually tangible and include, among others, food, water, shelter, and clothing.[11] Tangible resources are relatively easy to measure. Resources that can satisfy *psychological* needs are usually intangible and include what we may perceive through our senses, especially sights and sounds. Intangible resources are not easily measured. Love, a psychological need, is not met by the easily measured size and value of a present we give or receive for a birthday, but by *seeing* the present and the note attached to it. Sights and sounds that may satisfy our need for psychological comfort, contentment, self-esteem, and pride are not easily measurable resources. However, the intangibility and undefinability of resources needed to satisfy psychological needs do not render them less real for the organism than tangible resources that satisfy physical needs.

Tangible resources are obtained through such activities as fishing, mining, hunting or trading. They may also be obtained through remunerated work and profitable investment. All these and a range of other activities encompass a wide category of economic behaviour. Intangible resources are obtained through interactions between human beings.[12] Human interactions encompass a wide category of social, cultural, and political behaviour. Thus, to use shorthand terms, 'economics', in principle, should cater to the physical needs of human beings; socio-political interactions pertain to the psychological needs.

A distinction should also be made between *a resource* and its *sources*. A resource for satisfying a physical need may be water. A source of much of the water in Israel, for example, is Syria. Words of love are a resource for satisfying a psychological need, while their source may be a parent. In more general terms, sources of resources for satisfying physical needs may be found mainly in the material environment. However, sources of resources for satisfying psychic needs may be found mainly in the social environment.

Minding Our Needs

The exploration of the nervous system is important since, without at least some understanding of the nervous system, especially its connection to our two sets of needs, we cannot possibly understand human behaviour involved in satisfying these needs. The following section is devoted to a brief presentation about the nervous system or, more specifically, about the connection between the functioning of the nervous system and human behaviour toward the satisfaction of our two sets of needs.

How the human brain, the main component of the nervous system, functions has puzzled thinkers for centuries. Many different paths of research have been followed, and many theories have been proposed (Lumsden and Wilson, 1983; MacLean, 1973; Restak, 1979; Sagan, 1977; Sulloway, 1979; Symons, 1979). Despite the growing volume of exciting research in the past few decades, much has yet to be learned even by specialists. What may be counted as 'known' about the brain is that all our contacts and interactions with the outside world are made through it; our brain and our nervous system are always involved in the activities of other parts of our organism; and our nervous system plays a part in all our behaviour from the simplest to the most complex actions. The question that interests us here is how.

My propositions about brain functions are primarily extrapolated from the thesis of Paul MacLean, a medical doctor, who was Chief of the Laboratory of Brain Evolution and Behaviour at the National Institute of Mental Health from 1971 to 1985.[13] MacLean's thesis, as I understand it, is that the human brain is not one big, intelligent machine. Although the human brain has indeed evolved through natural selection, it has not supplanted but merely surpassed the more primitive brain of other animals and early humans. In other words, the process of biological evolution has not eliminated our more primitive brains, but built on them. Thus, other animals do not have the highly evolved brain that humans have, but all animals, including humans, have nervous systems that contain a primitive brain.

The foundation of the human brain is the neural chassis and parts of the mid-brain. The neural chassis provides the fundamental structure and organisation of the entire nervous system. It regulates circulation and respiration and other basic life functions. Three types of brains have evolved and formed layers over the neural chassis. The three basic brains, argues MacLean, show great differences in structure and chemistry. 'Yet all three must intermesh and function together as a *triune* brain' (MacLean, 1973, p. 7). They are:

(1) The R-complex, or the reptilian brain.[14] It is the oldest brain in our nervous system, situated on top of the neural chassis.

(2) The limbic system, or the old mammalian brain. It evolved through millions of years from the forebrain of the most advanced part of the reptilian.

(3) The neocortex, or the neo-mammalian brain, is the result of millions of years of evolution of the most developed part of the old mammalian brain.

The most advanced 'human' brain is the neocortex. It is the brain of reading, writing and arithmetic. With our evolved neocortex, we have the capacity to learn details of human history, provide our interpretation of an ideology, express feelings and views verbally and in writing, and study our own nature. The evolved parts of the human brain solve complex problems, but the primitive brain continues to function alongside or under the more evolved part of the brain.

Functions of the Triune Brain[15]

The human nervous system is the guiding mechanism that identifies and selects from among available resources those needed by the *human organism* for survival and well-being. In other words, the brain supervises the process through which the organism's needs are to be met. Our nervous system functions constantly and automatically to mediate the rest of the human organism with the needed tangible and intangible resources, so that our organism survives and attains a degree of well-being.

Specific parts of the brain do not commonly function alone but are assisted by other parts of the brain to perform certain functions. In addition, in my view, experts have concluded that if a specific part of the brain is damaged, other parts of the brain *could* come to serve as substitutes (Konner, 1982, Chapter 4). However, it is also my understanding that while the parts of the brain are interconnected and can be substituted, they are, to a considerable degree, specialised. It seems to me that MacLean's thesis supports this interpretation, as I shall illustrate here.

First, our R-complex, our reptilian brain, 'programmes stereotyped behaviours according to instructions based on ancestral learning and ancestral meaning' (MacLean, 1973, p. 8). Therefore, the R-complex appears to guide mammals, including humans, to do the tasks of selecting home sites, building shelters, mating and breeding.

Second, the limbic system is used by human beings and some lower animals to judge whether something is edible or not, or whether other animals are dangerous. More specifically, the lower part of the limbic system is 'primarily concerned with self-preservation both as it pertains to obtaining the requisites of life and avoiding the claws of injury and destruction' (MacLean, 1973, p. 15). When this part of the brain was surgically excised in wild monkeys, they lost their sense of fear (did not flee), became tame (did not fight), tried to eat objects such as metal nuts and bolts, and faeces (did not eat properly), and developed bizarre sexual behaviour (did not procreate) (MacLean, 1973, p. 15). In short, they lost their fundamental survival skills. In humans, the limbic system is also connected with the right hemisphere of the neocortex. Together they are responsible for the emotions of fear, anger, hatred, and love that *relate* to the functions of flight, fighting, killing, and reproduction. They are functions which guide the behaviour that promotes the two basic life principles of self-preservation and the preservation of the species.

Third, our neocortex, the new mammalian brain, has four major regions, or lobes: the frontal lobes (whose principal functions are believed to be deliberation and the regulation of action), parietal lobes (spatial perception), temporal lobes (variety of perceptual tasks), and occipital lobes (vision) (Sagan, 1977, p. 92). The neocortex is externally oriented. It receives information predominantly from outside sources through the eyes, ears, and somatic receptors of touch. Clinical research indicates that the various parts of the neocortex provide us with what we consider to be our human dimensions. We can live and act without the parietal lobes, but we would not understand what others say to us. We can exist and act without the frontal lobes, but we would lose our 'self', i.e., our conception of ourselves in relation to others.

Between Brains and Needs

This reinterpretation of MacLean's thesis on the triune brain is the basis for my overall proposition. The human brain 'acts' on the organism's behalf through different parts of the triune brain selecting resources that satisfy the needs of the organism. The selection is performed by a process called dichotomising (Flohr, 1987, p. 186). It involves the *memory bank*, located in various parts of the R-complex and the limbic system, where memory is stored both genetically and through nurture. Dichotomising occurs when incoming sensory material activates neuronal processes of selection, comparison and matching, resulting in either positive or negative reaction to the resource, or to the source of that resource (Davies, 1970). I also propose that the R-complex and the limbic system are mainly involved in the selection of resources to satisfy *physical* needs, and the neocortex is mainly involved in the selection of resources to satisfy *psychological* needs.

Satisfying Physical Needs

Resources for the satisfaction of physical needs are selected by the dominant channels of taste and smell -- the olfactory senses -- located primarily in the limbic system.[16] The limbic system and the R-complex either *accept* or *reject* a resource.[17] If the smell or taste of a resource matches with 'good' smells and tastes in the brain's memory bank, then the reaction of the brain will be favourable: eat or drink this. If the smell or taste of a resource does not match, or matches with 'bad' smells and tastes in the memory bank, then the reaction of the brain will be unfavourable: avoid this.[18]

As resources to satisfy physical needs are selected through the R-complex and the limbic system, and criteria for selecting resources are stored memories of tastes and smells, the *sources* of resources of tastes and smells that satisfy physical needs are not important, perhaps irrelevant. For example, Cuban sugar, a resource, packaged in a bag with a Red Star indicating the likely 'communist' source of that resource, would satisfy the physical need for sugar just as much as sugar from the United States packaged in a red-white-and-blue bag. The source of the resource is irrelevant to our more primitive brains.

Lower animals, without the evolved neocortex of human beings, must control the satisfaction of physical needs through the R-complex, the limbic system, and perhaps other primitive parts of their nervous system alone. Human beings can *supplement* the processes performed by the olfactory senses and other primitive channels with information received and processed through various parts of the neocortex. Political and ideological considerations performed by the neocortex can influence the dichotomising process. It is due to the intervention of the neocortex that sugar originating in Cuba, *considered to be* a hostile communist country, may be rejected. Nurture, laws, education, and brainwashing can affect the process of dichotomising the resources needed to satisfy our physical needs. Operating through our neocortex may bring us to exclude Cuba as a source of sugar, Iraq as a source of oil, Japan as a source of cars, or persons of other races or religions as sexual partners.

It is crucial for our assessment of the evolving future global order that, although our neocortex *can* influence the more primitive parts of our nervous system in selecting physical resources for our needs, it would be incorrect to assume that our neocortex can take over the process entirely. The proof of the pudding is still in its eating and not in its appearance. The colour, shape, presentation, or origin of the pudding may please our 'intelligent' eyes, but if it smells or tastes rotten, we won't eat it. The human behavioural response for the satisfaction of physical needs is ultimately controlled or supervised by the limbic system and the other more primitive parts of our brain. If they indicate that a certain food is edible and fresh, then it is, in fact, not intrinsically important whether the food comes from Texas, France, Timbuktu, or Cuba. Any part of the world may be a source for resources to satisfy our physical needs. Like most other animals, we humans satisfy our physical needs through our primitive brains.

Satisfying Psychological Needs

Satisfaction of psychological needs is regulated primarily by the frontal lobes of the neocortex. The information stored in the memory bank, which already contains sights and sounds as well as tastes and smells even in early infancy, is supplemented during the long process of childhood with the sights and sounds of parents, family, friends, and neighbours.[19] These images serve as the criteria to which later stimulation of sights and sounds, received from the outside world through our eyes and ears, is compared.

The process of selecting resources to satisfy psychological needs is the same as the process of selecting resources to satisfy physical needs. However, here the behavioural response toward the *sources* of a resource rather than to the resource itself is more direct. There is a more immediate behavioural reaction to the *source* of resources that satisfy psychological needs. The sight of a red flag may make one angry, but the anger will be directed toward the persons whom that flag represents. Here the neocortex is not merely *influential,* as in the case of physical needs, but reacts directly. *Sources* of sights and sounds tend to be regarded as a friend *or* foe. Thus, familiar *sights* and *sounds* stimulate friendly attitudes and behavioural responses toward other *human beings* (a smile, cooperation, embrace, care); unfamiliar sights and sounds create unfriendly attitudes and behavioural responses toward other human beings (frown, aggression, push, harm).

This neocortex guided attitude and behaviour toward the *source* of resources that satisfy psychological needs creates the human tendency to feel affinity to certain social environments. The closer I stay to my place of origin -- the family, neighbours, or clan in the village I was born -- the closer I am to the *sources* of resources that tend to satisfy my psychological needs, and the greater my chances of encountering pleasant sights and sounds. On the other hand, if I go and stay to live far away from my place of origin, the chances of encountering *sources* of pleasant sights and sounds may lessen, increasing the chances of feeling psychically threatened.[20]

The tendency toward the familiar *source* of resources of sight and sound may have important implications for society. Since human beings tend to cherish familiar sights and sounds and to suspect or feel threatened by unfamiliar ones, the appearance of a stranger is likely to disrupt our psychic comfort. The tendency of our brain-controlled organism will be to either avoid, segregate, or expel the stranger. Another option is to *assimilate* him or her through teaching or converting them to emanate sights and sounds familiar to me. Similarly, visiting or immigrating strangers might also want either to isolate themselves or to be assimilated in their new community.[21] It may not be surprising, therefore, that many immigrants to other countries and many rural families migrating to cities have tended to settle in closely knit *ethnic* neighbourhoods while their descendants have tried to be assimilated within a new social environment.

One may, of course, say, from a *sociological* perspective, that *ethnic* neighbourhoods are created because migrants coming from different *cultural* backgrounds want to stay in their familiar *cultural* environment. From the perspective of a cross-disciplinary brain, the migrants to a new country or to a city are *hearing* new sounds and *seeing* new faces which, in comparison with stored images in the memory bank, are found not to satisfy psychological needs. From that perspective, those forming or joining an ethnic neighbourhood can be said to be avoiding an environment of unfamiliar *sources* of sights and the potential threat from such *sources*.

Another facet of human behaviour may also appear in somewhat different light from the perspective of the brain-needs connection. From that perspective, conflict is not the outcome of an ingrained human nature, hence unavoidable, aggression toward other human beings, but instead is an optional aversive reaction to the sights and sounds that do not satisfy a psychological need. An actor perceiving threat from unfamiliar *sights* and *sounds* acts aggressively against the *source* of the perceived threat. If so, the Hobbesian 'war of all against all' is a brain-supervised attempt to eliminate threatening *sounds* and *sights* by destroying the *source* of the threat. The societal challenge is to find ways to neutralise or eliminate the threatening sights and sounds in an existing socio-political environment in order to pre-empt aggressive behaviour against the *source* of threat. Threats from unfamiliar sights and sounds can also be minimised through their *assimilation*. In that case, friendly or cooperative reaction may emerge. However, it can also be frequently observed: 'The amount of force needed to hold a society together varies with the heterogeneity of the elements composing it' (Waltz, 1954, p. 228).

Community, the State and Government

Without being associated with other human beings, it is difficult to find resources that satisfy one's psychic needs of love, pride, and self-esteem. Human beings are a *social* animal and, as such, are compelled to interact with each other. Individuals must be members in a community. The drive to satisfy psychological needs may sustain social interactions. It is the community that we shall first turn to before focusing on the state.

The Community

The family, be it a nuclear family, a tribe, or a clan, is the prototype of the many types of communities that have emerged since the dawn of history. Over the roughly 30,000 years between the appearance of *Homo Sapiens,* arguably some 35,000 years ago, and the rise of the first known political structure composed of several communities, the ancient

Egyptian empire some 5,000 years ago, human beings everywhere lived in relatively small communities. My concern here is how these communities may have satisfied human needs.

Satisfying Psychological Needs in the Community

The greater the chance of *hearing* familiar voices and *seeing* familiar sights, the greater the chance to satisfy psychological needs. A community is an aggregation of human beings as *sources* of resources to satisfy psychological needs, whose sights and sounds are familiar to each other. Familiarity of sights and sounds provides a sense of understanding, comfort, warmth, and personal security. Living in a community among familiar sources of sights and sounds can also help to neutralise inevitable personal and personality differences, and minimise, though not totally eliminate, manifestations of aggressive behaviour among community members.

The principle of *familiarity* that satisfies psychological needs favours permanent membership in the specific community into which one is born. Nevertheless, the satisfaction of psychic needs does not require membership in the same community throughout one's life. We *can* belong to a number of communities both simultaneously and in succession. We can also *familiarise unfamiliar* human beings from other communities, assimilate them into our community, or be absorbed by them. This has been commonly done in various ways throughout history. Marriage of a son from one community and a daughter from another creates a new community. The newly married couple, first together, later along with their children, become a new, psychic, needs-satisfying community.

Communities may be formed and split, created and re-created in a continuous search for the satisfaction of our psychic needs. Some may find satisfaction through life-long membership in one, others in several communities simultaneously or successively. The idea that human beings by their nature tend to remain forever loyal to one's original or to any one community or nation is a myth. Human beings pursue the satisfaction of their psychological needs.

Satisfying Physical Needs in the Community

Tangible resources for the satisfaction of physical needs may be obtained by members of a community in four optional ways. First, resources may be grown, produced, or found *in the site* where a community is located. Second, members of the community may *conquer and annex* inhabited territories with resources. Third, members of the community may obtain needed resources through some form of *exchange* with members of another community. Fourth, members of some communities could also *relocate* to an uninhabited new site with tangible resources.

As members of a social entity are attached not only to each other but also to the original site of the community, they tend to defend it if necessary. This historical fact may have contributed to another myth that human beings are territorial animals. From the cross-disciplinary perspective, however, human beings are not territorial but resource-seeking animals that must satisfy their physical needs. It is not the territory, *per se* that human beings regard so highly, but the resources in it. They are not inclined to defend a *territory*, but those *resources* of a specific territory that have satisfied their physical needs, and may satisfy them in the future. People are willing to abandon a 'territory' and relocate to another one, where resources needed to satisfy their needs are believed to be more available, as is indicated in the voluntary emigration throughout history.

The phrase 'safeguarding the territorial integrity of a state' is the product of the legal codification of the modern state, not a principle anchored in human nature. *Territorial integrity* is a notion ingrained through socialisation to inculcate attachment to *our* state for the purpose of securing a willingness to defend the boundaries of a state and prevent its division. Territoriality and territorial integrity, which contemporary governments are eager to propagate, have become central in politics. The notions of homeland, fatherland or motherland are often no more than exploitation of notions that pertain to the 'familiar' for political ends. The same is true of the call for soldiers to defend the territorial integrity of a state.

Governance in the Community

Authority is the *right* to do something while power is defined in terms of *capability*. The right to exercise power may stem from the *legitimate source* of authority. The legitimate source of authority may include God, a family tree, the people, age, or other factors. In the past, some communities considered sources of authority to be legitimate because it stemmed from the original founders of the community.

However, this relative uniformity, in regard to the source of authority, does not necessarily imply uniformity of community institutions and processes. Communities had internal division of labour and social stratifications. Some communities had highly hierarchical chains of command, with others non-hierarchical ones. In all probability, institutional forms varied according to specific indigenous norms which evolved through interactions among community members.

State and Government

In its common usage, the word *government* is a definitional component of the word *state*. D'Entreves, for example, defines the state as 'an organisation endowed with the capacity of exerting and controlling the use of force over a certain people and within a given territory' (1967, p. 32). Seton-Watson defines a state as 'a legal and political organisation, with the power to require obedience and loyalty from its citizens' (1977, p. 1). The first sentence of the introduction to the edited volume, *States & Societies*, reads: 'The state -- or apparatus of "government" -- appears to be everywhere, regulating the conditions of our lives from birth registration to death certification' (Held, 1983, p. 1).

The reason for this lack of a clear-cut distinction between state and government may be explained, in part, by the lasting impact of King Louis XIV's famous dictum: 'L'Etat c'est moi' (The state is me). In my impression, the post-World War II academic atmosphere in the United States may also be responsible for the ambiguous use of the terms. In the 1950s, a scholarly objection had arisen to the very use of both the terms state and government (Easton, 1953; Truman, 1951). Perhaps the concepts of state and government were even more obscured by the notions of *political development, nation-building* and *state-building*. At the time, colonies had either already inherited or were about to inherit colonial boundaries as their state boundaries. This practice was not questioned. In the midst of the Cold War, Western governments and political scientists were concerned instead with the unobtrusive exportation of 'authoritative allocation of [Western] values', i.e., Western ways of controlling populations within already delineated boundaries of states (Easton, 1953). Thus, the most influential scholars of the time posited four types of challenges to a *political system* in general and to newly independent states in particular: (1) state-building -- penetration and integration; (2) nation building -- loyalty and commitment; (3) participation -- pressure for decision making; and (4) distribution or welfare -- 'distribution of resources or values among different elements of the population' (Almond and Powell, 1966, pp. 35-37). These terms continue, to a considerable degree, to prevail and support the normative stand behind them.

On the other hand, a distinction between state and government appears, almost exclusively, in the literature on self-determination and secession. For example, Buchheit writes: 'the doctrine of national self-determination embraced the proposition that only legitimate form of *government* was self-government by natural political units, with its corollary that multinational *states* or empires... were ultimately illegitimate political entities' (1978, p. 4) (emphasis added).[22] Such a distinction between state and government must be made in order to accurately assess the process of change toward a future global order.

Distinctions between State and Government

By the word *state*, I refer to an internationally bordered territory and its inhabitants. The bordered territory of the state includes both material and human resources. It might also be added that most states have relatively scarce resources and relatively heterogeneous populations. Compared with the characterisation of state, government is controlled by a human being or a group of human beings within a state who deal with the challenges to the state. Government institutions exercise political and economic sovereignty within the state.[23]

The most important distinction between state and government is that states have their own histories separate from the histories of governments. The history of states includes changes in their boundaries, due to wars of conquest or secession, as changes in the size of populations due to emigration or immigration, as well as changes in the birth and death rates. The history of governments, in contrast, have included changes in the ways rulers used power internally and externally, changes in successions of governments, and changes in the ways governments gain power. Below are a few additional observations regarding the *difference* between state and government.

(1) A state may be conquered or annexed, while its government may continue to exist in exile. (France, for example, was occupied by German troops in 1940. A puppet Nazi government was set up in France, while a French government functioned in exile. One might also argue that France, the state, then had two governments.)

(2) A government may cease to function altogether while the state continues to exist. (This has happened, on occasion, in some African states. Perhaps the latest example is Rwanda.)

(3) Third, part of the population may move to another state, but may still be subject to the laws of the government of the original state.

The distinction between state and government may also guide the usage of the two terms.

(1) Governments represent a state, speak, and act for it; states cannot represent themselves, for example, in declaring wars.

(2) Governments, not states, intervene in the internal affairs of other states, either through foreign policy or use of armed forces (for example, governments of the United States sent troops to Vietnam).

(3) Governments, not states, intervene in the economy. State-intervention in the economy actually refers to government-intervention. In the same manner, state-ownership means that the government, or the party, regulates the economy.

(4) There is no such thing as state-society relations; there are government-society relations.

(5) Government has authority to *exercise* sovereign power, legitimate or not, within the state. If a government is democratic, sovereignty is *vested in* the population of the state.

Explanation of the concept of the state cannot be complete without examining two key terms: borders and sovereignty.

Borders

The borders of a state delineate a variety of material and human resources on the territory, as well as the size of heterogeneous populations. For example, the borders of Saudi Arabia enclose a large quantity and high quality of a single material resource, oil, whereas Switzerland may be noted for the high quality of its human resources. The borders of the former Soviet Union and the former Yugoslavia enclosed relatively large, socio-culturally heterogeneous populations, while those of Luxembourg enclose a relatively small and socio-culturally homogeneous population.

The location of borders of states is not 'natural'. They have been drawn by wars, open or secret treaties and other human acts. Since borders are arbitrary, the quantity and quality of human and material resources of states and the socio-cultural heterogeneity of states are also arbitrary. Boundaries of states have enlarged and shrunk over the centuries. Change of the arbitrary borders of states have at times produced smaller states, such as the change of borders of the former Soviet Union and the former Yugoslavia. The break-up of India in 1947, and more recently, the break-up of the former Soviet Union, Yugoslavia, Czechoslovakia, and Ethiopia have created economically poorer and socio-culturally more homogeneous states.

At times, there may have been good reasons for changing the boundaries of states, as in the case of Ethiopia, which ended a long, drawn out violent conflict by creating Eritrea. Governments have not tended to be primarily motivated by a consideration for satisfying needs. The political map of the world has changed over time, in some cases for good reasons. But these changes were not primarily made in order to adjust to the two sets of needs of human beings. It is the arbitrariness of borders and the resulting arbitrary human and resource composition of states that *necessitated,* throughout history, centralised authority and power in the hands of a ruler or government.

Sovereignty

The distinction between political sovereignty and economic sovereignty is often made but rarely defined. By political sovereignty, I refer to the exercise of sovereign power over relations among human beings in the population of a state, and between them and the institutions of that state. By economic sovereignty, I refer to the exercise of sovereign power over human and material resources in a state.

One of the central topics of discussion in recent years focused on the observation that multinational corporations or international organisations are taking over political and/or economic sovereignties from the state. This discussion takes for granted that *both* political and economic sovereignties are traditionally vested in the state and exercised by its government. The point I want to emphasise here is that whether or not multinational corporations or international organisations are *taking away* rights and powers is of secondary importance. Of primary importance is that, by accepting the traditional definition of the state, it is taken for granted that both political and economic sovereignties belong to the state.

Satisfying Needs within the State

The two sets of needs pose challenges to governments. These challenges are customarily met by satisfying the needs of those among the citizenry whose support was necessary for the maintenance of a government's power in office. When and where awareness of the right to resources is non-existent or low scale, the existence of the state is not seriously threatened internally. With the growing awareness and the accelerating intensity of demands to satisfy human needs in the post-Cold War era, however, the challenges to governments will prove insurmountable, resulting in the fading away of the state. The following section will focus on the challenges governments face in satisfying physical and psychological needs.

The Challenge of Satisfying Physical Needs

Three separate, though interdependent, factors are the most relevant to the satisfaction of physical needs: (1) the *availability and the potential availability* of human and material resources *within the state*, along with their quantity, quality and variety; (2) the ease of *obtaining* human and material resources from *outside* the boundaries of the state for use within the state; and (3) the method of *allocation* of available and obtained material resources to inhabitants of the state.

Potential availability of resources may be made accessible by redirecting present funds and technologies for development. It seems obvious that the greater the availability of high quality and large quantities of human and material resources within the state, the greater the pool available to satisfy physical needs. Such may be the case in the United States at present. It also seems obvious that, in such cases, obtaining outside resources is less necessary. As noted earlier, food, shelter, oil to heat homes, as well as a labour force, do not have to be *home-grown*. *Familiarity* is not important for the satisfaction of physical needs. Resources may come from any part of the world. Thus, while the bordered territory of a state may have been the only sovereign source of resources for governments of that state theoretically, in practice, resources could and have been obtained from outside its borders.

A list of means used to obtain both human or material resources from outside of the state have traditionally included the following: (1) trade and other forms of exchange; (2) colonialism (extending formal sovereignty, i.e., comprehensive political, military and economic control over material and human resources in foreign lands, often including settling in that state); (3) imperialism (not extending formal sovereignty, but only full or partial political and economic control over the other government and over a selected range of human and material resources, without settling in that state); (4) military conquest (annexation of a state, or part of a state, with its resources); (5) opening the state to immigration of cheaper and/or skilled human resources, including importing slaves; (6) obtaining resources from other states, foreign institutions or international organisations (material resources in the form of foreign aid, financial assistance in the form of loans, and human resources in the form of technical assistance); (7) regional economic cooperation, including, for example, free trade and customs arrangements that facilitate the exchange of resources; and (8) reduction of the number of human beings in a state in order to reduce the pressure on available material resources through limitation of immigration, encouragement of emigration, settling one's citizens in colonies, and expulsion or extermination of a section of the population.

All these options listed have been used by governments, especially in militarily strong states, often under their own 'morally acceptable' labels.[24]

On the Allocation of Material Resources

The decision regarding who gets what kind of material resources in a population of a state, along with how much and why, is a political decision about economic issues. The political decision making process itself might be guided by moral, philosophical, or ideological *principles*, such as 'competition is natural', 'private property is a God-given right', 'all property belongs to the society as a whole', 'each according to his or her needs', and so on. Based on one or a combination of these principles, governments might decide, for example, that (a) the available resources are to be equally distributed (everyone gets the *same* amount, quality and type of material resources); or (b) all human beings are to be provided with equal opportunity to compete for resources. Each of these two options has its inherent advantages and disadvantages from the point of view of satisfaction of physical needs. Equal distribution of resources might be sufficient for satisfaction of everyone's material needs, albeit on a low level (i.e., below the *human* level in many states). Also, if resources are equally distributed, one's incentive to develop more innovative products might be minimal.

The option of equal opportunity, on the other hand, may encourage innovation, satisfying the material needs of many. However, if human beings are expected to compete with each other to obtain and accumulate as much as each can, then the losers in the competition might be left without the resources to satisfy their material needs. In addition, the method of competition can easily lead to unfair competition and corruption.

Let us leave aside for the moment the various options and ask instead the following questions: How important are the particular principles that guide a government or ruler? Does it matter which guiding principle is followed by a ruler or government if human beings are driven to have their material needs satisfied? If the human being must satisfy his/her material needs, does it matter whether the guiding ideology is capitalism or socialism? From the cross-disciplinary perspective, the satisfaction or non-satisfaction of physical needs of the organism is the crucial criterion for every human being. Perhaps only those who have personally experienced physical deprivation in some form would fully appreciate that, ultimately, feeling hunger or extreme cold are among the primary motivations of behaviour. Principles on the allocation of goods are less important. Since physical needs must be satisfied, a human being with a full stomach and protective shelter will tend to adhere to a principle that is perceived to have created those favourable conditions and abhor a rival principle that is perceived to potentially deprive him or her of that condition. A hungry or homeless human being will tend to adhere to any guiding principle that satisfies, or promises, to satisfy his or her physical needs.

The Challenge of Satisfying Psychological Needs

It seems evident from the cross-disciplinary perspective that the human organism tends to gravitate toward 'familiar' *sources* of sights and sounds and shy away from the psychic discomfort that the unfamiliar sources of sights and sounds entail. The socio-cultural heterogeneity that exists in most states tends to generate unfamiliar sights and sounds to which human beings will tend to react. One possible reaction may be getting away from the unfamiliar sources of sights and sounds by isolating oneself *individually* from the rest of society. Perhaps one might try to do this by using drugs or committing suicide. A more common method of isolation is becoming a member of a specific community. Such communities have existed for long periods of time in the form of clubs, sects, gangs, and neighbourhoods.

Governments, in turn, have tended to encourage accommodation of socio-cultural heterogeneity among the citizenry of the state by encouraging socialisation to government, and societal norms in the family and formal education. In addition, in many states the threats of religious, moral, legal and extra-legal sanctions prevent non-compliance with the 'norms of society'. Such measures may produce fear of 'punishment'.

From the cross-disciplinary perspective, becoming a member of a *nation* is a neocortical process of *creating* familiar sources of resources among the non-familiar citizens of the state through neutralising socio-cultural heterogeneity within the state. Nationalism *from above* is an attempt by a government to activate a shared national identity among the population of a state.[25] A national identity created by nationalism *from above* has served as secular glue. It has replaced, or at least supplemented, religious glue and served to replace Marx's proletarian glue. Nationalism leads to the adoption of a national identity by positing a perceived threat. The perceived threat not only creates an unfamiliar *enemy*, but it also helps a ruler or government to advocate *national* defence, by a *national* armed forces, for the *body of the nation*. In other words, national security may be made to connote both security for the body of the neocortically created *nation*, as well as for the personal security of each *member* of that nation. Nationalism can also be used to create a legitimate source of authority that the government may rely on to justify its right to use force. National integration, solidarity and loyalty of citizens to the government are among the commonly used means and methods of neutralising the discomfort that unfamiliar sources of sights and sounds can create.

Conclusion

I noted in the introduction the premise that, as the Cold War ended, much of the repression and restraint directly associated with the conflict waned, making it possible for human beings to seek satisfaction of their needs more successfully than ever. In this concluding section, I shall briefly focus on the fading away of the state and on the future global order which is now being shaped by needs-propelled human behaviour.

My argument regarding the fading away of the state from a cross-disciplinary perspective on human beings is this: even if the satisfaction of *both* types of needs for all human beings were the aim of governments, accomplishing this aim is virtually impossible in socio-culturally heterogeneous, resource-poor states -- even with governments relying on a legitimate source of authority. In other words, however sincere a government's intentions may be, it will be unable to produce the results human beings are now fighting for. Satisfaction of human needs cannot be accomplished within the framework of a politically *and* economically sovereign state.

Looking from a cross-disciplinary perspective at human beings, my argument regarding the future global order is that the satisfaction of both sets of needs of human beings requires two different types of inter-linked entities. The satisfaction of psychological needs requires small, politically autonomous, community-like entities, whereas the satisfaction of physical needs requires building large, economically integrated communities encompassing shared human and material resources. The removal of constraints by Cold War confrontation, an accelerated striving for the satisfaction of human needs and the failure of the governments of most states to sustain the state will generate dynamics for change. Thus, the future global order will have to be composed of large economic frameworks, each enclosing a large number of politically autonomous entities, which people should be able to join and exit at will in their pursuit of both psychological and material needs.

The European Union now emerges as one such large economic community, while psychic needs are satisfied by the emergence of politically autonomous entities, such as Scotland, Catalonia, and the Basque country. Similar economic frameworks composed of politically autonomous entities will emerge elsewhere in the world. Such possibilities might emerge in Southeast Asia, partly as result of the apparent collapse of their ill-functioning 'globalised economies'. The Middle East could be another region for regional economic integration if the wider Arab-Israeli conflict is resolved.

In order to prevent another world war and other calamity, such a global transformation seems to me to be virtually inevitable for two main reasons: the spread and intensity of the human drive for satisfaction of needs and the fragile and artificial nature of state. States are not evolved communities. The feudal, manorial states in Europe, the absolutist state, and the modern state were not stages in the evolution of communities. The state is not the product of organic growth or of evolutionary change. The state has not naturally grown out of kinship and tribe. The state is often the product of accidental historical forces.

Desmond Morris compares the modern city to a human zoo: 'The modern human animal is no longer living in conditions natural for his species' (1969, pp. 8-9). Instead, he is '[t]rapped ... in a huge, restless menagerie where he is in constant danger of cracking under the strain'. The same may be said about the human animal in the state. Human beings have been forced into the state in the same way as animals are forced into a zoo. Animals trapped in zoos did not evolve into zoo animals; neither have humans confined in states evolved into state animals. Most governments have not been successful in satisfying human needs, and their capacities to do so in the future are very limited.

Notes

[1] In this chapter, 'cross-disciplinary' refers to a combination of some aspects of the social sciences with some aspects of the biological sciences. This is distinct from inter-disciplinary, by which I refer to a combination of fields within the social sciences.

[2] For a detailed examination of the connection between the social and natural sciences see Cohen (1995).

[3] Needless to say, I am far from the first to look at human needs in a cross-disciplinary context. In addition to a selected number of sources I shall refer to below, see also the important contributions of Sandole (1990) in relation to conflict resolution.

[4] A more explicit discussion of needs in terms of the human organism was presented by the historian Carroll Quigley (1961), who made an analytical distinction between potentialities, the range of static *capabilities* and needs, and the range of dynamic *requirements*.

[5] Most everyone speaks and writes about 'basic needs' or 'basic human needs'. I prefer 'human needs' as they are of the human organism, which is as 'basic' as one can get. I also think that others meant or implied the same, although without explicitly stating so for one reason or another. In any case, I do not see adding 'basic' as being useful.

[6] I am following the model of Quigley (1961) who listed two basic 'range[s] of human potentialities or human needs', the one *physical*, the other *psychic*, under which all other human potentialities and needs cluster. Each range of needs, or set of needs as I most often call them, includes a long list of specific needs.

[7] Realisation of one's spiritual being, creativity, and emotional expression may perhaps be also included among psychological needs.

[8] Subsequently, I shall usually refer to either one or the other set or type of needs in which the specific need might be located rather than to specific needs themselves. In occasional references to specific needs I tend to mention the most

obvious ones, such as food among the set of physical needs and freedom among the psychological needs. Note also that in all my references to 'freedom' I mean 'freedom from...', be it oppression, rule, domination, control, and so on, because I consider that to be the only *practical* meaning of the word 'freedom'.

[9] It does not seem necessary to elaborate here on the basic premise that all human beings of whatever religion, race, gender, in every part of the world are human beings, hence they all have the same two sets of human needs. However, it seems useful to point out, especially for those interested in human evolution, that *Homo Sapiens*, whom we are, emerged some 35,000 years ago and has had the same human organism, hence the same two sets of needs. Nevertheless, it may or may not be that the human brain has been as evolved as our brain is today. Since I am not sure, I am not arguing for the applicability of my thesis on human needs beyond some 10,000 years ago.

[10] A 200-pound person in a cold climate may need more food than a 120-pound person in a warm climate. Needs are universal; not their quantity or quality.

[11] I side-step here the important issue of body-mind connection which, in an elaborate case analysis, must be taken into account.

[12] It should be noted that the sight of a flag produced of man-made material may also produce satisfaction of a psychological need. In addition, sights and sounds of a physical environment, beautiful vistas for example, and interaction with dogs and cats may also produce psychic-needs satisfying resources.

[13] MacLean published his theory in many articles and in a book (1973) and has been extensively referred to, elaborated on, as well as criticised.

[14] The term reptilian does not refer to contemporary reptiles but to early ancestors of today's mammals.

[15] In exploration of the functions of the 'triune brain' I am modifying and to a degree adding on to MacLean's thesis.

[16] Shelter from extremities of weather are controlled by the even more primitive parts of the nervous system.

[17] I shall also propose that our dichotomising brain for the purpose of satisfying our needs also dichotomises in other contexts as well. It tends to dichotomise between up/down, left/right, clean/dirty, beautiful/ugly, friend/foe, and also liberal/conservative, communist/democrat, and so on. In other words,

dichotomising is also a guiding mechanism of human socio-political, economic, and all other types of behaviour. I also propose that we may or may not *learn* through life to conceive of a *continuum* between two dichotomised points and to identify a number of intermediate points located between two dichotomised points. It may be that the more educated we are, the finer are the distinctions, qualities and degrees, we 'discover'. But our brain is programmed to make either/or, dichotomised behavioural choices (Flohr, 1987).

[18] For another political scientist's view on the connection between the neuronal process and behaviour see Davies (1970, p. 102).

[19] Experiments with human infants have shown that two dots for eyes within an oval-face cut-out illustrates the genetic or ancestral input into the 'memory bank'. Peter C. Reynolds (1981, p. 89) summarised studies of facial expression first begun by Darwin: 'Several dozen ... studies by many researchers have confirmed that the facial configuration, particularly the eyes, is a potent elicitor of smiles in infants, but other sensory modalities such as voice and touch are also effective especially in very young infants of one to eight weeks'. Other experiments have shown that the disappearance or distortion of familiar faces can lead to crying, 'which suggests that fear and distress are resulting from violated expectations'. If the face does not match the stored features a psychic need is not satisfied, and this may be manifested through a frown. Similar processes occur with sounds, such as intonations of a voice, music, noise of the market place and explosions.

[20] Our feelings, attitudes and behavioural responses in unfamiliar, potentially threatening environments of unfamiliar *sources* of sights and sounds, such as in a foreign country, may also be positive, psychically satisfying. Reynolds (1981, p. 103) notes that 'distorted faces are widely used in horror movies, presumably because of their fear-inducing effects on humans in contexts of suspended disbelief'. It may also be that since *resources* satisfy or not psychological needs too, our behavioural reaction in a foreign country or in a horror movie will tend to be toward *resources* rather than to the *sources* of resources, for our visits to the foreign country and to the horror movie are temporary. The chances that foreigners or monsters would harm us are minimal or non-existent. Such encounters may even be useful in *reinforcing* our desire to return to the familiar *sources* of resources at home.

[21] Heiner Flohr (1987, p. 186), writing on prejudice, notes: 'Thinking in binary terms leads to an overaccentuation of properties and thus to distinctions between individuals and between groups. Prejudices thrive on polarisation, on the maximisation of differences between categories'. In regard to xenophobia, he

writes further below (p. 187): 'Group orientation provides several other indicators pointing to a biological basis of prejudices. One of them is the universal existence of xenophobia'.

[22] Sir Ernest Barker's note to his translation of Aristotle's *Politics* (Barker, 1948, p. xi) seems instructive: 'The word "state" comes to us from the Latin *status*, in its sense of standing or position: it meant, when we adopted it in the 16th century, the standing or the position of the person (or persons) in authority, so that Louis XIV was etymologically justified in saying *L'Etat, c'est moi!*; and though it has widened in the course of time to designate also the whole political community, it is still used today in its old sense (as when we speak of "state interference"), and its overtones are still the overtones of authority. How different are the suggestions of the word *polis*...'

[23] The word 'nation' is not interchangeable with the word 'state' either. The term 'nation' originates in the Latin term for birth and thus it denotes a large scale family that embraces the entire citizenry of the state. The use of the phrase 'nation state', in turn, implies that the population of a state is indeed such a large scale family. Political entrepreneurs and members of governments use the term 'nation' for its connotation of unity among their followers. If a *self*-perception of being a member of a nation exists among inhabitants of a state, they become a community. This may occur in such instances as war, 'national' holidays, international sporting events, and other specific occasions.

[24] Reaching beyond boundaries either in the form of trade, or wars of conquest, has not always been directly or completely related to obtaining human or material resources. The Crusades, for example, were motivated at least in some part by religious fervour; colonial expansion, at least for some governments, was to some degree motivated by a desire to spread Western civilisation. There have also been pre-emptive military conquests against perceived threats and for the personal aggrandisement of rulers. However, I propose that *most* transactions across boundaries of states have been related directly or indirectly, to scarcity of the amounts, quality and types of resources available within a state.

[25] Nationalism *from below* is a label for an attempt by a political entrepreneur to create a shared national identity among a group of human beings among the population within a state. Nationalism *from below* is often called sub-nationalism, ethnic nationalism, or sectarian-nationalism. Nationalism *from above* and *from below* may follow each other. For example, Nelson Mandela was first engaged in nationalism *from below*, attempting to create a shared national identity for the Blacks of South Africa; since he became President of South Africa, he has been engaged in nationalism *from above*, attempting to

create a shared national identity for all the inhabitants of South Africa. On the other hand, President Yeltsin attempted to produce nationalism *from above* for all the people of the Russian Federation; Judor Dudayev in Chechnya, was engaged in creating nationalism *from below* for Chechens. For activation of identity see Ronen (1979).

14 The Emergence of Regional Civil Society: Contributions to a New Human Security Agenda

TIMOTHY M. SHAW and SANDRA J. MACLEAN

> Above all, security in a post-Cold war world means that a far more extensive set of actors can take responsibility for setting the terms for their own peace and security, rather than passively receiving the prescriptions of state policymakers. This means that even if states remain the central agents of security for some time to come, they can no longer monopolise this function, especially in the identification of what is a threat to whom. Transnational religious organisations, environmental groups, human rights organisations, regional economic cooperatives, local communities, diasporas and refugees are just a few of the collectivities whose articulation of definitions and conditions for peace and security reflect the specific dimensions of their social and political life (Latham, 1995, p. 13).

> In a post-hegemonic world, the concept of region will assume a new importance as a possible mode of organising the international economic order, and obviously a better alternative than protectionist regression on the level of the nation state. This in my view is a realistic utopia (Hettne, 1990, p. 250).

Introduction

A 'new' security order, in which 'security' is defined as a state of human well-being rather than national integrity, is concerned not only with traditional 'high politics' issues of inter-state behaviours, but also with 'low politics' items such as drugs, health, crime, migrations, guns and landmines which have sub- and supra-state relevance and importance. Contributing to the construction of this 'new' order, various forms of cooperation and collaboration -- from informal coalitions to global conferences -- now exist among non-governmental organisations (NGOs) and between NGOs and official national and international governmental institutions in diverse areas of peacebuilding, the environment, gender relations, human rights and economic development. An important feature of many of these forms of cooperation is their dynamic and flexible regional character.

This chapter situates emerging analysis and discourse surrounding issues of 'human' security within the context of the ascendant and globalising neoliberalism of the post-bipolar world. It argues that novel 'bottom-up' forms of regionalism initiated by civil society are arising at least partly in response to the social disruptions, inequalities, and insecurities that are features of the currently dominant neoliberal order. The authors seek to identify the contributions which are being made by regional civil societies to the construction of a new 'human' security agenda. The chapter attempts to distinguish the relations and activities within and among civil societies that engender (but also those that impede) practices and discourses of 'security and development regionalisms'.

Security in the New International Divisions of Labour and Power

A new security discourse is emerging in the aftermath of the Cold War. In response to a changing environment characterised by a profusion of new issues and actors, traditional state-centric conceptualisations of security are giving way to a 'new' expanded agenda that now includes human needs and non-state actors. In the past, issues such as basic needs, human rights and the environment had been largely excluded from the list of items of interest to security and/or foreign policy experts. However, it is increasingly recognised that economic decline, ethnic rivalry and ecological degradation are central to many of the situations that threaten the world at present (Buzan, 1991; Klare, 1993). Moreover, in the past, it was widely accepted that the state alone had legitimate authority and its officials the appropriate expertise to deal with matters of international or world security. Yet, recently, new actors on the scene -- from new or revised institutions and regional organisations, to multinational corporations (MNCs), non-governmental organisations (NGOs), social movements and informal sectors -- have been assuming larger roles in influencing, setting or implementing policy (Kolodziej, 1992; Klare and Thomas, 1994). Whether acting autonomously or as sub-contractors to states, non-state actors are generally engaged in their own forms of political and diplomatic behaviour; as a consequence, they not only have significant effects on political processes and outcomes, but their involvement has added an unprecedented measure of complexity to security operations such as peacekeeping or peace-making (Weiss, 1998). However, while the inclusion of non-state actors imparts a more complicated and multi-dimensional character to security operations, it also creates possibilities for potentially more effective action, especially in areas of confidence-building, preventative and early-warning strategies, and peacebuilding.

While the rapid pace of change in the post-Cold War period has dramatically highlighted the changing nature of security, pressures toward such reconceptualisations predate the fall of the Berlin Wall. For example, over the past two decades, several United Nations commissions have encouraged the international community to support a reinvigorated multilateralism for dealing with the integrated issues of security, economics, the environment, development, and global governance.[1] Also, over that same period, changes have occurred in the study of world politics and security. Czempiel (1992, p. 255) notes, for instance, that 'globalists and transnationalists started to argue in the early 1970s that the issue-area of economic well-being had become as important as that of security'. Neo-institutionalists argued that economic interdependence described the nature of world politics as accurately as (if not more than) the political interests of individual states (Keohane and Nye, 1989). Regime theorists brought civil societies into the analytical complex, arguing that various non-state actors contribute to the establishment of transnational systems of governance in specific issue areas (Ruggie, 1975). And, over the past three decades, scholars from the 'normative' school of international relations (Brown, 1992), such as members of the World Order Model Project (WOMP), have argued that world security would be enhanced by multilateral efforts to identify common (global) goals and that, in addition to the military strength and political authority of states, normative values (of citizens as well as policy-makers) play significant roles in establishing and maintaining national and world order (e.g., see Falk, 1975; Falk, Kim and Mendlovitz, 1982).

For many years, the arguments of scholars from the normative school occupied a marginal position in security studies, overshadowed by the dominant realist perspective. However, in past two decades, the principles of realism have been challenged by scholars from various perspectives, including liberal neo-institutionalists, feminists, postmodernists, and post-Marxists (Neufeld, 1995). Furthermore, normative viewpoints have been gaining more credibility in foreign policy as well as academic circles.[2] As a result of these changes, positions which had been criticised in the past for their idealism now appear to many to have been more visionary than utopian, empirically grounded in the 'new' realism of the post-Westphalian world poised to enter the next millennium.

In the view of Robert Cox, and the growing number of scholars who have adopted his Gramscian historical materialist analytical approach, current revisionism may be attributed to a profound social change that has accompanied the unleashing of contemporary forces of economic globalisation. According to Cox, '(t)he market appears to be bursting free from the bonds of national societies, subjecting a global society to its laws' (1991, p. 335). This process has been furthered by the growing co-ordination of supportive influential organisations, including official bodies like the Organisation of Economics Cooperation and Development (OECD), the Bank of International Settlements (BIS), the International Monetary Fund (IMF), and 'unofficial forums like the Trilateral Commission, the Bilderberg conferences, or the... Mont Pelerin Society' (Cox, 1992, p. 30). The consensual network which links these 'official caretakers of the global economy' has created a level of 'governance without government'[3] which now constrains the decision making authority and autonomy of nation states. Being held increasingly accountable to the demands of a liberal global market, states are now less able to act independently in setting domestic policy. This 'internationalisation of the state' has, in Cox's view, eroded the social contract upon which modern democracies were based. As economic policy is increasingly directed toward the protection of transnational finance, there has been a concomitant need to 'insulate economic policy making from popular pressures' (p. 33). And, disturbing consequences of this process are 'the tendency toward limited democracy', a decline in state funding of social programmes, and increases in social and economic disparities (Cox, 1991, p. 335).

The 'disintegrating and alienating' consequences of globalisation have generated various measures and counter-measures by organisations and groups in civil society (Cox, 1992, p. 34). 'New' social movements seeking to promote ideological, cultural, and institutional changes on matters of peacebuilding, ecology, gender, and human rights have proliferated in response to modern (or post-modern) perceptions of insecurity in these areas. Since many NGOs are part of the 'new' social movements, their dramatic growth in numbers worldwide over the past three decades may also be attributed, in part, to a growing preoccupation with these humanistic concerns. However, the growth of NGOs has also been attributed to the downsizing of the state under neoliberal pressure, with the effect that social welfare needs must now be met by civil society organisations. Yet, whether conceived because of idealistic or functional concerns, many NGOs and 'new' social movements have played a significant role in advancing interest in 'human', as opposed to military/state, security.

Efforts by NGOs and social movements to establish the priority of human security have been bolstered in recent years by several international conferences on related issues[4] as well as by organisations such as the United Nations Development Programme (UNDP) and the United Nations Institute for Social Research (UNRISD). For example, in its *Human Development Report,* published annually since 1990, the UNDP has extended a notion of human security which blends concern for economic growth and social justice with an awareness of ecological limits and the need to preserve the environment for future generations, all within a framework that asserts the primacy of democracy, participation, and civil society (Plewes *et al.,* 1996, p. 216).

For its part, UNRISD has conducted meetings and published research that voices concern about 'the social effects of globalisation'.[5] Furthermore, it continues to explore the possibilities for establishing new global organisations, or revising existing international ones, in order to give official institutional form to a new social compact which appears to be forming between informal systems of governance and a nascent global civil society (UNRISD, 1995; see also Crouch and Marquand, 1995; MacLean, 1997; Mathews, 1997; Waterman, 1996).

Initiatives by many such development agents to expand the boundaries of the security agenda are unabashedly normative. Also, however, because official security actors now encounter a wide range of issues and actors in field operations, there is a noticeable reduction in the gap previously perceived to exist between 'high' politics issues of national self-interest, and 'low' politics items such as economics, identity, ethics and human dignity. The changing nature of security is demonstrated in the growing multiplicity of activities that are now included under operational mandates:

> ...the role of these operations is no longer confined to simply deploying a neutral presence between two belligerent parties. The aim of the new operations is the making, and indeed the building, of peace. This can involve electoral assistance, humanitarian aid, administrative activities, the rebuilding of roads and bridges, rural de-mining operations, the promotion of democracy, and the protection of human rights (Weiss and Gordenker, 1996, p. 9).

Besides the changed nature and array of the problems which security operants now encounter, the involvement of non-state actors with motivations other than strictly nationalist goals has helped to create a 'new' security agenda. Official organisations now usually involve NGOs in most, if not all, stages of security operations, from preventive diplomacy to crisis intervention and peace-making to reconstruction and peacebuilding (Weiss and Gordenker, 1996). As NGOs become involved in formal operations, they tend to take on roles as 'sub-contractors' to official actors, thus relinquishing some of their autonomy, but perhaps gaining a higher measure of legitimacy through association with state or inter-state authorities. However, in addition to the growing numbers of NGOs, which have become incorporated into the official structure, many others contribute to the outcomes of security situations indirectly or informally. For instance, NGOs that are outside the official security structures may play key roles in pre-crisis monitoring or confidence building, or in providing welfare and emergency care during periods of conflict or catastrophe. Moreover, many NGOs lead humanitarian efforts to meet basic needs and political struggles to strengthen civil societies. These developmental and democratising initiatives both have the potential to promote 'human' security by diminishing the danger in pre-crisis situations and to help build post-conflict communities during the peacebuilding phase.

To summarise, it appears that the recent revisionism in approaches to security results from the increasing juxtaposition of state and non-state actors, from an emerging integration of conventional strategic concerns with development imperatives, and from a growing acceptance that human needs are prior, or equal to, institutional interests. The complexity of the 'new security agenda' is complicated further by the increasingly interactive nature of the relations that exist among different levels of polity. In the changing world order, security -- state or human -- is affected by decisions, events, and processes in subnational and global political economies as well as in national contexts.

The 'New' Regionalism

A change in regional dynamics is one important effect of the altered and expanded security agenda. The recent proliferation of complex emergencies in the South, particularly in Africa, has highlighted the importance of regional issues and actors in the events leading to conflict in the subsequent crisis interventions, and in the post-crisis reconstructions (Shaw, 1996). Indeed, 'the region now seems to be most viable space within which to reassert political control and re-establish social security' (Swatuk, 1998, p. 4).

Conceptualisations of regionalism tend to include at least one of three possible dimensions of social interaction (Stubbs and Underhill, 1994, pp. 331-32). One dimension concerns the common interests, problems, or aspects of history which are shared by groups of proximal states in specific geographic areas. Another dimension, closely related to the first, involves the organisational structures that are established to deal with the collective needs of groups of neighbouring states. The third involves civil societies as well as states, consisting of forms of 'socio-cultural, political, and/or economic linkages that distinguish (certain geographical areas) from the rest of the global community' (Stubbs and Underhill, 1994).

Few traditional approaches to regionalism actually encompass all three dimensions. Most have tended to focus narrowly on the second, being concerned either with trade or market integration, or with security complexes. Certainly, functionalists and neo-functionalists[6] have recognised the interrelatedness of social, economic, and political aspects in explaining or prescribing inter- and transnational cooperation. However, the basic functionalist assumption that transnational interactions among civil societies in technical (or functional) areas would correspond to a linear progression in political integration has been challenged by persisting obstacles to cooperation. In particular, the resolute East-West differences that characterised the Cold War and the divisions which still persist between North and South have underscored the intransigent nature of competitive political solitudes (Cox, 1996, p. 507). Hence, both the unilinear evolutionism of functionalism -- both traditional or 'neo' forms

-- and the limited focus of statist and economistic perspectives are challenged by the profound changes now occurring in regional political economies. Therefore, to explain the complexities of contemporary forms of regional cooperation, a 'new' multifaceted approach has emerged which combines 'comparative, historical, and multilevel perspectives' (Mittelman, 1996, p. 189).

The pluralist nature of the 'new' regionalism theory reflects the complexity of the process it describes. Defined by Hettne (1990, p. 25) as 'political cooperation on the regional level to promote the region as a viable economic, cultural, and ecological unit', the 'new' regionalism differs from the 'old' by comprising a wider range of actors and issues and an expanded set of interactive relationships. It involves multiple transnational connections and levels of cooperation by non-state and informal actors as well as the institutional actors at national and international levels which are the central (indeed, often the only) players recognised in more traditional concepts of regionalism.

The 'new' regionalism emerges from the convergence of the three main factors associated with economic globalisation -- the changing nature and role of the state, the growing importance of other political actors, and the increasing strains on traditional systems of governance. Hence, both 'top-down' and 'bottom-up' pressures are driving the process. While 'top-down' initiatives often tend to support a view of regionalism as an inevitable stage or 'chapter' in the teleological process of globalisation (Mittelman, 1996, p. 189), at least some of the proliferating numbers of NGOs and new social movements represent 'bottom-up' social forces that are potentially counterhegemonic to (and transformative of) the dominant neoliberal order. Thus, the recent emergence and revitalisation of civil societies -- national and global *as well as regional* -- are partly the direct results of the threats to human security that are associated with globalisation. Yet, while the development of such 'democratisation' forces in civil societies may be mainly reactive responses to underlying structural change, they in turn are creating pressures for new types of social arrangements and thus have profound implications for restructuring formal and informal systems of governance.

Hettne (1997) describes one such arrangement as a 'new experiment with "security regionalism" and "developmental regionalism" in the peripheral regions'. Because of their marginal position in the world economy, states in the periphery tend to enter into cooperative arrangements in defence against, rather than in compliance with, globalisation. At the other end of the spectrum, opportunity rather than defence tends to be the motivating factor behind the 'neoliberal regionalism' that predominates in the industrialised core. For these countries, national self-interest is enhanced by possessing overlapping memberships in a 'transregional network' of trading groups (e.g., US and Canada in North America and Asia-Pacific groups), although ultimately the interactive nature of these blocs promotes the globalisation of trade rather than mercantilist regionalisms. Meanwhile, in balancing opportunity and defence, the 'open regionalism' of the semi-periphery is situated between the security and neoliberal versions; it tends to be a rather ambiguous response especially by Southeast Asian and Latin American trading blocs, driven by the desire on the one hand to participate fully in a global free market, and the need on the other to protect their less-developed economies from the trading bloc 'fortresses' of Europe and North America (Hettne, 1997, p. 14).

This typology separates the three main varieties of 'new' regionalism using the criterion of economic development. However, Hettne (1993, pp. 225-27) observes that common political and social solutions and identities also contribute to variations in degrees of 'regionness'. Hence, in comparative terms, Europe demonstrates the highest condition and most complex version of the 'new' regionalism in its advanced integration of security, political, and economic motivations. By contrast, the North American version of regionalism does not reflect a high degree of regionness, but cooperation is manifested primarily in economic relations, i.e., in the common market arrangement of the North American Free Trade Association (NAFTA). The Asia-Pacific area similarly lacks a strong 'regional self-consciousness', and various conflicting interests and several subregional identities persist. Nevertheless, the highly competitive nature of the global economy has intensified the level of interest in fostering closer regional relations -- particularly for economic, but increasingly also for security reasons. According to Hettne, the Third World most closely resembles Europe in terms of the degree of integration of economic, political, security, and social motivations -- in short, by demonstrating the wide range of criteria which establish the 'new' regionalism. However, whereas the European version reflects the triumph of 'benign (or neo-) mercantilist' interests, the 'security and development' regionalism in the periphery is driven to a large extent by the growing awareness that collective self-reliance may be the only option for any future development.[7]

Hettne has provided one of the most comprehensive treatments of the 'new' regionalism approach. Yet, despite the sophistication and nuance of his analysis, his typology is drawn by broad strokes in accord with the ontological categories of world systems theory. By viewing 'new' regionalism through different lenses, other scholars note that these categories intersect in interesting ways that do not necessarily correspond to legally or traditionally-labelled geopolitical space. Mittelman (1996, p. 191) observes, for example, that *macroregions* are a feature of the widening embrace of neoliberalism -- they co-ordinate capital flows within large circumscribed geographic areas and, at the same time, provide inter-regional linkages that promote globalisation. At the *subregional* level, factors such as 'historical legacies and economic forces' may be more important than geographic proximity in determining the terms of cooperation. And, as is the case in the formation of some subregional economic zones (SREZs), the interaction may be transnational or transborder without involving entire national economies. Finally, *microregions* with varying degrees of political/or economic autonomy are emerging within state borders. As examples of this phenomenon, Mittelman lists Catalonia, Lombardy, and Quebec.

Other forms of regionalism may exist based on alternative concepts of *regionness* held within civil societies. Indeed, in some regions, among different social groups divided by historical connections of race, class, ethnicity, *et cetera*, there may be multiple, widely divergent senses of regional identity. Niemann (1997) describes this situation in Southern Africa, for example. In that area, pre-colonial social interactions centred around traditional migratory routes formed one set of criteria on which regional identities were based; the colonial economy's needs for labour, transport, infrastructure, and political institutions created a second concept of regionness; while 'new' security items of the contemporary period -- the environment, human rights, democracy, and development -- constitute yet another nexus around which a new regional identity is emerging.

Regional responses by civil societies to these 'new' security issues exert pressure on state officials to expand their foreign policy frameworks. Yet, official structures tend to be resistant to change. As Vale (1996, p. 365) observes: '(t)his has been especially so in South Africa, where the security establishment was weaned on the Cold War, and, notwithstanding political changes, influential state-makers nurture traditional perspectives on security issues'. Nevertheless, emerging forces based on newly constructed regional identities in civil societies are a component of a *transformative multilateralism* that appears to be unfolding at present.[8] Referred to as features of a 'double movement' by Cox (1997, p. 107),[9] social reactions to the negative impacts of globalisation have the potential to radically transform the world order. According to Cox (1997, p. 107), widespread recent events including the Chiapas uprising in Mexico, workers' strikes in France, and revitalised support for communist leaders in parts of the former USSR represent attempts by groups in civil society to reassert social control over the global economic system. This is so because the process of globalisation has altered the system of rules, values, and expectations which had previously helped to maintain social stability and security. *Transformative multilateralism* involves the process(es) by which these various non-state counterforces articulate within existing forms of international organisation (Mittelman, 1997, p. 89). And, one important point of articulation is at the regional level.

'Bottom Up' Regionalism in the 'New' Security Agenda

There are infinite variations in the regional responses by non-state actors to the insecurities presented by globalisation. The reactions may be organised or diffuse, formal or informal, legal or criminal, and they may support single or pluralist interests. Among the more prominent actors are a diverse array of NGOs, many of which have formed transnational links in efforts to change social and/or political ideas and structures in areas of human security such as the environment, gender, and human rights. Migrant groups, consisting of workers from formal and informal sectors or refugees from political and economic crisis situations, present another set of civil society (re)actions which often have a clearly de-marked regional character. Less conspicuous, but nevertheless important, non-state agents of social change include members of criminal groups which conduct illegal trade on a regional scale in drugs, weapons, endangered species or stolen property.

Reflecting their diversity, non-state actors which advance regionalism do so for varied reasons, exerting pressure on official institutions at different political levels. In instances where threats to personal security such as disease, environmental degradation, crime, unemployment have a definite transregional character, national institutions are likely to be challenged to modify their foreign policy in one of two ways: by expanding the list of problems to be treated as items of 'security' (i.e., shifting the security agenda from state interest to human needs) or by relinquishing national responsibility for the problem to a regional institution. This may involve applying pressure to encourage the establishment of official forms of regional integration or revitalising existing transregional arrangements by bringing social concerns (and/or actors) into the decision making nexus. In some cases, organisations or social groups that wish to draw attention to issues that are of regional importance may circumvent the state to interact primarily with international governmental organisations (IGOs).

Regional and Global Civil Societies: Compatibilities and Contradictions

Some NGOs may function at a regional level or be concerned mainly with a particular issue of regional dimensions, but yet be more accurately described as constitutive of a global rather than regional civil society. Such organisations are part of an expanding worldwide transnational network of NGOs and research institutions that are consciously or functionally engaged in establishing a 'global identity' that centres around notions of global democracy, global governance, and global citizenship. Although the extent and even the existence of a global civil society remains somewhat controversial, a growing number of scholars nevertheless agree that the structure of collective action has changed, opening up ' a new space for theory and social action' at the global level (Escobar, 1995, p. 216). This is manifested in the proliferating transnational networks of Global Social Change Organisations (GSCOs) and Transnational Advocacy Non-Governmental Organisations (TANGOs), which adopt a world-view approach to development and 'new' security issues (de Sousa Santos, 1995; Cooperrider and Pasmore, 1991; Boulding, 1991). Some critical scholars, such as Cox (1994a & b), believe that this 'new space' offers unprecedented opportunities for democratic change led by non-state actors, although as yet, such opportunities are weakly or only intermittently seized. Others, however, believe that a radically-transformative (albeit still embryonic) global/transnational civil society has already emerged (Hunter, 1996; Macdonald, 1994).

In support of the latter view, at least some NGOs are engaged in conscious efforts to build a global civil society; these organisations are

'...presented, and present themselves, as an *alternative* model to the hegemonic ideology and methodology' of the present world order (Macdonald 1995, p. 119). However, because the membership in this group is diffuse, ever-changing and loosely co-ordinated, the degree to which it is counter-hegemonic, hence transformative, is not easily determined. But at least some measure of increased solidarity among these organisations is demonstrated in the pressures they have been able to assert collectively: 'first, to influence governments to change their positions and policies on a range of issues and, second, to create new modes and mechanisms of governance in those political spaces where they may not already exist' (Coate *et al.*, 1996, p. 100).

Both of these types of activity are often most effectively co-ordinated at the regional level. Yet, while they may draw mainly on regional connections as part of the process of building transnational linkages, or focus on a regional problem as a symptom of their broader concern, they are not necessarily or primarily inclined 'to promote the region as a viable economic, cultural and ecological unit' -- the motivating factor by which Hettne (1990, p. 250) defines the 'new' regionalism. One example in Southern Africa is the regional NGO, MWENGO.[10] According to its constitution, MWENGO exists for the purposes of defining a common (global) development paradigm, providing information webs for collecting and sharing information among members, creating stronger advocacy positions in national and international fora through alliance, and fostering connections between Northern and Southern NGOs and civil society's other agents for change. The sense of regionness which is associated with such organisations is part of a broader sense of identity within a global civil society. They draw on regional connections as part of a process to link up with a growing network of NGOs around the world that resist the dominant neoliberal system and 'the over-reliance placed on unaccountable open, free-market forces (which) aggravates, rather than alleviates, the current global social crises'.

Organisations such as MWENGO tend to promote the 'new' regionalism only indirectly through a functional need for like-minded, globally-oriented 'partners' in the area (a need that is heightened by the financial dependence of these NGOs on external donors, and the tendency of the latter to emphasise both 'partnerships' and 'regional development programmes') (MacLean, 1997). Still, some global change organisations may contribute significantly to the development of a sense of regionness;

that is, a condition prior to the maturation of a regional civil society. Many environmental NGOs are a case in point. Such organisations have tended to emerge from or be associated with the ecological movement whose members view environmental issues as a feature of a global problematic. Yet many of the more pressing environmental issues have a definite regional character and require regional solutions. Problems of water supply, desertification and air pollution transcend adjoining national boundaries and frequently affect environmental conditions in several neighbouring countries. Such problems may have natural causes, or they may result from, or be exacerbated by, war or other political events -- also with regional dimensions. The social consequences of environmental degradation, particularly transborder migrations of people, animals, pollution, or disease, demand regional solutions, even if the awareness of the problem is generated, at least in part, by an emerging sense of global citizenship.

Certainly, many NGOs operate at the regional level for practical reasons rather than a commitment to bring about a profound system change. Regional operation systems will tend to have a broader base of expertise available for dealing with local or national problems. Moreover, external funding agencies tend to encourage regionalisation of similar types of NGOs for the economies of scale it offers to the donors. However, even when motivated more by functional than ideological concerns, regionally based NGOs often contribute, even unwittingly, to the construction of a regional (and/or global) civil society. A variety of organisations, including women's groups, human rights organisations, and research and information institutes, contribute to the interconnections of a transnational civil society through their commitment to building capacity within individual NGOs, as well as connecting and informing NGOs from the grass-roots to the international level of operation. The resulting networks provide an infrastructure for transmitting a 'human security' discourse and for building a sense of global or regional identity. Civil society may coalesce around this identity to force the institutional changes that would bring 'new' security items to the forefront of official decision making.

Transformative Potential in Regional Civil Society

According to Hettne (1994, p. 135), the notion of 'global governance' is a 'realistic utopia'; that is, aspirations for its development are not necessarily overly idealistic or futile, but certainly premature. The 'new' regionalism is an emerging political solution to the disorder characterising the intermediate stage between the present Westphalian order and the one that will replace it. An important feature, then, of the 'new' regionalism is the articulation of social pressures for system change and the institutional structures and norms that have represented and supported the Westphalian order.

Numerous strategies and connections are involved in the processes by which 'bottom-up' pressures are being exerted to institutionalise regional action on 'new' security items, or to place regional concerns on national or international decision making agendas. In some instances, social groups have responded to crisis or insecurity by circumventing contemporary norms, conventions or institutions, and resorting to historical linkages and identities to settle power struggles or solve basic needs dilemmas. In many countries, the results of these seemingly atavistic gestures have ranged from escalations in ethnic rivalry to civil disorder and anarchy. At the same time, these events involve myriad political, economic, and social spillovers to the regional level as the interests, needs, and operational levels of the refugees, transnational corporations, military personnel, mercenaries and smugglers will tend to have regional dimensions and may only secondarily or incidentally coincide with national interests.[11] The serious implications presented by the variety of these actors has already been discussed in connection with the establishment of a 'new' human security agenda. It bears repeating here, however, to emphasise the relationship that exists between the 'new' human security model and the many 'bottom up' pressures which are contributing to the development of a 'new' regionalism (Shaw, 1998). It is also a credible rationale for the emerging tendency to 'regionalise' security operations by using troops from the regional commands closest for activities such as peacekeeping (Schwartzberg, 1997, p. 9).

In the recent past, many of these operations have involved clashes of identity, fuelled by resurrected ethnic or religious rivalries that appeared in many instances to have been laid to rest long ago. That antagonistic historical identities have resurfaced appears to support the view that the source of contemporary political crises in many developing countries may be traced to the imposition of modern (i.e. Western) models of governance and border placements that were either inappropriate or premature and only weakly or temporarily legitimised. Claims of nationhood and space by postcolonial powers did not necessarily, or usually, correspond to indigenous communities' historical perceptions of identity, and only superficial identification with the 'nation' and the 'nation state' occurred. Therefore, as the ability or will of states to protect or provide for their citizens has been compromised by forces of globalisation, peoples' tenuous identification with their 'imagined' national communities has tended to wither as they search for new solutions, often defined by regional connections among kin or ethnic group, rather than the political and legal boundaries of the state. Thus estranged to varying degrees from their citizens, states in the periphery have suffered additional strain on relations with their civil societies due to the harsh economic reforms that international financial institutions' (IFIs) have imposed on them as loan conditionalities since the early eighties. As one of us (Shaw, 1996, p. 36) has argued before, there is a probable connection between the structural adjustment programmes (SAPs), as these reforms are known, and the recent growth in numbers of complex emergencies. Indeed, these may be less exigent and more predictable than is widely supposed (i.e., they are structural consequences of the profound economic contractions which have resulted from SAPs).

Clearly, in many areas, the result of these stresses on the state and state system has been very destructive of both institutional authority and human security. Nevertheless, some 'bottom up' pressures on the state are potentially constructive. In particular, many recent efforts to establish or revitalise regional institutions may be seen as attempts to create new systems of governance that are in better alignment with prevailing social needs, expectations, relations and identities. Recent actions by non-state actors on issues of environmental and migration law in Southern Africa help to illustrate this point. Many environmental NGOs in the area encourage the development of regional strategies, institutions, and policies to deal with issues such as water usage and conservation of forestry, soil, or wildlife (Swatuk, 1997). Most of these organisations lead by example, with some (such as the Southern African Research and Documentation Centre [SARDC]) setting up regional networks for gathering and disseminating information on these issues, and others (such as Zimbabwe's Campfire programme) serving as models for similar initiatives throughout the region. Still others are involved in lobbying governments to adopt regional approaches, such as with recent efforts to establish a Trans Border Conservation Area in a triangle intersected by the countries of South Africa, Zimbabwe, and Mozambique (Duffy, 1997). Similarly, on the migration issue, there has been considerable pressure on South Africa to loosen restrictions on cross-border traffic based on the arguments that: (1) current constraints to movement are unenforceable and/or inhumane given that increases in migrancy rates are driven by human security problems; and (2) tight immigration policies impede economic integration in the region (Crush, 1996, p. 5).

It appears that efforts by non-state actors to have regional institutions deal with regional issues have had some measure of success: for example, the ECA's (Economic Commission for Africa) attempts to establish a Regional Centre for Civil Society Organisations (Shaw et al., 1998), and the Southern African Development Community's (SADC) incorporation of 'new' security items such as the environment on its agenda (Vale, 1996, p. 380). Moreover, SADC's recent Draft Proposal on the Free Movement of People in Southern Africa suggests that lobbying efforts by associations in civil society have been at least somewhat effective (Crush, 1996, p. 5). Nevertheless, despite the positive direction that is implied by one of the main organs for regional cooperation, in its efforts to promote a common approach to 'human security', the overall trend may be more negative. Other regional organisations, such as the Southern African Customs Union (SACU) and the Common Market for Eastern and Southern Africa (COMESA), do not even discuss security or acknowledge its linkage to the economic development issues with which they are concerned (Vale, 1996, p. 380). More importantly, there is significant resistance among state officials to transfer control from national authorities, even on issues of regional scale. As well, state officials tend to be very reluctant, often despite rhetoric to the contrary, to forgo traditional realist doctrine as the basis for setting foreign policy. As Vale (1996, p. 379) argues:

> (l)ooking at the debate on migration in South Africa, there is no reason to believe that significant progress is possible in the foreseeable future. Although leaders -- Nelson Mandela is an example -- have paid lip-service to the principle of reciprocal relations between the region's people, influential voices within the country's security community have promoted an alarmist response to the issue.... The discourse (among state officials) on migration has not moved beyond the confines of orthodox security thinking.

Resistance from the state notwithstanding, the momentum of the 'new' regionalism will most likely continue to grow in the periphery, not only because of the persistence of 'bottom up' action, but also because the latter is being augmented by forces from 'above'. Despite well-documented difficulties in the past with different forms of regional cooperation and various integration schemes in developing countries,[12] there has been a renewed impetus for states to enter into formal regional cooperation arrangements. While most of these organisations tend to conform to traditional ideas and patterns of cooperation or integration, the formation of some, like the Inter-Governmental Agency on Development (IGAD), suggest that 'new' security items are gradually becoming motivating factors for instituting formal regionalisms. Yet, it may be overly optimistic to expect that 'new' human security regionalisms will proliferate to the degree that they will reinforce the more positive of the 'bottom up' pressures for regional cooperation. Moreover, orthodox approaches to regional integration -- even of the 'development' variety favoured by countries in the periphery -- are unlikely to be compatible with many of the 'bottom up' regionalisms unless they are willing to incorporate the latter's concern for 'new' security issues.

Conclusions

Robert Cox has defined multilateralism as 'a commitment to maximum participation in a dialogue among political, social, economic and cultural forces as a means of resolving conflicts and designing institutional processes' (Mittelman, 1997, p. 89). Conforming to this definition are diverse strategies designed by various contemporary actors -- in formal and informal, official and unofficial capacities. What unifies their efforts is the search for means by which unprecedented levels and forms of insecurities may be eliminated or mediated. Since the 'new' security issues are at least partly the result of a failure of governance -- the inability of the present systems to maintain environments for the 'good life' of citizens -- the search involves the possibility of major institutional reform.

According to Hettne (1997, p. 3), the 'new' regionalism is one possible solution to the present institutional dilemma. As he defines it, the 'new' regionalism is a 'compromise between Westphalian and post-Westphalian political rationality', moving beyond reliance on the state alone for security needs but stopping short of plunging into the unknown area of global governance. Given this rather ambivalent position, the 'new' regionalism is a concept and process in flux. If it is to fill the existing institutional gap, as Hettne implies is possible, the disparate motivations and objectives that drive its various constituent processes will need to converge at some point. It would depend to a large extent upon the ability of existing regional organisations (as well as states) to incrementally adapt to the expanded set of issues and actors that confront officials at this time. It would seem to depend as well upon the ability of NGOs and others to strategise a collective approach to press for institutional reform. The plurality and divergent interests of civil society mitigates against a forceful collaborative effort in the near future. Nevertheless, at present, at least some of the 'bottom up' pressures encompassed by the 'new' regionalism provide one of the more effective vehicles for the construction of a 'new' human security agenda for the 21st century.

Notes

[1] These Commission Reports include the Independent Commission on International Development Issues (1980 and 1983); Independent Commission on Disarmament and Security (1982); World Commission on Environment and Development (1987); South Commission (1990); Commission on Global Governance (1995); International Commission on Peace and Food, (1994).

[2] For an example of the changing attitudes among practitioners, see a recent journal article by Canada's Minister of Foreign Affairs (Axworthy, 1997).

[3] This phrase is borrowed from the title of Rosenau and Czempiel's 1992 book which 'explores the ideational bases, behavioural patterns, and institutional arrangements that give structure and direction to the diverse forms of governance prevailing in different parts of the world' (p. i).

[4] Examples include the UN Conference on the Environment and Development in Rio de Janeiro (1992), the UN Conference on Population in Cairo (1994), the UN Social Summit in Copenhagen (1995), and the Beijing Conference on Women's Issues (1996).

[5] See for example, UNRISD's 1995 *States of Disarray* which bears '*the social effects of globalization*' as its sub-title.

[6] Functionalism is most often associated with the scholarship of David Mitrany while Ernst B. Haas, Karl W. Deutsch and Leon L. Lindberg are prominent proponents of the neo-functionalist approach.

[7] Hettne (1993, p. 222) uses the term 'neo-mercantilism' in essentially the same way that Buzan uses the term 'benign.... mercantilism'. According to the latter (1984, p. 608), 'The benign view sees a mercantilist system of large, inward-looking blocs, where protectionism is predominantly motivated by considerations of domestic welfare and internal political stability... Such a system potentially avoids many of the organisational problems of trying to run a global or quasi-global liberal economy... in the absence of political institutions on a similar scale. The malevolent view sees a return of the mercantilist dynamic of the... past, in which protectionism is motivated primarily by considerations of state power'.

[8] *Transformative multilateralism* is the focus of an ongoing study headed by Robert Cox and sponsored by the United Nations University (UNU). This MUNs (multilateralism and the United Nations) programme has a double mandate: the analytical component is concerned with exposing the relations among the various elements which comprise the complex post-Westphalian environment in which the United Nations now operates; a normative component involves commitments to 'the promotion of social equity, the diffusion of power among social groups and societies, the nonviolent means of dealing with conflict, the protection of the biosphere, and the mutual recognition of the values of different civilisations' (Cox, 1997, p. 105).

[9] Cox (1997, p. 107) has borrowed the term and concept of 'double movement' from Karl Polanski who was referring to a sequence of events that occurred with the Industrial Revolution in England. In the first movement, the economy was disembedded from society and, thus unfettered, dictated the terms of social relations, largely to the detriment of human needs. In response, social pressures emerged and intensified for protection against the negative aspects of the new economic order. This process was the 'double movement'.

[10] MWENGO is the acronym for Mwelekeo Wa NGO - Kiswahili for 'NGO Direction/vision' (MWENGO. *MWENGO Constitution*. Nairobi: Reprint by Kenpak Manufacturers and Printers Limited).

[11] Sub-Saharan Africa has provided the most dramatic recent examples with crises centred in such countries as Somalia, Rwanda, Burundi, Angola, Liberia, and Sierra Leone. However, various conflicts, often based on religious differences and having both national and regional dimensions, are also evident in the Middle East, Central and East Asia, and Northern Africa.

[12] For example, see the comprehensive comparative study by Blomqvist *et al.* (1993, pp. 48-67) of the Association of Southeast Asian Nations (ASEAN), the Central American Common Market (CACM), and the Latin American Free Trade Association (LAFTA).

15 Globalisation, Class and Cultural Identity at the End of Hegemony

JONATHAN FRIEDMAN

The Global Framework

Globalisation traps, balkanisation, class polarisation, the dominance of transnational companies and the subordination of transnational migrants are all part of the imaging broadcast over the global media, and they merge with experiences of fear and joy in the countdown to the next millennium; visions of freedom and multicultural enrichment for some, but visions of multiethnic conflict and marginalisation for others. There is no doubt that the economic changes that are occurring today need to be understood in order to account for the massive social changes that seem to be taking shape in the global arena. The general framework that has been suggested in my previous work (Friedman, 1994) is one which linked declining 'world' hegemony to decreasing homogeneity, increasing disorder and fragmentation in the larger social world. Simultaneously, increasing integration in smaller social worlds is expressed in a proliferation of cultural identities, ethnic, indigenous, national, religious and sexual struggling for autonomy and control of the larger arenas. Ascending areas within the global system were said to experience the inverse process, the suppression or ranking of cultural difference, national and regional integration. This framework was essentially cyclical and was based on a model of pulsating accumulation of wealth, centralisation and decentralisation, corresponding to political/cultural expansion versus contraction, a pattern that is said to characterise the entire history of commercial civilisations.

This kind of approach runs parallel to the recent work of Frank and Gills (1993) for world history, in general, and Braudel (1984) and Arrighi (1994) for the more recent European past. The model is a cyclical model of expansion/contraction and shift in a hegemonic centre of capital accumulation. Globalisation of financial capital occurs for Braudel and Arrighi as a product of the conjunction of declining old and rising new hegemonies, and so is nothing new for the contemporary situation since it is not a sign of the evolution of a new system. On the other hand, it might be countered that technological speed-up has finally, today, precluded the rise of new hegemons. Thus the rise of East Asia may harbour a tendency to a shift, but countries like Japan have not made it to the top as its predecessors, the US, UK, Spain, Portugal, Venice and Genoa. Rather the decentralised and rapidly shifting feature of globalisation may have become a permanent feature of the global system. The decline of Western hegemonies is evident and the social transformations involved in such declines are the subject of this analysis.

Social Structuration of the Global System

There are two parallel social processes, currently at work in the old hegemonic centres of the global system. The first of these is a process of fragmentation, both cultural and political, which takes the form of indigenisation, regionalisation, nationalisation (in the sense of nationalism) and the ethnification of immigrants. The other process is what I have referred to as a 'lift-off' at the apex of society, an increase in class polarisation which includes the globalisation of the world's upper classes and elites. These two processes are simultaneous aspects of the transformation of the world system, but they are also highly uneven processes. Verticalisation and horizontalisation discussed below have occurred primarily in declining hegemonic networks, while in East and Southeast Asia, the converse has been the norm, i.e., national and regional consolidation. The rise of indigenous movements, while globally orchestrated by an array of new international institutions and facilitated by international media and web sites, has not been successful in East and Southeast Asia, where increasingly powerful states have combined violence and accommodation in their strategies of integration. In the following discussion I have concentrated primarily on the Western sector, while emphasising the contrasting nature of developments in Asia.

Global processes are best understood as vectors of social fields that channel strategies and processes of identification. Thus, the globalisation of tribal elites as well as the globalisation of national and business elites is organised by the vectors of the same social field. The incorporation of such elites into global circuits of political and economic relations is a parallel process. If the same globalisation produces different results, this is because the local structures are very different from one another. Similarly the horizontal polarisation or fragmentation that characterises so many national societies today produces different results, depending on the state-society structures that are articulated to the global processes. While I begin with an analytical separation of the horizontal and vertical processes, they are in reality dialectically intertwined in ways that are crucial for understanding the current state of the world.

Parameters of Globalisation I: Horizontal Fragmentation

The decline of hegemony of the advanced industrial centres has led to a process that I have previously described in terms of fragmentation. It relates the decline of modernist identification to an increase in 'rooted' forms of identity, whether regional, indigenous, immigrant-ethnic or national. The modernist nation state is based on the identification of a subject population with a national project that defines its members in principle in terms of equality and political representativity. When this project ceases to function as an attractor, its subjects must look elsewhere. The modern nation state is founded upon a massive transformation of the world system in which a homogenising, individualising, and democratising process in the centre is combined with and dependent upon a hegemonic expansion in the rest of the world, the formation of a centre-periphery organisation. The modernist state is one in which the ethnic content of the nation is usually secondary to its function as a citizenry-based development project, in which cultural assimilation is a necessary by-product of the homogenisation of regional and contemporary differences that might weaken the unity of the national project. The decline of hegemony is also the decline in the unifying force of its mechanisms of identification. Those who were partly integrated and stigmatised move to establish themselves and those who were totally assimilated must search for new forms of collective belonging. This leads to a range of cultural identifications that fragment and ethnify the former political units, from ethnic to religious to sexual, all in the vacuum left by the disappearance of the future.

Indigenous populations have increased in size since the mid-1970s, not as a matter of biology but of identity choice. It is estimated that there are 350 million indigenous people and they have become increasingly organised as well as winning a series of battles over land and cultural autonomy. Sub-national regionalism is also on the increase and forms, for example, a powerful lobby in Europe today, aiming for a combination of a strong centralised Europe and a decentralised nation state. This has, like indigenous movements, been developing since the mid-1970s.

Migration is again a massive phenomenon in a destabilised world. But immigrants no longer come to their new countries simply to become good citizens. On the contrary, the ethnification of such groups has led to a strong tendency to diasporisation and to a cultural politics claiming recognition in the public sphere. In some cases this has led to a fragmenting of a former national unity. That is, rather than becoming assimilated to declining nation states, such groups maintain and develop transnational identities, cultures and social existences. National identity has become increasingly ethnified in this period as well in parallel with the ethnification of immigrants. This is expressed in the emergence of nationalist movements, and xenophobic ideologies that are themselves partially generated by economic crisis and downward mobility (see next section).

This process cannot be understood without placing it in the context of a weakened nation state structure as a specific form of relations between people and their representative governmental bodies. The decline of modernism is very much a product of the weakening of the state machine, its tendency in the 1970s toward bankruptcy and its general insecurity largely a result of the accelerating mobility of capital and taxable income. The transformation of the state is an issue in itself to which we must return. What is crucial here is that the focality of the state in identity formation is giving way to competing identities from indigenous, regional and migratory populations. This has also implied a decentralisation of resources within the state, along broadly ethnic lines, and an increasing division of powers, between the state as representative of the nation and the sub-groups that tend to displace it. This might be understood as temporary phenomenon. Certainly with respect to immigration earlier periods of our history are filled with debates concerning assimilation versus weaker forms of integration or even the formation of more loosely federal structures. Horace Kallen (1924) suggested during the early debates of this century that ethnic minorities ought to be given more autonomy as social entities and that the United States could become a kind of ethnic consociational democracy such as the regionalised states of Belgium and Switzerland. On the other hand there have rarely occurred situations in which the sub-groups themselves were so organised, and there was nothing like the strong multi-ethnic tendency that predominates today. From quite early on in the century, assimilation became the absolutely dominant policy in the United States. Wieviorka (1977) has reminded us that contemporary ethnic fragmentation is merely an aspect of a much broader cultural fragmentation, including gender, age, religion and most of the other cultural categories that constitute modern society.[1]

It is worth noting the difference between previous tendencies to multi-ethnicity, at the turn of the century, and the current situation. In the earlier period, while there were, as we said, debates on the reconstitution of society in multicultural terms, the same kind of debate was not present in Europe where assimilation was simply taken for granted.[2] Europe was still organised around the combination of a strongly ethnic state and a colonial world structure in which coming to the metropole was immediately understood as social mobility, an increase in status implying a will to assimilate to the superior. This was structured strongly enough to be more or less obvious to nationals as well as immigrants, regionals and indigenous peoples. While there were clearly differences in the constitution of nation states, such as the *jus sanguinis* of Germany and the *jus solis* of France, the process of assimilation was powerful in all cases. The high proportion of Polish labourers in German industrial development led to their eventual absorption into German national identity. The legal processes and cultural processes were not, of course, equivalent, and there was clearly both physical and psychological violence involved. While the conditions of assimilation are difficult to ascertain, I would argue that the ideological situation in earlier parts of the century was strongly nationalist while this situation has become reversed in the past decades. This reversal or ideological inversion is an important aspect of the general situation. Todd Gitlin (1995) has argued for the same identity shift in the United States. Earlier in the century, immigrants came to become part of the country whereas today they come to remain part of their countries of origin. Immigration in the current situation harbours strong tendencies to diasporisation. The latter must be understood in terms of a set of practices in which identification with a homeland is the basis for the organisation of cultural, economic and social activities that transgress national borders.

Consolidation in East and Southeast Asia as an Expression of Hegemonic Restructuring

An important contrast here is that while fragmentation is occurring in the old centres, Asia would seem to be heading in the opposite direction. Ideologies of the state and development are on the rise rather than the retreat in this area of the world. The rise of nationalism is itself a potential problem in the region, and, of course, processes of homogenisation remain very fragile. On the other hand there is little or no tolerance for separatism, nor for tendencies to establish conditions of Western style democratic confrontation. This is no mere cultural difference. One has only to return to the 19th century, to Victorianism, to Bismark, to ascertain the degree to which national growth was independent of democratic politics and all tendencies to political fragmentation. On the contrary, there are striking parallels between the ideology of Victorian England and neo-Confucianism.

I would suggest that these ideologies can be understood in structural and historical terms rather than in purely cultural terms. Indonesia, a country that has become increasingly consolidated after decades of internal strife, has a national 'discipline' movement, *Gerakan, Disiplin Nasional* (Hill,1994), and is actively engaged in forcefully integrating its internal others. The clear opposition to Western values and investment in an Asian way has led to consolidation within states rather than the fragmentation that has characterised the West. Even a society such as Singapore, founded on a colonial structure of pluralism, has struggled increasingly toward cultural unity, which in the 1980's has been referred to in terms of 'communitarian inclusionism' (Perry, Kong and Yeoh, 1997, p. 84). There is also a kind of 'vacuum cleaner' effect in the growth process which draws youths away from their local environments to centres of increasing employment and new forms of life. This includes both push and pull effects, but it is clearly expressed in the 100 million internal migrants in China.

There have been innumerable interpretations of the relation between cultural and political economic processes in the region. The 'Asian values' approach has been interpreted in simple cultural terms by business economists of the past decades, i.e., a more efficient way to run capitalism. But it is perhaps best seen as part of the content of the nationalisation process itself. If I have stressed the similarities between Victorianism and the larger family of nationalist ideologies associated with industrialism, this is not to deny the vast and various differences in real cultural forms, but to stress the strategic commonalities in the global system.[3] Certainly, the role of kinship networks in the structuring of all aspects of life implies a very different structure of the nation than that in the West. A recent article by Jayasuriya (1997) suggests that 'Asian values' represent a form of 'reactionary modernism', a concept developed by Herf (1982) in discussing the ideology that developed in Weimar Germany which was instrumental in the emergence of fascism. National-cum-traditionalist and authoritarian values were connected with the ideology of industrial development. The implications that this ideology has a lot in common with fascism is certainly interesting in structural terms, but it does not take into consideration the historical reaction to liberalism embodied in fascism, nor its working class and egalitarian core. This is quite a big difference with respect to the trajectories of fascism as opposed to the 'miracle' developments of Asia. The Victorian or even Bismarkian model thus seems better. It is important to note the degree to which Western discourse on Asia is so entirely ahistorical in this respect, assuming quite innocently that Western industrialism was somehow a product of the kind of liberal society to be found there at present. Any political history of Europe demonstrates, on the contrary, that industrialisation proceeded in an 'illiberal' regime until quite late.

The economic crisis may be said to reveal the degree to which nationalisation has occurred. In Indonesia there was clearly a nationalist mobilisation against Suharto. In Korea, the working class strikes and demands for state responsiveness are examples of the nationalisation of the population. Numerous calls by the state for discipline and even prayer (as in Thailand) have led to broad response at a national level. The close relation between state and capital in many of the crisis-ridden countries has been much discussed since the massive increase in easy credit was clearly channelled through these often quite personal networks. While this may be a socially specific aspect of the economies of the region which might be accounted for in terms of the history of the political structures involved, it was not recognised as a cause of the crisis until after the fact. The internal political conflicts that ensue from the crisis, as well as the possibility of a growing regionalism and nationalism in the face of the threat of global take-overs and other forms of intervention, should be staked out as an important area of research that might reveal deeper insights into the nature of social and political structures in the region.

Parameters of Globalisation II: Vertical Polarisation

While cultural and social fragmentation is occurring with various degrees of confrontation and violence in the former hegemonic regions of the world system, there is another process that has been discussed widely. Class stratification in the old centres is on the increase and often in quite astounding proportions. This is not, of course, a simple process and is definitely not limited to a combination of impoverishment and the enrichment of a capitalist class. The stratification process includes significant elites connected to public institutions, international bureaucracies and professional classes, all of whom depend in varying degrees on tax funds; their speculative growth and other sources of income that have been in one way or another transferred to the public sphere. I have referred to this earlier as the global pork barrel phenomenon, which plays an important role in consolidating global class identities and novel cultural discourses.

The economic parameters of this process in the old centres of the world system are well known through variations on common themes. Countries like Sweden with a low level of class differentiation and countries like the United States with a much higher level have experienced the same transformational vectors in the past decade, vectors that are common properties of a global dynamic. While the ratio of richest to poorest in Sweden is 2.7 as opposed to 5.9 for the US, the same kinds of changes have occurred. These are the economic vectors: the combination of global shift, speed-up and the changing composition of capital. The US has experienced the clearest example of this kind of change, where downward mobility since the 1970s has been a common denominator of the era. Flexible labour regimes have expanded, leading to a larger proportion of working poor. Incomes have stagnated or declined and mobility has become increasingly limited. In Europe unemployment has reached alarming proportions. In Sweden it was above 12% in the mid to late 1990s and has now declined, primarily due to public sector spending and make-work programmes. The private sector has continued to see a decline in employment that began in the 1970s.

The articulation of vertical polarisation and horizontal fragmentation takes on a variety of forms. At one extreme there is a cultural minimal state which is approximated in the United States, where individualism and a sacred private sphere have entailed a certain disinterested tolerance for cultural difference as long as it is not politicised. In continental Europe, on the other hand, the nation state has a much stronger cultural character, and multiculturalism here appears as a serious threat to the former social contract which has always been considerably stronger than in the United States. The economics of this are clearly expressive of the different natures of the nation state. In Europe the percentage of the population below the poverty line that is raised above that line by government support is between 40% and 60%, with the Scandinavian countries approaching 100%. The equivalent figure for the US is 0.5%. The US has an official poverty rate of over 15% for the nation as a whole, jumping to considerably more than 20% in some states. If one calculates in terms of families and raises the income to $25,000, which seems to be a more adequate definition of the threshold of subsistence adequacy, then the figure rises to 28% (Hacker, 1997, p. 229). More important, with an unemployment rate below 5%, these are, for the most part, the working poor. In both Europe and the US, the rate of ghettoisation has been extreme, and the formation of underclasses has been the formation of marginalised minorities as well, whose unemployment rates are often several times higher than those of the native born or more often those identified as 'real nationals'. Here of course there is a significant difference between polar extremes such as Sweden, where in the relatively well off welfare-supported ghettos unemployment reaches 90% or more, and states like California where entire industries are dependent on the influx of undocumented immigrants.

Downward mobility and de-industrialisation has been accompanied by an upward mobility in the upper echelons of society. It is reflected in reports of enormous incomes among the capitalist elite as well as increasing incomes among other political and cultural elites. The spate of scandals concerning credit cards, double salaries, long vacation-like trips and night club visits by politicians has led to a generalised crisis of confidence in the political elites. This crisis of accountability expresses an increasing rift between elites and the 'people'. The latter along with capitalists, who were always in such a position, have been assimilated into a global circuit of relations with similarly placed people, so that elite interests have become equivalent to a class for itself in many ways. The European Union has become a kind of super-national and weakly accountable political organ which makes increasing numbers of decisions that affect national level political situations. The salaries are considerably higher than those at the national level. And as there is no clearly defined social project, careers-in-themselves have become the *modus vivendi* of this massive reorganisation of Europe.

This kind of development at the regional and international level has produced new kinds of experiences for those involved. A person with such a career is very bound to his or her equivalents in the system. Representativity becomes less important than position itself. And the position may take on a new moral posture. The cosmopolitan is promoted to a new kind of legitimacy. It is increasingly associated with a series of agendas that may contradict those of the nation state itself. Recent expressions in Sweden have stressed a complex of multiculturalism, democratisation and globalisation as the new goals of world society. The very notion of having control over one's social existence has begun to take on a negative connotation. In recent interviews on the concept of people and peoplehood, or *folk,* in Sweden I discovered a certain inversion in values. While the notion of *folk* was taken over from the conservatives by the social democrats in the 1930's, it became associated with the notion of the people's will, with plebiscite, with concepts and symbols that expressed the notion of the 'captured state' or the 'captured elite'. A dominant class had been domesticated by ordinary working class people. Such words, just as nationalism, were associated with the progressive in the 50's through the 1970s. Today, however, there is an inversion of values. The notion of 'people' is associated with reaction, nationalism with essentialism. Multiculturalism has replaced older ideals of socialism. But then this is a view 'from afar', or from above, by a self-identified group that has constantly tried to liberate itself from the obsolete nation. In general, a formerly nationalist elite who may have seen 'the people' as a motley foreign mixture, today identifies itself as hybrid and views 'the people' as dangerous purists.

Hybridity and Class

The 'revolt of the elites' might well characterise this kind of development, but it only makes real sense in the nation state and its current transformation. Hybridity is a kind of top-down vision produced by this new positioning. Looking down on the new imploding urban zones with their diasporic minorities crowded into ethnic neighbourhoods, the new elites can marvel at a new-found cultural globalisation. Here they can consume the entire world, in the form of foods, and feasts of sight, from clothing to language to music. They can really experience their cosmopolitan desires in the new internationalised urbanity. The only problem is how to avoid the social realities of this celebrated world; the ghettoisation, marginalisation, criminalisation that have gone hand in hand with the more celebratory image. This can be achieved by remaining mere consumers and observers in a world of gated enclaves. What is good for eating might not be so pleasant in the kitchen.

The discourse of hybridity has an interesting logical structure (Friedman, 1997). It is at once cosmopolitan and postmodernist in its refusal of modernism. It is thus a re-investment of relativised cultures in a global scheme of cultural meetings. The new structure is a cultural ecumene, one that can only be understood from above. The new encompassing cosmopolitan elite is, thus, one that incorporates all the differences in the world, transforming them into the identity of the new authorities of the world.

There are numerous contradictions in this position which are not difficult to exemplify. One of the most salient representatives of hybrid identity is found in the much discussed book by Gloria Anzaldúa, *Borderlands/La Frontera: The New Mestiza* (1987) which details an identity based on border-crossing and mixture -- ethnic, national and sexual. The notion of the border as something to be straddled so as to be perpetually on both sides, is very different, of course than the daily lives of real border-crossers, especially the undocumented immigrants who cross over at great danger and whose life histories are replete with aversion and fear of precisely the border. There is clearly a class division in representations here. While there is a veritable culture industry that has grown up around the border-crossing identity among academics, the story at the lower end of the scale is quite different (Friedman, 1997). In Guatemala there is also a 'new mestizo' ideology, one that is rather widespread in Central America (Canclini, 1994). An elitist ideology harbours a logic that is implicitly anti-Indian. Maya can now be told that they are not pure and that all Guatemalans are part Indian. This implies, of course, that the legitimacy of Mayan land claims can be nullified. In Australia, perhaps the most immigrant-dense country in the world, the government, some years ago, launched a multicultural policy programme and a book called *Creative Australia* which was meant to recreate unity out of increasing diversity. On one occasion a representative literary scholar went to talk to a group of Aboriginal artists and intellectuals, presumably to entice them into the new multicultural project. He went on for some time about how mixed the Aborigines were as a population and that any other view of themselves was tantamount to *essentialism*, that favourite word of cultural studies. When he was through, an older man rose and looked the hybridist straight in the eyes,

I'm an essentialist mate, and if you don't like it you can bugger off!

There is clearly a conflict between hybridising elites and those who identify as indigenous. Canada, another state that has declared itself multicultural, has faced similar opposition from Indians who refuse to be classified as just another ethnic minority. They are the First Peoples, and this, of course, is more than cultural distinctiveness. It is about rights to land and political autonomy.

There is little evidence that hybridity works on the ground. Attempts to establish 'bi-racial' identity in the United States have had an interesting development. The bi-racial movement is primarily a middle class activity and it contains a strong strategy of distinction-making in which class mobility leads to attempts to separate oneself from a preceding, in this case, lower status identity. The attractor in this is 'whiteness'. The logical contradiction in this kind of identification lies between individual and collective identities. Every individual has a specific genealogy and is thus a very particular mixture. Collective creole identities in the past have always and continue to be closed ethnic identities just as non-mixed identities. The bi-racial movement split several years ago when Asian bi-racials protested at the dominance of African Americans. The new group took on the title, *Hapa* Forum, *hapa* being the Hawaiian word for 'half'. This is a normal product of the above contradiction. Any attempt to form a collectivity must also create boundaries and raise issues concerning the particular constituents of that identity. Hybrid identity only works as a discourse or as an individual identity or where the specificity of the hybridity is ignored. It is thus most suitable for elites where the only commonality of the identity is that it is position above the fragmenting multi-ethnic world below.

In my previous work (1997, 1998) I have discussed the logic of hybridity, arguing that it can be understood as a postmodern cosmopolitanism that combines an international identity with a revived culturalism, a kind of leaky essentialism. The problems of the fragmenting world are the result of essentialising differences. To solve this problem we have only to re-conceive the world in terms of mixtures of such essential things. Cosmopolitans in the earlier years of this century were true modernists who identified with a future of expanding knowledge, rationality, and experimentation, whether in arts or sciences. The new cosmopolitans are absorbed in issues of identity. This has strong parallels with an older racialism: before we were pure but now we are mixed. There were two opposing positions on hybridity in the racialism of the 19th and early 20th century. Hybrids were either sterile and weak or else they were superior in their very mixture. The latter position is logically identical to contemporary hybrid ideology. It should be noted that hybridity as a concept does not solve the issue of essentialism. Rather it reifies it by its very structure. The only way to identify a hybrid category is by specifying its genealogy, the origins of its constituents. Thus hybridity logically entails genealogical thinking and cultural genealogies necessarily reify collective identities.

However, as stated above, hybridity can indeed function as a class or elite identity in which the particularity of mixtures is never at issue. There is some evidence to suggest that hybridity among intellectuals is in some sense a reaction to multicultural politics in which difference became such a divisive issue as to preclude any permanent unity. Gilroy, for example, in his attempt to define a Black Atlantic identity as opposed to Afro-centric models has argued hybridity against those who invest in African roots. But this kind of identity is itself a practice of social differentiation argued in strangely objectivist terms. 'We trans-Atlantic blacks are not representatives of the African. We have more, we are a new combination, representatives of the postcolonial conditions of the world. Just as the new mestizo's we represent a new people, dare I say 'race', that shall inherit the earth, or at least point the way to the future.' Homi Bhabha is perhaps the purest representative of hybridity as a new class ideology (1994) and his use of the term is much more generalised to practically all forms of in-between-ness to which he refers with the term 'third space'.

> For a willingness to descend into that alien territory -- where I have led you -- may reveal that the theoretical recognition of the split-space of enunciation may open the way to conceptualising an *inter*national culture, based not on the exoticism of multiculturalism or the *diversity* of cultures, but on the inscription and articulation of culture's *hybridity*. To that end we should remember that it is the 'inter' -- the cutting edge of translation and negotiation, the *in-between* space -- that carries the burden of the meaning of culture. It makes it possible to begin envisaging national, anti-nationalist histories of the 'people'. And by exploring this Third Space we may elude the politics of polarity and emerge as others of our selves (Bhabha, 1994, p. 38).

The connection between the restructuration of global classes and the emergence of hybridity has been made previously (Dirlik, 1994; Friedman, 1997, 1998). I would argue that there is a truly massive ideological transformation involved here which I have referred to in terms of cosmological inversion. This includes some of the phenomena described above which are included in the discourse of anti-nationalism, anti-essentialism, multiculturalism and hybridity. In a certain sense this is a reversal of the ideology of common goals and superordinate social projects common to a former left and a nationalism which was part of both left and right ideologies. The lift-off of the state produces a new populism that appears as reactionary, but which, in reality, is very much more complex. It re-imagines the former left as the new conservatism. As democracy, globalisation and multiculturalism become slogans of self-identified progressive politicians, it becomes immoral to demystify the structural adjustment inherent in such projects.

Paradoxes of Globalisation

The globalising tendencies and massive capital flows in the world create the kind of pork barrels referred to above. These flows interact with the fragmentation process, often splitting it by creating micro-classes. The example of the Maori is of importance here. The Maori indigenous movement made important inroads into New Zealand politics in the 1970s and 1980s. This led to numerous concessions, both cultural and economic. The restoration of tribal lands led ultimately to the establishment of 'tribal capitalism' (Rata, 1997) in which the tribal units were able to run fisheries while maintaining their conical clan structures. This created a new hierarchy of control within the tribal units since those closest to the central lineages were those who controlled the capital. The Maori today control a third of New Zealand's fisheries, but in an unequal way. More seriously, those Maori who do not have genealogical access to tribal land remain in their urban slums. They make up between 40 and 50% of the Maori population. Thus the Maori success story has created a class division within the group that did not exist previously. Throughout the world, NGO's are helping to create similar kinds of divisions. The same kind of class division occurred quite a few years ago among the Sami, between the small minority of reindeer owners and those who had been cut off from this livelihood and lost their territorial rights. There is also a considerable skim-off within the Fourth World that has created a travelling class of tribal representatives based largely around UN organs and those who stay home. Now this new class does not represent a hybrid ideology as such, but they might be seen as minor actors in the multiculturalisation of the world in which the hybrid encompassers represent the ideological apex. The globalisation of fragmentation consists in driving a class wedge through the ethnic groups themselves, leading to a whole new set of internal conflicts. My own work in the Hawaiian movement contains instances of increasing divisions between central actors and grassroots people which in some cases has led to the withdrawal of support for new 'chiefs'. There are international consultant firms today who specialise in what they call the 'sovereignty business', specialised that is in milking the funds that are destined for indigenous groups.

At the same time indigenisation has been a powerful factor of identification among the marginalised populations and underclasses of the declining hegemons. The ideologies of the New Rights in Europe, the Militia groups in the US are evidence of this. Many of these groups have strongly indigenous ideologies, invoking anti-universalism, local autonomy, nationhood over citizenship, 'tribal' religion and anti-modernist holism. There are African American Indian tribes such as the Washitaw who are allied with the Republic of Texas, there are numerous examples of cooperation between Black Power organisations and the Ku Klux Klan, primarily under the common banner of anti-statism, anti-cosmopolitanism and separatism.

Figure 1: The Dialectic of Hybridisation and Indigenisation

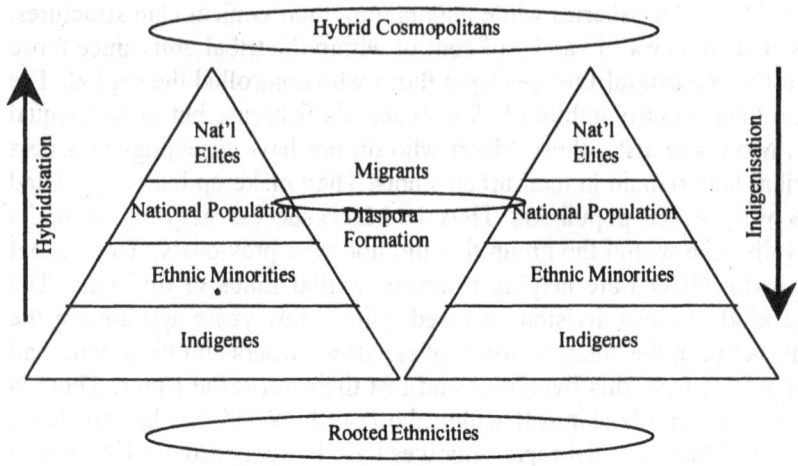

These tendencies, summarised in Figure 1, are not isolated from one another. They all interact on the Internet and are thoroughly embedded in the world systemic processes that we have discussed. The world processes that become salient in this model are the combined and seemingly contradictory phenomena of increasing cultural fragmentation in substantial parts of the world at the same time as there is an apparent increase in global unity in the form of communication, capital flows and global elite formations. These simultaneities are organised by a single nexus of global political economic processes and form the basis for the differential identity politics that are sometimes referred to in terms of 'glocalisation', the globalisation of the local and the localisation of the global. The latter metaphors, however, are not expressions of cultural processes in themselves but aspects of more powerful forces of local/global articulation. Class and ethnicity, vertical and horizontal polarisation are the two contradictory formations that emerge from the dynamics of globalisation.

Notes

[1] This generalised fragmentation is clearly expressed in the deconstruction of gender identities, both in intellectual discourse and in much middle class experimentation. Here roles are reversed and varied in the extreme and identities are reduced to acts. Judith Butler (1990) has gone so far as to suggest that there are no gender identities other than those that are imposed externally by the State or related Foucauldian power structure.

[2] As Noiriel has noted, 'It is somewhat suprising that Halbwachs (my note: a noted French sociologist) attributed the appearance of the Chicago school to the specificity of the immigrant experience in Chicago itself ... At the same time there were as many immigrants in France as there are today ... What was missing, then, was the sociologist, not the object' (Noiriel, 1996, p. 13).

[3] There is an interesting and growing literature on these issues which we can not deal with here (Robison, 1995; Khoo, 1995; Rodan, 1995; Tu, 1991; Tønnessson and Antlöv, 1996).

Bibliography

Abizaid, J. (1993), 'Lessons for Peacekeeping', *Military Review*, March, pp. 11-19.
ACDA (1996), *World Military Expenditures and Arms Transfers*, Washington DC: Government Printing Office.
Acharya, A. (1994), *An Arms Control Race in Post-Cold War South-East Asia: Prospects for Control*, Singapore: Institute of Southeast Asian Studies.
Adler, E., ed. (1992), *The International Practice of Arms Control*, Baltimore: Johns Hopkins University Press.
Ajayi, J.F.A. (1997), 'The Legacy of Colonialism in Post-Colonial Conflicts in Africa', in K. Volden and D. Smith, eds. *Causes of Conflict in the Third World*, Oslo: Idégruppen om Nord/Sør, International Peace Research Institute, pp. 23-32.
Albin, C. (1993), 'The Role of Fairness in Negotiation', *Negotiation Journal*, vol. 9, pp. 223-244.
Albrecht, U. (1990), 'The Role of Military R & D in Arms Build-ups', in N.P. Gleditsch and O. Njølstad, eds., *Arms Races: Technological and Political Dynamics*, London: Sage, pp. 87-104.
Albrecht, U., Lock, P. and Cohen, J. (1994), 'Germany - the Reluctant Eurofighter Partner', in R. Forsberg, ed., *The Arms Production Dilemma, Contraction and Restraint in the World Aircraft Industry*, Cambridge, MA: MIT Press, pp. 177-192.
Albrow, M. (1996), *The Global Age*, Cambridge: Polity.
Alger, C.F. (1989), 'Peace Studies at a Crossroads: Where Else?', in G. Lopez, ed., *Peace Studies: Past and Future*, Newbury Park: Sage, pp. 127-162.
Alger, C.F. (1995), 'Building Peace: a Global Learning Process', in M.M. Merryfield and R.C. Remy, eds., *Teaching about International Conflict and Peace*, New York: State University of New York Press, pp. 127-162.
Alger, C.F. (1996), 'The Emerging Tool Chest for Peacebuilders', *International Journal of Peace Studies*, vol. 1, no. 2, pp. 21-45.
Alker, H.R. (1996), *Rediscoveries and Reformulations*, Cambridge: Cambridge University Press.
Allison, G. (1971), *The Essence of Decision: Explaining the Cuban Missile Crisis*, Boston: Little-Brown.
Allison, G.T. and Morris, F.A. (1975), 'Armaments and Arms Control: Exploring the Determinants of Military Weapons', *Daedalus*, Summer, pp. 99-129.
Allison, G.T. (1983), 'What Fuels the Arms Race?' in J.F. Reichart and S.R. Sturm, eds., *American Defence Policy*, Baltimore: Johns Hopkins University Press, pp. 463-480.
Almond, G.A. and Powell, G.B. (1966), *Comparative Politics: a Developmental Approach*, Boston: Little, Brown and Co.

Ambler, R. (1990), 'Ghandian Peacemaking', in P. Smoker, R. Davies and B. Munske, eds. *A Reader in Peace Studies*, New York: St. Martin's Press, pp. 199-205.
Anthony, I., ed. (1991), *Arms Export Regulations*, Oxford: Oxford University Press.
Anthony, I., et al. (1997), 'The Trade in Major Conventional Weapons', in *SIPRI Yearbook 1997. Armaments, Disarmament and International Security*. Oxford: Oxford University Press, pp. 267-342.
Anzaldua, G. (1987), *Borderlands/La Frontera: The New Mestiza*, San Fransisco: Aunt Lute Books.
Arend, A.C. and Beck, R.J. (1993), *International Law and the Use of Force*, London: Routledge.
Arrighi, G. (1997), 'Globalization, State Sovereignty, and the "Endless" Accumulation of Capital', Paper presented at the States and Sovereignty in the World Economy Conference, University of California, Irvine.
Augsburger, D.W. (1992), *Conflict Mediation Across Cultures: Pathways and Patterns*, Louisville, KY: Westminster, John Knox.
Auvinen, J. (1997), 'Political Conflict in Less Developed Countries 1981-89', *Journal of Peace Research*, vol. 34, no. 2, pp. 177-195.
Axelrod, R. (1984), *The Evolution of Cooperation*, New York: Basic Books.
Axworthy, L. (1997), 'Canada and Human Security: The Need for Leadership', *International Journal*, vol. 52, no. 2, pp. 183-196.
Ayoob, M. (1998), 'Subaltern Realism: International Relations Theory Meets the Third World', in S.G. Neumann, ed., *International Relations Theory and the Third World*, New York: St. Martin's Press, pp. 31-54.
Ball, D. (1993), 'Arms and Affluence: Military Acquisitions in the Asia-Pacific Region', *International Security*, vol. 18, no. 3, pp. 78-112.
Ball, N. (1988), *Security and Economy in the Third World*, Princeton: Princeton University Press.
Barker, E. (1948), *The Politics of Aristotle*, Oxford: Clarendon Press.
Barnett, R. (1970), *The Economy of Death. A Hard Look at the Defense Budget, the Military Industrial Complex and What You Can Do About Them*, New York: Antheneum.
Behnke, A. (1997), 'Sleeping with the Enemy: the Western Involvement with Bosnia and the Problem of Security', Paper presented at the 38th Annual ISA Conference, Toronto.
Bercovitch, J., Anagnoson, J. and Wille, D. (1991), 'Some Conceptual Issues and Empirical Trends in the Study of Successful Mediation in International Relations', *Journal of Peace Research*, vol. 28, pp. 7-17.
Bercovitch, J. and Houston, A. (1996), 'The Study of International Mediation: Theoretical Issues and Empirical Evidence', in J. Bercovitch, ed., *Resolving International Conflicts. The Theory and Practice of Mediation*, Boulder, CO: Lynne Rienner, pp. 11-35.
Bercovitch, J. and Langley, J. (1993), 'The Nature of the Dispute and the Effectiveness of International Mediation', *Journal of Conflict Resolution*, vol. 37, pp. 670-691.
Bhabha, H. (1994), *The Location of Culture*, London: Routledge.

Blechman, B.M. (1983), 'Do Negotiated Arms Limitations Have a Future?', in J.F. Reichart and S.R. Sturm, eds., *American Defence Policy*, Baltimore: Johns Hopkins University Press, pp. 408-419.

Blomqvist, H.C., Lindholm, C., Lundahl, M., Schauman, S., and Oden, B., eds. (1993), 'Some Experiences from Regional Cooperation between Third World Countries', in *Southern Africa after Apartheid: Regional Integration and External Resources*, Uddevalla: Nordiska Afrikainstitute, pp. 48-67.

Bonta, B.D. (1996), 'Conflict Resolution Among Peaceful Societies: The Culture of Peacefulness', *Journal of Peace Research*, vol. 33, no. 4, pp. 403-420.

Borg, M. (1987), *Jesus: A New Vision*, New York: Harper and Row.

Boulding, E. (1991), 'The Old and New Transnationalism: An Evolutionary Perspective', *Human Relations*, vol. 44, no. 8, pp. 789-805.

Boulding, K.E. (1989), *Three Faces of Power*, Newbury Park: Sage.

Boulding, K.E. (1975), 'Can There be a National Policy for Stable Peace?', in K.E. Boulding, ed., *Collected Papers of Kenneth Boulding*, Boulder: Colorado Associated University Press.

Boutros-Ghali, B. (1992), *An Agenda for Peace*, New York: United Nations.

Boutros-Ghali, B. (1995), *An Agenda for Peace*, 2nd ed., New York: United Nations Department of Public Information.

Bradshaw, Y. and Wallace, M. (1996), *Global Inequalities*, Thousand Oaks: Pine Forge Press.

Brams, S.J. (1990), *Negotiation Games. Applying Game Theory to Bargaining and Arbitration*, New York: Routledge.

Braudel, F. (1984), *The Perspective of the World*, New York: Harper and Row.

Brogan, P. (1992), *World Conflicts*, London: Bloomsbury.

Brown, C. (1992), *International Relations Theory: New Normative Approaches*, London: Wheatsheaf.

Brown, L.R. (1977), *Redefining National Security*, Worldwatch Paper No. 14, Washington DC: Worldwatch Institute.

Brundtland, G.H., et al. (1987), *Our Common Future. World Commission on Environment and Development*, Oxford: Oxford University Press.

Buchheit, S.C. (1978), *Secession: The Legitimacy of Self-Determination*, New Haven: Yale University Press.

Bull, H. (1987), *Hedley Bull on Arms Control*, London: Macmillan.

Bull, H. (1995), *The Anarchical Society. A Study of Order in World Politics*, Houndmills, Basingstroke: Macmillan.

Burton, J.W. (1990a), *Conflict: Resolution and Prevention*, New York: St. Martin's Press.

Burton, J.W., ed. (1990b), *Conflict: Human Needs Theory*, London: Macmillan.

Burton, J.W. and Dukes, F. (1990), *Conflict: Practices in Management, Settlement & Resolution*, London: Macmillan.

Butler, J. (1990), *Gender Trouble*, London: Routledge.

Büttner, V. and Krause, J., eds. (1995), 'Rüstung Statt Entwicklung? Sicherheitspolitic, Militärausgaben und Rüstungskontrolle' *in Der Dritten Welt*, Baden-Baden: Nomos Verlagsgesellschaft.

Buzan, B. (1984), 'Economic Structure and International Security: The Limits of the

Liberal Case', *International Organization*, vol. 38, no. 4, pp. 597-624.

Buzan, B. (1987), *An Introduction to Strategic Studies. Military Technology and International Relations*, London: Macmillan.

Buzan, B. (1991), *People, States and Fear*, Boulder: Lynne Rienner.

Buzan, B. (1997), 'Rethinking Security after the Cold War', *Cooperation and Conflict*, vol. 32, no. 1, pp. 5-28.

Buzan, B. and Wæver, O. (1997), 'Slippery? Contradictory? Sociologically Untenable? The Copenhagen School Replies', *Review of International Studies*, vol. 23, no. 2, pp. 241-250.

Calhoun, C. (1997), *Nationalism*, Buckingham: Open University Press.

Cambon, J. (1931), *The Diplomatist*, London: Philip Allan.

Campbell, D. (1992), *Writing Security. United States Foreign Policy and the Politics of Identity*, Minneapolis: University of Minnesota Press.

Canclini, H. (1994), *Hybrid Culture*, Minneapolis: University of Minnesota Press.

Carlson, D. and Comstock, C. (1986), *Citizen Summitry*, New York: Jeremy Tarcher.

Carnegie Comission on Preventing Deadly Conflict, ed. (1997), *Preventing Deadly Conflict*, New York: Carnegie Commission of New York.

Carnevale, P. and Henry, R. (1989), 'Determinants of Mediation Tactics in Public Sector Disputes', *Journal of Applied Social Psychology*, vol. 19, pp. 469-488.

Carnevale, P.J.D. (1986), 'Mediating Disputes and Decisions in Organizations', *Research on Negotiation in Organizations*, vol. 1, pp. 251-269.

Carnevale, P.J.D. and Pruitt, D.G. (1992), 'Negotiation and Mediation', *Annual Review of Psychology*, vol. 43, pp. 531-582.

Carroll, L. (1962), *Alice's Adventures in Wonderland and Through the Looking Glass*, Harmondsworth: Penguin Books.

Carter, A. (1989), *Success and Failure in Arms Control Negotiations*, Oxford: Oxford University Press.

Chan, S. (1997), 'In Search of Democratic Peace: Problems and Promise', *Mershon International Studies Review*, vol. 41, no. 1, pp. 59-91.

Chopra, J. and Weiss, T.G. (1992), 'Sovereignty Is No Longer Sacrosanct: Codifying Humanitarian Intervention', *Ethics and International Affairs*, vol. 6, pp. 95-117.

Choucri, N. and North, R. (1989), 'Lateral Pressure in International Relations: Concept and Theory', in M.I. Midlarsky, ed., *Handbook of War Studies*, Boston: Unwin Hyman, pp. 289-327.

Cigar, N. (1995), *Genocide in Bosnia. The Policy of 'Ethnic Cleansing'*, College Station: Texas A&M University Press.

Clapham, C. (1996), *Africa and The International System. The Politics of State Survival*, Cambridge: Cambridge University Press.

Claude, I. (1955), *National Minorities, an International Problem*, Cambridge: Harvard University Press.

Clausewitz, C. von (P. Paret and M. Howard, trans) (1976), *On War*, Princeton: Princeton University Press.

Coate, R.A, Alger, C.F. and Lipschutz, R. (1996), 'The United Nations and Civil Society: Creative Partnerships for Sustainable Development', *Alternatives*, vol. 21, no. 1, pp. 93-122.

Coddington, A. (1968), *Theories of the Bargaining Process*, Chicago: Aldine.

Cohen, I.B. (1995), *Interactions: Some Contacts between the Natural Sciences and the Social Sciences*, Cambridge: Massachusetts Institute of Technology.

Cohen, R. (1997), *Negotiations Across Cultures. International Communication in an Interdependent World*, Washington, D.C.: United States Institute of Peace Press.

Cohen, Y., Brown, B.R. and Organski, A.F.K. (1981), 'The Paradoxical Nature of State Making. The Violent Creation of Order', *American Political Science Review*, vol. 75, no. 4, pp. 901-10.

Cohn, C. (1987), 'Sex and Death in the Rational World of Defense Intellectuals', *Signs*, vol. 12, no. 4, pp. 687-718.

Coles, R. (1990), *The Spiritual Life of Children*, Boston: Harper Collins.

Collins, A. (1996), 'The Security Dilemma', in J. M. Davis, ed., *Security Issues in the Post-Cold War World*, Cheltenham: Edward Elgar, pp. 181-195.

Commission on Global Governance, (1995), *Our Global Neighborhood*, Oxford: Oxford University Press.

Cooperrider, D.L. and Pasmore, W.A. (1991), 'The Organization Dimension of Global Change', *Human Relations*, Special Series Edition, vol. 44, no. 8, pp. 763-787.

Copson, R.W. (1994), *Africa's Wars and Prospects for Peace*, London: M.E. Sharpe.

Cordesman, A.H. (1993), *After the Storm. The Changing Military Balance in the Middle East*, Boulder: Westview.

Council of Europe (1950), *European Convention on Human Rights*, Strasbourg.

Council of Europe (1992), *European Charter for Regional or Minority Languages*, Strasbourg.

Council of Europe (1995), *Convention on the Protection of National Minorities*, Strasbourg.

Cox, R. (1991), 'The Global Political Economy and Social Choice', in D. Drache and M.S. Gertler, eds., *The New Era of Global Competition: State Policy and Market Power*, Montreal: McGill-Queen's, pp. 335-350.

Cox, R. (1992), 'Global Perestroika', in R. Miliband and L. Panitch, eds., *Socialist Register 1992*, London: Merlin, pp. 26-43.

Cox, R. (1994a), 'The Crisis on World Order and the Challenge to International Organization', *Cooperation and Conflict*, vol. 29, no. 2, pp. 99-113.

Cox, R. (1994b), 'Global Restructuring: Making Sense of the Changing International Poltical Economy', in R. Stubbs and G.R.D. Underhill, eds., *Political Economy and the Changing Global Order*, Toronto: McClelland & Stewart, pp. 45-59.

Cox, R. (1996), *Approaches to Order*, Cambridge: Cambridge University Press.

Cox, R. (1997), 'An Alternative Approach to Multilateralism for the Twenty-First Century', *Global Governance*, vol. 3, no. 1, pp. 103-116.

Crosson, J.D. (1991), *The Historical Jesus: The Life of a Mediterranean Jewish Peasant*, San Fransisco: Harper Collins.

Crouch, C. and Marquand, D. eds. (1995), *Reinventing Collective Action: from the Global to the Local*, Oxford: Blackwell.

Crush, J. (1995), 'Introduction: Imagining Development', in J. Crush, ed., *Power of Development*, London: Routledge, pp. 1-26.

Crush, J. (1996), 'A Bad Neighbour Policy? Migrant Labour and the New South

Africa', *Southern African Report*, vol. 12, no. 1, pp. 3-5.

Czempiel, E-O. (1992), 'Governance and Democratization', in J. Rosenau and E.-O. Czempiel, eds., *Governance Without Government: Order and Change in World Politics*, Cambridge: Cambridge University Press.

Dahrendorf, R. (1957), *Soziale klassen und Klassenkonflikt in der Industriellen Gesellschaft*, Frankfurt am Main: Janke, Neuendorfer & Schelsky.

Dahrendorf, R. (1988), *The Modern Social Conflict. An Essay on the Politics of Liberty*, Berkeley: University of California Press.

David, S.R. (1996), 'Internal War: Causes and Cures', *World Politics*, vol. 49, no. 4, pp. 552-576.

Davies, J. (1970), 'Ions of Emotion and Political Behavior: a Prototheory', in A. Somit, ed., *Biology and Politics*, Paris: Mouton, pp. 97-125. De Sousa Santos, B. (1995), *Towards a New Common Sense: Law, Science and Politics in the Paradigmic Transition*, New York: Routledge.

de Waal, F. (1989), *Peacemaking Among Primates*, Cambridge: Harvard University Press.

D'Entreves, A.P. (1967), *The Notion of the State*, Oxford: Oxford University Press.

Dessler, D. (1994), 'How to Sort Causes in the Study of Environmental Change and Violent Conflict', in N. Græger, N. Smith and D. Smith, eds., *Environment, Poverty, Conflict*, Oslo: International Peace Research Institute, pp. 91-112.

Destexhe, A. (1994), 'The Third Genocide', *Foreign Policy*, vol. 97, pp. 3-17.

Diehl, P. (1992), 'What Are They Fighting for? The Importance of Issues in International Conflict Research', *Journal of Peace Research*, vol. 29, pp. 333-344.

Diehl, P. (1994), *International Peacekeeping*, Baltimore, MD: Johns Hopkins University Press.

Diehl, P., Druckman, D. and Wall, J. (1998), 'International Peacekeeping and Conflict Resolution: A Taxonomic Analysis with Implications', *Journal of Conflict Resolution*, vol. 42, pp. 33-55.

Dirlik, A. (1994), 'The Postcolonial Aura: Third World Criticism in the Age of Global Capitalism', *Critical Inquiry*, Winter, pp. 328-356.

Dixon, W.J. (1994), 'Democracy and the Peaceful Settlement of International Conflict', *American Political Science Review*, vol. 88, no. 1, pp. 14-32.

Donnelly, J. (1995), 'The Past, the Present and the Future Prospects', in M. Esman and S. Telhami, eds., *International Organization and Ethnic Conflict*, Ithaca: Cornell University Press.

Donohue, W.A. and Kolt, R. (1992), *Managing Interpersonal Conflict*, Newbury Park, CA: Sage.

Doran, C. (1989), 'Power Cycle Theory of Systems Structure and Stability: Commonalities and Complementarities', in M.I. Midlarsky, ed., *Handbook of War Studies*, Boston: Unwin Hyman, pp. 83-111.

Doty, R. L. (1996), *Imperial Encounters. The Politics of Representation in North-South Relations*, Minneapolis: University of Minnesota Press.

Druckman, D. (1977), 'Boundary Role Conflict: Negotiations as Dual Responsiveness', *Journal of Conflict Resolution*, vol. 21, pp. 639-662.

Druckman, D. (1978), 'The Monitoring Function in Negotiation: Two Models of

Responsiveness', in H. Sauermann, ed., *Contributions to Experimental Economics: Bargaining Behavior*, Tubingen, FRG: J.C.B. Mohr, pp. 344-374.

Druckman, D. (1980), 'Social-psychological Factors in Regional Politics', in W.J. Feld and G. Boyd, ed., *Comparative Regional Systems*, New York: Pergamon, pp. 18-55.

Druckman, D. (1994), 'Determinants of Compromising Behavior in Negotiation: a Meta-Analysis', *Journal of Conflict Resolution*, vol. 38, pp. 507-556.

Druckman, D. and Bjork, R.A., eds. (1994), *Learning, Remembering, Believing: Enhancing Human Performance*. Washington DC: National Academy Press.

Druckman, D., Broome, B. and Korper, S.H. (1988), 'Value Differences and Conflict Resolution: Facilitation or Delinking?', *Journal of Conflict Resolution*, vol. 32, pp. 473-488.

Druckman, D. (1993), 'An Analytical Agenda for Conflict and Conflict Resolution', in D.J.D. Sandole and H. van der Merwe, eds. *Conflict Resolution. Theory and Practice. Integration and Application*, Manchester: Manchester University Press, pp. 25-42.

Duffy, R. (1997), 'The Environmental Challenge to the Nation State: Superparks and National Parks Policy in Zimbabwe', *Journal of Southern Africa Studies*, vol. 23, no. 3, pp. 441-451.

Dukes, F. (1993), 'Public Conflict Resolution: a Transformative Approach', *Negotiation Journal*, vol. 10, no. 1, pp. 45-57.

Dundes, A. (1984), *Sacred Narrative: Readings in the Theory of Myth*, Berkeley and Los Angeles: University of California Press.

Easton, D. (1953), *The Political System. An Inquiry into the State of Political Science*, New York: Knopf.

Eide, E.B. (1997), 'Conflict Entrepreneurship: A Few Post-Yugoslav Reflections on the "Art" of Waging Civil War', in A. McDermott, ed., *Humanitarian Force*, PRIO Report 4/97, pp. 41-69.

Elangovan, A.R. (1995), 'Managerial Third-Party Dispute Intervention: A Prescriptive Model of Strategy Selection', *Academy of Management Review*, vol. 20, pp. 800-830.

Enserink, B., Smit, W.A. and Elzen, B. (1992), 'Directing a Cacophony: Weapon Innovation and International Security', in W.A. Smit, J. Grin and L. Voronkov, eds., *Military Technological Innovation and Stability in a Changing World*, Amsterdam: VU University Press, pp. 94-123.

Enzenberger, H.M. (1994), *Civil Wars. From L.A. to Boston*, New York: The New Press.

Escobar, A. (1995), *Encountering Development: the Making and Unmaking of the Third World*, Princeton: Princeton University Press.

Escobar, A. (1995), 'Imagining a Post-Development Era' in J. Crush, ed., *Power of Development*, Routledge, London & New York, pp. 212-247.

Esman, M. (1994), *Ethnic Politics*, Ithaca: Cornell University Press.

Esser, J.K., Calvilio, M.J., Scheel, M.R. and Walker, J.L. (1990), 'Oligopoly Bargaining: Effects of Agreement Pressure and Opponent Strategies', *Journal of Applied Social Psychology*, vol. 20, pp. 1256-1271.

Falk, R.A. (1975), *A Global Approach to National Policy*, Cambridge: Harvard

University Press.
Falk, R.A., Kim, S.S. and Mendlovitz, S., eds. (1982), *Toward a Just World Order*, Boulder: Westview.
Ferguson, J. (1990), *The Anti-Politics Machine: Development, Depoliticization and Bureaucratic Power in Lesotho*. Cambridge: Cambridge University Press.
Fetherston, A.B. (1994), *Toward a Theory of United Nations Peacekeeping*, New York: St. Martin's Press.
Fetherton, A.B. (1998), 'Transformative Peacebuilding: Peace Studies in Croatia', Paper presented at the 39th Convention of the International Studies Association, Minneapolis.
Fischer, D. (1984), *Preventing War in the Nuclear Age*, Totowa, NJ: Rowan and Allanheld.
Fisher, R. (1964), 'Fractionating Conflict', in R. Fisher, ed., *International Conflict and Behavioral Science: The Craigville Papers*, New York: Basic Books.
Fisher, R. (1994), 'Generic Principles for Resolving Intergroup Conflict', *Journal of Social Issues*, vol. 50, pp. 47-66.
Fisher, R. (1997), *Interactive Conflict Resolution*, Syracuse: Syracuse University Press.
Fisher, R. and Brown, S. (1988), *Getting It Together*, Boston: Houghton Mifflin.
Fisher, R. and Ury, W. (1981), *Getting to Yes: Negotiating Agreement Without Giving In*, 2nd edition. New York: Penguin Books.
Fisher, R., Ury, W. and Patton, B. (1991), *Getting to Yes. Negotiating an Agreement Without Giving In*, New York: Penguin Books.
Flohr, H. (1987), 'Biological Bases of Prejudice', *International Political Science Review*, vol. 8, no. 2, pp. 183-192.
Forcey, L. (1989), 'Introduction to Peace Studies', in L. Forcey, ed., *Peace: Meanings, Politics, and Strategies*, New York: Praeger, pp. 3-14.
Frady, M. (1992), 'The Outsider, II', *New Yorker*, February, 2, pp. 41-80.
Frank, A.G. and Gills, B. (1993), *The World System: Five Hundred Years or Five Thousand*, London: Routledge.
Friedman, J. (1994), *Cultural Identity and Global Process*, London: Sage.
Friedman, J. (1997), 'Global Crises, The Struggle for Cultural Identity and Intellectual Pork-Barreling: Cosmopolitans, Nationals and Locals in an Era of De-hegemonisation', in P. Werbner, ed., *The Dialectics of Hybridity*, London: Zed Press, pp. 70-89.
Friedman, J. (1998), 'The Hybridisation of Roots and the Abhorrence of the Bush', in M. Featherstone and S. Lash, eds., *Spaces of Culture: City, Nation, World*, London: Sage.
Galtung, J. 'Self-Reliance and Global Interdependence: Some Reflections on the "New International Economic Order"', Unpublished manuscript, Oslo: University of Oslo.
Galtung, J. (1969), 'Violence, Peace and Peace Research', *Journal of Peace Research*, vol. 6, pp. 167-191.
Galtung, J. (1975), *Peace: Research, Education, and Action*, Copenhagen: Christian Ejlers.
Galtung, J. (1980), 'The Basic Needs Approach', in K. Lederer, ed., *Human Needs*,

Cambridge: Oelgeschlager, Gunn & Hain Publishers, Inc., pp. 55-125.

Galtung, J. (1986), 'Peace Theory: an Introduction', in E. Lazlo and J.Y. Yoo, eds., *World Encyclopedia of Peace*, New York: Pergamon Press, pp. 251-260.

Gandhi, M.K. (1938), *Hind Swaraj, or Indian Home Rule*, Ahmedabad: Navajivan Publishing House.

Gandhi, M.K. (Desai, V.G., trans) (1950), *Satyagraha in South Africa*, Ahmedabad: Navajivan Publishing House.

George, P. (1997), 'Military Expenditure', *SIPRI Yearbook 1997. Armaments, Disarmament and International Security*, Oxford: Oxford University Press, pp. 163-210.

Gibson-Graham, J.K. (1996), *The End of Capitalism (as we knew it)*. Oxford: Basil Blackwell.

Giddens, A. (1985), *The Nation State and Violence*, Cambridge: Polity.

Giddens, A. (1990), *The Consequences of Modernity*, Cambridge: Polity.

Gilpin, R. (1988), 'The Theory of Hegemonic War', *Journal of Interdisciplinary History*, vol. 18, no. 4, pp. 591-613.

Girard, R. (1987), *Things Hidden Since the Foundation of the World*, Stanford: Stanford University Press.

Gitlin, T. (1995), *The Twilight of Common Dreams: Why America is Wracked by Culture Wars*, New York: Henry Holt.

Gleditsch, N.P. (1990), 'Research on Arms Races', in N.P. Gleditsch and O. Njølstad, eds., *Arms Races: Technological and Political Dynamics*, London: Sage, pp. 87-104.

Gleditsch, N.P. (1998), 'Armed Conflict and the Environment: A Critique of the Literature', *Journal of Peace Research*, vol. 35, no. 3, pp. 381-400.

Goldgeier, J.M. and McFaul, M. (1992), 'A Tale of Two Worlds: Core and Periphery in the Cold-War Era', *International Organization*, vol. 46, no. 2, pp. 467-491.

Goldman, A. (1994), 'The Centrality of "Ningensei" to Japanese Negotiating and Interpersonal Relationships: Implications for US-Japanese Communication', *International Journal of Intercultural Relations*, vol. 18, pp. 29-54.

Goldstein, J.S. (1994), *International Relations*, New York: Harper Collins.

Gottlieb, S. (1997), *Defense Addiction. Can America Kick the Habit?* Boulder: Westview Press.

Gouldner, A.W. (1960), 'The Norm of Reciprocity: A Preliminary Statement', *American Sociological Review*, vol. 25, pp. 161-178.

Gow, J. (1994), 'Nervous Bunnies: The International Community and the Yugoslav War of Dissolution, the Politics of Military Intervention in a Time of Change', in *Military Intervention in European Conflicts*, L. Freedman, ed., Oxford: Blackwell, pp. 14-33.

Gow, J. (1997), Triumph of the Lack of Will: International Diplomacy and the Yugoslav War, London: Hurst & Co.

Gray, C.S. (1992), *House of Cards. Why Arms Control Must Fail*, Ithaca, NY: Cornell University Press.

Greenhalgh, L. and Kramer, R.M. (1990), 'Strategic Choice in Conflicts. The Importance of Relationships', in R.L. Kahn and M.N. Zald, eds., *Organizations and Nation States. New Perspectives on Conflict and Cooperation*, San

Fransisco: Jossey-Brass Publishers, pp. 181-220.

Gregg, R. (1935), *The Power of Nonviolence*, Philadelphia: J.B. Lippincott.

Guetzkow, H.S. and Alger, C.F. (1963), *Simulation in International Relations: Developments for Research and Teaching*, Englewood Cliffs: Prentice-Hall.

Gurr, T.R. (1970), *Why Men Rebel*, Princeton: Princeton University Press.

Gurr, T.R. (1994), 'People Against States: Ethnopolitical Conflict and the Changing World System', *International Studies Quarterly*, vol. 38, no. 3, pp. 347-378.

Hacker, A. (1997), *Money: Who Has How Much and Why*, New York: Scribner.

Hahn, P.C. (1986), *Korean Jurisprudence, Politics and Culture*, Seoul: Yonsei University Press.

Hammond, G.T. (1993), *Plowshares into Swords. Arms Races in International Politics, 1840-1991*, Columbia, SC: University of South Carolina Press.

Hansen, L. (1997), 'Past as Preference: Civilization and the Politics of the "Third" Balkan War', Paper presented at the 38th Annual ISA Conference, Toronto.

Harbottle, M. (1992), *What is Proper Soldiering?* Oxon, England: Centre for International Peacekeeping.

Hardin, R. (1995), *One For All. The Logic of Group Conflict*, Princeton, NJ: Princeton University Press.

Hauge, W. (1997), 'Development and Conflict', in K. Volden and D. Smith, eds., *Causes of Conflict in the Third World*, Oslo: Idégruppen om Nord/Sør International Peace Research Institute, pp. 33-51.

Hauge, W. and Tanja Ellingsen (1998), 'Beyond Environmental Scarcity: Causal Pathways to Conflict', *Journal of Peace Research*, vol. 35, no. 3, pp. 299-317.

Hedges, C. (1997), 'Studying Bosnia's US Prisoners of War', *New York Times*, Sunday, March 30, pp. 6Y.

Held, D. (1983), 'Introduction: Central Perspectives on the Modern State', in D. Held, ed., *States and Societies*, New York: New York University Press, pp.1-55.

Herf, J. (1982), *Reactionary Modernism*, Cambridge: Cambridge University Press.

Hettne, B. (1990), *Development Theory and the Three Worlds*, Harlow: Longman.

Hettne, B. (1993), 'Neo-Mercantilism: The Pursuit of Regionness', *Cooperation and Conflict*, vol. 28, no. 3, pp. 211-232.

Hettne, B. (1994), 'The Regional Factor in the Formation of a New World Order', in Y. Sakamoto, ed., *Global Transformation: Challenges to the State System*, Tokyo: The United Nations University Press, pp. 134-165.

Hettne, B. (1997), 'Development, Security and World Order: a Regionalist Approach', Paper presented at the International Development Studies and International Development Association, Dalhousie University, Halifax, Canada.

Hill, H., ed. (1994), *Indonesia's New Order: the Dynamics of Socio-economic Transformation*, Honolulu: University of Hawaii Press.

Hirst, P. and G. Thompson (1995), *Globalization in Question*, Cambridge: Polity.

Hoffman, S. (1995), 'The Politics of Military Intervention', *Survival*, vol. 37, no. 4, pp. 29-51.

Holsti, K.J. (1996), *The State, War, and the State of War*, Cambridge: Cambridge University Press.

Holsti, K.J. (1998), 'International Relations Theory and Domestic War in the Third World', in S.G. Neuman, ed., *International Relations Theory and the Third World*, New York: St. Martin's Press, pp. 103-132.

Homans, G.C. (1961), *Social Behavior: Its Elementary Forms*, New York: Harcourt, Brace and Wold.

Homer-Dixon, T. (1991), 'On the Threshold: Environmental Changes as the Causes of Acute Conflict', *International Security*, vol. 16, no. 2, pp. 76-116.

Homer-Dixon, T. (1994), 'Environmental Scarcities and Violent Conflict: Evidence from the Cases', *International Security*, vol. 19, no. 1, pp. 146-171.

Hopmann, P.T. (1995), 'Two Paradigms of Negotiation: Bargaining and Problem-Solving', *The Annals of the American Academy of Political and Social Science*, vol. 542, pp. 24-47.

Hopmann, P.T. (1996), *The Negotiation Process and the Resolution of International Conflicts*, Columbia, SC: University of South Carolina Press.

Horowitz, D. (1985), *Ethnic Groups in Conflict*, Berkeley: University of California Press.

Howard, M. (1981), *Clausewitz*, Oxford: Oxford University Press.

Howard, M. (1983), *The Causes of War and Other Essays*, London: Temple Smith, pp. 7-22.

Hunter, A. (1996), 'Globalization From Below? Promises and Perils of the New Internationalism', *Transnational Associations*, vol. 4, pp. 202-207.

Ignatieff, M. (1993), *Blood and Belonging: Journeys into the New Nationalism*, New York: Farrar, Straus and Giroux.

Ignatieff, M. (1994), *Blood and Belonging. Journeys into the New Nationalism*, London: Penguin.

Independent Commission on International Development Issues (Brandt Commission) (1980), *North-South: Programme for Survival*, Cambridge, MIT Press.

Independent Commission on International Development Issues (Brandt Commission) (1983), *Common Crisis North-South: Cooperation for World Recovery*, London, Pan.

Independent Commission on Disarmament and Security (Palme Commission) (1982), *Common Security: A Blueprint for Survival*, New York, Simon and Schuster.

International Commission on the Balkans (1996), *Unfinished Peace*, Washington DC: Carnegie Endowment.

International Commission on Peace and Food (1994), *Uncommon Opportunities: An Agenda for Peace and Development*, London: Zed.

International Institute for Strategic Studies (1997), *The Military Balance 1996/97*, Oxford: Oxford University Press.

Intrilligator, M.D. and D.L. Brito (1993), 'Richardsonian Arms Race Models', in M.I. Midlarsky, ed., *Handbook of War Studies*, Ann Arbor: Michigan University Press, pp. 219-236.

Isard, W. (1988), *Arms Races, Arms Control, and Conflict Analysis: Contributions from Peace Science and Peace Economics*, Cambridge: Cambridge University Press.

Ivie, R.L. (1954), 'Metaphor and the Rhetorical Invention of Cold War "Idealists"', *Communication Monographs*, vol. 54, pp. 165-181.
Jabri, V. (1994), *Discourses on Violence. Conflict Analysis Reconsidered*, Manchester: Manchester University Press.
Jacobs, J. (1996), *Edge of Empire: Postcolonialism and the City*, London: Routledge.
Jackson Preece, J. (1997a), 'Minority Rights in Europe: From Westphalia to Helsinki', *Review of International Studies*, vol. 23, no. 1, pp. 75-92.
Jackson Preece, J. (1997b), 'National Minority Rights vs. State Sovereignty in Europe: Changing Norms in International Relations', *Nations and Nationalism*, vol. 3, no. 3, pp. 345-364.
James, W.S. (1911), 'The Moral Equivalent of War', in *Memories and Studies*, W.S. James, ed., New York: Longmans, Green & Co.
Jayasuriya, K. (1997), 'Asian Values as Reactionary Modernization', *Nordic Newsletter of Asian Studies*, vol. 4, pp. 19-27.
Jenkins, S. (1997), 'Ulster of the Balkans', *The Times*, December 17.
Jeong, H. (1995), 'Alternative Development Strategies and Regeneration of Social Space for Human Development', *Peace & Change*, vol. 20, no. 3, pp. 329-347.
Jervis, R. (1976), *Perception and Misperception in International Politics*, Princeton: Princeton University Press.
Jervis, R. (1997), *System Effects. Complexity in Political and Social Life*, Princeton: Princeton University Press.
Jewett, R. and Lawrence, J.S. (1977), *The American Monomyth*, Garden City: Anchor Doubleday.
Johanson, R.C. (1993), 'Unilateral Initiatives', in R.D. Burns, ed., *Encyclopedia of Arms Control and Disarmament*, New York: Charles Scribner's Sons.
Johnston, D.W. (1967), 'The Use of Role Reversal in Intergroup Competition', *Journal of Personality and Social Psychology*, vol. 7, pp. 135-142.
Kahn, J. (1983), 'Arms Interaction and Arms Control', in J.F. Reichart and S.R. Sturm, eds., *American Defense Policy*, Baltimore: John Hopkins University Press, pp. 393-408.
Käkönen, J. (1992), 'The Concept of Security -- From Limited to Comprehensive', in, J. Käkönen, ed., *Perspectives on Environmental Conflict and International Relations*, London: Pinter Publishers, pp. 146-155.
Kaldor, K. (1982), 'Warfare and Capitalism', in E.P. Thompson, ed., *Exterminism and Cold War*, Oxford: Verso, pp. 261-288.
Kaldor, K. (1991), *The Imaginary War*, Oxford: Blackwell.
Kaldor, K., ed. (1997), *New Wars*. London: Pinter.
Kaldor, M. (1981), *The Baroque Arsenal*, New York: Hill and Wang.
Kallen, H. (1924), *Culture and Democracy in the United States*, New York: Arno Press.
Kaplan, M. (1957), *Systems and Process in International Politics*, New York: John Wiley and Sons.
Kaplan, R. (1994), 'The Coming Anarchy', *The Atlantic Monthly*, vol. 276, no. 2, pp. 44-76.

Kaplan, R. (1996), *The Ends of the Earth. A Journey at the Dawn of the 21st Century*, New York: Random House.

Karambayya, R. and Brett, J.M. (1989), 'Managers Handling Disputes: Third-Party Roles and Perceptions of Fairness', *Academy of Management Journal*, vol. 32, pp. 687-704.

Karim, W. J. (1996), 'Anthropology Without Tears: How a "Local" Sees the "Local" and the "Global"', in H. Moore, ed., *The Future of Anthropological Knowledge*, London: Routledge, pp. 115-138.

Kaufman, C. (1996), 'Possible and Impossible Solutions to Ethnic Civil Wars', *International Security*, vol. 20, no. 4, pp. 136-175.

Keane, J. (1996), *Reflections on Violence*, London: Verso.

Keashly, L. and Fisher, R.J. (1996), 'A Contingency Perspective on Conflict Interventions: Theoretical and Practical Considerations', in J. Bercovitch, ed., *Resolving International Conflicts. The Theory and Practice of Mediation*, Boulder: Lynne Rienner, pp. 235-261.

Keegan, J. (1994), *A History of Warfare*, New York: Random House, Vintage.

Keohane, R.O. and Nye, J.S. (1989), *Power and Interdependence*, 2nd ed., Glenview, IL: Scott, Foresman and Co.

Khoo, B.T. (1995), *The Paradoxes of Mahathirism*, Kuala Lampur: Oxford University Press.

Kim, J.H., Wall, J.A., Solm, D.W. and Kim, J.S. (1993), 'Community and Industrial Mediation in South Korea', *Journal of Conflict Resolution*, vol. 37, pp. 361-381.

King, M.L. (1967), *Where Do We Go From Here: Chaos or Community?* New York: Harper and Row.

Kingsbury, B. (1992), 'Claims by Non-state Groups in International Law', *Cornell International Law Journal*, vol. 25, no. 3, pp. 481-513.

Kittani, I. (1995), 'Peacemaking and Peacekeeping for the Next Century', Paper presented at the 25th Vienna Seminar; Government of Austria, International Peace Academy, Vienna.

Klare, M.T. (1993), 'The New Challenges to Global Security', *Current History*, April, pp. 155-161.

Klare, M.T. and Thomas, D.C., eds. (1994), *World Security: Challenges for a New Century*, 2nd ed., New York: St. Martin's Press.

Kohn, H. (1944), *The Idea of Nationalism*, New York: Macmillan.

Kohn, H. (1955), *Nationalism: Its Meaning and History*, Princeton: Princeton University Press.

Kohut, A. and Toth, R.C. (1994), 'Arms and the People', *Foreign Affairs*, vol. 73, no. 6, pp. 47-61.

Kolb, D.M. (1987), 'Corporate Ombudsman and Organizational Conflict', *Journal of Conflict Resolution*, vol. 31, pp. 673-692.

Kolodziej, A. (1992), 'Renaissance in Security Studies? Caveat Lector!', *International Studies Quarterly*, vol. 36, no. 4, pp. 421-438.

Konner, M. (1982), *The Tangled Wing: Biological Constraints on the Human Spirit*, New York: Hold, Reinhart and Winston.

Krause, K. (1992), *Arms and the State: Patterns of Military Production and Trade*, Cambridge: Cambridge University Press.

Krause, K.R. (1993), 'Controlling the Arms Trade Since 1945', in R.D. Burns, ed., *Encyclopedia of Arms Control and Disarmament*, New York: Charles Scribner's Sons, pp. 1021-1039.

Kressel, K. (1972), *Labor Mediation: an Exploratory Survey*, Albany, NY: Association of Labor Mediation Agencies.

Kressel, K., et al. (1994), 'The Settlement Orientation vs. The Problem-solving Style in Custody Mediation', *Journal of Social Issues*, vol. 50, pp. 67-84.

Kressel, K. and Pruitt, D. (1985), 'Themes in the Mediation of Social Conflict', *Journal of Social Issues*, vol. 41, pp. 179-196.

Kressel, K. and Pruitt, D.G. (1989), 'Conclusion: A Research Perspective on the Mediation of Social Conflict', in K. Kressel and D.G. Pruitt, eds., *Mediation Research*, San Francisco: Jossey-Bass, pp. 1-8.

Kyi, A.S. (1991), *Freedom from Fear and Other Writings*, Harmondsworth: Viking Penguin.

Laclau, E. and Mouffe, C. (1985), *Hegemony and Socialist Strategy: Towards a Radical Democratic Politics*, London: Verso.

Lall, A. (1966), *Modern International Negotiation: Principles and Practice*, New York: Columbia University Press.

Lassonde, L. (1997), *Coping with Population Challenges*, London: Earthscan.

Last, D. and Eyre, K.C. (1995), *Combat and Contact Skill in Peacekeeping: Surveying Recent Canadian Experience in UNPROFOR*, Unpublished manuscript, The Lester B. Pearson Canadian International Peacekeeping Training Centre.

Latham, R. (1995), 'Thinking about Security after the Cold War', *International Studies Notes*, vol. 20, no. 3, pp. 9-16.

Lederach, J.P. (1995a), *Beyond Prescription: Perspective on Conflict, Culture, and Training*, Syracuse: Syracuse University Press.

Lederach, J.P. (1995b), *Preparing for Peace. Conflict Transformation Across Cultures*, Syracuse: Syracuse University Press.

Lederach, J.P. (1997), *Building Peace. Sustainable Reconciliation in Divided Societies*, Washington, D.C.: United States Institute of Peace Press.

Levy, J. (1989), 'The Causes of War: a Review of Theories and Evidence', in P.E. Tetlock, J. L. Husbands, R. Jervis, P. C. Stern and C. Tilly, eds., *Behavior, Society and Nuclear War*, New York: Oxford University Press, pp. 209-333.

Levy, M.A. (1995), 'Is the Environment a National Security Issue?', *International Security*, vol. 20, no. 2, pp. 35-62.

Lewicki, R. and Sheppard, B. (1985), 'Choosing How to Intervene: Factors Affecting the Use of Process and Outcome Control in Third Party Dispute Resolution', *Journal of Occupational Behavior*, vol. 6, pp. 49-64.

Lijphart, A. (1977), *Democracy in Plural Societies*, New Haven: Yale University Press.

Lijphart, A. (1984), *Democracies: Patterns of Majoritarian and Consensus Government in Twenty-one Countries*, New Haven: Yale University Press.

Lim, R. and P. Carnevale (1990), 'Contingencies in the Mediation of Disputes', *Journal of Personality and Social Psychology*, vol. 58, pp. 259-272.

Little, A. and Silber, L. (1996), *Yugoslavia: Death of a Nation*, New York: Penguin.

Little, D. (1994), *Sri Lanka: The Invention of Enmity*, Washington, DC: The United States Institute of Peace Press.

Luckham, R. (1984), 'Of Arms and Culture', *Current Research on Peace and Violence*, vol. 7, no.1, pp. 1-64.

Lumsdon, C.J. and Wilson, E.O. (1983), *Promethean Fire: Reflections on the Origin of the Mind*. Cambridge: Harvard University Press.

Lund, M. (1996), *Preventive Diplomacy and American Foreign Policy*, Washington DC: United States Institute for Peace.

Lynd, S. and Lynd, A. (1995), *Nonviolence in America: a Documentary History*, Maryknoll: Orbis.

Lynn-Jones, S.M. (1995), 'Offense-defense Theory and its Critics', *Security Studies*, vol. 4, no. 4, pp. 660-691.

MacDonald, L. (1994), 'Globalizing Civil Society: Interpreting International NGOs in Central America', *Millennium*, vol. 23, no. 2, pp. 267-286.

MacDonald, L. (1995), 'Unequal Partnerships: the Politics of Canada's Relations with the Third World', *Studies in Political Economy*, vol. 47, pp. 111-141.

MacLean, P.D. (1973), *A Triune Concept of the Brain and Behaviour*, Toronto: University of Toronto Press.

MacLean, S.J. (1997), *NGO Partnerships and Sustainable Democratic Development: With Lessons from a Canadian-Zimbabwean Case Study*, Unpublished doctoral dissertation, Department of Political Science, Dalhousie University, Halifax, Canada.

MacNeill, W.H. (1982), *The Pursuit of Power*, Oxford: Blackwell.

MacQueen, G. (1992), 'Marking and Binding: an Interpretation of the Pouring of Blood in Nonviolent Direct Action', *Peace and Change*, vol. 17, no. 1, pp. 60-81.

Maggiolo, W.A. (1971), *Techniques of Mediation in Labor Disputes*, Dobbs Ferry, NY: Oceana.

Mahoney, L. and Eguren, L. (1997), *Unarmed Bodyguards: International Accompaniment for the Protection of Human Rights*, West Hartford: Kumarian.

Mann, M. (1986), *The Sources of Social Power*, Cambridge: Cambridge University Press.

Mann, M. (1987), 'The Roots and Contradictions of Modern Militarism', *New Left Review*, vol. 162, pp. 135-150.

Mansfield, E.D. and Snyder, J. (1996), 'Democratization and the Danger of War', *International Security*, vol. 20, no. 1, pp. 5-38.

Markusen, A. and Yudken, J. (1992), *Dismantling the Cold War Economy*, New York: Basic Books.

Marrus, M. (1985), *The Unwanted*, Oxford: Oxford University Press.

Martin, S., ed. (1996), *The Economics of Offsets: Defence Procurement and Countertrade*, Amsterdam: Harwood Academic Publishers.

Maslow, A. (1943), 'A Theory of Human Motivation', *Psychological Review*, vol. 50, pp. 370-396.

Mason, P. (1995), 'The United Nations Guidelines for Regional Approaches to Disarmament', *Disarmament*, vol. 18, no. 2, pp. 49-71.

Mathews, J.T. (1997), 'Power Shift', *Foreign Affairs*, vol. 76, no. 1, pp. 50-66.

Matthew, R.A. (1997), 'Rethinking Environmental Security', in N.P. Gleditsch et al., eds., *Conflict and the Environment*, London: Kluwer Academic Publishers, pp. 71-99.

Maturana, H. and Varela, F. (1987), *The Tree of Knowledge*, Boston: Shambala.

Mayall, J. (1990), *Nationalism and International Society*, Cambridge: Cambridge University Press.

Mayall, J. (1998), 'Sovereignty, Nationalism and Self-determination', Paper presented at the International Studies Association Conference, Minneapolis.

McGrew, A. (1992), 'Conceptualizing Global Politics', in A. McGrew and P.G. Lewis, eds., *Global Politics*, Cambridge: Polity.

McLaughlin, M.E., Carnevale, P. and Lim, R.G. (1991), 'Professional Mediators' Judgements of Meditation Tactics: Multidimensional Scaling and Cluster Analysis', *Journal of Applied Psychology*, vol. 76, pp. 465-472.

McMichael, P. (1996), *Development and Social Change*, Thousand Oaks: Pine Forge Press.

McSweeney, B. (1996), 'Identity and Security: Buzan and the Copenhagen School', *Review of International Studies*, vol. 22, no. 1, pp. 81-93.

Merchant, C. (1980), *The Death of Nature*, San Fransisco: Harper and Row.

Merry, S. (1989), 'Mediation in Non-industrial Societies', in K. Kressel and D.G. Pruitt, eds., *Mediation Research*, San Francisco: Jossey-Bass, pp. 68-90.

Mingione, E. (1996), 'Urban Poverty in the Advanced Industrial World: Concepts, Analysis and Debates', in E. Mingione, ed., *Urban Poverty and the Underclass*, Oxford: Blackwell, pp. 3-40.

Mirsky, Y. (1995), 'Jewish Perspectives', in D. Smock, ed., *Perspectives on Pacifism*, Washington, DC: United States Institute for Peace, pp. 21-27.

Mitchell, C. and Banks, M. (1996), *Handbook of Conflict Resolution. The Analytical Problem-solving Approach*, London: Pinter.

Mitrany, D. (1966), *A Working Peace System*, Chicago: Quadrangle.

Mittelman, J.H. (1996), 'Rethinking the "New Regionalism" in the Context of Globalization', *Global Governance*, vol. 2, pp. 189-213.

Mittelman, J.H. (1997), 'Restructuring the Global Division of Labour: Old Theories and New Realities', in S. Gill, ed., *Globalization, Democratization and Multilateralism*, London: Macmillan, pp. 77-103.

Modelski, G. (1978), 'The Long Cycle of Global Politics and the Nation State', *Comparative Studies in Society and History*, vol. 20, pp. 214-235.

Møller, B. (1991), *Resolving the Security Dilemma in Europe. The German Debate on Non-offensive Defence*, London: Brasseys.

Møller, B. (1992), *Common Security and Non-offensive Defense: A Neo-realist Perspective*. Boulder, London: Lynne Rienner Publishers, UCL Press.

Møller, B. (1995), *Dictionary of Alternative Defense*, Boulder: Lynne Reinner Publishers, Adamantine Press.

Møller, B. (1996), 'Common Security and Non-offensive Defence: Are They Relevant for the Korean Peninsula?', in B-M. Hwang and Y-S. Han, eds., *Korean Security Policies Towards Peace and Unification*, Seoul: Korean Association of International Studies, pp. 241-291.

Møller, B. (1997), *Resolving the Security Dilemma in the Gulf Region. Cooperative*

Security, Arms Control and Defensive Restructuring, Occasional Papers Series, Abu Dhabi: Emirates Center for Strategic Studies and Research.

Møller, B. and Voronkov, L., eds. (1996), *Defence Doctrines and Conversion*, Aldershot: Dartmouth.

Moore, J. (1996), *The UN and Complex Emergencies: Rehabilitation in Third World Transitions*, Geneva: United Nations Research Institute for Social Development.

Morris, D. (1969), *The Human Zoo*, New York: A Delta Book.

Moskos, C. (1993), 'The Military in a Warless Society', Paper presented at the British Military Studies Group, London.

Mouffe, C. (1994), 'For a Politics of Nomadic Identity', in G. Robertson *et al.*, eds., *Travelers' Tales. Narratives of Home and Displacement*, London: Routledge, pp. 105-113.

Mouritzen, P. (forthcoming), *The Idea of Civic Participation: Problems and Promises of Political Community*, European University Institute, Florence, Italy.

Muellner, L. (1996), *The Anger of Achilles: Menis in Greek Epic*, Ithaca: Cornell University Press.

Murray, H.A. (1938), *Explorations in Personality*, 3rd ed., New York: Alfred A. Knopf.

Myers, N. (1996), *Ultimate Security: the Environmental Basis of Political Stability*, Washington DC: Island Press.

Nagler, M. (1997), 'Peacemaking and Nonviolence Today', *ReVision*, vol. 20, no. 2, pp. 12-17.

Nathan, L. (1998), 'A South African Policy Framework on Peace Initiatives in Africa', *South African Political & Economic Monthly*, vol. 11, no. 3, pp. 25-30.

Neale, M.A. and Bazerman, M.H. (1983), 'The Role of Perspective-taking in Negotiating under Different Forms of Arbitration', *Industrial and Labor Relations Review*, vol. 36, pp. 378-388.

Neufeld, M. (1995), *The Restructuring of International Relations Theory*, Cambridge: Cambridge University Press.

Neumann, I.B. (1996), 'Self and Other in International Relations', *European Journal of International Relations*, vol. 2, no. 2, pp. 139-174.

Nicholson, M. (1989), *Formal Theories in International Relations*, Cambridge: Cambridge University Press.

Nicholson, M. (1992), *Rationality and the Analysis of International Conflict*, Cambridge: Cambridge University Press.

Nickalls, J. and Fox, G. (1952), *Journal of George Fox*, Cambridge: Cambridge University Press.

Nicolaïdis, K. (1996), 'International Preventive Action: Developing a Strategic Framework', in R.I. Rodberg, ed., *Vigilance and Vengeance*, Washington DC, Cambridge: Brookings Institution, World Peace Foundation.

Niemann, M. (1997), 'Southern Africa as Social Space', Paper presented at the Annual Meeting of the International Studies Association, Toronto.

Noiriel, G. (1996), *The French Melting Pot: Immigration, Citizenship and National Identity*, Minneapolis: University of Minnesota Press.

North Atlantic Treaty Organization (1995), *NATO Handbook*. Brussels.
O'Leary, M. (1994), 'The Political Regulation of National and Ethnic Conflict', *Parliamentary Affairs*, vol. 47, no. 1, pp. 94-115.
Ohlson, T. and Stedman, S.J. (1994), *The New is Not Yet Born. Conflict Resolution in South Africa*, Washington, DC: The Brookings Institution.
Organization for Security and Cooperation in Europe (1990), *Charter of Paris for a New Europe*, Prague.
Organization for Security and Cooperation in Europe (1990), *Copenhagen Document*, Prague.
Organization for Security and Cooperation in Europe (1991), *Geneva Report on National Minorities*, Prague.
Organization for Security and Cooperation in Europe (1991), *Moscow Document*, Prague.
Organization for Security and Cooperation in Europe (1992), *Helsinki Document*, Prague.
Organization for Security and Cooperation in Europe (1994), *Budapest Document*, Prague.
Paige, G. (1968), *The Korean Decision: June 24-30, 1950*, New York: The Free Press.
Paige, G. (1977), 'On Values and Science: the Korean Decision Reconsidered', *American Political Science Review*, vol. 71, no. 4, pp. 1603-1609.
Parkman, P. (1988), *Nonviolent Insurrection in El Salvador*, Tuscon: University of Arizona.
Pastor, R. (1993), 'Forward to the Beginning: Widening the Scope for Global Collective Action', *International Journal*, vol. 48, no. 4, pp. 641-667.
Pepinsky, H.E. and Quinney, R. (1991), *Criminology as Peacemaking*, Bloomington: University of Indiana.
Perry, M.L. Kong and Yeoh, B. (1997), *Singapore: a Developmental City State*, New York: Wiley.
Pinkley, R.L. (1995), 'Impact of Knowledge Regarding Alternatives to Settlement in Dyadic Negotiations: Whose Knowledge Counts?', *Journal of Applied Psychology*, vol. 80, pp. 403-417.
Plant, R. (1993), 'The Justifications for Intervention: Needs before Contexts', in I. Forbes and M. Hoffman, eds., *Political Theory, International Relations and the Ethics of Intervention*, Basingstoke: St. Martin's Press, pp. 104-112.
Plewes, B.G. Sreenivasan and Dramin, T. (1996), 'Sustainable Human Development as a Global Framework', *International Journal*, vol. 51, no. 2, pp. 211-234.
Podell, J.E. and Knapp, W.M. (1969), 'The Effect of Mediation on the Perceived Firmness of the Opponent', *Journal of Conflict Resolution*, vol. 13, pp. 511-520.
Posen, B. (1993), 'The Security Dilemma and Ethnic Conflict', in M. Brown, ed., *Ethnic Conflict and International Security*, Princeton: Princeton University Press, pp. 103-124.
Prabhu, R.K. and Rao, U.R. (1960), *The Mind of Mahatma Gandhi*, Ahmedabad: Navajivan Publishing House.
Pred, A. and Watts, M. (1992), *Reworking Modernity*, New Brunswick: Rutgers University Press.

Prein, H. (1984), 'A Contingency Approach to Conflict Resolution', *Group and Organizational Studies*, vol. 9, pp. 81-102.
Princen, T. (1992), *Intermediaries in International Conflict*, Princeton: Princeton University Press.
Pruitt, D. and Carnevale, P. (1994), *Negotiation in Social Conflict*, Pacific Grove: Brooks/Cole Publishing Co.
Pruitt, D.G. (1971), 'Indirect Communication and the Search for Agreement in Negotiations', *Journal of Applied Social Psychology*, vol. 1, pp. 205-239.
Pruitt, D.G. and Johnson, D. (1970), 'Mediation as an Aid to Face Saving in Negotiation', *Journal of Personality and Social Psychology*, vol. 14, pp. 239-246.
Pruitt, D.G. and Rubin, J.Z. (1986), *Social Conflict: Escalation, Stalemate, and Settlement*, New York: Random House.
Przeworski, A. (1995), *Sustainable Democracy*, Cambridge: Cambridge University Press.
Pursell, C.W. Jr., ed. (1972), *The Military Industrial Complex*, New York: Harper and Row.
Putnam, L.L. and Poole, M.S. (1987), 'Conflict and Negotiation', in F.M. Jablin, L.L. Putnam, K.H. Roberts and L.W. Porter, eds., *Handbook of Organizational Communication Yearbook*, Newbury Park, CA: Sage.
Putnam, L.L. and Wilson, S.R. (1982), 'Communication Strategies in M. Burgood, ed., Organizational Conflicts: Reliability and Validity of a Measurement Scale', in *Communication Yearbook*, Beverly Hills, CA: Sage.
Pyarelal (1932), *The Epic Fast*, Ahmedabad: Navajivan Publishing House.
Pyarelal, and Nayar, S. (1991), *In Gandhiji's Mirror*, Delhi: Oxford University Press.
Quigley, C. (1961), *The Evolution of Civilizations*, Indianapolis: Liberty Press.
Ramberg, B., ed. (1993), *Arms Control without Negotiation. From the Cold War to the New World Order*, Boulder: Lynne Reinner Publishers.
Rapoport, A. (1989), *The Origins of Violence: Approaches to the Study of Conflict*, New York: Paragon House.
Rasmussen, J.L. (1997), 'Peacemaking in the Twenty-First Century. New Rules, New Roles, New Actors', in I.W. Zartman and J.L. Rasmussen, eds., *Peacemaking in International Conflict. Methods and Techniques*, Washington, DC: The United States Institute of Peace Press, pp. 23-50.
Rata, M. (1997), 'Global Capitalism and the Revival of Ethnic Traditionalism in New Zealand: The Emergence of Tribal-Capitalism', Unpublished doctoral dissertation, University of Auckland, New Zealand.
Rathjens, G. (1973), 'The Dynamics of the Arms Race', in H. York, ed., *Arms Control. Readings from the Scientific American*, San Francisco: Freeman, pp. 177-187.
Reardon, B. (1990), 'Feminist Concepts of Peace and Security', in P. Smoker, R. Davies, and B. Munske, eds. *A Reader in Peace Studies*, New York: St. Martin's Press, pp. 136-143.
Redclift, M. (1996), *Wasted: Counting the Costs of Global Consumption*, London: Earthscan.

Reisman, M.W. (1990), 'Sovereignty and Human Rights in Contemporary International Law', *American Journal of International Law*, vol. 84, pp. 866-876.
Renner, M. (1989), *National Security: The Economic and Environmental Dimensions*, Worldwatch Paper No. 89, Washington DC: Worldwatch Institute.
Reno, W. (1995), *Corruption and State Politics in Sierra Leone*, Cambridge: Cambridge University Press.
Reno, W. (1998), *Warlord Politics and African States*, Boulder: Lynne Rienner.
Resnick, S. and Wolff, R. (1987), *Knowledge and Class: a Marxian Critique of Political Economy*, Chicago: University of Chicago Press.
Restak, R.M., MD. (1979), *The Brain: the Last Frontier*, New York: Warner Books.
Reynolds, P.C. (1981), *On the Evolution of Human Behavior*, Berkeley: University of California Press.
Richardson, L. (1960), *Strategies of Deadly Quarrels*, Chicago: Quadrangle.
Rieff, D. (1994), 'Accomplice to Genocide', *War Report*, vol. 28, pp. 35-40.
Rieff, D. (1995), *Slaughterhouse: Bosnia and the Failure of the West*, New York: Simon & Schuster.
Ringmar, E. (1996), *Identity, Interest and Action. A Cultural Explanation of Sweden's Intervention in the Thirty Years War*, Cambridge: Cambridge University Press.
Risse-Kappen, T. (1995), 'Democratic Peace - Warlike Democracies? A Social Constructivist Interpretation of the Liberal Argument', *European Journal of International Relations*, vol. 1, no. 4, pp. 491-517.
Roberts, A. (1994), 'The Crisis in UN Peacekeeping', *Survival*, vol. 36, no. 3, pp. 93-120.
Roberts, A. (1995), 'Communal Conflict as a Challenge to International Organization', *Review of International Studies*, vol. 21, no. 4, pp. 401-416.
Robison, R. (1995), 'Ideology and the Politics of Asian Values', *The Pacific Review*, vol. 9, no. 3, pp. 309-327.
Rodan, G. (1995), *Political Oppositions in Industrializing Asia*, London: Routledge.
Rogin, M.P. (1987), *Reagan, The Movie, and Other Episodes in Political Demonology*, Berkeley: University of California Press.
Romm, J. (1993), *Defining National Security: the Nonmilitary Aspects*, New York: Council on Foreign Relations Press.
Ronen, D. (1979), *The Quest for Self-determination*, New Haven: Yale University Press.
Rønnfeldt, C. (1997), 'Three Generations of Environment and Security Research', *Journal of Peace Research*, vol. 34, no. 4, pp. 473-482.
Ross, W.H., Conlon, D.E. and Lind, A. (1990), 'The Mediator as a Leader. Effects of Behavioral Style and Deadline Certainty on Negotiation', *Group and Organizational Studies*, vol. 15, pp. 105-124.
Rothman, J. (1997), *Resolving Identity-based Conflicts in Nations*, Organizations, and Communities, San Fransisco: Jossey-Bass Publishers.
Rouhana, N.N. and Kelman, H.C. (1994), 'Promoting Joint Thinking in International Conflicts: An Israeli-Palestinian Continuing Workshop', *Journal of Social Issues*, vol. 50, pp. 157-178.

Rubin, J. (1994), 'Models of Conflict Management', *Journal of Social Issues*, vol. 50, no. 1, pp. 33-45.
Rubin, J., Pruitt. D. and Kim, S.H. (1994), *Social Conflict, Escalation, Stalemate and Settlement*, New York: McGraw Hill.
Ruggie, J.G. (1975), 'International Responses to Technology: Concepts and Trends', *International Organization*, vol. 29, no. 3, pp. 557-583.
Rummel, R.J. (1995), 'Democracies ARE Less Warlike Than Other Regimes', *European Journal of International Relations*, vol. 1, no. 4, pp. 457-479.
Sachs, W., ed. (1992), *The Development Dictionary*, London: Zed Books.
Sagan, C. (1977), *The Dragons of Eden*, New York: Ballantine Books.
Sandler, T. and Hartley, K., eds. (1995), *The Economics of Defense*, Cambridge: Cambridge University Press.
Sandole, D.J.D. (1990), 'The Biological Basis of Needs in World Society', in J.W. Burton, ed., *Conflict: Human Needs Theory*, London: Macmillan, pp. 60-88.
Sarkesian, S.C., ed. (1972), *The Military Industrial Complex: A Reassessment*. Beverly Hills: Sage.
Saunders, H.H. (1991), 'Officials and Citizens in International Relationships: The Dartmouth Conference', in V.D. Volkan, J.V. Montville and D.A. Julius, eds., *The Psychodynamics of International Relationships*, Lexington: Lexington Books, pp. 41-69.
Schell, J. (1984), *The Abolition*, London: Picador.
Schellenberger, J.A. (1996), *Conflict Resolution. Theory, Research and Practice*, Albany: SUNY Press.
Schelling, T.C. (1986), 'What Went Wrong with Arms Control', in Ø. Østerud, ed., *Studies of War and Peace*, Oslo: Norwegian University Press, pp. 90-109.
Schelling, T.C. and M.H. Halperin (1985), *Strategy and Arms Control*. New York: Pergamon-Brassey's.
Schneider, H. (1973), 'Friedensverständniss in Vergangenheit und Gegenwart', in R. Weiler and V. Zsifkovits, eds., *Interwegs zum Frieden*, Vienna: Herder.
Scholte, J.A. (1997), 'Global Capitalism and the State', *International Affairs*, vol. 73, no. 2, pp. 427-452.
Schulte-Sasse, J. and Schulte-Sasse, L. (1991), 'War, Otherness, and Illusionary Identification with the State', *Cultural Critique*, Fall, vol. 19, pp. 67-95.
Schwartzberg, J.E. (1997), 'A New Perspective on Peacekeeping: Lessons from Bosnia and Elsewhere', *Global Governance*, vol. 3, no. 1, pp. 1-16.
Sebenius, J.K. (1992), 'Negotiation Analysis: A Characterization and Review', *Management Science*, vol. 38, no. 1, pp. 18-38.
Semb, A.J. (1992), *The Normative Foundation of the Principle of Non-intervention*, PRIO Report 1/1992, Oslo: International Peace Research Institute.
Senghaas, D. (1972), *Rustung und Militarismus*, Frankfurt: Suhrkamp Verlang.
Senghaas, D. (1990), 'Arms Race Dynamics and Arms Control', in N.P. Gleditsch and O. Njolstad, eds., *Arms Races: Technological and Political Dynamics*, London: Sage, pp. 15-30.
Senghaas, D. (1995), 'Zivilisierung und Gewalt: Wie Den Frieden Gewinnen?', in W.R. Vogt, ed., *Frieden als Zivilierungsproject - Neue Herausforderungen and die Friedens- und Konfliktforschung*, Baden Baden: Nomos Verlag, pp. 37-55.

Senghaas, D. (1995a), 'Provokation -- Ein Verhanntes Mittel der Mediation', *Friedensforum*, vol. 4, pp. 21-23.

Seton-Watson, H. (1977), *Nations and States*, Boulder: Westview Press.

Shapiro, M. (1992), 'That Obscure Object of Violence: Logisitics, Desire, War', *Alternatives*, vol. 17, no. 4, pp. 453-477.

Shapiro, M. (1995), 'Return of the Apparatchiks', *International Herald Tribune*, January, 16.

Sharp, G. (1970), *Exploring Nonviolent Alternatives*, Boston: Porter Sargent.

Sharp, G. (1973), *The Politics of Nonviolent Action*, Boston: Porter Sargent.

Sharp, J.M.O. (1997), *Honest Broker or Perfidious Albion. British Policy in Former Yugoslavia*, London: Institute for Public Policy Research.

Shaw, M. (1988), *Dialectics of War: An Essay on the Social Theory of War and Peace*, London: Pluto.

Shaw, M. (1991), *Post-military Society*, Cambridge: Polity.

Shaw, M. (1994), *Global Society and International Relations: Sociological Concepts and Political Perspectives*, Cambridge: Polity.

Shaw, M. (1997), 'The State of Globalization', *Review of International Political Economy*, vol. 4, no. 3, pp. 497-513.

Shaw, T.M. (1996), 'Beyond Post-conflict Peacebuilding: What Links to Sustainable Development and Human Security?', *International Peacekeeping*, vol. 32, no. 2, pp. 36-48.

Shaw, T.M. and Adibe, C. (1995-6), 'Africa and Global Developments in the Twenty- First Century', *International Journal*, vol. 51, no. 1, pp. 1-26.

Shaw, T.M., MacLean, S.J. and Orr, K. (1998), 'Peacebuilding and African Organizations: Towards Subcontracting and/or a "New" Sustainable Division of Labour', in K. van Walraven, ed., *Early Warning and Conflict Prevention: Limitations and Possibilities*, Dordrecht: Kluwer.

Sheppard, B.H. (1984), 'Third Party Conflict Intervention: A Procedural Framework', *Research in Organizational Behavior*, vol. 6, pp. 141-190.

Shimko, K.L. (1991), *Images and Arms Control: Perceptions of the Soviet Union in the Reagan Administration*, Ann Arbor: University of Michigan Press.

Shusta, R.M. (1995), *Multicultural Law Enforcement. Strategies for Peacekeeping in a Diverse Society*, Englewood Cliffs: Prentice-Hall.

Silbey, S. and Merry, S. (1986), 'Mediator Settlement Strategies', *Law and Policy*, vol. 8, pp. 7-32.

Singer, D. (1996), 'Armed Conflict in the Former Colonial Regions: From Classification to Explanation', in L.v.d. Goor, K. Rupesinghe, and P. Sciarone, eds., *Between Development and Destruction: An Enquiry into the Causes of Conflict in Post-colonial States*, The Hague: Netherlands Ministry of Foreign Affairs; The Netherlands Institute of International Relations, pp. 35-49.

Singer, D. and Small, M. (1972), *The Wages of War, 1816-1965: A Statistical Handbook*, New York: Wiley.

Singer, M. and Wildawsky, A. (1993), *The Real World Order: Zones of Peace/Zones of Turmoil*, Chatham, NJ: Chatham House Publishers.

Singh, J. (1995), 'Arms Race in the Region: Myth and Reality', *Strategic Analysis*, vol. 18, no. 5, pp. 595-610.

Sisk, T. (1996), *Power Sharing and International Mediation in Ethnic Conflicts*, Washington, DC: The United States Institute of Peace Press.

Siverson, R.M. and Diehl, P.F. (1993), 'Arms Races, The Conflict Spiral, and The Onset of War', in M. Midlarsky, ed., *Handbook of War Studies*, Ann Arbor: Michigan University Press, pp. 195-218.

Slater, D. (1995), 'Challenging Western Notions of the Global: Geopolitics of Theory and North-South Relations', *The European Journal of Development Research*, vol. 1, no. 7, pp. 366-388.

Slotkin, R. (1973), *Regeneration Through Violence: The Mythology of the American Frontier, 1600-1860*, Middletown: Wesleyan University Press.

Smith, D. (1997a), 'Interventionist Dilemmas and Justice', in A. McDermott, ed., *Humanitarian Force*, Oslo: International Peace Research Institute, pp. 13-39.

Smith, D. (1997b), *The State of War and Peace*, London, New York: Penguin.

Snyder, G.H. and Diesing, P. (1977), *Conflict Among Nations: Bargaining, Decision Making, and System Structure in International Crisis*, Princeton, NJ: Princeton University Press.

South Commission (headed by Julius Nyerere) (1990), *The Challenge to the South*, Oxford University Press, New York.

Starr, H. (1997), 'Democracy and Integration: Why Democracies Don't Fight Each Other', *Journal of Peace Research*, vol. 34, no. 2, May, pp. 153-162.

Stedman, S.J. (1992), 'The New Interventionists', *Foreign Affairs*, vol. 72, no. 1, pp. 1-16.

Stedman, S.J. (1995), 'Alchemy For a New World Order: Overselling "Preventive Diplomacy"', *Foreign Affairs*, vol. 74, no. 1, pp. 14-20.

Stedman, S.J. (1996), 'Negotiation and Mediation in Internal Conflict', in M.E. Brown, ed., *The International Dimensions of Internal Conflict*, Cambridge: The MIT Press, pp. 341-376.

Stedman, S.J. (1997), 'Spoiler Problems in Peace Processes', *International Security*, vol. 22, no. 2, pp. 5-53.

Stern, P.C. and Druckman, D. (1995), 'Has The "Earthquake" of 1989 Toppled International Relations Theory?', *Peace Psychology Review*, vol. 1, pp. 109-122.

Stoltzfus, N. (1996), *Resistance of the Heart: Intermarriage and the Rosenstrasse Protest in Nazi Germany*, New York: Norton.

Strathern, M. (1980), 'No Nature, No Culture: The Hagen Case', in C. MacCormack and M. Strathern, eds., *Nature, Culture and Gender*, Cambridge: Cambridge University Press, pp. 174-22.

Stubbs, R. and Underhill, G.R.D. (1994), 'Global Trends, Regional Partners', in R. Stubbs and G. Underhill, eds., *Political Economy and the Changing Global Order*, Toronto: MacClelland & Stewart, pp. 331-335.

Sulloway, F.J. (1979), *Freud: Biologist of the Mind*, New York: Basic Books.

Summers, D.A., Taliaferro, J.D., and Fletcher, D.J. (1970), 'Judgement Policy and Interpersonal Learning', *Behavioral Science*, vol. 15, pp. 514-521.

Swatuk, L.A. (1997), 'The Environment, Sustainable Development, and Prospects for Southern African Regional Cooperation', in L.A. Swatuk and D.R. Black, eds., *Beyond the Rift: the New South Africa in Africa*, Boulder: Westview, pp. 127-151.

Swatuk, L.A. (1998), 'Space, Security, Sovereignty: The New Regionalism in the New Southern Africa', Paper presented at the Annual Conference of the International Studies Association, Minneapolis.

Swedish MFA. (1997), *Preventing Violent Conflict: A Study. Executive Summary and Recommendations*, Stockholm: Ministry for Foreign Affairs.

Symons, D. (1979), *The Evolution of Human Sexuality*, Oxford: Oxford University Press.

Tedeschi, J.T. and Bonoma, T.V. (1977), 'Measures of Last Resort: Coercion and Aggression in Bargaining', in D. Druckman, ed., *Negotiations: Sociopsychological Perspectives*, Beverly Hills: Sage, pp. 213-241.

Thee, M. (1990), 'Science-based Military Technology as a Driving Force Behind the Arms Race', in N.P. Gleditsch and O. Njølstad, eds. *Arms Races: Technological and Political Dynamics*, London: Sage, pp. 105-120.

Thibaut, J. (1968), 'The Development of Contractual Norms in Bargaining: Reflection and Refinement', *Journal of Conflict Resolution*, vol. 12, pp. 102-112.

Thomas, K.W. (1992), 'Conflict and Negotiation Processes in Organizations', in M. D. Dunnette and L. M. Hough, eds., *Handbook of Industrial and Organizational Psychology*, Palo Alto, CA: Consulting Psychologists Press.

Thornberry, P. (1991), *International Law and the Rights of Minorities*, Oxford: Clarendon Press.

Tishkov, V. (1997), *Ethnicity, Nationalism and Conflict In and After the Soviet Union: The Mind Aflame*, London: Sage.

Tjonneland, E.N. and Vraalsen, T. (1996), 'Toward Common Security in Southern Africa: Regional Cooperation After *Apartheid*', in A. Adedeji, ed., *South Africa and Africa: Within or Apart?*, London, Zed in association with The African Center for Development and Strategic Studies (ACDESS), pp. 193-214.

Tønnesson, S. and Antlov, H., eds. (1996), *Asian Forms of the Nation*, vol. 23, Nias Institute of Asian Studies, Richmond Surrey: Curzon Press.

Touvall, S. and Zartman, I.W., eds. (1985), *The Man in the Middle: International Mediation in Theory and Practice*, Boulder: Westview.

Truman, D.B. (1951), *The Governmental Process*, New York: New York University Press.

Tu, W., ed. (1991), *The Triadic Chord: Confucian Ethic, Industrial East Asia and Max Weber*, Singapore: Institute of East Asian Philosophy.

Ungar, S. (1992), *The Rise and Fall of Nuclearism: Fear and Faith as Determinants of the Arms Race*, University Park: Pennsylvania University Press.

United Nations (1966), *International Covenant on Civil and Political Rights*, New York.

United Nations (1992), *Declaration on the Rights of Persons Belonging to National or Ethnic, Religious and Linguistic Minorities*, New York.

United Nations Development Programme (1990-1998), *Human Development Report, Annual Editions*, New York: Oxford University Press.

United Nations Research Institute for Social Development (1995), *States of Disarray: the Social Effects of Globalization*, Geneva: UNRISD.

Uyangoda, J. (1996), 'Militarization, Violent State, Violent Society: Sri Lanka', in K.

Rupesinghe and K. Mumtaz, eds., *Internal Conflicts in South Asia*, London: Sage, pp. 118-130.

Vale, P. (1996), 'Regional Security in Southern Africa', *Alternatives*, vol. 21, no. 3, pp. 363-391.

Van de Vliert, E. (1985), 'Conflict and Conflict Management', in H. Thierry, P.J.D. Drenth and C.J.D. Wolff, eds., *A New Handbook of Work and Organizational Psychology*, Have, England: Erlbaum.

Van Evera, S. (1994), 'Hypotheses on Nationalism and War', *International Security*, vol. 18, no. 4, pp. 5-39.

Vasquez, J. (1983), 'The Tangibility of Issues and Global Conflict: A Test of Rosenau's Issue Area Typology', *Journal of Peace Research*, vol. 20, pp. 179-182.

Vasquez, J.A., Johnson, J.T. and Jaffe, S., eds. (1996), *Beyond Confrontation: Learning Conflict Resolution in the Post Cold War Era*, Ann Arbor: University of Michigan Press.

Väyrynen, R. (1991), 'To Settle or to Transform: Perspectives on the Resolution of National and International Conflicts', in R. Väyrynen, ed., *New Directions in Conflict Theory. Conflict Resolution and Conflict Transformation*, London: Sage, pp. 1-25.

Väyrynen, R. (1994), 'Violence, Resistance, and Order in International Relations', in Y. Sakamoto, ed., *Global Transformation. Challenges to the State System*, Tokyo: The United Nations University Press, pp. 385-411.

Väyrynen, R. (1996), *The Age of Humanitarian Emergencies*, Helsinki: United Nations University Press.

Väyrynen, R. (1998), 'Enforcement and Humanitarian Intervention: Two Faces of Collective Action by the United Nations', in C.F. Alger, ed., *The United Nations System: Potential for the Twenty-First Century*, Tokyo: United Nations University Press, pp. 54-88.

Wæver, O. (1995), 'Securitization and Desecuritization', in R.D. Lipschutz, ed., *On Security*, New York: Columbia University Press, pp. 46-86.

Wæver, O. (1996), 'European Security Identities', *Journal of Common Market Studies*, vol. 34, no. 1, pp. 103-132.

Wæver, O. et al. (1993), *Identity, Migration and the New Security Agenda of Europe*, London: Pinter.

Walcott, C., Hopmann, P.T. and King, T.D. (1977), 'The Role of Debate in Negotiation', in D. Druckman, ed., *Negotiations: Socio-psychological Perspectives*, Beverly Hills: Sage, pp. 193-217.

Walker, J. (1993), 'International Mediation in Ethnic Conflicts', in M. Brown, ed., *Ethnic Conflict and International Security*, Princeton: Princeton University Press, pp. 165-180.

Wall, J.A. (1981), 'Mediation: An Analysis, Review, and Proposed Research', *Journal of Conflict Resolution*, vol. 25, pp. 157-180.

Wall, J.A. (1995), *Negotiation: Theory and Practice*, Glenview, IL: Scott Foresman.

Wall, J.A. and Blum, M. (1991), 'Community Mediation in the People's Republic of China', *Journal of Conflict Resolution*, vol. 35, pp. 3-20.

Wall, J.A. and Callister, R.R. (1995), 'Conflict and its Management', *Journal of*

Management, vol. 21, pp. 515-558.
Wall, J.A. and Rude, D. (1985), 'Judicial Mediation: Techniques, Strategies, and Situational Effects', *Journal of Social Issues*, vol. 41, pp. 47-64.
Wall, J.A. and Stark, J. (1996), 'Techniques and Sequences in Mediation Strategies: A Proposed Model for Research', *Negotiation Journal*, vol. 12, pp. 231-239.
Wallensteen, P. (1994), *Från Krig till Fred: Om Konfliklösning i det Globale Systemet*, Stockholm: Amlqvist & Wiksell.
Wallensteen, P. (1998), *The 1997 Executive Seminar on Preventing Conflicts: Past Record and Future Challenges. Executive Summary*, Uppsala: Uppsala University, Department of Peace and Conflict Research.
Wallerstein, I. (1980), *The Modern World System II: Mercantilism and the Consolidation of the European World Economy 1600-1750*, New York: Academic Press.
Walt, S.M. (1985), 'Alliance Formation and the Balance of World Power', *International Security*, vol. 9, no. 4, pp. 3-43.
Walton, R.E. and McKersie, R.B. (1965), *A Behavioral Theory of Labor Negotiations: An Analysis of a Social Interaction System*, New York: McGraw-Hill.
Waltz, K.N. (1954), *Man, the State, and War: A Theoretical Analysis*, New York: Columbia University Press.
Waterman, P. (1996), 'A New Global Solidarity Praxis for a World in which "The Future Is Not What It Used To Be"', *Transnational Associations*, vol. 3, pp. 63-80.
Wattanayagorn, P. and Ball, D. (1995), 'A Regional Arms Race?', *The Journal of Strategic Studies*, vol. 18, no. 3, pp. 147-174.
Weber, M. (1978), *Economy and Society*, Vol. 1, Berkeley: University of California Press.
Weber, T. (1993), 'From Maude Royden's Peace Army to the Gulf Peace Team: An Assessment of Unarmed Interpositionary Peace Forces', *Journal for Peace Research*, vol. 30, no. 1, pp. 45-64.
Weber, T. (1996), *Gandhi's Peace Army: The Shanti Sena and Unarmed Peacekeeping*, Syracuse: Syracuse University Press.
Weiss, T.G., ed. (1998), *Beyond UN Subcontracting: Task-sharing with Regional Security Arrangements and Service-providing NGOs*, London: Macmillan.
Weiss, T.G. and Gordenker, L., eds. (1996), *NGOs, the UN, and Global Governance*, Boulder: Lynne Reinner.
Welch, D. (1993), *Justice and the Genesis of War*, Cambridge: Cambridge University Press.
Wendt, A. (1992), 'Anarchy is What States Make of It: The Social Construction of Power Politics', *International Organization*, vol. 46, no. 2, pp. 391-425.
Werna, E., Blue, I. and Harpham, T. (1996), 'The Changing Agenda for Urban Health', in M.A. Cohen, ed., *Preparing for the Urban Future. Global Pressures and Local Forces*, Washington D.C.: The Woodrow Wilson Center Press.
Westing, A. (1986), *Global Resources and International Conflict*, Oxford: Oxford University Press.

White, N.D. (1993), *Keeping the Peace: The United Nations and the Maintenance of International Peace and Security*, Manchester: Manchester University Press.
Wiberg, H. (1990a), 'Arms Races, Formal Models and Quantitative Tests', in N.P. Gleditsch and O. Njølstad, eds., *Arms Races: Technological and Political Dynamics*, London: Sage, pp. 31-57.
Wiberg, H. (1990b), 'Armament Dynamics - Why Worry?', in N.P. Gleditsch and O. Njølstad, eds., *Arms Races: Technological and Political Dynamics*, London: Sage, pp. 352-375.
Wievorka, M. (1977), 'Un Nouveau Paradigme de la Violence', in M. Wievorka, ed., *Un Nouveau Paradigme de la Violence*, Paris: l'Harmattan, pp. 9-57.
Wiberg, H. (1976), *Konfliktteori och Fredsforskning*, Stockholm: Scandinavian University Books.
Willett, S.M. Clarke and Gummet, P. (1994), 'The British Push for the Eurofighter 2000', in R. Forsberg, ed., *The Arms Production Dilemma. Contradiction and Restraint in the World Aircraft Industry*, Cambridge: MIT Press, pp. 139-160.
Witte, R. (1996), *Racist Violence and the State: A Comparative Analysis of Britain, France and the Netherlands*, New York: Longman.
World Commission on Environment and Development (Brundtland Commission) (1987), *Our Common Future*, Oxford University Press, Oxford.
Xenos, N. (1996), 'Refugees: the Modern Political Condition', in M.J. Shapiro and H.R. Alker, eds., *Challenging Boundaries*, Minneapolis: University of Minnesota Press, pp. 233-246.
Zartman, I.W. (1991), 'Negotiations and Prenegotiations in Ethnic Conflict: the Beginning, the Middle and the Ends', in J.V. Montville, ed., *Conflict and Peacemaking in Multiethnic Societies*, New York: Lexington Books, pp. 511-534.
Zartman, I.W., Druckman, D., Jensen, L., Pruitt, D.G. and Young, H.P. (1996), 'Negotiation as a Search for Justice', *International Negotiation*, vol. 1, no. 1, pp. 79-89.
Zebich-Knos, M. (1998), 'Global Environmental Conflict in Post-Cold War Era: Linkage to an Extended Security Paradigm', *Peace and Conflict Studies*, vol. 5, no. 1, pp. 26-40.
Zechmeister, K. and Druckman, D. (1973), 'Determinants of Resolving a Conflict of Interest: A Simulation of Political Decision Making', *Journal of Conflict Resolution*, vol. 17, pp. 63-88.
Zipes, J. (1997), 'Tales Worth Telling', *Utne Reader*, September-October, vol. 42.
Zunes, S. (1994), 'Unarmed Insurrections Against Authoritarian Governments in the Third World: A New Kind of Revolution', *Third World Quarterly*, vol. 15, no. 3, pp. 403-426.

Index

Afghanistan 71, 72, 138
Africa
  arms race in 101, 102, 104;
  decolonialisation 67, 181, 183,
    184, 187, 189
  ethnonational groups 181
Albania 185, 187
Algeria 142, 236
Amnesty International 30
Angola 71, 72, 152
Arab-Israeli conflict 152, 249, 282
Armenia 187, 193
Arms
  developing countries 94, 101
  expenditures 89, 93-95, 98-101
  global arms trade 77, 100-104
  offensive/defensive weapons 31, 92
Arms control 89
disarmament 8, 16, 30, 31, 40, 41, 89-92, 100
  General and Complete Disarmament (GCD) 90, 91
  gradualism 90, 92
  Missile Technology Control Regime 102
  Non-Proliferation Treaty (NPT) 102
  prisoner's dilemma 103
  stability and 78, 90, 101
  supplier constraints 101-104
  trade regulations 101-103
  United Nations and 16, 91, 147
  verification 106, 109

Arms races
  Action-Reaction Phenomena (ARP) 84-86, 103
  classical arms race theory 83-86
  costs 89, 93-95, 97, 98, 100, 101
  'defensive races' 34, 85
  defensive restructuring 91, 92, 94-99, 103
  diversion of resources 89, 93
  Military-Industrial Complex (MIC) 74, 87
  multipolar and bipolar 95
  outbreak of war 83, 88, 89
  peace research and 5, 6, 32, 83
  'Red Queen races' 82, 88-92, 96, 98
  regional 94-104
  residual 94, 95, 100
Asia-Pacific (*See* Northeast Asia, South Asia, Southeast Asia)
  crisis 99, 283, 315
  decolonialisation 67, 181-184, 187, 189
  values 314, 315
Australia 320
Austria 156, 185
Azerbaijan 187, 192

Bangladesh 186
Borders 276-278
  'borders of violence' 64-66, 68
  ethnonational 180, 181, 184, 303
  globalisation and 68, 228, 292, 298
  postcolonial 67, 181, 184-186, 274
  resources 26, 272, 274, 276, 278

Bosnia-Hercegovina 152, 163-167, 173, 175, 243, 244
  Bosnia Contact Group 164, 165
  ethnic cleansing and 173, 176, 190
  identity and 59, 60
  United States and 163-165, 167, 173
Botswana 138
Boulding, K. 21, 236
Boutros-Ghali, B. 29, 161, 164, 179
Britain 66, 185, 239, 248
Burton, J. 5, 31, 262
Burundi 166, 174, 304n
Buzan, B. 55-58, 84, 87, 216, 298, 307n

Cambodia 71, 72, 236
Canada 320
Capitalism
  alternatives to 227, 228
  development of 64, 69, 220
  elites 71, 72, 310, 311, 316-321, 324
  globalisation and 224, 226, 231, 310, 312, 322, 324
  noncapitalism 223-231
  state ideology 280
  tribal 322, 323
    land rights 319, 320, 322, 323
Central Europe
  ethnonationalism 187, 192
Chechnya 175, 176, 236
  independence and 188, 193, 204
  OSCE and 204, 206
China 73, 146, 220, 314
  arms 97-100, 104
  Taiwan and 186
  Tibet and 186, 253
Civil Rights Movement 244, 246
Civil/internal war (*See* War, Yugoslavia) 56, 70, 71, 137, 167-169, 176
  elites and 71, 72

international intervention 106, 139, 161-164, 167, 275
  prolongation of war 77, 243
  neorealist theory 6, 7, 138, 139
  periphery violence 138, 139, 145
  postcolonialism and 170, 176
  total war and 74-76
Clark, M. 239, 241
Clausewitz 58, 59, 74, 171
Clinton, B. 243
Cold War (*See* War)
  arms race and 94, 95
  inter-bloc war 66, 67, 70
  stability 66, 70, 186, 187
  Third World conflict 22-27, 66-68, 70, 94, 95, 184, 213, 218-220
  "total" war 65, 74-76
Colonialism 170, 185, 176, 279, 289
  dismantling of 66, 67, 70, 72, 185
  United Nations and 19, 20, 183
Congo (ex-Zaire) 72, 137
Council of Europe (COE) 180, 190, 195-198, 200-206
Croatia 182, 183, 187, 188, 193, 201
  Krajina and 187, 188, 204
Cuba 4, 103
Conflict (*See* conflict escalation, conflict management; conflict prevention; conflict resolution; conflict theory, identity, nationalism, security, violence)
  anomie 154, 155
  causes 4, 5, 7, 8, 10, 25, 38, 45, 52, 88, 138, 151, 168, 169, 173, 213, 218, 219
  class 154-156, 227, 310, 316, 317, 319, 320
  complexity 135, 143-146, 148-150, 152, 153, 158
  political mobilisation 30, 74, 75, 172, 174-177, 218, 315
  power 6, 7, 10, 21, 50, 63, 64, 142, 146-148, 273, 274

relative deprivation 169, 174, 218, 221
research 3-10, 157
situational 50, 154, 155
structural 5, 7, 9, 22-24, 50, 59, 67, 71, 136, 137, 143, 148, 167, 171, 205, 212, 233, 252
zones 136, 138, 142, 145, 153
Conflict escalation
Bosnia 163-167
Chechnya (1994-6) 175, 188, 204
Cold War 22
de-escalation 152
ethnic mobilisation 136, 165, 169, 302
preventative diplomacy 29, 161, 165, 291, 300
research 157, 162, 166
Conflict management, 7, 17, 80, 105, 106, 137, 144, 146, 152-154, 157
criticism 140-142, 144-147, 149, 151, 155, 156
strategies 157, 158
Conflict prevention (*See* peace-building; peace-making; peacekeeping)
conflict escalation 161-162
diplomacy 29, 40, 291, 294
early warning systems 162-164, 167, 219
intervention 77, 139, 161-164, 167, 243, 275
Kosovo 164, 165, 187, 188, 253
lack of will 162-165, 167
mechanisms 161
NATO 22, 24, 28, 165
obstacles to 162, 166
realpolitik 7, 164, 203, 291, 305
theory 7
United Nations 29, 163, 164, 167
Conflict resolution
approach 138-146

criticism 140-142, 144-147, 149, 151, 155, 156
compromise 114, 118, 122, 140, 166
contingency model 119, 153, 159
group processes 145, 151
justice 6, 8, 148, 245, 246
mediation 139-142, 146-149, 152, 155
minority rights and 182
negotiation 143-146, 149, 154
cultural style 143
principled 139, 140
neutrality 147, 148, 155, 156
peripheral violence 138, 139
power 142, 143, 146-148, 151
transformation 149-153
social change 7, 150-153, 292, 298, 310
social constructivism 150
Conflict theory
anomie 155, 156
approach 149
behavioural 4, 50, 239
complexity 135, 143-146, 148-150, 152, 153, 158
game theory 83, 144, 145, 160n
idealist traditions 4, 6, 7, 293
Marxism 7, 67, 226, 292
narrative 49, 52-54
poststructuralism 47, 53-55, 60, 225
identity and, 53-55, 57
relative deprivation 169, 174, 218, 221
Cox, R. 292, 295, 298, 300, 306, 307n, 308n
Culture 233, 236, 238, 239, 249, 252
'armament culture' 78
behaviour and 263, 264, 270
consciousness 236, 238, 241, 245, 246, 254, 257

globalisation and 61, 63-66, 69, 78
human needs 263, 264, 270, 281
immigration and 156
multiculturalism 185, 276, 24, 281, 317, 318, 320-322
norms 240, 280
obstacles to negotiations 143, 154
peace 136, 149, 150, 235, 236
'sacred narratives' 240, 252
state 136, 182, 273
violence and 8, 33, 150, 151, 234-236, 239, 254, 255
Cyprus 95
Czechoslovakia 185, 237, 244, 276

Dahrendorf, R. 155, 156
Democracy
  anarchy 7, 137, 145
  civil society 296f, 292-301
  civilisational perspective 136
  conflict and 136-138, 145, 150, 154, 168, 186, 205, 294
  conflict resolution and 144
  democratisation 72, 79, 106, 109, 120, 135-139, 144, 148, 153, 169, 275, 309-311, 318, 187
  nationalism 154, 311, 314
  power-sharing 151, 153
  market mechanisms 136, 292, 301
  new world order 137, 154, 168, 280, 292, 296, 318
  peace 136, 137, 168
  transition 72, 77, 137, 138, 153, 187
Democratic People's Republic of Korea (DPRK) (*See* Korea)
Development
  aid 23
  ecological imbalances 16, 26, 30, 39, 41, 42, 290, 293
  industrial 22, 219, 220
  informal economy 237
  political 274

postdevelopment 223-231
poverty 8, 23, 24, 135, 168
productivity and 23, 227, 229
natural resource exploitation 27
regional cooperation and 290-306
self-reliance 16, 35-37, 297
socio-economic projects 311
sustainable development 8, 26
traditional model of 7
United Nations Development Programme (UNDP) 135, 293
Dudayev, D. 175, 188, 286n
Dukes, F. 5, 141, 149

East Timor 185
Economy (*See* Development, Environment)
  behaviour and 264, 268
  informal 227
  international system and 24, 35, 65, 66, 169, 173
  economic growth model 219, 220
  processes 135
  well-being 291, 293
Ecology (*See* Environment)
  balance 16, 26, 30, 39, 41, 290, 293
  global security 8, 213, 218-221, 290
  holism 8
  political 216
  systems 40, 42, 62
Egypt 96, 137
El Salvador 152
Environment (*See* Ecology)
  degradation of 8, 26, 219, 220, 290, 301
  development 26, 216, 219, 220, 293
  exploitation 219, 220
  'place-based' consiousness 227, 228, 230, 231
  political economy 219, 220
  pollution 25, 26, 214, 219, 220,

population 217-220, 275, 276, 278
regional 301-304
resource conservation 214, 216, 218, 276
resource competition 268-270, 272-274, 276, 278
securitisation 215-217
security 211-221
sustainable development 8, 26
Third World 25-27, 213, 218, 219, 220
threats 26, 212-215, 219, 268, 272-274, 290
UNCED Stockholm, Rio de Janeiro conference 26, 30, 307n
Eritrea 277
Ethiopia 166, 218, 277
Ethnic
cleansing 167, 176, 190, 191, 193, 205, 208
mobilisation 136, 167, 176
identity 173-175, 182
European Union 7, 79, 318
assimilation 9, 156, 312, 313, 315
Council of Europe (COE) 180, 190, 195-198, 200-206
identity 48, 185, 313, 317
minority rights and 180, 181, 185
multi-ethnicity 156, 313, 317

France 66, 185

Galtung, J. 5, 35, 36, 233, 237, 262, 263
Gandhi, M.K. 7, 33, 236, 243-256
as a 'cultural hero' 236, 249
Charkha 252-254
constructive programme 236, 247-256
Hind Swaraj (Home Rule) 248
'peace march'/ 'Great march' 246, 248, 251
principled nonviolence 33, 236, 243, 244, 247, 252, 255
Satyagraha 245, 247, 248, 251, 252, 255
'soul force' 244, 246, 247
strategic nonviolence 243- 245
Germany
Holocaust and 76, 190
identity and 156, 190, 313
Globalisation 61
centre – periphery 135-138, 139, 145, 296, 297, 303
conflict resolution 138, 139, 144
civilisational perspective 136
communication 62, 74, 324
cyclical expansion/contraction 308
democracy 79, 136-138, 144, 153
ecology 62, 290
economy 282, 291-293
elites 7, 71, 72, 310, 311, 316-319
emerging global order 7, 63, 67, 70-74, 261, 281, 282, 292, 296
ethnification 319
fragmentation 72, 135, 137, 179, 187, 309-311, 314, 320, 322-324n
horizontal/vertical 135
global authority 69, 292, 309
globality 61, 62, 64-69, 73, 78-80
homogeny 309, 311
marketisation 62-64, 68, 69
non-state actors and 299, 300
process 62-64, 311, 314
regionalism 278, 289-291, 293-306, 309-313, 315-318
social transformations 79, 154, 292, 293, 296, 298-303, 310
social/cultural 62, 63, 136, 143
state relations 63-70, 296
undermining 62, 136, 292
territorial boundaries 26, 180, 272, 273
transformation 298, 299, 312

war 61-80
warlord politics 137
Governance
  Commission on Global
    Governance 29
  global commons 29, 291, 300,
    302
Government
  civil society and 136, 290-306
  human needs and satisfaction 169,
    276-279, 281, 282, 293, 302
  legitimacy and 136, 137, 273-275,
    277, 280, 281, 290
  nation-building 274, 280, 281
Greece 95, 189
Greenpeace 30
Group of 77 24
Group of Seven 66
Guatemala 319-321
Gurr, T. 168, 169, 172, 174, 221

Haiti 28, 249
Hettne, B. 290, 296, 297, 301, 302,
  306, 307n
Holsti, K.J. 135, 138
Homer-Dixon, T. 169, 172, 211, 217
Horowitz, D. 169, 172, 174
Human needs
  behaviour 261-267, 269-271, 280,
    281, 285n
  brain and 261, 262, 264-270,
    285n
  civil society and 293, 296, 298
  community and 271-274, 282
  cross-disciplinary analysis of 261,
    262, 270, 272, 280, 281, 282n
  culture 263, 264, 270, 281
  physical/material 262, 263, 281,
    283n, 284n
  psychological/psychic 262-264,
    267, 269, 270-272, 278, 31, 282
  evolution 265-267, 284n
  triune 265-267, 284n
  limbic system 265-269
  nervous system 264-266, 268
  neocortex 265-269
  R-complex 265-268
  satisfaction of needs 261-264,
    267-272, 277-282, 293, 302
Hungary 34, 185

Identity
  assimilation 269-272, 270, 312,
    314
  Black-Atlantic 321
  Bosniak 59, 60
  class/elite identity 48, 154-156,
    310, 316, 317, 319-321, 324
  collective 56, 269-273, 303, 320,
    321
  conceptions of, 46-53, 151, 310,
    311
  cosmopolitanism 319, 321
  cultural 48, 182, 309, 311, 321
  essentialism 320, 321
  ethnification 185, 310-313, 319
  formation of 51-53, 55, 312, 319
  hybrid identity 48, 318-322
  imagined community 54, 303
  inclusion and exclusion 49-54,
    151, 154, 171, 269-273, 314
  indigenisation 310, 311, 324
  homogenisation 309-311
  multiculturalism 143, 309, 313,
    317, 318, 320-322
  national 59, 60, 174, 176, 270,
    271, 274, 280, 303, 310-312,
    315
  'new *mestizo*' 319, 321
  outbreak of war 45-60, 173
  regional 297, 298, 301, 303, 312
  religious 155
  representation of 53-55
  societal security 56, 269-274
India 72, 142, 239, 248, 254, 276
  Bangladesh 186
  Goa 186
  partition 181

Indonesia 72, 314
  East Timor 186
  nationalist movement and 315
  West Irian 186
International Monetary Fund (IMF) 66, 292
International system
  borders of violence 64-66, 276
  centre-periphery 135-138, 139, 145, 296, 297, 303, 311
  decolonialisation 22, 23, 67, 76, 137, 181, 184, 239, 248, 274
  democratisation 72, 79, 153, 309-311, 318
  Developed Countries (DC) 22
  division of labour 290-294
  empires 20-22, 64-67, 70, 72, 185
  European domination 64, 66, 67, 70
  growth of international trade and communication 22-27, 62, 64, 65, 74, 310, 324
  internal conditions 73, 138, 139
  international communications equity 16, 24, 25, 39, 41, 42
  international economic equity 16, 23, 24, 35, 37
  minority rights and 182-219
  sovereignty 179, 180, 275, 281
  strong and weak states 72, 135-137
  regionalisation 290-306, 310
  rich-poor gap 22-24, 135, 169, 220
  two-zone model 138, 153, 154
  world economy 135-137, 292
Iran 71, 73, 75
Iraq 71, 73, 75, 96, 101, 180, 204
Israel 96, 118, 152, 249, 282
Izetbegovic, A. 175

Jackson, J. 245
Japan 98, 126

King, M.L., Jr.
  Civil Rights Movement and 244
  nonviolent power and 245, 246
Korea 75, 99, 103
Kurdistan 20, 71, 180, 188, 201
Kuwait 71, 96, 106
Kyi, Aung San Suu 246

Latin America
  decolonialisation 181, 187
  new states 181, 185, 272
Lebanon 105
Liberia 72, 137, 152
Libya 103
Lund, M. 161, 162

MacLean, P. 261, 265-267
Malaysia 100
Mali 138
Malvinas/Falkland Islands 31, 186
Maori 322, 323
Mexico 298
Middle East 72, 282
Military (*See* Security, Peacekeeping)
  alternative defence 8, 31, 83, 89-92
  balance of power 15, 40, 41, 96, 99
  citizen defence 8, 16, 33, 34, 40, 41, 237
  collective security 16-18, 22, 40, 41, 91
  conversion 8, 16, 32, 40, 41
  defence 281, 272-274, 281, 306
    costs 34
  deterrence 8, 15, 17, 21, 34, 39-41
  Non-offensive defence (NOD) 8, 16, 32, 33, 34, 40, 41, 91, 92
  Military-Industrial Complex (MIC) 74
  threats 88, 181-183, 272-274, 290, 296, 306
Milosevic, S. 174, 175

Minority
  independence and 180, 184, 186
  OSCE and 180, 186
  rights 179-208
Mouffe, C. 47, 48
Movements
  bi-racial movement 320
  Civil Rights Movements 244, 246
  Hawaiian 320, 323
  independence 186, 187
  indigenous 310-312, 314, 319-324
  nationalist 312, 314, 315, 324
  peace/nonviolent 33, 34, 236-238, 244, 245-250, 252
  secessionist 183-186, 188, 274
  social 290, 292, 293, 298, 299
Mozambique 72, 138, 152

Nationalism (*See* Movements) 151, 280, 281, 286n, 289n, 322
  democracy 151, 153
  ethnonationalism 179, 180, 286
  from above/ below 280, 286n, 289n
  multi-ethnic state 309-311
  rise of 297, 310, 312, 314, 315
Nigeria 137
Non-governmental organisations (NGOs)
  civil society 30, 39, 41, 136, 137, 290-306
  human rights 30, 289, 290
  minority rights 179, 180
  Peoples Organisations (POs) 16, 30-33, 41
  regional cooperation 290, 292-306
  security 293-306
Nonviolence (*See* Gandhi, M.K.; King, M.L., Jr.)
  as a way of life 247, 248, 251
  citizen defence 8, 33, 34, 238
  civil disobedience 33
  culture 236, 238
  Czechoslovakia 238, 244, 276

Hungary 34, 185
power and 34, 244
'principled' 33, 236, 243, 244, 247, 252, 255
social change 7, 33, 237, 240, 244, 245, 249, 252, 254, 255, 292, 298
'strategic' 33, 243-245
North Atlantic Treaty Organisation (NATO) 22, 24, 28, 99, 165, 211
Northeast Asia 98
Northern Ireland 31, 152, 185

Organisation for Economic Cooperation and Development (OECD) 66, 292
Organisation for Security and Cooperation (OSCE) 180, 186, 194-198, 200, 201, 204-206

Pakistan 72, 97, 98, 181, 239
Peace (*See* peace-building, peacekeeping, peace-making, nonviolence)
  culture 136, 143, 149, 150, 159n, 233, 236, 238, 249, 253, 255
  democracy 79, 135-139, 144, 153, 169
  diplomacy 14-17, 21, 29, 40, 41, 291
  education 37-42, 149, 150, 289
  feminist perspective 16, 36, 37, 41, 42
  human well-being 6, 7, 211, 216, 289-306
  positive/negative 7, 8, 16, 21, 27, 37
  research 3-10, 157, 233, 289
    armament dynamics 5, 83
    behavioural school 4, 50, 239
    'emancipatory empiricism' 6, 9
    scientific approaches 4-6
    strategic studies and 6, 291
    theoretical traditions 4, 6-10

social justice 33, 293
zones of peace 136, 142, 145, 153
Peace-building
  functionalism 6, 16, 18, 21, 35, 295
  human rights 8, 16, 20, 28, 30, 36, 37, 40, 41, 290
  multiculturalism 6, 185
Peace Brigades International 249
Peacekeeping
  Bosnia 110, 111, 129, 187
  conflict management 7, 105, 107, 113, 117, 129, 154, 157
  cultural environment 124-126, 132
  Cyprus 31, 105, 111
  implementation 109-114, 119, 124
    contingency approach 119, 152
    pragmatic approach 119, 154
  Lebanon 105
  mediation 108-110, 112-116, 119, 129, 139-142, 146-149, 152, 155
  negotiations 108, 112-115, 120, 123, 128, 129, 139-146, 151, 154
  neutrality 116, 120
  military peace operations 106, 107, 291, 293
    collective enforcement 106, 109, 130, 204
    election supervision 106, 109, 130, 293
    humanitarian assistance 28, 77, 106, 107, 109, 130, 131, 137, 139, 142, 156, 157, 243, 293, 294
    observation 106, 109
  primary party strategy
    distributive/ integrative process 108, 109, 127, 128
    goal-setting 120-122, 124, 125
    outcomes assessment 121-123
    strategy development 122-124

Somalia 107, 131, 138, 142, 201, 204, 218
Persian Gulf 53, 95, 97, 103, 214
the Philippines 100, 186
Poland 185, 244
Political
  culture 312
  identity 151, 274
  system 24, 35, 65, 66, 169, 173, 274
  norms 274, 280
Population
  displacement 278, 299, 304, 305
Post-Cold War
  democracy, democratisation 72, 77, 79, 137, 153, 169, 187, 318
  ethnonationalism 179-208
  global power structure 21, 23, 296
  hegemony, decline of 309-311
  instability 180, 187, 188, 194
  regionalism 290, 293-306
  security 290, 291
  warlord politics 137

Rapoport, A. 142, 169, 172
Region
  ASEAN 99-101, 296, 297, 308n
  conceptualisations of 295, 297
  cooperation 278, 290, 293-306
  'new' regionalism 296, 297, 301-303
  organisations 297, 298, 301, 305
  subregional economic zones (SREZs) 298
Republic of Korea (ROK) (see Korea)
Rights
  civil and political 20, 184
  human 8, 188, 289, 290, 294
  minority 179-208
Ringmar, E. 49-53, 60
Russia 103, 153, 211
Rwanda 72, 174, 236, 253, 254, 275

Saudi Arabia 101, 276
Security (*See* Military)
  collective 91, 153
  Copenhagen School of Security
    Studies 45, 54-60
  decision-making 6, 289, 305
  dilemma 84, 92, 103
  economic aspects of 291
  environmental 211-221, 289, 290
  functional cooperation 6, 295
  global 37, 135-138, 183, 293
  human 8, 289, 293-306
  national 87, 90, 91, 99, 103, 212-215, 218-220, 281, 282, 290, 305, 306
  multilateralism 291, 298, 306
  regionalism 289-306
  resource protection 137, 214, 272-274
  post-Cold War 290, 291, 293-306
  securitisation 56-60
  sovereignty 56, 73, 103, 213, 275-279, 281
  United Nations and 91, 243
Self-determination 19-22, 36, 40, 41, 274
  criteria 181-186
  minority rights and 179-208
  sovereignty and 180, 181, 187, 188, 192, 198, 207, 208, 281
  state 179, 182, 274, 276
  United Nations and 20, 183, 184
Senegal 137
Sierra Leone 72, 137
Singapore 100
  'communitarian inclusionism' 314
Social
  change 7, 33, 150-153, 292, 298
Somalia 72, 138, 142
South Africa 72, 152, 248, 298, 304
South Asia 97
Southeast Asia
  arms races 99-101
  ASEAN 99-101, 296, 297

crisis 99, 283, 315
nationalism 310, 314, 315
strategies of integration 310, 314
values 315
Sovereignty 73, 275-278
  economic 275, 277, 281, 282
  environmental 26, 212, 213
  multinational organisations 7, 274, 277, 290, 291
  political 275-277, 281
  state 180, 181, 187, 188, 192, 198, 207, 208, 275-277, 281
Soviet Union 187, 276
Sri Lanka 152, 176, 236, 249
State
  borders 184-186, 272, 274-276, 282, 292
  civil society 136, 290-306
  collapse 71, 72, 76, 135-138, 157, 186, 277, 281, 282, 312
  human needs and 261-263, 271, 278, 281, 282, 283n, 284n, 293
  international relations 69, 179
  legitimacy 136, 182-184, 273, 290, 303
  modernist 309-312
  multiculturalism 143, 185, 187, 276, 280, 281, 309-312, 313, 318, 320-322
  post-Cold War 278, 282, 289, 292, 296
  postcolonial 67, 137, 138, 181, 183, 184, 186
  sociological perspective 262, 268, 270
  state/nation-building 274, 280-282
  territorial integrity 181, 184-187, 272-274
Sudan 138
Sweden 156, 316-318

Third World 22-27, 66-68
  arms race and 94, 95
  environment 25-27, 213, 218-220

postcolonialism 67, 179-181, 184, 303
minority rights 184
'new' regionalism and 297, 303
Tibet 186, 253
Transnational
  economy 292, 296-298
  migration 8, 191, 301, 304, 309
  organisations 7, 290-306
Tudjman, F. 175
Turkey 95, 96, 137, 188

United Nations
  Charter 18-20, 22, 27, 28, 39, 182, 183, 186
  colonialism 19, 20, 183, 184
  General Assembly 243
  global policing 77-80, 91
  institutional weaknesses 69, 73
  human rights and 20, 28, 30, 79, 183, 184
  League of Nations 15, 17, 39, 180
  minority rights system 180, 182, 183-186, 189, 191, 196
  multilateralism 291, 293, 298, 306
  peacekeeping, 29, 73, 77, 78, 204, 243
  preventative diplomacy 29, 163
  Security Council 18
  self-determination and 19, 20, 182-184, 187
United States
  class polarisation 154-156, 316, 317, 320, 321
  cultural fragmentation 179, 313, 316, 317, 320, 321, 323, 324n
  immigration 155, 156, 313
  multi-ethnicity 154-156, 169, 185, 309-313, 317, 319-321
  NAFTA 297
  violence and 154-156, 254

Vietnam 75, 100, 214, 275
Violence
  against nature 234, 235
  borders of 64-66, 276
  causes 5-10, 150-153, 168, 169, 173
  centre - periphery 137-139, 145
  class 154-156, 310, 316-320
  culture of 8, 234-236, 239, 254, 255
  international intervention 139, 161-164, 167, 275
  media and 237-242, 250, 252-255
  paradigms of 234, 235, 237, 241-244, 247, 249
  power and 155, 273, 274
  structural violence 5, 7, 252
  urban 155, 156, 319

Wæver, O. 55-58
Wallerstein, I. 135
War (See civil war, Cold War, Post-Cold War)
  causes of 4, 7, 45, 52, 88, 168, 169, 173, 244
  civil 137, 138, 155, 168
  conditions for 168, 173, 174, 176
  degenerate warfare 77-80
  democracy and 72, 137, 138, 153, 168, 169
  guerrilla warfare 75
  identity 45-60, 77, 151, 169, 272-274
  outbreak of 45-60
  total war 65, 74-76
  violisation 56, 58-60
Warsaw Pact 22, 24
Witness for Peace 249
World Bank 66
World War I; 15, 17, 19, 180, 185
World War II; Second World War 65-67, 183, 185

Yugoslavia 174, 244, 254, 276
  Badinter Arbitration Commission 167, 186
  identity 59, 60, 276